OUT OF OAKLAND

A volume in the series

The United States in the World

Edited by Mark Philip Bradley, David C. Engerman, Amy S. Greenberg, and Paul A. Kramer

A list of titles in this series is available at www.cornellpress.cornell.edu.

OUT OF OAKLAND

Black Panther Party Internationalism during the Cold War

Sean L. Malloy

Cornell University Press
Ithaca and London

First published 2017 by Cornell University Press
First printing, Cornell Paperbacks, 2017

Printed in the United States of America

Library of Congress Cataloging-in-Publication Data

Names: Malloy, Sean L. (Sean Langdon), 1972– author.
Title: Out of Oakland : Black Panther Party internationalism during the Cold War / Sean L. Malloy.
Description: Ithaca : Cornell University Press, 2017. | Series. The United States in the world | Includes bibliographical references and index.
Identifiers: LCCN 2016052423 (print) | LCCN 2016054021 (ebook) | ISBN 9781501702396 (cloth : alk. paper) | ISBN 9781501713422 (pbk. : alk. paper) | ISBN 9781501712708 (epub/mobi) | ISBN 9781501712715 (pdf)
Subjects: LCSH: Black Panther Party—History. | Black power—United States—History—20th century. | United States—Race relations—Political aspects—History—20th century. | Internationalism—History—20th century. | Anti-imperialist movements—United States—History—20th century. | Cold War—Political aspects.
Classification: LCC E185.615 .M275 2017 (print) | LCC E185.615 (ebook) | DDC 322.4/20973—dc23
LC record available at https://lccn.loc.gov/2016052423

Cornell University Press strives to use environmentally responsible suppliers and materials to the fullest extent possible in the publishing of its books. Such materials include vegetable-based, low-VOC inks and acid-free papers that are recycled, totally chlorine-free, or partly composed of nonwood fibers. For further information, visit our website at www.cornellpress.cornell.edu.

To Lia

"Even renowned hack historians have found that
The people only bound back when they pound back"
—The Coup, "Ghetto Manifesto"

Contents

Acknowledgments   xi

Introduction: "Theory with No Practice Ain't Shit"   1

1. "Every Brother on a Rooftop Can Quote Fanon": Black
   Internationalism, 1955–1966   18

2. "Army 45 Will Stop All Jive": Origins and Early Operations
   of the BPP, 1966–1967   46

3. "We're Relating Right Now to the Third World": Creating
   an Anticolonial Vernacular, 1967–1968   70

4. "I Prefer Panthers to Pigs": Transnational and International
   Connections, 1968–1969   107

5. "Juche, Baby, All the Way": Cuba, Algeria, and the Asian
   Strategy, 1969–1970   130

6. "Gangster Cigarettes" and "Revolutionary Intercommunalism":
   Diverging Directions in Oakland and Algiers, 1970–1971   161

7. "Cosmopolitan Guerrillas": The International Section and
   the RPCN, 1971–1973   187

8. The Panthers in Winter, 1971–1981   211

Epilogue: "Our Demand Is Simple: Stop Killing Us":
From Oakland to Ferguson   241

Notes   257

Index   295

Acknowledgments

It took countless people to make this book possible. Not everyone named here will share my conclusions about the Black Panther Party (BPP), and the mistakes are all mine, but I want to thank at least some of the many people who helped me. These include all the staff at Cornell University Press, particularly my editor Michael J. McGandy, as well as the series editor David Engerman at Brandeis. Michael has been involved with this book since its inception, and aside from his monstrous instance on having only a single space after periods he has been everything an author could ever wish for as both a sounding board and advocate. David provided insightful advice, particularly on the introduction and conclusion, that helped me better frame some of my core arguments. My sincere thanks also to the two anonymous peer reviewers whose feedback on my draft manuscript was invaluable. Chris Dodge's copyediting also contributed greatly to the readability of this book.

The University of California, Merced, has been my academic home for over a decade, and the students, faculty, and staff have been a constant source of inspiration and support. While UCM has grown too large to thank everyone by name, I want to particularly highlight my colleagues and unindicted coconspirators in History, Critical Race and Ethnic Studies

(CRES), and the graduate program in Interdisciplinary Humanities (IH). Mario Sifuentez, Anneeth Kaur Hundle, David Torres-Rouff, Jan Goggans, Ma Vang, Kit Myers, Kevin Dawson, Sholeh Quinn, Daniel Rios, and Kim McMillon are among the many comrades who have made UCM such a wonderful environment for scholarship, teaching, and activism. Gregg Herken brought me to UCM back in 2005 and for that I will always be thankful. While I cannot thank everyone by name, I want to acknowledge the contributions of the hardworking support staff at UCM and particularly highlight Becky Smith, Megan Topete, Alisha Kimball, Fatima Paul, and Simrin Takhar for all their help over the years. They make the work of teachers and scholars possible and too often go unmentioned.

Outside of UCM, I want to extend thanks to the terrifyingly smart and always generous Mark Padoongpatt for his feedback. Kevin Fellezs has left UCM for Columbia, but his advice and counsel over pizza and Sapporo were crucial in the early stages of this book. Steven Salaita is the model of a committed and compassionate scholar whose courage and tenacity has been an inspiration. Thanks also go to the staff at the Bancroft Library at UC Berkeley and Special Collections at Stanford University for assistance with the Eldridge Cleaver and Huey P. Newton collections respectively. Adrienne Fields (Artists Rights Society), and Liz Kurtulik Mercuri (Art Resource) were immensely helpful in securing the rights to reprint artwork by Emory Douglas. The work done by Joshua Bloom and Waldo E. Martin in ensuring that the near-complete run of the *Black Panther* newspaper was collected and digitized made my research, and that of future scholars of the BPP, considerably easier.

Most importantly, my family has supported and inspired me. My parents Jim, Treacy, and Judy helped shape both my values and my curiosity. My wife Patricia has offered not only love and support but also a daily example of no-bullshit commitment to social justice. My daughter Lia is a constant source of wonder and inspiration. I love you all.

OUT OF OAKLAND

Introduction

"Theory with No Practice Ain't Shit"

On October 15, 1966, two young men in Oakland, California, drafted the charter for a new organization they dubbed the Black Panther Party for Self-Defense. Demanding "Land, Bread, Housing, Education, Clothing, Justice and Peace," their ten-point program was a ringing call for Black Power and self-determination.[1] Minister of Defense Huey P. Newton and Chairman Bobby Seale were not the first to use the panther icon. Earlier that year, Stokely Carmichael (later known as Kwame Ture) and the Student Nonviolent Coordinating Committee (SNCC) had joined local activists in Alabama in founding the Lowndes County Freedom Organization, which adopted a black panther as its symbol. The LCFO was sometimes referred to as the Black Panther Party, and its logo was soon adopted by a number of black organizations in the urban North and West.[2] Newton and Seale's Black Panther Party for Self-Defense was one of two similarly named groups in Northern California. A rival Black Panther organization was located across the bay in San Francisco.[3] The Oakland-based Panthers, however, soon distinguished themselves from their contemporaries to become arguably the most visible representatives of the black freedom struggle during the late 1960s and early 1970s.

Dropping "Self-Defense" from its name in early 1968 at Newton's behest, the Black Panther Party (BPP) quickly expanded from a small, West Oakland neighborhood group to a national organization with chapters in sixty-eight cities across the United States.[4] In 1970 the party established an international section in Algeria, under Minister of Information Eldridge Cleaver, that would serve as an officially recognized embassy for the BPP and a beacon for U.S. revolutionaries abroad, attracting figures ranging from Black Power skyjackers to fugitive LSD guru Timothy Leary. Engaging directly with the expanding Cold War in the Third World, BPP representatives cultivated alliances with the governments of Cuba, North Korea, China, North Vietnam, and the People's Republic of the Congo. Newton personally offered "an undetermined number of troops" from the ranks of the BPP to aid the struggle of the National Liberation Front (NLF) against the United States in South Vietnam.[5] The Panthers also pursued links with the Fatah party led by Yasser Arafat and attended meetings of the Palestine Liberation Organization (PLO) in Jordan and Kuwait. In addition to these direct connections, the party boasted support groups and emulators as far afield as India, New Zealand, Israel, Japan, Great Britain, West Germany, and Scandinavia.[6]

The government of the United States responded to the rise of the BPP by launching an unprecedented campaign to infiltrate, undermine, and destroy it. FBI director J. Edgar Hoover declared in 1969, "The Black Panther Party, without question, represents the greatest threat to the internal security of the country."[7] The party became the number one target of the bureau's covert Counterintelligence Program (COINTELPRO) and the subject of 233 of its 295 known operations. The CIA also kept tabs on the party though its MH/CHAOS program.[8] A congressional committee echoed Hoover in declaring that "through its deliberately inflammatory rhetoric and through the actual arming and military training of its members, [the BPP] contributed to an increase in acts of violence and constitutes a threat to the internal security of the United States."[9] The State Department, meanwhile, pressured the Panthers' foreign allies, most notably Algeria. In October 1971, Secretary of State Henry Kissinger invoked the specter of the Panthers in his meeting with Premier Zhou Enlai in preparation for Richard Nixon's visit to China, speaking of "the average American, not Huey Newton."[10]

The origins, rise, and decline of the BPP have been explored from multiple angles by participants, journalists, and scholars over the last decades. Given the dispersed nature of the party, with local chapters often enjoying a great deal of autonomy, and the many changes that took place from its foundation in 1966 through its demise in the early 1980s, no single account of the party has fully elucidated its diverse (and sometimes divergent) history.[11] To even speak of a singular Black Panther Party is in some ways misleading, as there were often significant divisions between the party's national headquarters and local chapters as well as within and between its leadership and grassroots supporters. Gender, class, region, and even age combined to produce significant differences in the experiences of party members over the course of the Panthers' existence. Rather than attempt to survey the history of the party in its entirety, *Out of Oakland* examines the Panthers in an international and transnational context with specific reference to the party's relationship to the Third World and the Cold War during the 1960s and 1970s. Exploring the history of the BPP through an international lens reveals continuities that are not immediately visible in a domestic context as well as highlighting crucial points of contention and change in the party's development.

"[W]e saying that theory's cool," proclaimed Illinois BPP chairman Fred Hampton in 1969, "but theory with no practice ain't shit."[12] In keeping with Hampton's injunction, this book examines both the ideological roots of the BPP's international engagement and the party's attempts to put it into practice. A core theme of *Out of Oakland* is the link between the Panthers' domestic analysis and operations and their international engagement with revolutionary governments and movements. From the beginning, Panther leaders drew on a long tradition of anticolonial theory and practice in order to make sense of the situation facing black Americans. Though initially focused on the daily problems afflicting the residents of cities such as Oakland, the leaders' anticolonial analysis prepared them to quickly cultivate international alliances as they turned outward in response to U.S. government repression. These foreign contacts, in turn, not only provided practical support for the BPP and its efforts in the United States but also helped party leaders further refine their anticolonial critique of American society. Nor was the relationship entirely one-sided. Although their impact on foreign governments was limited, the Panthers helped to inspire activists ranging from Mizrahi Jews in Israel to Pacific Islanders in New Zealand and the Red Army Faction (RAF) in West Germany.

At its peak in the late 1960s and early 1970, the BPP's domestic and international efforts were mutually reinforcing in both theory and practice. This productive synthesis of local and global was a major factor in the ability of the Panthers to survive and even grow in the face of intense pressure from law enforcement agencies. There were also potential tensions in these relationships, however, and it was not always easy to explain to working-class black Americans why North Korean leader Kim Il-sung was on the front page of the *Black Panther* newspaper. A similar set of perils and opportunities lurked within the diverse foreign alliances pursued by the BPP. *Out of Oakland* makes distinctions between the party's state-level international relationships with foreign governments and its grassroots transnational organizing with fellow activists and supporters around the world. While these efforts could be complementary, each had its strengths and weaknesses, and at times advocates for each of the two approaches within the party clashed dramatically.

The focus of *Out of Oakland* is on the BPP's national leaders, who played the primary roles in directing the party's international and transnational engagements. There remains much work to be done in order to understand how the party's local chapters and their diverse rank-and-file membership experienced, embraced, and contested these connections. And while scholars have explored how some of the party's transnational allies framed their relationship to the BPP within the context of their own struggles, lack of archival access has made it more difficult to trace the internal calculations of the Panthers' state-level allies in places such as Cuba, North Korea, Vietnam, and China. But while necessarily incomplete in its coverage, *Out of Oakland* offers a number of insights into the origins, evolution, and legacy of the Black Panther Party's international engagement and the ways in which it intersected with larger developments in the Third World, the Cold War, and the black freedom struggle. In doing so, the book links the rich scholarship on the black freedom struggle and black internationalism with the nuanced approach to the changing international environment that characterizes the best literature on race and U.S. foreign relations.[13]

The Long March from Bandung to Oakland

One of the central questions surrounding the Black Panther Party is how a small, local organization founded in an impoverished West Oakland neighborhood by two community college students vaulted to international prominence in such a short time. Though the charisma, bravery, intelligence, and media savvy of the party's leaders undoubtedly played a role, there is another major explanation for the BPP's seemingly improbable success. The Panthers were able to build on a foundation of intellectual and practical work by activists who had previously sought to link the condition of African Americans to peoples in the Third World struggling for independence. The organization that Newton and Seale founded in Oakland in 1966 was neither an aberration nor an exception. As scholar Nikhil Pal Singh observed, "A more or less consistent tradition of radical dissent can be traced, in which black activists and movements produced political discourses that strained the nation-form, stretching the boundaries of U.S. liberal and democratic thought and issuing a political challenge—still unmet—to achieve lasting equalitarian transformation of social life in general, both within and beyond US borders."[14] In addition to continuing a long tradition of armed self-defense in the African American community, the Panthers also drew upon the intersections between black internationalism, the emergence of a global postcolonial order in the wake of World War II (highlighted by the 1955 Afro-Asian Conference in Bandung, Indonesia), and the radicalization of Third World anticolonialism that accompanied the Cuba and Algerian revolutions, the crisis in the former Belgian Congo, and the escalating U.S. war in Vietnam in the early 1960s.

The Panthers inherited not only a body of anticolonial theory, as represented by works such as Frantz Fanon's *Wretched of the Earth*, but also a vocabulary and set of analytical tools honed over the previous decade by figures such as Malcolm X, Amiri Baraka (LeRoi Jones), Lorraine Hansberry, Robert F. Williams, Shirley Graham Du Bois, Wanda Marshall, Ahmad Muhammad (Max Stanford), Vicki Garvin, and Harold Cruse. By the mid-1960s, a consensus had developed among a subset of activists that black Americans were not citizens denied their rights (as argued by the liberal civil rights movement) but rather a colonized people scattered throughout the ghettos and Black Belts of the United States. When Newton referred to Oakland police as an "occupying army" and black Oaklanders as colonial subjects, he was drawing directly from this rich rhetorical and ideological legacy.[15] The Revolutionary Action Movement (RAM) further expanded Cruse's formulation of revolutionary nationalism to posit that black Americans had a vanguard role to play in the international struggle against imperialism by virtue of their unique position "behind enemy lines" inside the United States.[16] This vision of African Americans as an anticolonial vanguard was crucial to the BPP's domestic and international strategy.

At the core of both the Panthers' foreign and domestic operations was the doctrine of "revolutionary nationalism," first posited by Cruse in 1961 and later developed by RAM in the middle of the decade. Reinterpreting the tradition of black nationalism in light of Third World anticolonialism,

Zimmer

revolutionary nationalism sought to link self-determination to a larger project of socialist revolution in the United States and around the world. In this
analysis, the oppression faced by black Americans was the result of both
racism and capitalism, and the two forces could not be separated from one
another domestically or internationally. In light of the deep historical links
between white supremacy and capitalism, it would not be possible to liberate black America without also liberating the entire United States (and the
rest of the world) from racialized colonialism. Revolutionary nationalism
thus provided a tool for organizing within racial and ethnic communities while its adherents remained committed to the long-term prospect
of worldwide socialist revolution rather than retreating into factionalized
separatism.

Even as the BPP remained largely focused on local issues in its early
years, Third World anticolonialism, as reflected through the lens of the
urban African American experience, played a crucial role in the party's origins and operations. Carrying loaded firearms and donning striking uniforms comprising black beret, black leather jacket, and powder-blue shirt,
Newton, Seale and a handful of other early party members patrolled the
streets of Oakland in late 1966 and early 1967. In exposing and confronting the daily exercise of colonial power in black neighborhoods they also
sought to reconcile the anticolonialism espoused by figures such Fanon
with the realities confronting black Americans as a minority living inside a
First World superpower. The result was a strategy that mixed street theater,
radical pedagogy, and community organizing while building a foundation
for a revolution that would link black Americans with their brothers and
sisters in the Third World.

The Evolving Internationalism(s) of the BPP

While numerous scholars have noted the BPP's internationalism, few have
seriously wrestled with its evolving and often contested manifestations. Just
as the BPP existed in dialogue with a black freedom struggle in the United
States that was far from monolithic, so too was it connected to a shifting and sometimes clashing cast of international actors that included both
nation-states and nongovernmental organizations. Internally, meanwhile,
the BPP was marked by diverse—and sometimes divergent—approaches
to foreign relations, even within the relatively limited circle of the party's national leadership. Yet most historical accounts treat the Panthers'

internationalism as unitary and frozen in time, usually in the late 1960s at the height of the Vietnam War and militant Third World anticolonialism. Ultimately the significance of texts such as Fanon's *Wretched of the Earth*, Ernesto "Che" Guevara's *Guerrilla Warfare*, and *Quotations from Chairman Mao Tse-Tung* (more popularly known as the "Little Red Book") to the Panthers and other participants in the U.S. Third World Left cannot be detached from the changing domestic and international context in which they were produced and consumed.[17]

The era in which the BPP was born, evolved, and ultimately dissolved was marked by dramatic changes in both the Cold War and the Third World (often overlapping with one another). The aftermath of the Cuban and Algerian revolutions, the Sino-Soviet split, the escalation of the Vietnam War followed by eventual U.S. withdrawal, President Richard M. Nixon's visit to China, Soviet-American détente, the Arab-Israeli wars of 1967 and 1973, armed liberation struggles in sub-Saharan Africa, and the spread of neoliberal globalization were among the many factors that influenced the evolution of the Black Panthers. Domestic developments, including the arrest and trial of Panther cofounder Newton and the escalating police and federal crackdown on the BPP, also spurred the development of the party's internationalism while producing divisions within its ranks over the merits of foreign entanglements and guerrilla warfare.

The first major turning point in the Panthers' evolving international engagement came with the passage of the 1967 Mulford Act in California. The law, which was targeted directly at the BPP, prohibited the open display of loaded weapons, a tactic that had been critical to the party's early operations activism in Oakland. In its wake, the Panthers embraced a new form of anticolonial organizing that built upon, and in some cases transformed, the ideological links to the Third World they had inherited from their predecessors. Newton and Seale had initially downplayed these connections in favor of direct action. By late 1967, however, they embraced what I refer to as an "anticolonial vernacular" that sought to locate and define Third World anticolonialism in a fashion that was easily legible to a mass audience in the United States.

In the pages of the *Black Panther* newspaper, the speeches of party leaders, and the drawings of Panther artists Emory Douglas and Tarika Lewis, the party blended Third World symbols and rhetoric, a loosely Marxist economic analysis, and a distinctive verbal and visual style influenced by urban African American idioms and argot. As Eldridge Cleaver explained it, "We're relating right now to the Third World."[18] The result was one of

Figure 1. Panther revolutionary artist Emory Douglas collaborated with the Cuban Organization of Solidarity of the People of Asia, Africa, and Latin America (OSPAAAL) to promote a day of "Solidarity with the African American People" timed to coincide with the anniversary of the August 1965 Watts uprising. 1968. Photo courtesy of Emory Douglas/Art Resource, NY

the most comprehensive and successful efforts to embed Third World anti-colonialism in the specific context of black life in the United States. As the Panthers expanded in largely decentralized fashion in this period, with local chapters enjoying a great deal of autonomy, the party's anticolonial vernacular provided a common vocabulary that was as important as the gun or iconic black berets in cementing an identity for the BPP. By casting the problems facing African Americans in terms of their relationship to a broad of set of political and economic processes rather than simply stressing racial or cultural identity, the Panthers also opened up the possibility of alliances with both white radicals and other communities of color inside the United States.

A second major turning point came with Newton's arrest on charges of killing a police officer and wounding another during a late-night shoot-out on the streets of Oakland. Newton's high-stakes trial, which opened in July 1968, forced the party to scramble for allies. In the process, Panther leaders supplemented the party's anticolonial vernacular with more practical efforts at alliance building. Although they tentatively sought contacts with foreign governments and international organizations such as the United Nations, the most fruitful of the BPP's overseas alliances in 1968–69 came via transnational links to activists in western Europe and Japan. These connections brought much-needed publicity, financial support, and legitimacy at a time when the party's cofounder and minister of defense was fighting for his life in an Oakland courtroom. They also, however, exposed some of the tensions and limits inherent to transnational organizing. Just as the Panthers' anticolonial vernacular could romanticize and oversimplify the complex relationship between black Americans and the Third World, the party's transnational partners sometimes relied on an Orientalist exoticization of black Americans, particularly black masculinity, to facilitate these alliances. More practically, even at their best there were limits to the kind of support that non-state actors, many of which operated inside the borders of countries allied to the United States, could offer to the BPP in its revolutionary struggle.

A third evolution of the Panthers' international engagement followed in the wake of another confrontation with Oakland police, this time involving Cleaver. Following a disastrous attempt to ambush police officers in retaliation for the assassination of Martin Luther King Jr. in April 1968, Cleaver fled the United States rather than return to jail. Arriving in Cuba on the eve of 1969, he planned to supplement the BPP's anticolonial vernacular and transnational alliances with more formal connections to revolutionary governments in the Third World that could provide safe haven, arms, and training for the party and its members. His ultimate goal was to return to the country he dubbed "Babylon" at the head of a "North American Liberation Front" that would overthrow the U.S. government by force.[19] Cleaver's plans were frustrated by the unwillingness of his Cuban hosts to invoke the further ire of the United States on his behalf. Cast out by the government of Fidel Castro and sent packing to Algeria in June 1969, the Panthers' minister of information was forced to improvise a new strategy. He and his wife, Kathleen Cleaver, embraced a more direct engagement with Cold War geopolitics in Asia. As part of their "Asian strategy," the Cleavers and the BPP pursued state-level contacts with socialist governments in the region, most notably in Vietnam and North Korea. These relationships paid some impressive short-term dividends. It was support from the party's Asian allies that convinced the Algerian government to recognize and fund the international section of the BPP in Algiers, giving the Panthers their first institutional foothold outside the United States. These connections also facilitated Eldridge Cleaver's leadership of the U.S. People's Anti-Imperialist Delegation, an eleven-member group of U.S. activists that embarked on a six-week tour of revolutionary Asia, including North Korea, North Vietnam, and China in 1970.[20]

The Asian alliances pursued by the Cleavers and the international section provided the Panthers a legitimacy that did not depend on the whims of the U.S. government, but they also left the BPP exposed to the shifting winds of Cold War politics. The winding down of the Vietnam War, the stirrings of détente, and Nixon's visit to China undermined the BPP's international strategy and left the party increasingly isolated on the world stage. Moreover, in attempting to cultivate foreign allies, the Panthers often had to tailor their message to appeal to governments that in most cases had only superficial knowledge of, and concern for, blacks in the United States. Internal disputes over the wisdom of such alliances, fueled in part by the FBI, helped to fragment the BPP in 1971, leading to a permanent break between Eldridge Cleaver (who favored both guerrilla warfare and Cold War–inspired alliances) and Newton (who wanted to pursue a strategy more rooted in local community organizing), followed by bloody infighting between their respective factions. Though most accounts of the Cleaver-Newton conflict have focused on its disastrous repercussions for the BPP at home, the split in the party also played out beyond the borders of the United States as both sides scrambled to define and legitimize themselves internationally.

The final iterations of the BPP's evolving approach to international and transnational connections played out in the 1970s in the wake of the Cleaver-Newton split. The split produced at least three separate organizations, each of which claimed to be the true heir to the legacy of the party. The surviving Oakland-based BPP under the leadership of Newton and Elaine Brown was the largest of these three factions. Abandoning both Cold War geopolitics and the flirtation with guerrilla warfare that marked the early years of the party, the post-split BPP refocused on community service and local politics in Oakland. Guided by a theory that Newton dubbed "intercommunalism," the Panthers repositioned local activism as a reaction to the rise of neoliberal globalization and the declining significance of the nation-state. In practice, this entailed focusing on local politics and on providing community services to Oakland residents through the party's "survival programs" while pursuing transnational connections to like-minded activists around the world. Though Newton's efforts to reorient the Panthers fell victim to government repression, party infighting, and his own weaknesses (including an escalating struggle with drug addiction), intercommunalism was a sophisticated theoretical analysis that presaged later debates over globalization.[21]

In Algeria, the rump international section of the BPP pursued a different form of transnational organizing in the early 1970s. Reorganizing under the banner of the Revolutionary People's Communications Network (RPCN), the Cleavers and their allies sought to weather the storm caused by both the BPP split and the geopolitical realignment that accompanied Nixon's visit to China by building links among groups still committed to revolutionary anticolonialism in the United States and around the world. While Newton and the BPP stressed community service, Eldridge Cleaver lionized the efforts of the Palestinian Black September guerrilla group and its strategy of stateless, anticolonial violence that exploited "the landscape of technology, the channels and circuits of our environment" in order to strike across borders against "all pigs and pig structures."[22] Deprived of their former Asian allies and struggling to hold together a fractious community of American exiles, the RPCN's leaders failed to put this new strategy into practice. The Algerian government, which was seeking a closer economic relationship with the United States, grew tired of the troublesome Panther contingent, and by the end of 1972 the international section had dissolved, and the Cleavers fled to France.

Initially the RPCN had hoped to work with the third of the major groups that came out of the 1971 BPP split: the Black Liberation Army

(BLA). The BLA was largely composed of former Panthers from the New York City and West Coast chapters of the party who rejected Newton's turn toward reformist local politics and community service. In the wake of the split, BLA cells organized and undertook guerrilla actions in the service of revolutionary nationalism, including targeted assassinations of police officers. Quickly forced underground, estranged from Newton's BPP, and cut off from the Cleavers' increasingly embattled operations in Algeria, the BLA lacked an effective aboveground political apparatus to complement its military operations. As a result, the group was unable to leverage its sporadic acts of violence into a meaningful debate over the colonial status of black Americans, much less bring about a revolution. By 1973 the majority of BLA leaders were either imprisoned or killed, though the group experienced a brief and violent resurgence at the end of the decade.

The Legacy of the Panthers

Anthropologist Renato Rosaldo has identified a strain of ideology in American and European accounts of indigenous societies, ranging from works of fiction such as *Out of Africa* and *A Passage to India* to scholarly articles and monographs, that he dubbed "imperialist nostalgia." Its central characteristic is a peculiar inversion in which colonial elites came to romanticize the very cultures and peoples they had helped to destroy.[23] Privileged scholarly and journalistic chroniclers must be wary of something similar when it comes to the Black Panther Party. It is easy for scholars to romanticize the Panthers at a time when the threat that they posed to the institutions of white privilege (including the university system itself) seems nothing more than a colorful memory. To do so, however, is to do violence to the history and the memory of the party. While the Panthers could be media-savvy, calculating, and charismatic, their daily struggles on a local, national, and international level were grounded in the grim material reality of white supremacy, state violence, and racialized capitalist inequality. The BPP was dedicated to piercing the comforting illusions of liberalism and American exceptionalism, and party members were profoundly unromantic in confronting both the challenges they faced and the many setbacks they experienced in pursuit of their revolution.

The Panthers ultimately failed in their quest for a revolutionary remaking of U.S. society as part of a worldwide anticolonial uprising against capitalism and white supremacy. They left a substantial legacy, ranging from Oakland mayoral politics to the practical community work of their various survival programs and the enduring images of armed, leather-clad black men and women. But any honest assessment of the Panthers must grapple with their fundamental failures as measured by the party's own ten-point program. By the early 1970s, it was clear that the forces represented by "Pig Nixon" and "that jive punk, the dickless motherfucker" Ronald Reagan had triumphed on the national and international stage while a vastly reduced Panther contingent struggled for relevance in Oakland and behind bars.[24] "If there is one unavoidable truth about the Black Panther Party," wrote former Philadelphia Panther Mumia Abu-Jamal, "it is this: it lost its long battle for institutionalization and the primary realization of its revolutionary political objectives. It did not establish revolutionary power, due to reasons both internal and external."[25]

External factors undoubtedly played an important role in the demise of the Panthers and their failure to bring about the revolution. Police and government repression, most notably by COINTEPRO, not only took a direct toll on the party's membership through jail terms and killings. It also undermined the bonds of trust that held the party together, instilling chronic fear and paranoia about agents provocateurs and infiltration. As Kansas City Panther and international section member Charlotte O'Neal told me, "That COINTELPRO did a job on us, brother."[26] Whatever one makes of the BPP and its members, it is doubtful that the Boy Scouts of America could have survived the level of subversion and repression unleashed by COINTELPRO and local police against the Panthers. Developments on the international stage, including détente, Sino-American rapprochement, the winding down of the Vietnam War, and the changing internal and national security politics of the party's partners in the Third World also dealt a critical blow to the BPP. Just as the escalation of Vietnam War and the rise of militant anticolonialism helped to fuel the party's growth in the 1960s, the shifting winds of the Cold War and divisions within and between its Third World allies contributed to the Panthers' unraveling in the 1970s.

As Abu-Jamal conceded, however, external pressures were not the only factor that undermined the BPP. Among the challenges facing the party as it grew was a leadership structure based in Oakland that was patriarchal, hierarchical, and often wary of allowing local chapters too much autonomy. Women were involved in the party from the beginning, and on paper the Panthers were committed to gender equality in pursuit of the revolution.

Figures such as Kathleen Cleaver, Connie Mathews, Elaine Klein, and Denise Oliver were pivotal in facilitating the BPP's transnational and international connections. Much research remains to be done on the role that Panther women played in interpreting and contesting the party's efforts at foreign engagement at the grassroots level. Prior to the 1971 split, however, BPP women were usually assigned subordinate roles. Panther men expected them to conform to traditional gender norms—to support and nurture their male comrade—or to prove their worth to the struggle by "picking up the gun" and embracing gendered notions of citizenship through violence. Elaine Brown recalled, "If a black woman assumed a role of leadership, she was said to be eroding black manhood, to be hindering the progress of the black race. She was an enemy of black people."[27] Not all female Panthers agreed with Brown's assessment. Kathleen Cleaver argued that "[w]hen women suffered hostility, abuse, neglect, and assault—this was not something arising from the policies or structure of the Black Panther Party, something absent from the world—that's what *was* going on in the world. The difference that being in the [BPP] made was that it put a woman in a position when such treatment occurred to contest it."[28] Nevertheless, it is undeniable that the party, at least at the national level, was male-dominated for much of its early history and never offered a truly intersectional analysis that placed concerns about heteropatriarchy and misogyny on par with a critique of white supremacy and capitalism. While there was a rich strain of intersectional black feminist internationalism that both predated and survived the BPP, the party's guiding lights tended to be figures such as Malcolm X, Amiri Baraka, and Harold Cruse rather than Lorraine Hansberry, Vicki Garvin, or Shirley Graham Du Bois.[29]

In the wake of the split, women such as Brown, Ericka Huggins, Joan Kelley, and Donna Howell assumed more prominent roles in the leadership of the Oakland-based BPP, while Assata Shakur and Kathleen Cleaver were critical players in the BLA and RPCN respectively. During this period, some BPP and RPCN members also engaged in more explicitly addressing the underlying origins of women's' oppression while linking it to the struggles against capitalism and white supremacy.[30] The heyday of the Panthers' internationalism, however, corresponded to a period in the party's history when men dominated the national leadership and gendered notions of violence and manhood shaped the BPP's approach to anticolonialism. In this respect, ironically, the party's leadership had much in common with the U.S. foreign policy establishment that they so vehemently opposed. Given my focus on the Panthers' national leadership, the bulk of this book deals with male figures. In doing so, I have tried to pay attention to the way in which gender shaped decision making within the party and its approach to international relations as well as the shifts that accompanied the move away from male domination in the early 1970s. Among the many areas requiring further attention, however, are the ways in which both women and men at the grassroots level interpreted, supported, and contested the party's international engagements.

In light of the BPP's many internal contradictions and its failure to achieve lasting institutional achievements, some observers have gone so far as to suggest that the Panthers were little more than an artifact of sensational media coverage and white liberal guilt. A group of congressional representatives declared in 1971 that the BPP was "largely a creation of the mass media" and that "[t]he publicity given to this relatively small group of criminal misfits has enabled them to make some gains among a tiny minority of young Negroes and to raise considerable funds from gullible whites." This viewpoint was expressed with dripping sarcasm in Tom Wolfe's infamous *New York* magazine article "Radical Chic: That Party at Lenny's," which used a fund-raising event hosted by Leonard Bernstein as an excuse to skewer the Panthers and their white supporters.[31] In a review of recent scholarship on the Black Power era, Harvard law professor Randall L. Kennedy embraced a softer version of this argument, conceding the legitimacy of the party's origins but questioning whether the Panthers' frequent coverage in the media was "an accurate reflection of their activity and influence, or a reflection of journalists' hunger for the sensational (albeit marginal)?"[32] These critiques, however, fail to engage with the underlying ideological and practical innovations that brought the BPP to public attention in the first place. While small in sheer number of members, particularly compared to liberal civil rights organizations such as the NAACP, the Panthers attracted outsized attention not simply due to splashy news coverage but because they offered a powerful alternative worldview and proceeded to act on it both domestically and internationally.

For all their weaknesses and failings, the Panthers offered a challenge to capitalism and white supremacy that directly confronted American liberals' complicity in both of those oppressive forces as well as the violence that undergirded daily life for people of color in the United States and around the world. Central to this analysis, and crucial to the party's growth and endurance, was an approach that was fundamentally international both in its critique and its connections. While often criticized for being divisive, the BPP was at the forefront of a movement among those seeking to link people of color in the United States, antiracist white allies at home and in Europe, and governments and movements in the Third World. Though messy and flawed in practice, the Panthers' coalition-building efforts were far more ambitious and inclusive then those of contemporary movements that either confined their ambitions within the borders of United States or insisted that class and race were somehow mutually exclusive categories in organizing for revolution.[33]

This book pulls no punches in critiquing the sometimes shallow and tenuous nature of the connections that the BPP forged with its allies overseas. The party's ambitions, however, were not only laudable but also remarkably successful given their modest origins in a decaying West Oakland neighborhood and the intense repression and opposition that its members faced from the U.S. government and its allies. In their anticolonial analysis of black life in the United States and U.S. foreign policy, the Panthers were right more often than they were wrong. The same cannot be said of many of the party's opponents at a time when the "domino theory" and reflexive anticommunism dominated U.S. foreign policy and liberal lions such as Daniel Patrick Moynihan were blaming the plight of black Americans on "the deterioration of Negro family."[34] Stripped of the blinders of liberalism, the Panthers offered insights into racialized violence in American cities and the Third World that often eluded the "best and brightest" in Washington, the press corps, and the academy. As a scholar of U.S. foreign relations, it is my firm conviction that the world would have been a better place if Henry Kissinger and Robert S. McNamara had spent the latter part of the 1960s in jail rather than Huey P. Newton and Bobby Seale. The violence of the Panthers paled in comparison to that unleashed by the well-dressed, well-mannered "wise men" of the U.S. establishment who oversaw a genocidal war in Vietnam, a wasteful and dangerous nuclear arms race, and a nation characterized by deep structural inequality that manifested itself in the daily violence of poverty and white supremacy.

Although their opponents often exaggerated the party's commitment to violence and capacity for revolution, they were not wrong to see the BPP, with its anticolonial analysis and vernacular wedded to local, national, international, and transnationalism activism, as a threat to a U.S. state deeply implicated in institutionalized white supremacy at home and abroad. The Panthers were profoundly "uncivil" in their condemnation of "the motherfuckers . . . fucking up the people's freedom" and in their willingness to expose and transcend the limits of American exceptionalism in pursuit of a revolutionary coalition that crossed both color lines and national borders.[35]

Viewed in these terms, it is unsurprising that the national security apparatus of the U.S. government responded harshly to this challenge. "That [the party] survived and functioned at all in the face of the State's overt and covert oppression," observed Abu-Jamal, "especially for the extended period that it did, is a startling testament to the vision of its founders and the gritty will of its membership."[36] *Out of Oakland* follows the injunction of former BPP and BLA member Nuh Washington, who declared from behind bars, "Our history, the good and the bad, must be analyzed and summarized for other revolutionaries.... Let us learn from our mistakes and not feel ashamed. After all, we did a lot, knowing little."[37]

Chapter 1

"Every Brother on a Rooftop Can Quote Fanon"

Black Internationalism, 1955–1966

In November 1964, Robert F. Williams addressed an audience in Hanoi in the Democratic Republic of Vietnam (DRV). Williams, a former U.S. marine, had been the head of the Monroe, North Carolina, chapter of the National Association for the Advancement of Colored People (NAACP) before fleeing into exile after an armed confrontation with the Ku Klux Klan resulted in federal charges. Arriving in Cuba in 1961, he operated under the protection of Fidel Castro's revolutionary government while publishing a newspaper (the *Crusader*) and hosting a radio show (*Radio Free Dixie*) in which he blasted white supremacy and promoted black unity with the Third World. Williams also traveled extensively in Asia, and it was on one of these trips that he arrived in Hanoi in 1964 to deliver a message of solidarity. Describing African Americans as a "captive people" suffering under "mainland American colonialism," Williams ridiculed the 1964 Civil Right Act as "a farce of the first magnitude" while endorsing "the right of all oppressed people to meet violence with violence." Following the example set by "our brothers of Vietnam, Cuba, the Congo, Mozambique, and throughout Asia, Africa and Latin America," he declared, "our oppressed people are turning the streets of racist and imperialist America into battlegrounds of resistance."[1]

Williams's Hanoi declaration predated the events most commonly associated with the rise of black militancy in the United States, including the 1965 Watts rebellion in Los Angeles, the June 1966 "March Against Fear," which heard Stokely Carmichael's rallying cry of "Black Power," and the formation of the Black Panther Party for Self-Defense (BPP) in Oakland in October of that year. It also took place at a time when few in the United States were openly opposing the Vietnam War, much less endorsing "the right of our brothers of Vietnam to defend themselves against the armed aggression, repression and tyranny of U.S. imperialism."[2] Williams's journey, which took him from North Carolina to Havana, Hanoi, and Beijing during the first half of the 1960s, provided inspiration to other black activists who would expand upon his efforts to link the black freedom struggle in the United States to the Third World and the expanding Cold War in Asia. It also represented the culmination of trends that had begun in the aftermath of World War II and continued to develop throughout the 1950s and 1960s.

This chapter explores the intersection of the domestic and international developments that shaped the creation of black-led movements that looked beyond the borders of the United States for support and legitimacy in the 1960s. By the mid-1960s, the notion that black Americans should seek solidarity with the Third World rather than looking to Washington for help had attracted advocates ranging from Williams to Malcolm X, Lorraine Hansberry, Amiri Baraka, Vicki Garvin, Harold Cruse, and groups such as the Revolutionary Action Movement (RAM). The successes—and failures—of these pioneering figures helped pave the way for a new generation of activists, including key figures in the birth and development of the BPP. The meteoric rise of the Black Panthers to national and international prominence in the latter half of the 1960s was in large part made possible by the development of links between the Third World and black America in the preceding decade.

"Two, Three, or Many Vietnams": The Evolution of Third World Anticolonialism

From nineteenth-century abolitionist Martin R. Delany's sojourn in Africa through W.E.B. Du Bois's involvement in pan-African conferences, Marcus Garvey's Universal Negro Improvement Association (UNIA), and the left-leaning anticolonialism of the African Blood Brotherhood (ABB) in the 1920s and the Council on African Affairs (CAA) during the 1940s,

African American activists had long sought to link their struggles in the United States to the international realm.[3] Du Bois's 1903 declaration that "the problem of the twentieth century is the problem of the color-line,— the relation of the darker to the lighter races of men in Asia and Africa, in America and the islands of the sea" set the tone for a global program of analysis and activism.[4] Black internationalism, however, was never a monolithic phenomenon, and it underwent significant changes over time. With most of Africa and Asia in the grips of colonial rule during the first half of the twentieth century, there were relatively few opportunities for black Americans to seek effective allies outside the United States. In part because it was disproportionally represented by diasporic elites based in the United States or Europe, pan-Africanism prior to World War II was often tinged by the paternalistic attitude of Western advocates who hoped to "civilize" and "uplift" the mother continent.[5] The rapid spread of decolonization in the wake of World War II and the emergence of an independent Third World in the 1950s changed this dynamic, shifting the leadership of the anticolonial movement toward indigenous nationalist leaders in Asia, Africa, and the Middle East.

The term "Third World," identifying those nonaligned states outside the U.S.- or Soviet-led Cold War blocs, was coined in 1952 by French demographer Alfred Sauvy.[6] It was the Asian-African (or Bandung) Conference, however, that gave substance to the notion of a new group of nations with their own agenda independent of the superpowers. Like the sprawling nation of islands that played host to the conference, Indonesia, the twenty-nine states that gathered in Bandung in April 1955 were defined by their diversity. Representing some 1.5 billion people, these African, Asian, and Middle Eastern nations encompassed a dizzying variety of languages, religions, cultures, and forms of government. There were, however, several themes that not only united the participants at Bandung but also potentially linked them to communities of color in the United States.[7] Opposition to the linked forces of white supremacy and colonialism was the keynote of the conference. Many of the assembled states represented, including the five conference organizers (India, Pakistan, Indonesia, Burma, and Ceylon—now Sri Lanka), were less than a decade removed from winning their independence after a prolonged period of European colonial rule. Even nations such as China, which had remained at least nominally independent, had spent much of the century struggling to maintain their dignity and territorial integrity in the face of repeated colonial encroachments. The common experience of racialized colonialism provided a potential link between otherwise disparate nations and peoples. "We are united," exclaimed Indonesian president Sukarno in his opening address, "by a common detestation of colonialism in whatever form it appears. We are united by a common detestation of racialism."[8] Historian Cary Fraser has asserted, "The Afro-Asian conference was midwife to an international order in which the politics of race was an essential factor in the calculus of power."[9] In fact, race had long been an "essential factor" in the international colonial order created by the West. Bandung's contribution was to not only acknowledge this reality, but also to explicitly challenge the racial ideology of white supremacy that sustained colonialism. Among the ten principles formally adopted by the conferees on April 24, 1955, was the "[r]ecognition of the equality of all races and of the equality of all nations large and small."[10] Enunciated at Bandung by independent states that combined to account for more than half the world's population, this combination of anticolonialism and antiracism offered people of color around the world an alternative lens with which to view their place on the world stage.

The post-Bandung landscape was dominated not by loose transnational coalitions of diasporic anticolonial activists, but rather by postcolonial national governments in the Third World. "As a naked celebration of diplomatic protocol and the elevated status of its participants," historian Jeffrey James Byrne observed, "the [Bandung] conference suggested that statesmanship was the ultimate expression of individual and national liberation. The organizers' formalization of Third World relations introduced a new sense of hierarchy to the anti-imperialist scene."[11] This shift posed both opportunities and dangers for African Americans. Nations led by former colonial subjects and fellow victims of white supremacy and now boasting their own borders, armed forces, communications networks, and seats at the United Nations could make for powerful allies. It remained unclear, however, if these newly independent states were willing to go beyond rhetorical support for colonized peoples still struggling for their freedom. Many Third World nations had their own internal problems with ethnic minorities and were reluctant to set the precedent that anticolonial solidarity or racial affinity should trump national sovereignty, particularly if it meant directly challenging an economic and military superpower such as the United States. And unlike the early days of the pan-African movement, when figures like Du Bois had operated on equal footing with fellow black internationalists, in a post-Bandung world African Americans would be approaching these new nations as supplicants.

The repressive domestic atmosphere of the 1950s initially hampered the ability of African Americans to even attempt to navigate the postcolonial landscape. In the decade that followed, however, the rapid spread of decolonization combined with developments in the Cold War to provide new potential allies and models in the Third World. Of particular relevance to the evolution of the U.S. Black Power movement was the emergence of revolutionary governments in Cuba and Algeria. The triumph of Fidel Castro and the Cuban revolution in 1959 and the victory of the Algerian Front de Libération Nationale (FLN) in its war for independence from France two years later offered a new template for Third World liberation. In both cases guerrilla warfare campaigns brought to power governments that were committed not only to a form of socialism at home, but also to exporting anticolonial insurgency. The anticolonialism and antiracism enunciated at Bandung remained central in the 1960s, but in Cuba and Algeria these values found new and more aggressive champions willing to directly confront First World colonial powers. In the process they provided both practical and ideological support for a new generation of black activists in the United States.

Though Cuban foreign policy oscillated considerably during the 1960s, a recurring theme in the early years of Castro's government was that its survival depended on the success of other revolutions in the Western Hemisphere and beyond. This doctrine, epitomized in Ernesto "Che" Guevara's call for "two, three or many Vietnams . . . throughout the world," went beyond rhetoric to include material support for insurgencies from Bolivia to the former Belgian Congo. The combination of Guevara's *foco* theory of guerrilla warfare, which held that small groups of committed rebels could successfully initiate a revolutionary struggle without waiting for a mass popular uprising, and Castro's willingness to commit his government to providing direct assistance in support of this proposition, pushed the boundaries of Third World anticolonialism much further than had been contemplated at Bandung.[12] Among the first recipients of aid from the new Cuban government was the Algerian FLN. After successfully ousting the French in 1962, the new Algerian government under Ahmed Ben Bella went on to offer material support and a base of operations to groups ranging from the Palestine Liberation Organization (PLO) to the African National Congress (ANC) and the South Vietnamese National Liberation Front (NLF).[13] By the latter half of the 1960s, Cuba and Algeria would become important destinations for the Black Panthers and other African American revolutionaries seeking shelter and support.

Beyond their practical contributions to a more militant strain of anti-colonialism, the Cuban and Algerian revolutions also led to a sharpened focus on the links between race, culture, nationalism, and revolution in both the Third and First Worlds. Although its domestic record when it came to confronting the legacy of white supremacy in Cuban society was mixed, internationally Castro's government enthusiastically expanded on the anti-racism of Bandung by linking its support for revolution in Africa and Latin American to a solidarity rooted in the experience of racialized Western colonialism.[14] Nor were Cuban efforts to link race, revolution, and anti-colonialism confined to the Third World. From Castro's dramatic visit to Harlem in September 1960 (where he and the Cuban delegation to the UN stayed at the Hotel Theresa) to hosting a range of African American dissidents and exiles, the new revolutionary government actively cultivated links to the black freedom struggle in the United States throughout the first half of the 1960s.[15]

While less directly relevant to the situation of African Americans, the Algerian revolution ended up producing arguably the single most impor-tant statement on race, identity, and decolonization in the twentieth cen-tury. The Martinique-born and French-educated psychiatrist Frantz Fanon authored several landmark studies on race and colonialism in the 1950s and early 1960s. His most influential work, and the one that won him the attention of Black Power advocates in the United States, was born of his experience fighting with the FLN in Algeria. *The Wretched of the Earth*, published shortly before Fanon's death in 1961, linked the struggle for Third World independence to a decolonization of the mind among racial-ized colonial subjects. As part of this process, Fanon argued, violence against colonial oppressors was "a cleansing force" that "rids the colonized of their inferiority complex, of their passive and despairing attitude."[16] Anticolonial violence was not new—the Mau Mau revolt in Kenya, for example, had attracted international attention and divided the civil rights community in the United States during the 1950s.[17] Nor did Fanon uncritically celebrate violence as a solution to all of the problems ailing the colonized world. But in linking the willingness to forcefully confront racialized oppression to an exploration of the psychological effects of colonialism and white supremacy on its victims, Fanon provided a potential bridge between decolonization in the Third World and the struggles of people of color in the First World. He also challenged Marxist notions that the industrial working class was the sine qua non of revolution. Fanon highlighted not only the rural peasantry but also the lumpenproletariat, "the pimps, the hooligans, the unemployed, and the petty criminals," as "one of the most spontaneously and radically revolutionary forces of a colonized people." By the mid-1960s, *The Wretched of the Earth* was known as the "black bible" among African American militants, with *Liberation* editor and activist Daniel Watts declaring that "[e]very brother on a rooftop can quote Fanon."[18]

Collectively the Cuban and Algerian revolutions helped to crystallize a new, more militant expression of anticolonial internationalism. In word and deed, the Cuban and Algerian governments born of revolution cultivated the notion of a shared struggle that pitted oppressed subjects everywhere against colonialism and white supremacy. Che Guevara's insistence that "[s]olidarity among peoples does not now come from religion, customs, tastes, racial affinity or its lack. . . . [but] from a similarity in economic social conditions and from a similarity in desire for progress and recuperation" expressed a logic that would become central to the efforts of the BPP and other groups to link their struggle to those of Third World peoples.[19] From the striking images of bearded guerrillas to widely circulated texts such as Guevara's *Guerrilla Warfare* and Fanon's *The Wretched of the Earth*, the Cuban and Algerian revolutions nurtured a populist anticolonial internationalism whose reach far exceeded the more tempered vision outlined at Bandung. In the United States, these developments contributed to the ideological development of black internationalism and anticolonialism well before the BPP turned to Cuba and Algeria for more practical material support in the late 1960s and early 1970s.

Two other developments in the early 1960s influenced the evolution of Third World anticolonialism in a way that would have long-lasting repercussions for the more militant wing of the black freedom struggle in the United States. The first was the Sino–Soviet split and the ensuing competition for leadership in the Third World between the two former allies. While the Soviet Union under Nikita Khrushchev distanced itself from the legacy of Stalin and gradually sought a less confrontational relationship with the United States, Chinese leaders rejected the notion of peaceful coexistence and denounced Soviet "revisionism" as cowardly and reactionary. In practice, this translated into substantial Chinese support for revolutionary movements in the Third World coupled with aggressively anti-American rhetoric.[20] Ideologically, Maoism's modification of Marxism to give nationalism an equal place with proletarian internationalism was attractive to both Third World anticolonalists and black nationalists in the United States. This was particularly so compared to the ossified party line offered by Moscow and often echoed by the leadership of the Communist Party USA

(CPUSA).[21] But the abstract appeal of Maoism as a doctrine cannot be divorced from the practical impact of Chinese foreign policy in the 1960s, particularly in comparison to the more conciliatory stance of the Soviet Union. Mao was not simply the author of the "Little Red Book" but also the leader of a large, powerful, and (after 1964) nuclear-armed nonwhite nation that was willing to risk conflict with the United States and its allies in support of anticolonialism and antiracism. This included not only aid to the Third World but also direct outreach to African Americans. In response to urging by Robert F. Williams, in August 1963 Mao issued a statement linking the "evil system of colonialism and imperialism" to the advent of the African slave trade and offering Chinese solidarity with the black freedom struggle in the United States.[22] As with Algeria and Cuba, it was the combination of action and ideology that made China an attractive model to some black activists during the 1960s.

A final major factor in the evolution of the Third World political project in the 1960s, as well as the birth of the BPP and similar groups in the United States, was the increasingly heavy-handed interventionism of the U.S. government. The 1956 Suez crisis—in which British, French, and Israeli forces invaded Egypt in response to President Gamal Abdel Nasser's decision to nationalize the Suez Canal—and the bitter French resistance to Algerian independence had served notice that Europe was not entirely ready to concede to the anticolonial mandate laid down at Bandung.[23] By the early 1960s, however, the United States had assumed the mantle of the most visible interventionist power in the Third World. The U.S. government's complicity in the ousting and subsequent murder of Congolese prime minister Patrice Lumumba in 1961 was particularly important in creating a perceived community of interest including African American activists and the Third World. Lumumba, whose defiant portrait would later become a fixture atop the international news section of the *Black Panther* newspaper, had helped lead resistance to Belgian rule and took office as Congo's first independent prime minister in June 1960 with harsh words for the country's former colonial master. Within days of independence, the new prime minister confronted a Belgian-backed secessionist movement in the mineral-rich province of Katanga as well as a mutiny within the army, which had remained under the control of Belgian officers even after independence. When the UN delayed responding to Lumumba's urgent request for aid to put down the secessionist forces, he expressed a willingness to accept Soviet assistance. Shortly afterward, Lumumba was removed from power in a CIA-supported coup (which followed an abortive American plan to assassinate the Congolese prime minister). Captured while trying to rally his forces several months later, Lumumba was turned over to secessionist forces and executed by a firing squad supervised by Belgian officers on January 17, 1961.[24]

The tangle of neocolonialism and Cold War intrigue that surrounded Lumumba's death was a harsh reminder of the limits of formal independence in the Third World. Reflecting the global attention focused on decolonization and its discontents, news of Lumumba's murder provoked angry protests from Cairo to London to Tokyo. In the United States, the most dramatic reaction took the form of a demonstration inside the gallery of the UN Building on February 15, 1961. Loosely organized by a coalition of black nationalist groups and artists, including Maya Angelou, Abbey Lincoln, Amiri Baraka, Rosa Guy, and jazz drummer Max Roach, some sixty protesters expressed their anger at UN secretary general Dag Hammarskjold for failing to save Lumumba. The demonstration, which coincided with a speech by U.S. representative Adlai Stevenson, disrupted a meeting of the Security Council and escalated into a running battle with police in and around the UN Building. That evening some two hundred protesters attempted to march on Times Square while chanting their support for Lumumba and his legacy of resistance to colonialism before being turned back by police and regrouping in Harlem.[25]

The UN "riot" (as the *New York Times* dubbed it) was a significant moment in the rise of Third World–oriented black internationalism in the United States. Daniel Watts, one of the protest organizers, argued that "the spontaneous demonstrations in the Security Council marked the beginning of the departure of Negro militants from passive, peaceful, largely legalistic protests."[26] Perhaps more significantly, the UN protest foreshadowed the efforts of the BPP and other groups to use Third World rhetoric and symbols to build a grassroots domestic coalition among urban African Americans. The protesters who gathered at the UN in mid-February 1961 were a diverse lot, ranging from jazz musicians to members of the Cultural Association of Women of African Heritage (CAWAH), the International Muslim Society, and the Universal African Legion. The demonstrations reflected these diverse roots as protesters joined their chants of "Congo, yes! Yankee, no!" with cries of "Viva Nasser!" (for the Egyptian president) and demands that the word "Negro" be abolished and replaced with "Afro-American."[27] Though Afrocentric and black nationalist groups played an important role in the Lumumba protests, the fact that many of their slogans were modified from those employed during the Cuban revolution illustrated the broad

↑ push - pull factors

appeal of a synthetic Third World identity that transcended any one nation or even continent.[28] As scholar Cynthia Young observed, "The fact that the Lumumba protest occasioned the articulation of a new black identity demonstrates how 1960s anticolonialism and black cultural politics were mutually constitutive. A new black American identity . . . resulted from a transnational consciousness, one that drew on anticolonial critiques for its political analysis and international legitimacy."[29] More specifically, the UN protest also foreshadowed the BPP's later effort to construct an anticolonial vernacular that melded Third World rhetoric and symbols with the concerns and sensibilities of urban black Americans.

The Bay of Pigs fiasco in Cuba in April 1961 and the landing of U.S. marines during the 1965 Dominican crisis also helped to draw attention to the role of the U.S. government in oppressing people of color around the world. Nothing was more important in this respect, however, than the Vietnam War. President Lyndon B. Johnson's escalation of the war in 1964–65 helped to unite an otherwise fractious Third World and provided a potential link to black Americans who saw themselves as fellow victims of racialized U.S. violence. "U.S. intervention in Vietnam," concluded historian Lien-Hang Nguyen, "made Hanoi's war the most visible national liberation struggle in the Third World and revolutionaries in the Global South took heed. Although the Vietnam War unfolded in a tiny part of Southeast Asia, it was ubiquitous."[30] Journalist I.F. Stone was more blunt in assessing the radicalizing effect of the war, declaring, "Lyndon Johnson may precipitate what Che Guevara alone could never accomplish."[31] Just as the war in Vietnam helped to unite many in the Third World against U.S. aggression, so did it help to provide a common frame of reference for the predominantly white New Left and elements of the emerging Black Power movement. Within the United States, the war generated opposition not just on college campuses but also among elements of the black freedom struggle, including SNCC and RAM.[32]

The impact of the Vietnam War on the evolution of both Third World anticolonialism and the black freedom struggle was vividly illustrated at the Tricontinental Conference of Asian, African and Latin American Peoples held in Havana in January 1966, nine months prior to the founding of the BPP. The delegates gathered in Cuba for the conference continued to champion the core values of antiracism and anticolonialism. The Havana meeting was notable for adding Latin America to the Afro-Asian solidarity movement created at Bandung, but also, as David Kimche observed, "because this was the first time that such a conference openly called on its members to embark on the course of armed struggle and openly preached revolution to those operating in independent countries."[33] The final declaration of the Tricontinental Conference not only proclaimed "the right of the people to meet imperialist violence with revolutionary violence" but also specifically identified the United States as the world's leading imperialist power, with a particular emphasis on its role in Vietnam.[34] The explicitly anti-American character of many of the conference's proclamations, as well as the participation of both China and the USSR, marked a move away from nonalignment toward a more direct confrontation with "Yankee imperialism." At the same time, the conference also moved to establish links between the Third World and communities of color inside the United States. Chinese delegate Wu Hsueh-chien hailed "our United States Negro brothers in their just struggle against racial discrimination and for democratic rights," and the conferees passed a resolution linking the 1965 Watts rebellion to the shared struggle "against racism and U.S. imperialism in a common cause with the Vietnamese brothers."[35]

Malcolm X, Robert F. Williams, and the Tragedy of African American Diplomacy

By the early 1960s, the waning of McCarthy-era travel restrictions combined with the rise of revolutionary governments in the Third World to create unprecedented opportunities for black activists to move beyond rhetorical internationalism. Now they could engage in ad hoc diplomacy aimed at cultivating allies in a global struggle against white supremacy. Malcolm X and Robert F. Williams stood at the forefront of African American efforts to engage internationally in the first half of the 1960s. Moving beyond the broad-based transnationalism represented by the pan-African movement in the first half of the twentieth century, Malcolm and Williams engaged directly with the governments of postcolonial states in the Third World. Although tentative and fraught with dangers, their pioneering efforts helped to distinguish the internationalism of the emerging Black Power movement from both the previous generation of black anticolonialists and the contemporary liberal civil rights movement. At the same time they laid the groundwork for the BPP's later attempts to create an institutional African American presence in the Third World.

After breaking with Elijah Muhammad and the Nation of Islam (NOI) in March 1964, Malcolm X expanded upon his earlier efforts to internationalize the black freedom struggle. Seeking to bridge the gulf that separated black Americans from Third World people, Malcolm stressed their common experience as victims of racialized oppression while suggesting that anticolonial violence might be necessary to achieve black freedom in the United States. "The same conditions that prevailed in Algeria that forced the people, the noble people of Algeria, to resort eventually to the terrorist-type tactics that were necessary to get the monkey off their backs," he declared in May 1964, "those same conditions prevail today in America in every Negro community." Anticipating the later efforts of the BPP, Malcolm highlighted police brutality and economic exploitation as examples of the ways in which white supremacy afflicted people of color from Harlem to Algiers while emphasizing the role of capitalism in generating and sustaining racialized oppression.[36] He also sought to demonstrate that an alliance with the Third World could reap practical benefits for African Americans. While people of color were a minority in the United States, by linking with the Third World they could become part of a global majority of color. Elevating their struggle from the national terrain of the civil rights movement to an international appeal for human rights would allow African Americans to "take it into the United Nations, where our African brothers can throw their weight on our side, where our Asian brothers can throw their weight on our side, where our Latin-American brothers can through their weight on our side, and where 800 million Chinamen are sitting there waiting to throw their weight on our side."[37]

While his life was cut short before he could fully explore the possibilities of an alliance with the nations of the Third World, Malcolm X began to lay the groundwork for such an approach in 1964–65. During two trips to Africa and the Middle East he attempted to win practical support for the black freedom struggle in the United States from Third World governments. Most ambitiously, he traveled to the July 1964 meeting of the Organization of African Unity (OAU) in Cairo in order "to represent the interests of 22 million African-Americans whose *human rights* are being violated daily by the racism of American imperialists." His goal was not simply to win sympathy from the OAU but also to prompt them to take action by using their power to arraign the United States for its treatment of black Americans before the UN Commission on Human Rights.[38] But while he was warmly received and accorded official observer status at the meeting, Malcolm was unable to convince the OAU to support his UN resolution. This setback highlighted a recurring problem facing advocates of an alliance with the Third World. While African Americans might benefit from such external pressure, it was unclear what they could offer in return, particularly in comparison to the benefits of maintaining friendly relations with the U.S. government. Though Malcolm attempted to convince the assembled nations that "[y]our problems will never be fully solved until and unless ours are solved," his rhetoric and charisma were little match for the lure of U.S. economic and military aid. The power of what he referred to as "dollarism" to trump Third World solidarity with communities of color in the United States would be a recurring challenge for Black Power advocates in the 1960s and 1970s.[39]

Though Malcolm X was the most visible pioneer in establishing links between black Americans and the Third World during the early 1960s, several other groups and individuals also made important contributions. A community of African Americans living in Ghana, including W.E.B. and Shirley Graham Du Bois, Maya Angelou, Vicki Garvin, William Alphaeus Hunton, and Alice Windom were instrumental in linking the black freedom struggle in the United States to developments in the postcolonial African nation most closely associated with pan-Africanism under the rule of Kwame Nkrumah. Garvin, Angelou, and Windom played a particularly pivotal role in introducing Malcolm to the shifting currents of black internationalism in the context of African decolonization.[40] Representatives from SNCC, including John Lewis and James Foreman, also spent a month touring Africa in the fall of 1964, meeting with African leaders and crossing paths with Malcolm in Kenya.[41] It was Robert F. Williams, however, who provided the most successful example of practical alliance building in the Third World prior to the efforts of the Black Panther Party.

Williams had drawn national attention in the late 1950s when he organized and armed black residents of Monroe, North Carolina to defend themselves against attacks by the Ku Klux Klan. His outspoken support for the Cuban revolution as part of the Fair Play for Cuba Committee (FPCC) won Williams an invitation to visit the island, and he was personally received there by Castro in June 1960. The following month he made a return trip as head of a delegation that included poet and playwright Amiri Baraka and cultural critic Harold Cruse.[42] In the aftermath of an August 1961 incident in Monroe, in which Williams led the armed defense of his neighborhood against the Klan, he was indicted by the FBI and chose to flee the country rather than surrendering to the authorities. Welcomed by Castro's government, Williams was allowed access to Cuban presses for his *Crusader* newspaper and a fifty-thousand-watt transmitter that beamed his *Radio Free Dixie* program across the southeastern United States three times a week.[43]

The key to Williams's success in forming working alliances in the Third World, one that the BPP would later embrace, was in his choice of allies and willingness to directly engage with Cold War geopolitics. The nonaligned African states that Malcolm X approached in 1964 had much to lose and little to gain from pressuring the United States over its domestic record on race relations. In addition to risking access to U.S. military or economic aid, many of these new nations were wary of setting the precedent that racial or ideological solidarity should trump national sovereignty.[44] Castro's revolutionary government, however, had no such concerns in the early 1960s. Already locked in a bitter struggle with the United States and committed to exporting its revolution, the Cubans welcomed Williams as a natural ally. While the personal rapport between Castro and Williams may have facilitated this relationship, both sides had pragmatic reasons for working with one another. Cuban leaders scored a propaganda victory by highlighting U.S. racial troubles and exposing cracks in the façade of Cold War liberalism. Williams, meanwhile, received a high-profile platform for his views as well as protection from the U.S. government.

Williams's ad hoc diplomacy highlighted both the opportunities and pitfalls of directly engaging with the Cold War in the Third World. The rise of a more militant anticolonialism, exemplified by the Cuban and Algerian revolutions, combined with the polarizing effects of U.S. intervention in Vietnam to create potential new allies for black Americans. These revolutionary states were not only willing to directly challenge the United States but were also far more attuned to the issues of race, culture, and nationalism that animated the American Black Power movement than the Soviet Union or its Warsaw Pact allies (or, for that matter, the CPUSA). However, in casting their lot with revolutionary states in the Third World, Williams and those who later followed in his footsteps (including the BPP) faced a new set of problems. Not only did such alliances alienate some potential supporters in the United States, they also placed black activists at the mercy of governments whose interests did not always coincide with their own. The bonds of anticolonialism, racial affinity, and international proletarian solidarity were seldom strong enough to override more narrow calculations of national interest by even the most revolutionary of governments. As John Gronbeck-Tedesco observed in his study of Cuba and the U.S. Left, "While Cuba's tricontinentalism crafted a multiracial, multicultural and multinational community, it was at the same time a state discourse, which employed the transnational dynamic towards nationalist ends."[45]

Williams witnessed the limits of Cuban solidarity firsthand during his exile. Although initially welcomed by Castro, by the mid-1960s he found himself left out in the cold as a result of changes in Cuban politics and national security policy. As Castro's government fell increasingly into the Soviet orbit, the adventurous revolutionary spirit exemplified by Che Guevara was replaced by a more cautious policy aimed at avoiding a direct confrontation with the U.S. government. The Cuban government also increasingly followed an orthodox Marxist line that downplayed the possibility of an imminent black revolution in the United States in favor of the kind of longer-term, class-based alliance with white workers advocated by Moscow and the CPUSA. The existence of a large Afro-Cuban population, including many who still experienced discrimination even after the revolution, also made Cuban leaders wary of the domestic implications of Black Power even as they publicly hailed many of its leaders in the United States.[46] Increasingly constrained by the evolving domestic and international politics of the Cuban government, Williams relocated to China in July 1965. From Beijing he lashed out at his former Cuban hosts, lamenting that "the bourgeois oriented power structure of some socialist states, even one with a black and white population, would prefer to preserve the white reactionary anti-communist power structure in racist America, their natural enemy, than to see a just, democratic, fraternal socialist state brought about by the revolutionary action of oppressed blacks."[47] While the ability to cultivate multiple partners in the Third World somewhat alleviated the dangers of relying on foreign governments for support, as non-state actors with limited resources at their disposal Williams and other Black Power activists struggled to bargain on equal terms with their sometimes reluctant hosts. As Williams biographer Timothy B. Tyson concluded, "A hard truth for all who admire Williams's courage and leadership in the freedom movement is that, snared in exile, he became less a player than a pawn in the Cold War."[48]

Beyond the tactical difficulties that Malcolm X and Robert F. Williams encountered in trying to forge alliances in the Third World during the early 1960s, both men also struggled with the more fundamental question of how to apply the militant anticolonialism represented by Guevara and Fanon in the context of black life in the United States. Though Malcolm insisted that "we're just as thoroughly colonized as anybody else," his anticolonialism shifted after leaving the NOI to emphasize local control over urban black communities rather than working toward an independent homeland.[49] "The political philosophy of black nationalism," he asserted in April 1964, "means that the black man should control the politics and the politicians in his own community; no more."[50] While this was perhaps a more practical goal than the NOI's plan for complete secession, it remained unclear exactly how the alliances that Malcolm sought to cultivate in Africa and elsewhere would translate into better living conditions for African Americans in Harlem, Detroit, and Watts. And while his rhetoric was clearly influenced by the Cuban, Algerian, and Vietnamese struggles for independence, Malcolm's Organization of Afro-American Unity (OAAU) was not a guerrilla *foco* but rather a fairly conventional domestic pressure group. Indeed, with its emphasis on bread-and-butter issues affecting African Americans, the OAAU had more in common with the NAACP than with the NLF or the FLN.[51]

Had he not been assassinated in February 1965, Malcolm might have found a way to better integrate the militant anticolonialism of Che Guevara and Frantz Fanon with his emphasis on black nationalism as a form of local community control. But Robert F. Williams struggled with a similar dilemma throughout the decade as he sought to reconcile Third World solidarity and anticolonial violence with his evolving approach to civil rights within the United States. While his tactics distressed the national leadership of the NAACP, Williams's goals, including the integration of public facilities and the elimination of racial discrimination in hiring, remained well within the mainstream of the liberal civil rights movement during the 1950s and early 1960s. Prior to his flight from the United States, Williams employed guns as a complement to nonviolent protest and a tool of self-defense against racist aggression rather than as part of an effort to launch a guerrilla war or overthrow the government. Even his controversial call to "meet violence with violence" and "stop lynching with lynching" came in response to the failure of the U.S. government to intervene in the South to protect African Americans. Actor and civil rights activist Julian Mayfield, who accompanied Williams on his second tour of Cuba in 1960, suggested that his flirtation with Castro's government was actually part of a larger plan to pressure the U.S. government to act more decisively on civil rights.[52] To this extent, Williams was still following the blueprint of the NAACP and the liberal civil rights movement, albeit with a novel set of allies and tactics. BPP founder Huey P. Newton acknowledged the influence of Williams's armed self-defense tactics, but he disapproved of "the way [Williams] had called on the federal government for assistance; we viewed the government as an enemy, the agency of a ruling clique that controls the country."[53]

The dichotomy between Williams's militant rhetoric and relatively mainstream vision of civil rights reform was heightened in the aftermath of his August 1961 flight to Cuba. In an influential 1964 article in the pages of the *Crusader*, "USA: The Potential of a Minority Revolution," Williams called for "an urban guerrilla war" and urged black Americans to stockpile "[h]and grenades, bazookas, light mortars, rocket launchers, machine guns and ammunition." But even as he embraced armed struggle and the examples set by Cuban, Algerian, and Vietnamese guerrilla fighters, he continued to celebrate "America's true cause and commitment to her Constitution, democratic principles and the rights of man" and hailed the black contribution to "our beloved country," the United States.[54] Though Williams was adopted as a figurehead by groups seeking both the violent overthrow of the U.S. government (RAM) and a separate black homeland (the Republic of New Afrika), his militant rhetoric masked a reformist agenda that remained little changed from his days in the NAACP. Harold Cruse perceptively observed the tension inherent in Williams's advocacy of guerrilla warfare tactics in service of goals that ultimately differed little from those of the liberal civil rights movement. "One can objectively shoot a Klansman 'defensively' or 'offensively,'" Cruse remarked, "but to succeed in shooting one's way into voting rights, jobs, and 'desegregated' public facilities calls for much deeper thought than certain revolutionaries seem to imagine."[55]

It is hardly surprising that the initial efforts at Black Power diplomacy in the Third World in the early 1960s ran into both practical and theoretical difficulties. The combination of a rapidly evolving international environment, one in which the Third World itself was seldom united, and the disproportionate military and economic influence wielded by the U.S. government created a challenge for even the most savvy emissaries. Moreover, the domestic legacy of McCarthy-era repression and Cold War conformity put black activists of the early 1960s in the difficult position of building these relationships virtually from scratch, with little in the way of practical examples to follow. Pioneering black internationalists such as W.E.B. Du Bois, Paul Robeson, and Vicki Garvin, as well as organizations such as the NOI and the Council on African Affairs (CAA) could provide inspiration, but they offered no firm institutional or ideological foundation on which to build a black relationship with the Third World. Even as Malcolm X and Robert F. Williams struggled to implement a form of Black Power diplomacy, however, other figures within the movement were closing the circle by importing the theory and practice of decolonization to the United States.

"Black Is a Country": Black Arts and Revolutionary Nationalism

The repressive political atmosphere of the 1950s meant that American activists had had little choice but to look overseas to find a friendly venue to explore the intersection between the black freedom struggle and Third World anticolonialism. But as the political power of McCarthyism waned and the liberal civil rights movement forced contention of the American system of apartheid into the political mainstream, opportunities opened up in the 1960s for those interested in fusing domestic and international developments to pursue novel strategies for black liberation within the United States. In an illustration of the intersection between the Third World and the origins of the Black Power movement, two key figures in this process were part of the delegation that Williams brought to Cuba in July 1960. Amiri Baraka, still named LeRoi Jones at the time, a beatnik poet and playwright living in New York's Greenwich Village, found the trip to be a transformative experience. Seeing "a whole lot of young dudes my own age who were walking around with guns" jolted Baraka into believing that revolution was possible not only in the Third World but also perhaps in the United States.[56] Though he would later play a direct role in the formative years of the BPP, Baraka's contribution to the party's origins predated his stint as a visiting artist at San Francisco State University (SFSU) in 1967. As a pivotal figure in the Black Arts Movement, Baraka melded nationalism and Third World anticolonialism in creating a "post-American" identity that, in the words of historian Melanie McAlister, existed "outside of, and in opposition to, the expanding role of the United States on the world stage."[57]

Baraka's essays, plays, and poems in the early 1960s echoed a number of themes later championed by the BPP, including a rejection of the middle-class leadership of the liberal civil rights establishment, skepticism about the goal of integration, and a ringing call for "a literal murdering of the American socio-political stance, not only as it directly concerns American Negroes, but in terms of its stranglehold on most of the modern world." The way in which he expressed this critique, with an emphasis on urban African American vernacular and a flourish of rhetorical violence ("poems that shoot guns . . . wrestle cops into alleys and take their weapons leaving them dead") also anticipated the Panthers' anticolonial vernacular during the latter half of the 1960s.[58] Perhaps most importantly, Baraka championed the link between urban black nationalism and the Third World that would later become a crucial part of the Panthers' appeal in the late 1960s. His 1962 declaration that "[i]n America, black *is* a country" drew on traditions of black nationalism going back to Marcus Garvey and the NOI while situating it as "only a microcosm of the struggle of the new countries all over the world."[59] Grappling directly with the land question that had plagued previous black nationalist ventures, Baraka argued that rather than fixating on secession or emigration, "[w]hat the Black Man must do now is look down at the ground upon which he stands, and claim it as his own." Specifically, African Americans should build up a base of power where they were already concentrated: in "[b]lack cities all over this white nation. Nations within nations."[60] Facilitating this vision of urban black nationalism in the heart of a First World superpower was the notion of African Americans as part of a global nonwhite majority. Building on themes espoused by Malcolm X, Baraka insisted that "[t]he only difference between the Congo and, say, Philadelphia, Mississippi is the method the white man employs to suppress and murder." Baraka thus saw "establishing an honest connection [with] . . . the rest of the nonwhite world" as crucial to the success of black nationalism in the United States.[61] The Third World would have an incentive to come to the aid of this movement because "no other nation on earth is safe, unless the Black Man in America is safe. . . . And there is only one people on the planet who can slay the white man. The people who know him best. His ex-slaves."[62]

Baraka's emphasis on a form of virtual sovereignty centered in urban black communities and validated by a connection to the Third World was an important innovation that extended the work of Malcolm X. Attuned to the rising wave of militant anticolonialism in the Third World, Baraka cited Fanon and the struggle in Vietnam among his inspirations in seeking to build "a National Liberation Front that would include all groups and aspirations" as part of the "war of liberation going on now in America."[63] Like Malcolm, Baraka was often vague with respect to the question of how, precisely, this kind of militant anticolonialism would work on a practical level for a minority group within the United States. But along with other Black Arts Movement figures such as Larry Neal, Sonia Sanchez, Marvin X (Marvin Jackmon), and Askia M. Touré (Roland Snellings), Baraka produced cultural works that were both cosmopolitan and firmly rooted in a sharp and sometimes profane urban African American vernacular. Taking up Fanon's notion of "combat literature . . . [that] calls upon a whole people to join in the struggle for the existence of the nation," Baraka's works in the early to mid-1960s helped provide the cultural foundation for a cosmopolitan black nationalism with an affinity for the Third World.[64]

Harold Cruse, who had accompanied Baraka on the July 1960 Cuban tour led by Robert F. Williams, played an even more direct role in the early 1960s efforts to forge links between the African American freedom struggle and anticolonial revolution in the Third World. In a 1962 article in *Studies on the Left*, "Revolutionary Nationalism and the Afro-American," Cruse addressed the domestic implications of anticolonialism in a way that influenced an entire generation of activists and provided the theoretical underpinnings of the BPP's ideology. "From the beginning," he declared, "the American Negro has existed as a colonial being."

> His enslavement coincided with the colonial expansion of European powers and was nothing more or less than a condition of domestic colonialism. Instead of the United States establishing a colonial empire in Africa, it brought the colonial system home and installed it in the Southern states. When the Civil War broke up the slave system and the Negro was emancipated, he gained only partial freedom. Emancipation elevated him only to the position of a semi-dependent man, not to that of an equal or independent being.[65]

African Americans' history as colonial subjects not only gave them something in common with the new nations of the Third World, it also had important implications for their domestic struggles. As with the former European colonies in Asia, Africa, and the Middle East, the situation facing African Americans was "much more than a problem of racial discrimination; it [was] a problem of political, economic, cultural, and administrative underdevelopment."[66] In the face of centuries of white supremacy and systematic colonial exploitation, Cruse wrote, "it is impossible for American society as it is now constituted to integrate or assimilate the Negro."[67] Cruse thus provided a theoretical model that both explained the inherent limits of the liberal civil rights movement and pointed to the need for a domestic revolution on par with decolonization in the Third World.

The notion of African Americans as a colonized people within the United States was not new. As early as 1852, Martin R. Delany had declared that American blacks were "a nation within a nation," comparing their situation to that of the Irish in Great Britain or Poles in Russia.[68] The 1928 "Black Belt" thesis of the Communist International (Comintern) was also based on this premise, and the NOI later offered a non-Marxist variation. But Cruse, a former CPUSA member who had broken with the party over what he perceived to be its domination by a narrow group of white leaders,

updated the notion of internal colonization to better fit the international
and domestic situation of the early 1960s.[69] In his broad critique of Western
society and the historical role of capitalism in creating and sustaining racial
inequities, Cruse retained elements of his former commitment to Marxism. But rather than looking to Europe or to an alliance with the white
working class, he insisted that "[t]he revolutionary initiative has passed to
the colonial world, and in the United States is passing to the Negro, while
Western Marxists theorize, temporize and debate."[70] Cruse's concept of
"revolutionary nationalism" melded the urban-centric black nationalism
of Marcus Garvey and the NOI with the anticolonial internationalism
of Bandung and a nonsectarian Marxist emphasis on the world-ordering
power of capitalism.

Like Garvey and the NOI, Cruse distrusted interracial organizations
and called for the creation of independent, black-run cultural, economic,
and political institutions. Unlike many black nationalists, however, Cruse
did not believe that these separatist organizations should be an end in and
of themselves. Rather, there were organizing bodies through which black
Americans would play a vanguard role in the revolutionary decolonization
of U.S. society as a whole. As both an analytical framework and a prescrip-
tion for social change, Cruse's revolutionary nationalism was crucial in the
development of the BPP and other urban Black Power organizations. It
provided a new generation of activists with a "useable past" (in harking back
to Garvey) while simultaneously linking black nationalism to the militant
Third World anticolonialism that had captured the imagination of younger
African American activists in the 1960s. Revolutionary nationalism validated the sentiment among some activists and intellectuals that separation
from white society was necessary to affect meaningful social change. At
the same time, Cruse's analysis held out hope that black-run organizations
could instigate a revolution that would eventually refashion the political,
economic, and cultural landscape of the entire United States rather than
remaining forever confined to the urban ghetto or the southern Black Belt.
In this respect, Cruse's revolutionary nationalism bridged the difference
between Marxism and black nationalism by way of the Third World.

A self-described "critical Kamikaze fighter on the cultural front,"
Cruse's strengths as a commentator were not matched by a similar tal-
ent for organizing or coalition building.[71] Relentlessly critical of commu-
nists, the liberal civil rights movement, and Black Power militants whom
he believed to be insufficiently thoughtful, Cruse was never able to fully
articulate a plan for implementing the kind of revolutionary changes that

he deemed necessary in U.S. society. Though prescient in identifying the difficulties that Robert F. Williams and those who followed in his footsteps (including the BPP) would have in "shooting one's way" into a more just society, Cruse's call for a "cultural revolution" that involved seizing control of "the entire American apparatus of cultural communication and placing it under public ownership" was if anything more ambitious and impractical.[72] And while he identified the black freedom struggle as part of a world-wide anticolonial movement, his insistence on "the uniqueness of Negro cultural complexities in America" led Cruse to be skeptical of the kind of international alliances pursued by Williams and Malcolm X.[73] Astute in observing the practical limits of Third World solidarity, Cruse's analysis left unanswered the question of how a domestic minority population could succeed in making a revolution in the United States without some sort of outside support. His most important contribution to the evolution of the black freedom struggle in the 1960s was to influence other activists who elaborated on the implications of revolutionary nationalism in the process of building grassroots organizations.

The Revolutionary Action Movement and the "Bandung World"

The Revolutionary Action Movement represented the most ambitious effort to synthesize the contributions of Cruse, Robert F. Williams, Malcolm X, the Black Arts Movement, and the Old Left during the early 1960s and was the single most influential organization in the origins of the BPP. While it never attracted the same level of public attention or popular participation as SNCC or the Black Panthers, as Robin Kelley and others have noted, RAM played a crucial role in the evolution of the U.S. Black Power movement, particularly with respect to its relationship the Third World and the Cold War.[74] The group originated in the spring of 1962 with student organizing efforts in Ohio led by Muhammad Ahmad (then known as Max Stanford), Wanda Marshall, Donald Freeman, and handful of African Americans affiliated with Students for a Democratic Society (SDS). Returning to his hometown of Philadelphia the following year, Ahmad helped bring RAM from the campus to the community. By the mid-1960s, the organization had branches in Philadelphia, Cleveland, New York, Oakland, and Detroit, as well as direct ties to Baraka, Williams (appointed the organization's leader in exile) and Malcolm X. RAM leaders also sought guidance from leftists and former CPUSA members, including "Queen Mother" Audley Moore, Harry Haywood, and James and Grace Lee Boggs.[75]

For all its eclectic influences, it was Cruse's revolutionary nationalism that played the most important role in shaping RAM's agenda. Ahmad explicitly cited Cruse's 1962 article "Revolutionary Nationalism and the Afro-American" as crucial to the group's formation, and in the years that followed he and other RAM leaders both embraced and subtly modified this doctrine. The group's twelve-point program declared that "black people in the U.S.A. are a captive nation suppressed and that their fight is not for integration into the white community but one of national liberation."[76] But while organized along racial and nationalist lines, RAM did not limit its goals to celebrating black culture or pursuing self-determination within their own communities. Rather, the organization's leaders insisted that "in order for Black America, Africa, Asia and Latin America to obtain universal self-determination . . . the present economic and political structure of White America . . . must be totally changed." Thus, while RAM theorists called for black Americans to "search deeply within their psyches, their everyday customs, actions and characteristics to revive their latent Africanism [and] renew their original culture," they sought to harness cultural nationalism in service of a socialist revolution that would liberate the entire country.[77] Following Cruse's lead, they embraced a form of socialism that acknowledged the intersectional nature of white supremacy and capitalism and sought to build an alternative while avoiding the sectarian disputes that had long plagued the U.S. Left.

RAM made two significant revisions to Cruse's formulation of revolutionary nationalism, both of which were later incorporated by the BPP. First, RAM leaders insisted that any successful revolution in the United States would inevitably entail violence. "Brooklyn is no different than Johannesburg—except distance," they declared, "[and we] feel that armed struggle is applicable in all cases."[78] Second, RAM went much further than Cruse in eliding the differences between African Americans and the peoples of the Third World. The American revolution would be part of a larger global struggle against capitalism and white supremacy, with the ultimate goal of "a world government under the dictatorship of the Black Underclass."[79] Key to this ambitious agenda was a very broad definition of what it meant to be black. In a 1964 manifesto, Ahmad declared that "black people of the world," which he defined as including "darker races, black, yellow, brown, red, [and] oppressed peoples," were "all enslaved by the same forces." Using this logic, he concluded that black nationalism "is really internationalism."[80]

Historically, "[a]ll of the Bandung, non-white peoples have been victims of
the system that has been formed by the European, built on the concept of
his racial superiority, in order to justify his 'minority' rule of the world." As
a result of four hundred years of racialized oppression, "all non-European
people . . . have similar if not the same cultural histories and have a common
destiny." As Donald Freeman explained it, this "common bondage unites
black America with the majority of mankind."[81]

The notion that a shared history as victims of white supremacy and capitalism linked African Americans to the rest of the nonwhite world had deep
roots in the history of black internationalism. W.E.B. Du Bois had drawn
similar connections in writing of the global significance of the color line at
the dawn of the twentieth century, and groups as diverse as the NOI, the
Comintern, and the CAA had previously advocated versions of this argument. It was in exploring the contemporary nature of this relationship that
RAM made its most important contribution during the early 1960s. RAM
leaders went beyond Du Bois, Cruse, and even Malcolm X in insisting
that African Americans were not only participants in a global anticolonial
struggle but also its natural leaders. In the global struggle "between capitalist and socialist forces . . . the Afro-American revolutionists have a vanguard
role . . . by virtue of their unique four hundred year endurance of 'Charlie's inhumanism' and their strategic domestic bondage within his 'belly.'"
Having helped build the wealth and power of United States through their
own forced labor, it was now the "prophetic mission" of black America "to
annihilate the 'imperialist beast' that its toil created."[82]

RAM's understanding of African Americans as an anticolonial vanguard poised to strike from inside the First World had practical implications
for the conduct of the black freedom struggle in the United States. Most
importantly, it meant that revolutionary nationalists in the United States
should act immediately, without waiting for outside support or approaching
foreign nations or international organizations as supplicants (as Malcolm X
attempted with the OAU in 1964). While acknowledging that "we must
unite with the 'Bandung' forces," RAM's leadership declared that it was
"defeatism" to insist that the revolution could not be successful without
lining up such support ahead of time. By virtue of their position as an
anti-imperialism *foco* within the United States, African Americans could,
through their own actions, create the conditions that made such an alliance
possible.[83] Although RAM leaders overestimated both the vulnerability of
the U.S. government and the willingness of other nations to come to their
aid, this analysis helped to embolden a new generation of black militants to

act on the assumption that their struggles would naturally garner support from a sympathetic Third World.

Another important contribution of RAM theorists to black internationalism in the 1960s was to acknowledge and address the divisions within both the Third World and socialist blocs. Conscious of the shift from the broad-based transnational anticolonialism that had characterized the period before decolonization to a Third World internationalism rooted in newly independent nation states, RAM leaders realized that this new environment required them to distinguish between potential allies. While all non-white peoples may have historically experienced similar oppression, not all Third World governments were equally committed to confronting the United States as the contemporary leader of the world's imperialist powers. Thus, even as they identified themselves with the "Bandung World" and celebrated Third World anticolonialism, RAM leaders explicitly rejected the notion of nonalignment that had emerged at that conference and was later institutionalized in the form of the Non-Aligned Movement (NAM). "Nonalignment is *betrayal*," RAM insisted, "because it subordinates *international freedom (humanism)* to *national neo-colonialism*."[84] Attuned to disputes on this issue within the Third World, RAM publications condemned nations and groups (including the OAU) that they believed to be overly accommodating to the United States while celebrating the confrontational stance of Algeria, Cuba, and Vietnam, as well as the militant line laid down at the 1966 Tricontinental Conference in Havana. RAM leaders also paid close attention to the Sino-Soviet split. Scornful of the Soviet policy of peaceful coexistence, they cast their lot instead with Mao's China. The appeal of China for RAM had as much to do with that nation's willingness to support revolution around the world, even at the risk of provoking the United States, as it did with the doctrinal nuances of Maoism. "[T]he Black American radical and China are the paramount polarizers of the globe," RAM declared, as both were "dedicated to precipitating Armageddon."[85]

For all of RAM's contributions to black internationalism, the group struggled with both conceptual and practical problems from the very beginning. Its plans for attracting international support hinged on mounting a guerrilla warfare campaign that would topple the U.S. government. On the surface, this seemed a hopeless proposition. How could a minority group, not all of whom would be willing to join the struggle, hope to overthrow the government of the most powerful nation on the planet? Even sympathetic historians such as Robin Kelley have criticized RAM's seemingly naive plans for a ninety-day military victory against the U.S. establishment (a notion they took directly from Williams).[86] RAM leaders did give serious thought to how to overcome these seemingly insurmountable odds. Their answer was strikingly similar to that offered by the military apostles of aerial bombing as the future of warfare during the 1920s and 1930s. Like the interwar Anglo-American strategic bombing enthusiasts who had argued that a few well-placed bombs would bring speedy victory, RAM leaders believed that advanced capitalist economies were vulnerable to even the slightest of disruptions. "What we must understand," they argued, "is that 'Charlie's' system runs like an IBM machine."

> But an IBM machine has a weakness, and that weakness is its complexity. Put something in the wrong place in an IBM machine and it's finished for a long time. And so it is with this racist, imperialist system. Without mass communications and rapid transportation, this system is through.[87]

Building on Williams's vision of U.S. cities as sites of military action, RAM strategists believed they had identified the soft underbelly of U.S. industrial capitalism. A relatively small group of rebels could initiate "sabotage in the cities—knocking out the electrical power first, then transportation." The resulting disruption would bring the ruling class to its knees, encourage further uprisings among disaffected domestic groups, and trigger a flood of support from fellow revolutionaries overseas.[88]

The seductive notion that a handful of attacks by urban guerrillas could paralyze the entire U.S. political and economic system would continue to appeal to some black militants through the early 1970s. There was, however, little evidence to suggest that this strategy amounted to more than wishful thinking. The experience of World War II had belied prewar predictions that advanced industrial economies were so fragile that they would immediately collapse once the bombs started falling. Harold Cruse, who had witnessed the effects of bombing firsthand while serving in the U.S. Army in Europe and North Africa, perceptively observed the limits of a strategy aimed at bringing about a revolution by lobbing a handful of bombs. "If [Robert F.] Williams had been to war in Europe," declared Cruse, "he would have seen that nothing sabotages capitalistic property more thoroughly than the war machine of the enemy. But that did not matter, for the capitalist owners simply rebuilt their property and proceeded to exploit it as before, under the same system."[89] This equation would hold as true in Watts, Newark, and Detroit as it had in Hamburg, Cologne, and West Berlin. Absent a strategy for leveraging property destruction into fundamental political and economic change, urban insurrections would be nothing more than a minor inconvenience for those whose property was directly targeted.

As it was, RAM never tested its thesis about the viability of urban guerrilla warfare in the United States. For all the talk of being a vanguard party, RAM's leaders actually trailed behind the urban black masses in their willingness to engage in direct action. Characterized by a small, mostly middle-class membership, the group never built a substantial base of potential revolutionaries. The group's decision to "go underground" in 1965 further weakened its ability to engage in grassroots organizing.[90] RAM publications hailed the August 1965 Watts uprising as proof that "our people are learning through struggle" and compared the "the Black Freedom Fighters of Watts" to their Cuban comrades in their willingness to challenge "the kingpin of the atomic menace."[91] But Watts and the score of other urban disturbances that followed were spontaneous affairs in which RAM played no role in organizing or directing. While law enforcement officials charged the group with planning such actions, there is no evidence to suggest that RAM ever did more than discuss them in theoretical terms. A similar disconnect between theory and practice applied to RAM's approach to the Third World. While RAM publications promoted black internationalism and some members toured Cuba, the organization made little or no effort to translate its rhetoric of Third World solidarity into practical alliances. For all their cosmopolitanism, RAM's leaders never really grappled with the difficult task of building and maintaining relationships across geographic, cultural, and linguistic barriers. In large part, this failure stemmed from the assumption that no such efforts were necessary. Fueled by a form of African American exceptionalism, Ahmad and other RAM leaders were convinced that such alliances would flow naturally as other nations came to recognize their vanguard position in the worldwide anticolonial struggle. As Donald Freeman confidently predicted, "Once we create a revolutionary Black Political Party Asia, Africa and Latin America will indicate their solidarity with more than words."[92]

RAM's problems were further compounded by a combination of factors, including police and FBI repression as well as internal disputes over ideology and tactics. For all its bold plans for attacking white supremacy and capitalism, the group was largely male-dominated, never seriously engaged with the role of patriarchy as an axis of oppression, and frequently fell into romanticized notions of gendered violence and manhood in its plans for black liberation. As a group, it had little to show in the way of tangible accomplishments during its brief existence. Longer term, however, RAM had a major influence over the direction of the black freedom struggle during the 1960s. Individual members and local chapters spread the doctrine of revolutionary nationalism as they cross-fertilized with other emerging Black Power groups in this period, including SNCC, UHURU in Detroit, the Afro-American Institute in Cleveland, and the Black Arts Movement and the literary group UMBRA in New York City.[93] RAM's various publications, most notably the quarterly journal *Black America*, had a major impact on the development of a Third World Left in the United States. In melding black nationalism, anticolonial internationalism, and anticapitalism in the pages of *Black America* and elsewhere, RAM, in the words of Robin Kelley, "elevated revolutionary black nationalism to a position of critical theoretical importance for the Left in general."[94] RAM's theoretical and practical contributions had a particularly lasting impact in Oakland, where the organization and its offshoots played a direct role in the birth of the Black Panther Party.

Chapter 2

"Army 45 Will Stop All Jive"

Origins and Early Operations of the BPP,
1966–1967

In the fall of 1962, the Cuban missile crisis came to the streets of Oakland, California. In response to the blockade of Cuba announced by President John F. Kennedy on October 22, the Progressive Labor Movement (PL) held a demonstration outside of Merritt College in the predominantly African American neighborhood of North Oakland. Founded by dissident members of the CPUSA less than a year earlier, PL rejected Soviet "revisionism" while expressing vigorous support for both Maoism and Fidel Castro's revolutionary government in Cuba. Though the majority of speakers at the rally comprised, in the words of one observer, "a socialist group of white boys," its location insured that Oakland's black population was also well represented.[1] Among them was twenty-year-old Merritt student Huey P. Newton. Newton, who was then affiliated with the Afro-American Association (AAA), a nascent Bay Area black nationalist group, had not been invited to speak. In the aftermath of the rally, however, he was at the center of a spirited debate in front of an audience of several hundred people near the entrance to the campus. When Bobby Seale, another Merritt student, stepped up to defend the efforts of the federal government and the NAACP to pass civil rights legislation, Newton fired back that new laws were not the answer. Picking up on a theme most powerfully enunciated by Malcolm X, Newton argued that so long as the government refused to enforce the existing laws on the books, black people were better off taking care of themselves than looking to Washington for help.[2]

Four years after their impromptu debate in the shadow of the Cuban crisis, Newton and Seale cofounded the Black Panther Party for Self-Defense. By the end of the 1960s, the BPP had gone from an Oakland neighborhood group to a sprawling organization with dozens of chapters scattered around the United States, an international section headquartered in Algeria, and a weekly newspaper with a circulation of over 139,000. Cuba, meanwhile, became a magnet for exiled Panthers, eventually including Newton himself.[3] Newton and Seale's initial encounter in 1962 offers a revealing glimpse into the overlapping forces that shaped the birth and early operations of the BPP, including developments in the Third World and the Cold War, the growth of urban black nationalism and the ensuing tension with the liberal civil rights movement, the evolution of the U.S. Left outside the boundaries of the CPUSA, the role of institutions of higher education as centers of protest and activism, and the political geography and demographics of the San Francisco Bay Area.

Key to the theory and practice of the BPP during its early years was an understanding of urban black neighborhoods as colonized spaces that needed to be liberated before African Americans could truly be free. Drawing from Frantz Fanon, Mao Zedong, Che Guevara, and pioneering black internationalists such as Malcolm X and Robert F. Williams, the Panthers embraced a form of revolutionary nationalism that posited the dire conditions facing black Oaklanders as part of a worldwide system of oppression linked to capitalism and white supremacy. In doing so, the BPP's founders built directly on their experiences with other organizations, particularly the Revolutionary Action Movement (RAM), as well as lessons drawn from the daily lives of people of color in the Bay Area. Where Newton and Seale parted ways with their predecessors was in their efforts to translate the lessons of Third World anticolonialism into practical action in the context of urban black America.

Bandung by the Bay: Revolutionary Nationalism Comes to Oakland

The San Francisco Bay Area was fertile ground for a movement that fused black nationalism with Third World anticolonialism and a radical critique of capitalism and the Cold War. Well before the advent of the BPP, a number of local groups were at work on the theory and practice of these various elements, though often in relative isolation. From C.L. Dellums and the Brotherhood of Sleeping Car Porters (founded in 1926), through the battle to organize the waterfront in the 1930s and the diverse coalition behind the 1946 Oakland general strike, the Bay Area had a long tradition of cosmopolitan activism.[4] The history of East Bay unionism included links with the CPUSA and other groups expressing larger critiques of capitalism and imperialism. BPP chief of staff David Hilliard recalls in his autobiography, "When I'm growing up, Communist Party members openly recruit at the docks and in union halls, and there's no stigma attached to their ideas or practice. The political environment encourages the idea of internationalism; solidarity is the watchword, and we are surrounded by examples of people collectively asserting their power."[5] During the 1950s, Oakland was home to one of the most vibrant chapters of the CPUSA-affiliated Civil Rights Congress (CRC), which petitioned the United Nations to charge the U.S. government with genocide for its treatment of African Americans. In the early 1960s, local PL representatives joined the Young Socialist Alliance (YSA), Socialist Workers Party (SWP), and the UC Berkeley chapter of the CPUSA's W.E.B. Du Bois Club in staging Bay Area rallies and offering a critique of capitalism and its role in the systematic exploitation of domestic communities of color and Third World people. As historian James Smethurst observed, one result of the Bay Area's long and relatively continuous history of radical activism was that "the public campaigns and organization of the Left were a part of the cultural memory of young Black militants in ways that were unusual elsewhere."[6]

The Bay Area also had close connections to the development of both the military industrial complex and oppositional movements that questioned U.S. Cold War policies. The industrial base and strategic location for staging men and material across the Pacific that had made the region so important during World War II (and drawn so many African Americans from the South in search of jobs) contributed to making the Bay Area a crucial cog in the Cold War military buildup that began with the Korean War and continued through the Vietnam War era. The region was home to numerous military installations and defense contractors as well as two universities, the University of California, Berkeley (UCB) and Stanford, that helped create the scientific, technological, and intellectual architecture of U.S. Cold War strategy.[7] Not coincidentally, the Bay Area also gave birth to a series of vibrant movements that questioned the logic of both the Cold War and U.S. actions in the Third World. As early as May 1960, students at UCB staged a dramatic public challenge to the domestic effects of the Cold War by interrupting hearings of the House Committee on Un-American Activities (HUAC) in San Francisco.[8] The escalating war in Vietnam, the continuing tensions between the United States and Cuba, and the fallout from the Congo crisis all played out in the streets of the Bay Area during the 1960s. The 1962 PL-sponsored rally in support of Cuba outside the gates of Merritt College is one example of the way in which developments in the Third World and U.S. foreign policy intersected with the development of the black freedom struggle in the East Bay. The Berkeley-based Vietnam Day Committee (VDC) led several high-profile marches attempting to close the Oakland induction center, and its November 1965 demonstration ended in DeFremery Park in West Oakland, which would soon become a hub for Panther organizing and rallies.[9] Although anti–Vietnam War and Cold War–related activism in the Bay Area were often dominated by a combination of middle-class students and "socialist . . . white boys," by virtue of sheer geographic proximity these demonstrations made an impact on the development of black activism in the East Bay during the 1960s.

Developing in parallel with primarily white antiwar activism on campuses and in the streets of the Bay Area was an emerging black nationalist scene. During the 1920s, Oakland had hosted a chapter of Marcus Garvey's Universal Negro Improvement Association (UNIA). In the 1950s and 1960s, the Nation of Islam (NOI) had temples in San Francisco and West Oakland, and Malcolm X's May 1961 visit to UCB (where he had to speak off campus due to opposition from the university administration) stimulated broad local interest in black nationalism.[10] Among the local organizations that sprang up in the wake of Malcolm's visit was the Afro-American Association. Founded by UCB law student Khalid al-Mansour (then known as Donald Warden) and a handful of others in 1962, the AAA encouraged the cultivation of black pride and self-reliance while rejecting the liberal civil rights movement's emphasis on integration. Al-Mansour's charisma and his emphasis on rediscovering the black past attracted young activists ranging from Newton and Seale to Ronald Everett, who would later found the US Organization in Southern California under the name Maulana Karenga, and future Oakland mayor Elihu Harris. Though primarily focused on promoting cultural pride and black capitalism in the tradition of Marcus Garvey, the AAA also drew links to contemporary anticolonial struggles in Africa. At rallies, reading groups, and on his weekly Bay Area radio show, al-Mansour frequently invoked figures such as Kwame Nkrumah, Patrice Lumumba, and Kenyan leader Jomo Kenyatta.[11] Black nationalist organizations such as the AAA, meanwhile, coexisted with other formal and informal activism by people of color in the Bay Area. As scholar Jason M. Ferreira observed, "The notion of revolutionary Third Worldism was profoundly facilitated . . . [not only] by the sheer fact that many individuals within these Bay Area organizations had known each other for years," but also because "Black and Brown and Yellow and Red San Franciscans were connected, by buses, by schools, by neighborhoods, by cultures, and ultimately by histories."[12]

Public colleges and universities on both sides of the San Francisco Bay played a crucial role in nurturing a cosmopolitan strain of black activism in the early to mid-1960s. UC Berkeley was home to an NAACP chapter led by J. Herman Blake, who would later collaborate on many of Newton's writings, including his autobiography. The UCB chapter distinguished itself by inviting Robert F. Williams to speak on campus in March 1961 at a time when he was out of favor with the NAACP's national leadership. As with Malcolm's visit later that year, Williams's Bay Area appearance under the auspices of the Fair Play for Cuba Committee (FPCC) helped stimulate discussion about armed self-defense and the international dimensions of the black freedom struggle. The international orientation of black activism on the UCB campus was also fueled by the presence of a growing number of students from Ghana and Kenya during the early 1960s, an inadvertent side effect of U.S. Cold War policies aimed at using access to American higher education as a tool for winning support from these newly independent nations.[13] Even predominantly white organizations such as Students for a Democratic Society (SDS) played a role in spreading black nationalism at UCB. In October 1966 the Berkeley SDS chapter sponsored a major Black Power conference on campus that included an appearance by Stokely Carmichael (Kwame Ture) as well as local activists such as Mark Comfort.[14] Across the bay at San Francisco State University (SFSU), the Black Student Union (BSU) fused the emerging West Coast Black Power scene with the more established East Coast Black Arts Movement. As part of a larger effort to expand the black studies curriculum and faculty at SFSU in 1966–67, the BSU invited Amiri Baraka, Sonia Sanchez, and Askia Touré to campus as visiting faculty. They would interact with local students, artists, and activists including Bobby Seale, George Murray, and Eldridge Cleaver (who would go on to become, respectively, chairman, minister of education, and minister of information in the BPP).[15]

Merritt College in North Oakland played the most important role in bringing from the classroom to the community the emerging fusion between urban black nationalism, anticapitalism, and Third World anti-colonialism. Newton and Seale both attended Merritt in the early 1960s, and Newton later cited influences ranging from Marxism to the logical positivism of A.J. Ayers and the writings of Mao Zedong as examples of the ways in which the education he received there shaped his approach to black liberation.[16] But it was Merritt's location as a hub linking higher education, activism, and the surrounding black community in Oakland that accounted for its disproportionally influential role in the Bay Area Black Power movement. Though it had had few African Americans students when it opened in 1946 as a business and trade school, Oakland's shifting demographics, combined with the effects of the California Master Plan for Higher Education, led to a rapid rise in black enrollment at Merritt during the 1960s. While nearby UC Berkeley remained out of reach for most black Oakland residents, community colleges like Merritt offered a more accessible alternative. With a 40 percent black student body by the late 1960s, it featured, in the words of historian Martha Biondi, "the largest concentration of Black students at a predominantly white institution in the United States."[17]

The shift in the composition of Merritt's student body led to corresponding pressure to revamp the college's academic programs. The college offered its first black history course in 1964, and in the years to come student activism impelled the creation of one of the nation's pioneering black studies programs.[18] Unlike nearby UCB, where black students tended to be more isolated from both their peers and the surrounding community, Merritt was tightly integrated into the North Oakland neighborhood where it was located. Historian Donna Murch described the boundary between Merritt and the surrounding community as "completely porous," with students and local residents mingling on campus and eating together at the school cafeteria. Joining this mixture of students and local residents was a diverse group of local and national organizations, including the NOI, the AAA, and PL, that took advantage of Merritt's central location and ties to the community to stage rallies and recruit members.[19]

As a result of Merritt's spatial and demographic situation, when students such as Newton and Seale read Frantz Fanon's *The Wretched of the Earth* or *The Selected Works of Mao Tse-Tung* they experienced them not as exotic foreign imports but as organically related to the activism and debate that took place on campus and as part of the Bay Area's cosmopolitan Black Power and leftist scene. Newton recalled a seamless blending of classroom and street, with "rap sessions [taking] place all over, in cars parked in front of the liquor store on Sacramento Street near Ashby in Berkeley, outside places where parties were being held, and sometimes inside."[20] Figures such as Malcolm X, Amiri Baraka, Harold Cruse, and Robert F. Williams had wrestled with the challenge of reconciling their struggle at home and developments in the Third World with little in the way of examples to guide them. In contrast, young activists in the Bay Area in the mid-1960s not only had the precedents set by these pioneers to draw upon, but also a vibrant local environment in which to attempt to translate black nationalism and Third World anticolonialism into practice both at Merritt and beyond. As Murch observed, Merritt acted as a kind of proving ground where young activists not only developed skills and connections that they could then apply in the nearby community but also had a chance to exercise power in a way that would have been impossible in larger and more established institutions such as the NAACP, NOI, or Left/labor organizations such as PL.[21]

Starting in 1964, a small group of individuals affiliated with Merritt began to weave together the tangled threads of black nationalism, Third World anticolonialism, and anticapitalism, giving birth to a series of new organizations in the East Bay. Huey Newton is generally credited with being the driving force behind the creation of the BPP, but Bobby Seale also played a pivotal role in bringing revolutionary nationalism to Oakland. Born in 1936 in Dallas, Seale came to Northern California with his family during the 1940s. Dishonorably discharged from the air force in February 1959 following a confrontation with his commanding officer, Seale returned to Oakland and enrolled at Merritt while holding down a variety of jobs that ranged from metallurgical work on the Gemini rocket project to work as a standup comedian at local nightclubs.[22] Although he identified as a supporter of the NAACP when he first met Newton in 1962, Seale subsequently rejected the liberal civil rights movement and joined al-Mansour and the AAA. Like Newton, however, Seale eventually found the AAA to be too conservative, and in 1964 he left to join a small, informal study group centered around black nationalism and Third World anticolonialism, a group whose members included Ernest Mkalimoto Allen, Mamadou Lumumba (Kenn M. Freeman), and Isaac Moore. Allen, who had also been a student at Merritt before transferring to UCB, took part in a PL-sponsored trip to Cuba. During his visit to the island in 1964, Allen had a chance encounter with Muhammad Ahmad and other RAM-affiliated activists who were there to visit with Robert F. Williams in exile. Inspired by this meeting, Allen returned to the East Bay and helped to transform what had been an informal study group into the Oakland chapter of RAM.[23]

RAM in Oakland had a small, mostly underground membership (Newton later characterized it as "more intellectual than active"), and its major contribution was in the realm of theory and ideology.[24] Starting in late 1964, Allen, Lumumba, Seale and a handful of others began publishing *Soulbook*, a quarterly journal dedicated to "jazz, economics, poetry, [and] anti-imperialism." Though nominally independent and attracting a wide range of contributors, *Soulbook* was tightly linked to Oakland RAM and followed the national organization in promoting revolutionary nationalism and Third World anticolonialism. In an editorial accompanying the first issue, *Soulbook*'s founders insisted that while "this Journal and all ensuing issues of it must be produced, controlled, published and edited by people who are sons and daughters of Africa," their goals were not confined to promoting a parochial form of black nationalism. Rather, they insisted that it would ultimately require "a radical socio-economic transformation within the United States before the freedom of the Black man in the U.S., the Congo, and anywhere else . . . can be won and guaranteed for all time."[25] This linkage between black nationalism, socialist revolution, and the Third World was characteristic of the approach pioneered by Harold Cruse in the early 1960s and subsequently adapted by Muhammad Ahmad and other RAM leaders. Like them, the editors of *Soulbook* also offered an interpretation of the Cold War that cast the Soviet Union as "America's clandestine ally" and "'white' as any Mississippi peckerwood," while hailing Mao's China for both the development of a nonwhite form of Marxism and for directly challenging the United States.[26]

Of particular significance to the development of black internationalism in the Bay Area and beyond was the way in which *Soulbook* integrated the Third World into a domestic context. Though by no means the first black publication to highlight the Third World, *Soulbook* was distinguished by the depth of its coverage—which went beyond current events to feature long, citation-packed pieces on subjects ranging from the history of Tanzania to the relationship between the United Nations and the former Belgian Congo and reports from the Tricontinental Conference in Havana.[27] *Soulbook* also went to great lengths to let voices from the Third World speak for themselves, translating and publishing pieces by Frantz Fanon, Aimé Césaire, and Senegalese intellectual and activist Cheikh Anta Diop and reprinting pro-independence statements from Puerto Rican nationalist leaders in both English and Spanish.[28] In its very layout, *Soulbook* elided the differences between the black experience in the United States and the anti-colonial struggles of the Third World. Rather than confining these voices to a separate "international" section of the journal, *Soulbook's* editors intertwined news and opinions from the Third World with articles exploring the domestic issues facing African Americans. In similar fashion, the journal bridged the gap between cultural nationalists and socialist revolutionaries with poetry and plays by Black Arts Movement luminaries such as Amiri Baraka, Larry Neal, Carol Freeman, and Sonia Sanchez, dense doctrinal exegeses by former CPUSA member Harry Haywood, reviews of Mao Zedong's writings, and works by such lesser known figures as future BPP minister of education George Murray.

Soulbook and the Oakland chapter of RAM played a crucial role in building the intellectual foundations of a Third World–oriented Black Power movement on the West Coast. Ultimately, however, both ventures suffered from many of the same tensions that characterized RAM's operations elsewhere. For all of its internationalism, *Soulbook* offered little in the way of practical guidance on how black Americans might forge meaningful relationships with their brothers and sisters in the Third World. Like those of the national organization, Oakland RAM's leaders often operated under the assumption that as the revolutionary vanguard inside the United States they would naturally win recognition and support from fellow world revolutionaries without the hard work of building relationships across languages, cultures, and societies. The most glaring unresolved issue that beset *Soulbook* and Oakland RAM, however, was how to translate ideology into action at home in the United States. While embracing what Kenn Freeman dubbed "Fanonismo" and declaring that "in the best tradition of the Bandung Conference . . . Afroamerica is more and more struggling to become DECOLONIZED," *Soulbook* was generally silent on the question of how this might work at either a local or national level.[29] Indeed, for all its eclectic content, *Soulbook* seldom touched on the issues that most directly affected the daily lives of the East Bay's African American population. The inaugural issue, for example, featured a literary critique of Mark Twain's *Pudd'nhead Wilson* and an annotated bibliography on apartheid in South Africa but nothing about the chronic unemployment, poverty, and police brutality that plagued the neighborhoods surrounding the journal's place of publication. And unlike the NOI's *Muhammad Speaks* or the *Black Panther* newspaper, both of which succeeded in reaching a mass audience in urban African American communities, *Soulbook's* dense and often citation-heavy prose limited its potential appeal to a select and highly educated few. Its most important contribution to the practical development of the black freedom struggle was indirect: *Soulbook* and Oakland RAM served as incubators for individuals who would attempt to apply revolutionary nationalism and Third World anticolonialism directly to the communities where they lived.

"Uncle Sammy Call Me Full of Lucifer": Newton, Seale, and the Formation of the BPP

Born in 1942 in Monroe, Louisiana, Huey Pierce Newton was three years old when his family (which included his parents Walter and Armelia and his six older siblings) joined the thousands of African Americans who were drawn to the Bay Area by the World War II defense boom. The West Oakland neighborhood where Newton grew up was emblematic of the plight of African Americans in the urban West and North, as well as the failure of both government and the liberal civil rights movement to address the enduring structural issues of poverty, inequality, and institutionalized white supremacy. As deindustrialization erased wartime economic gains, most black Oaklanders found themselves with neither the means to follow the jobs into the white suburbs nor the political and economic clout to control the institutions in their own community. By the mid-1960s, the city's African American unemployment rate hovered around 20 percent, and nearly half of the families in West Oakland lived below the poverty line.[30] In addition to these economic woes, police brutality, political underrepresentation, decaying housing and infrastructure, and a lack of adequate schools, medical care, and other public services were among the daily problems confronting Oakland's black population. It was, Newton later described, "almost like being on an urban plantation, a kind of modern-day sharecropping."[31]

There was little in Newton's early years to suggest that he would go on to become an international icon or, in the words of Bobby Seale, "the baddest motherfucker ever to set foot in history."[32] A rebellious student who had barely learned to read by the time he graduated from Oakland Technical High School in the late 1950s, Newton drifted into hustling and petty crime, including pimping, armed robbery, burglary, and credit card fraud. As a teenager, he was a member of a local gang known as "the Brotherhood" and won notoriety in the streets of West Oakland as a "bad dude" and fearless street brawler.[33] He enrolled at Merritt (then called Oakland City College) in the fall of 1959, but the experience was not an immediately transformative one. "As soon as I finished my classes," he later recalled,

"I would go down to the block . . . and drink wine, gamble, and fight." Newton studied law in large part to defend himself against the criminal charges that he confronted with some regularity in the early 1960s, including allegations of theft leveled by the dean of the college. He kept up this dual life as hustler and student until 1964, when he was sentenced to six months in prison for felony assault after stabbing a man with a steak knife at a party. Newton spent much of his sentence in solitary confinement, including the infamous "soul breaker" cell in the Alameda County Jail. He emerged on parole more disciplined and focused, returning to Merritt in 1965 just as it was becoming the epicenter of the Bay Area's cosmopolitan Black Power scene.[34]

Prior to his time behind bars, Newton had drifted in and out of several of the groups that often uneasily coexisted as part of the Bay Area's eclectic mix of black nationalism and leftist activism. In addition to occasionally attending local NOI mosques, he was briefly involved with the AAA but broke with the organization over al-Mansour's conservative black capitalism and what Newton felt to be an unwillingness to engage with the practical issues facing the "brothers on the block." Though Newton later praised al-Mansour for his emphasis on black pride and history, he was disillusioned with his "refusal to deal with the Black present." Newton also attended PL meetings and signed up to take the same Cuban trip that inspired Ernest Allen to found the Oakland chapter of RAM, but he withdrew at the last moment. Though he embraced socialism while at Merritt after reading Marx and Mao, he found that PL was "just a lot of talk and dogmatism, unrelated to the world I knew."[35] Upon his release from prison, Newton reconnected with Seale and through him was introduced to RAM. Although this too proved to be a short-lived association, RAM's fusion of black nationalism, socialism, and Third World anticolonialism was crucial in informing the later development of the BPP. The doctrine of revolutionary nationalism, as initially propounded by Harold Cruse and adapted by RAM in the mid-1960s, would become central to the identity of the Panthers. But it was what RAM was *not* willing to do in terms of putting decolonization into practice at the community level that inspired Newton to join with Seale in forming a new organization in October 1966.

The dispute that culminated in the formation of the BPP centered on the Soul Students Advisory Council (SSAC), a Merritt campus group formed in the mid-1960s. The SSAC organized students and local activists around the issues of building a black studies curriculum at Merritt and hiring more African American instructors and administrators. But while the demand for black studies was able to unite cultural nationalists, revolutionary nationalists, and even otherwise apolitical students, the issue of moving the group's activities beyond the campus proved to be more divisive. Newton and Seale had sought a wider agenda for the SSAC from the beginning—at their suggestion the group's first rally centered on the issue of black men being drafted to fight in the Vietnam War.[36] The turning point came in March 1966 when the two men were arrested following a public reading of Ronald Stone's antiwar poem "Uncle Sammy Call Me Full of Lucifer" (which had recently been published in *Soulbook*) on Berkeley's Telegraph Avenue. Seale was standing on the table of a sidewalk cafe and loudly reciting the poem, which concluded with the ringing declaration "fuck your motherfucking self . . . I will not serve," when police arrived and a scuffle ensued. Though the charges were later dropped, Newton and Seale used funds from the SSAC treasury to retain a lawyer. From this incident they took the notion that the group should put its resources to work on combating police brutality off campus. Several weeks after the Berkeley incident, Newton and Seale observed an African American being stopped on the street by police without apparent cause. They followed the officers back to the station and used SSAC funds to bail out the arrested man in the hope that doing so would create awareness of the student organization in the local black community.[37]

Building on their initial efforts to join antiwar activism, campus organizing, and community-centered protests against police brutality, Newton proposed that the SSAC stage a public demonstration outside the gates of Merritt College on Malcolm X's birthday (May 19) while openly carrying firearms. The demonstration would not only serve notice to the Merritt administration but also impress the local community with the determination of the SSAC to stand up for all African Americans in Oakland. At the time of Newton's proposal, however, the SSAC was increasingly dominated by RAM members who hoped to use it as a front group on campus. Following the line set by the national organization, Oakland RAM rejected actions such as that proposed by Newton as likely to bring unwanted attention, choosing instead to confine their operations to the realm of rhetoric and propaganda. After a contentious meeting, the RAM-dominated leaders of the SSAC rejected Newton's proposal as "suicidal" and chastised both Newton and Seale for their use of funds from the group's treasury. "The Soul Students Advisory Council, RAM, the Muslims, and the Afro-American Association were not offering these brothers and sisters anything concrete,"

Newton later declared, "much less a program to help them move against the system."[38]

"We Want Freedom": The Ten-Point Program and Picking up the Gun

Having declared "Later for these dudes" to RAM, *Soulbook*, and the SSAC, Newton and Seale set about creating their own organization.[39] On October 15, 1966, they sat in the library of the North Oakland Service Center and crafted a ten-point program for a new organization, the Black Panther Party for Self-Defense. The party's name and logo were borrowed from the Lowndes County Freedom Organization (LCFO), an Alabama group organized to run African American candidates for political office on an independent, all-black ticket. But while the LCFO inspired a number of activists outside the South to take up the panther name and iconography (including some RAM members in the Bay Area who formed their own version of the Panthers in 1966), the form and substance of the BPP's ten-point-program owed its biggest debt to the pioneers of urban black nationalism in the North and West.[40] Borrowing directly from a device employed by the NOI, the program included a list of demands ("What We Want"), each backed by a brief statement analyzing the situation facing black people in the United States ("What We Believe").[41] In substance, it was focused on the right of black communities to assert local control over housing, education, employment, police, and the justice system. Its first point—"We want freedom. We want power to determine the destiny of our black community"—echoed Malcolm X's assertion in April 1964 that "[t]he political philosophy of black nationalism means that the black man should control the politics and the politicians in his own community."[42]

On its face, the BPP's foundational document appeared narrowly nationalist in orientation, sharing little in common with RAM's celebration of the "Bandung World" and call for a global socialist revolution. In both rhetoric and substance, the ten-point program was overwhelmingly focused on the domestic problems facing urban black America. Of the ten points, only one was directly linked to contemporary international or foreign policy issues. In calling for African American men to be exempt from the draft, Newton and Seale insisted, "We will not fight and kill other people of color in the world who, like black people, are being victimized by the white racist government of America." While later revisions would add more overtly internationalist elements, the October 1966 version directly invoked only two sources of authority in legitimating its demands: the U.S. Constitution and the Declaration of Independence.[43] Figures such as Che Guevara, Mao Zedong, Frantz Fanon, and Patrice Lumumba, who would later dominate the Panthers' rhetoric and iconography, were absent from the BPP's charter. Absent too were explicit invocations of Marxism or Maoism and a coherent critique of capitalism. Though condemning "the robbery by the white man of our black community," the ten-point program was not explicitly anticapitalist, instead taking the form of a broad call for "land, bread, housing, education, clothing, justice and peace" without endorsing any specific doctrinal approach.[44]

Newton later characterized the BPP in these early years as "just plain nationalists or separatist nationalists," and this explanation has been accepted uncritically by a number of scholars.[45] In fact, despite the relatively narrow focus of the ten-point program, Newton and Seale were deeply immersed in the black internationalism that characterized ventures such as Oakland RAM and *Soulbook* from the very beginning. In particular, they embraced the notion of black Americans as a colonized people (rather than citizens denied their rights) whose struggle for freedom should be modeled on that of Third World revolutionaries rather than the reformism of the liberal civil rights movement. Building on the work of RAM and other Black Power pioneers, including Malcolm X and Harold Cruse, the Panthers offered an international analysis of race and racism in which capitalism played a mutual constitutive role with white supremacy at home and abroad. "The white racist oppresses black people not only for racist reasons," declared Newton in May 1967, "but because it is also economically profitable to do so."[46] This equation was not unique to the United States or to black people. In a statement prepared for a 1967 demonstration at the California State Capitol in Sacramento, Newton linked the plight of African Americans in Oakland and the nations of the Third World to "the fact that towards people of color the racist power structure has but one policy: repression, genocide, terror, and the big stick."[47] Thus, even as they focused their actions locally, from the very beginning the Panthers situated themselves as part of a global struggle against capitalism and white supremacy. Where Newton and Seale broke with RAM and the SSAC was over how to translate this ideology into practice at the local level.

RAM and its various chapters, front groups, and publications primarily focused on a middle-class, educated audience, a strategy that flowed naturally out of its origins as a student group. Though RAM chapters attempted to engage with the local community in the early 1960s, the group's decision to go underground in 1965 restricted its visible operations to the publication of journals and pamphlets that had limited appeal outside a select group of already committed activists.[48] In forming the BPP, Newton and Seale had a very different audience in mind. While hailing figures such as Mao and Che Guevara as "kinsmen" and declaring that "the oppressor who had controlled them was controlling us, both directly and indirectly," Newton wrote in his autobiography that BPP leaders "did not want merely to import ideas and strategies; we had to transform what we learned into principles and methods acceptable to the brothers on the block."[49] In an example of the way in which the local interacted with the international in the formation of the party, Fanon provided an important intellectual justification for this approach. As Seale described it, "Huey understood the meaning of what Fanon was saying about organizing the lumpen proletariat first, because Fanon explicitly pointed out that if you didn't organize . . . the brother who's pimping, the brother who's hustling, the unemployed, the downtrodden, the brother who's robbing banks, who's not politically conscious . . . that if you didn't relate to these cats, the power structure would organize these cats against you."[50] The Panthers in their early incarnation appeared to be "just plain nationalists" in large part because they deliberately downplayed their internationalist influences while seeking to reach a local audience.

Guns played the most visible role in the Panthers' early efforts to move beyond study groups, campus activism, and academic-style publications in appealing to "the poor, uneducated brothers off the block."[51] In a piece entitled "Guns Baby Guns" published in an early edition of the *Black Panther* newspaper, Newton captured the party's early focus on firearms as both a tool and symbol:

> Army 45 will stop all jive
> Buckshots will down the cops
> P38 will open prison gates
> Carbine will stop a war machine
> 357 will win us our heaven
> And if you don't believe in lead, you are already dead.[52]

The inspiration for this strategy came from a variety of sources, especially Malcolm X's rhetorical embrace of armed self-defense and the practical examples provided by Robert F. Williams and the armed civil rights groups such as Louisiana's Deacons for Defense and Justice. Seale and Newton also invoked both the anticolonialism of the American Revolution and the constitutional protections of the Second Amendment in claiming the right to bear arms.[53] In a 1967 article, scholars Aristide and Vera Zolberg observed that groups such as the Panthers were tapping into the old American archetype of the Minuteman, suggesting that "[t]he Molotov cocktail is but a McLuhanish extension of his self through a new medium, gasoline. The adoption of this role-model by the Negro is the greatest proof yet that the Negro is an American."[54] In the case of the BPP, however, these domestic inspirations coexisted seamlessly with examples provided by Third World guerrilla movements. In addition to Fanon and his emphasis on the violent nature of decolonization, Newton also cited "Brother Mao Tse-Tung" as well as the example of the Vietnamese NLF in explaining the BPP's decision to "pick up the gun" in the first year of the party's operations. "Mao and Fanon and Guevara all saw clearly that the people had been stripped of their dignity," Newton later explained, "not by any philosophy of mere words, but at gunpoint. They had suffered a holdup by gangsters, and rape; for them, the only way to win freedom was to meet force with force."[55]

In a local context, Newton and Seale's prominent display of firearms in promoting the BPP stemmed primarily from a belief that such actions were the most effective way to spread their message of anticolonialism among a working-class African American audience unlikely to ever pick up an issue of *Soulbook*, attend a clandestine RAM meeting, or wrestle with a translation of *The Wretched of the Earth*. In explaining their plan for an armed demonstration that ultimately led them to break with the SSAC, Newton described guns as "a recruiting device":

> I felt we could recruit Oakland City College students from the grass roots, people who did not relate to campus organizations that were all too intellectual and offered no effective program of action. Street people would relate to Soul Students if they followed our plan; if the Black community has learned to respect anything, it has learned to respect the gun.[56]

The party's first weapons came from Japanese American activist Richard Aoki, "a Third World brother we knew [who] . . . had guns for a motherfucker: .357 Magnums, 22's, 9mm's, what have you."[57] The way in which Newton and Seale expanded this initial arsenal was indicative of their commitment to blend their international influences with their perception of local conditions in the East Bay. Though strongly influenced by Mao's concept of "people's war" and his non-Western interpretation of Marxism, Newton concluded that parroting Maoist rhetoric was not the best way to recruit the "brothers on the block." Rather, he and Seale "initially used [Mao's] Red Book as a commodity" by selling it to "[white] radicals on the campus" at UC Berkeley in order to raise money to buy guns. As Seale explained it, "at first the guns would be more valuable and more meaningful to the brothers on the block, for drawing them into the organization; then in turn we taught them from the Red Book."[58]

"Patrolling the Pigs": Anticolonial Activism in the East Bay, 1966–1967

Between the weapons provided by Aoki and shotguns purchased at a local department store with funds raised through sale of the Red Book, Newton and Seale were able to amass a small arsenal not long after founding the BPP in October 1966. But while they could draw on a rich vein of domestic and foreign sources to legitimate their embrace of the gun as recruiting device, the BPP's founders faced a greater challenge in figuring out how to implement it into the daily operations of their new party. From the beginning, there were tensions and potential contradictions in the BPP's attempts to apply anticolonialism at the local level. The party's original name (the Black Panther Party for Self-Defense) and Newton's signature column in the BPP newspaper ("In Defense of Self-Defense") were indicative of a carefully delineated approach to the use—or threat—of violence. This relatively cautious attitude carried over into the Panthers' early operations in the East Bay. Newton not only invoked constitutional protections for the carrying of firearms but also insisted that BPP members pay strict attention to California gun codes in handling and displaying them.[59] The party's early emphasis on self-defense and attention to legal detail were hardly the hallmark of an armed insurrection. It is difficult to imagine Algerian freedom fighters, the NLF, or Che's guerrilla *focos* consulting and abiding by local guns laws in conducting their operations. Indeed, one of the early critiques of the BPP raised by RAM members in Oakland was that by openly displaying firearms, Newton and Seale were inviting state repression without a corresponding military or political plan for seizing power.[60]

Responding to RAM criticism, Newton not only reaffirmed the Panthers' commitment to revolution but also directly invoked the examples set by Castro and Che in Cuba as well as "the revolution in Kenya, the

Algerian Revolution, Fanon's *The Wretched of the Earth,* the Russian Revolution, the works of Chairman Mao Tsetung, and a host of others." In an early editorial in the BPP newspaper, "The Correct Handling of a Revolution," he positioned the party's decision to display firearms in an open and legal manner as only the first step in a larger campaign. Acting as a "Vanguard Party," the Panthers would initially employ their guns in order to "raise the consciousness of the masses through educational programs and certain physical activities the party will participate in." Avoiding acts of spontaneous and unorganized violence such as the Watts uprising (which Newton criticized as lacking direction), the BPP would build a base of support through aboveground activities such that when finally driven underground they would have already created the nucleus for a well-organized guerrilla army, which could then move against the power structure militarily. When the time came, "guns and defense weapons, such as handgrenades, bazookas, and other necessary equipment, will be supplied by taking these weapons from the power structure, as exemplified by the Viet Cong." Using this logic, Newton concluded that the government oppression unleashed by the party's public organizing efforts would actually be beneficial in the long run as, "the greater the military preparation on the part of the oppressor, the greater is the availability of weapons for the black community."[61]

The most visible of the Panthers' early attempts to employ firearms as way of mobilizing and educating the black community was a tactic that Newton and Seale dubbed "patrolling the pigs." Armed with loaded weapons and a stack of law books, the two men drove around their West Oakland neighborhood and conspicuously followed Oakland police officers as they conducted their business. Attempts to monitor police conduct in black neighborhoods were not new. The Oakland chapter of the Civil Rights Congress had protested police brutality in the 1950s, and the more recent example of the Community Action Patrol (CAP) in Los Angeles had directly inspired Newton and Seale to focus their attention on the daily operations of the Oakland Police Department (OPD).[62] But Newton and Seale's decision to openly carry weapons, as opposed to the notebooks and two-way radios employed by CAP, marked a crucial difference in their underlying strategy. In "patrolling the pigs," Newton and Seale went beyond defending their homes or protecting peaceful civil rights protesters to directly confront the exercise of police power in black neighborhoods. In doing so, they made both symbolic and material contributions to the development of an indigenous anticolonialism that linked older traditions of black nationalism with the insights of Fanon and other inspirations from the Third World.

An early account of the BPP's police patrol operations by *Ramparts* magazine correspondent Gene Marine captured their ability to simultaneously highlight the violence of the state and offer local residents a counter-example of practical anticolonial organizing. Recounting an incident in which Newton and Seale refused to back down when several squad cars of police challenged their right to brandish their weapons, Marine observed:

> The crowd that watched Huey Newton, a round of ammunition ostentatiously jacked into the firing chamber of his M-1 [rifle], face down a squad of Oakland police was not thinking about colonies and mother countries; most had never heard of Fanon. But whatever the validity of the theory, they knew the truths from which it grew: that they are oppressed people, that the police normally treat them with contempt and regard them as less than human, and that a small band of black men had stood up in defiance of every taboo to insist on their own humanity.[63]

This was a dramatic example of Newton's strategy of using guns as way to "educate through action," translating the militant anticolonialism articulated by RAM and in the pages of *Soulbook* into actions aimed squarely at the "brothers on the block." Invoking the Cuban revolution, Newton explained that "Che and Fidel . . . could have leafleted the community and they could have written books, but the people would not respond. They had to act and the people could see and hear about it and therefore become educated on how to respond to oppression."[64]

The symbolic importance of "picking up the gun" has attracted widespread attention from scholars of the BPP. But as originally envisioned by Newton and Seale, "patrolling the pigs" was only the prelude to a series of actions aimed at expanding the party's reach in the local community and beyond. The initial goal of the BPP's police patrols was to educate and recruit within the East Bay's black communities. Ultimately, however, the BPP would mobilize "black people . . . under well organized machinery" in order to "smash police terror and domestic colonialism, and to shatter the war-mongering racist foreign policy that holds the rest of our Third World brothers and sisters in a vicious bind."[65] This dual program of remaking American society while linking African Americans with the Third World was drawn directly from the ideology of revolutionary nationalism espoused by RAM and its various organs earlier in the decade. The BPP distinguished itself, however, not only by its use of the gun as a recruiting tool but also by its early efforts at community-level organizing, which were intended to serve as a steppingstone to the more ambitious revolutionary goals that the party's founders shared with RAM. The first of these efforts took place not in Oakland but in nearby Richmond, California.

Early in the morning of April 1, 1967, Denzil Dowell, was shot in the back and killed by a Contra Costa County sheriff who had pursued him in connection with a suspected burglary in North Richmond. Dowell, a twenty-two-year-old African American man, was unarmed at the time of his shooting. Outraged by the killing and lack of police accountability, Dowell's family contacted Mark Comfort, an Oakland community organizer, who in turn introduced them to the BPP.[66] The Panthers initially responded by holding a protest rally in Richmond while openly displaying their firearms. In the months that followed, however, the BPP expanded its efforts into a larger campaign against "community imperialism" in Richmond. Rather than simply protesting the actions of local police, the Panthers challenged the "abject, colonial status" of North Richmond in which "the power structure taxes them while allowing them no representation." In response, they sought "in the interest of black people to incorporate the area into an independent city that will not be at the cruel mercy of the racist swine, the bloodsucking parasites, who are content to allow black people to wither away." By incorporating, the residents of North Richmond would "be in control of their own police force, their own school system, and they will have the power to tax the businesses in the area, like Standard Oil Company."[67]

On the surface, the BPP's campaign to incorporate North Richmond fit comfortably into a tradition of urban black nationalism with roots as far back as Marcus Garvey's UNIA and more direct links to the NOI and figures such as Malcolm X, Amiri Baraka, and James and Grace Lee Boggs. Certainly there was nothing inherently revolutionary about the claim, as expressed in the *Black Panther* newspaper in May 1967, that "[t]he core city is becoming more and more heavily populated by black people; as a result. . . . [h]e will be able to elect political representatives and he will be able to hold such political representatives accountable to the black community."[68] What distinguished the Panthers' early efforts at community organizing from previous examples of urban black nationalism, however, was the way in which they contextualized them against a larger international backdrop. From the beginning, the BPP's call for black self-determination

ocal level drew on connections to other anticolonial struggles. "In
and time, when oppressed people all over the world are moving to
e their lives," asserted BPP minister of information Eldridge Cleaver
in June 1967, "there is absolutely no good reason why the people of North
Richmond can't significantly improve their lot by taking steps to incorporate an independent city."[69]

The Panthers also linked local self-determination in places such as Oakland or North Richmond to the larger goal of remaking American society
as a whole. While incorporating North Richmond and similar efforts at
local self-determination would have immediate benefits for the residents
in terms of increased control over city services and functions, these liberated communities would also serve as the nucleus for a larger revolutionary movement. Newton argued that as black Americans lacked substantial
economic or political clout, they should embrace a form of military power,
"arming themselves from house to house, block to block, community to
community, throughout the nation."[70] In leveraging the gun as a way to
organize and assert power on a local level, the BPP would slowly build the
basis for a larger revolutionary movement centered in urban, black America.
Picking up a theme advanced by RAM and Robert F. Williams from exile
earlier in the decade, Newton insisted that "America can not stand to fight
every Black country in the world and fight a civil war at the same time."
Building one community at a time, the Panthers would ultimately be poised
to move both politically and militarily to dismantle the American Empire
from within.[71]

"The Hour of Doom": Sacramento, the Mulford Act, and the Limits of Self Defense

In the six months following its formation in October 1966, the BPP made
significant strides in advancing the work begun by RAM and its various
front organizations. Combining street theater with acts of personal courage
and community organizing, Newton and Seale helped to bring revolutionary nationalism and Third World anticolonialism to the streets of the East
Bay. With their guns, striking uniforms (black beret, black leather jacket,
and powder-blue shirt), and acts of individual bravery, the Panthers suc-
ceeding in reaching the "brothers on the block" in ways that more cere-
bral organizations such as RAM and *Soulbook* were never able to manage.
The BPP's operations, including their efforts to sell Mao's Red Book on

the UCB campus and at local antiwar demonstrations, also drew attention from white students and activists, opening up the possibility of alliances beyond the black community. But for all their initial successes, by
April 1967 the nascent BPP was in the midst of a crisis that threatened its
continued existence.

Though they were more successful than RAM in raising their public
profile in the black community, the Panthers still struggled to gain members. The dramatic actions that drew attention from the local community
also set the bar for membership at a level too high for most black residents
of the East Bay. While they might admire Newton and Seale's courage, few
Oakland residents were willing to pick up the gun and join them in facing
down the OPD. The BPP's small base of perhaps forty members (not all of
whom were active at any one time) was not necessarily critical. Newton
self-consciously positioned the Panthers as a vanguard party that would
lead by example rather than as a mass-membership organization. But even
on those terms, the party struggled to gain traction for much of the first
year of its existence. Neither the police patrols nor the BPP's early efforts
at community organizing ended up producing much in the way of tangible
accomplishments. Panther demonstrations did convince the city of Oakland to place a new stoplight at a dangerous West Oakland intersection, but
other than that they had little to show for their efforts.[72] As Harold Cruse
had warned some years earlier in reference to Robert F. Williams, guns
might succeed in grabbing attention, but short of a full-scale insurrection,
which the BPP was not prepared to initiate, they were not particularly
useful for accomplishing practical goals such as ending police brutality or
gaining control over city services.[73] The BPP also struggled during its early
operations to draw meaningful links to nations, movements, and individuals
outside the United States. In reacting to what Newton believed to be the
overly intellectual approach of RAM and *Soulbook*, the Panthers did not
dwell on the theoretical complexity of applying Third World anticolonialism in the context of the United States. Though BPP leaders were heavily
influenced by thinkers such as Fanon and Mao in 1966–67, their preferred
tactic of educating through direct action limited their ability to explicate
the nature of the connections between African Americans and others in
anticolonial struggles around the world.

With a thin base of local support and no practical ties to international
or transnational allies, the BPP was highly vulnerable to state repression in
1966–67. As RAM leaders had predicted, the Panthers' armed public demonstrations drew a swift counter-response. The most damaging blow took

the form of a 1967 bill in the California legislature that prohibited the public carrying of loaded weapons by private citizens. The Mulford Act, named after conservative Alameda County representative David Donald Mulford, whose district encompassed parts of Oakland and nearby Berkeley, was aimed squarely at the BPP's organizing efforts.[74] The law made it difficult for the Panthers to continue operating as an aboveground, legal organization while simultaneously confronting the daily exercise of the state's police power and planning for an armed rebellion. Newton had acknowledged from the beginning that such a development was inevitable, but the Mulford Act forced it on the party preemptively at time when it was unable to offer an effective response either in the form of massive public demonstrations or an underground military campaign. Newton responded with a high-stakes gamble.

On May 2, 1967, a delegation of thirty Panthers arrived in Sacramento. Led by Chairman Bobby Seale, a subset of the group clad in black leather jackets and berets and carrying loaded weapons marched toward the California State Capitol. Upon reaching the front steps, Seale read aloud Newton's "Executive Mandate Number One" to a small crowd of reporters. Declaring that "the hour of doom" had arrived, Newton's statement specifically targeted the Mulford Act and "legislation aimed at keeping the black people disarmed and powerless." It also, however, sought to connect the BPP's local efforts and larger historical and international developments by linking the contemporary treatment of black Americans to "the genocide practiced on the American Indians and the confining of the survivors on reservations . . . the dropping of atomic bombs on Hiroshima and Nagasaki, and now the cowardly massacre in Vietnam."[75] Prompted by reporters, the Panthers went into the building itself and briefly appeared on the floor of the California State Assembly before being ejected by guards. Upon exiting, Seale read Newton's statement again several times at the request of a growing crowd of print and television reporters before accidentally crossing paths with Governor Ronald Reagan, who was meeting "an eighth grade social studies class on the Capitol's west lawn for a fried chicken lunch." The governor beat a hasty retreat, prompting one Panther to cry, "look at Reagan run." The Panthers then got in their cars and dispersed to a local gas station to prepare for the journey back to Oakland. It was there at the station that they were arrested by police and charged with various Fish and Game code violations, relating to their weapons, and conspiracy to invade the capitol building.[76]

The Sacramento demonstration catapulted the BPP from an East Bay neighborhood group to national notoriety. Television cameras captured dramatic images of the Panther "invasion," while the press from coast to coast reported on the "grim-faced, silent young men armed with guns" and the "antiwhite Black Panther party . . . with bandoliers of shells draped across their shoulders."[77] An editorial in the *Washington Post* perhaps inadvertently reinforced the Panthers' anticolonial analysis in declaring the scene at Sacramento to be "something . . . that could happen . . . only in the Congo or in Outer Slobovia."[78] For his part, Governor Reagan lamented the BPP's action as "a ridiculous way to solve problems that have to be solved among people of goodwill," adding, "There's no reason why a citizen should be carrying loaded weapons on the street today." But while successful in garnering attention, the Sacramento demonstration did not offer an immediate solution to the problems besetting the Panthers. If anything, it led to increased public support for both the Mulford Act and a police crackdown on the Panthers. Newton later conceded that while "our tactic at Sacramento was correct at that time . . . it was also a mistake in a way."[79]

The Mulford Act passed the legislature and was signed into law by Governor Reagan in July 1967. Even prior to the passage of the new law, the arrest of the Sacramento demonstrators and increased policy scrutiny tied up Panther resources and made it difficult to mobilize even small-scale patrols or protests. Kathleen Cleaver later recalled, "By then the organization [Newton] led had lost its cohesion, particularly after the Chairman [Seale] and other key Panthers started serving the six-month jail sentences they received for the Sacramento demonstration. The party had no funds to continue renting its storefront office in Oakland, and no meetings were being held."[80] Meanwhile, the increased police and media attention did nothing to stimulate the growth of the party at the local level. By October 1967, David Hilliard estimated that the BPP's membership had fallen to as few as a dozen members.[81] Having had little success with community organizing, forced to abandon the armed theatrics that had defined the party's early operations, and unready to commit to underground guerrilla warfare, BPP leaders had little choice but to steer the party in a new direction in the aftermath of Sacramento. While guns would remain an important part of the Panthers' image and public presentation, starting in mid-1967 the party began a shift away from direct action such as "patrolling the pigs" in favor of a new form of anticolonial activism.

Chapter 3

"We're Relating Right Now to the Third World"

Creating an Anticolonial Vernacular, 1967–1968

In December 1968, BPP minister of information Eldridge Cleaver addressed an audience at the Berkeley Community Center in one of his last public appearances before fleeing the country for exile in Cuba. He condemned colonialism and militarism in raw terms, declaring, "Fuck anyone who crosses their own frontier and oppresses another people." Summing up the BPP's strategy and orientation, Cleaver said, "We're relating right now to the Third World." Rather than looking to the U.S. government or the liberal civil rights establishment for help, the Panthers would "make a coalition with every people in the world who has been fucked over by another people."[1]

Both the form and content of Cleaver's statement represent an important moment in the BPP's evolution. The party changed dramatically in 1967–68 in response to a combination of internal and external developments. The institutional changes (covered in the next chapter) were the most visible, as the Panthers expanded from a neighborhood group with a handful of members to a national organization with branches scattered across the United States and supporters and emulators around the world. This dramatic expansion was made possible by an accompanying evolution in the BPP's identity and self-presentation that was less visible but had long-lasting implications.

Figure 2. The *Black Panther* newspaper was the primary vehicle for BPP's anticolonial vernacular as well as an important source of party funds and a tool for organizing chapters across the United States. March 6, 1969. Photo courtesy of Emory Douglas/Art Resource, NY.

In response to the restrictions of the Mulford Act, increased police harassment, and their inability to mobilize significant support at the local level, the party's leaders were forced to embrace new strategies for survival by mid-1967. Guns remained an important part of the BPP's public image, and behind the scenes the party continued to amass a stockpile of weapons in anticipation of an eventual confrontation with the state. In their day-to-day activities, however, the Panthers shifted away from highly visible armed actions such as "patrolling the pigs" in favor of new forms of party-building. One of the most important of these involved returning to the international influences that had helped shape the birth of the party by marrying their streetwise sensibilities to a more explicit discussion of the ways in which the U.S. black freedom struggle intersected with Third World anticolonialism. Cleaver, who joined the BPP in February 1967 shortly after being released from prison, played an important role in this evolution. Under his guidance, the *Black Panther* newspaper became the primary vehicle for a colorful anticolonial vernacular that combined Third World–inspired imagery and rhetoric with a nondoctrinaire Marxism and a distinctive verbal and visual style influenced by urban African American idioms and argot. Emory Douglas, a San Francisco City College student and aspiring visual artist who joined the party at the same time as Cleaver, oversaw the graphics and layout for the newspaper. Douglas and fellow Panther artist Tarika Lewis provided a striking visual complement to the

What to make of this? How serious?

party's evolving ideology. At its most effective, the BPP's anticolonial vernacular seamlessly mixed the global and the local, embedding a diverse set of international influences in the daily experiences of the "brothers on the block" who formed the party's rank and file.

The ideological content of the BPP's anticolonial discourse was not always easy to isolate from the jumbled pastiche of Third World symbols and colorful language that characterized the *Black Panther* and other party outlets in 1967–68. As Panther minister of education Raymond "Masai" Hewitt put it:

> Call us Red or Black or vice versa. We dig Chairman Mao, Ho Chi Minh, we have a profound love for Fidel Castro. I am not talking about their own individual ideological lines. We dig what they are doing.[2]

This very pastiche was itself a sort of statement, setting apart the BPP from the narrow black nationalism of groups such as Maulana Karenga's US Organization and the doctrinaire Marxism of the CPUSA and its rivals on the communist Left (such as PL). Other key premises of the party's anticolonial vernacular, drawn from revolutionary nationalism, included an emphasis on the colonial status of black Americans, a rhetorical and symbolic emphasis on the centrality of violence in the process of both colonialism and decolonization, and the assertion that white supremacy and capitalism were inextricably linked as historical forces. Collectively these propositions created the basis for a transnational and transhistorical narrative that linked the BPP to people of color in the United States and around the world in a struggle for self-determination.

As the party continued to evolve and grow in the late 1960s, its anticolonial vernacular provided a common thread that helped to tie together the Panthers and their supporters in the United States and around the world. It also, however, contained a number of contradictions and ambiguities that contributed to the BPP's growing pains. While the party's broad-ranging anticolonial rhetoric helped to build a cohesive identity and win support from outside the black community, it created tensions with cultural nationalists and pan-Africanists. By the end of 1968, figures ranging from Karenga in Los Angeles to former SNCC chairman Stokely Carmichael had publicly attacked the BPP for its embrace of Marxism and willingness to ally with white activists. More broadly, in embracing international partners, the Panthers ran into many of the same dilemmas that had confronted Malcolm X, Robert F. Williams, and RAM earlier in the decade. What, precisely, did it mean for black Americans living in a First World superpower to relate to the Third World? While the BPP's anticolonial vernacular sought to elide the differences between the black condition in the United States and anticolonial struggles in Asia, Africa, and Latin America, questions about how to translate these theoretical links into practical action remained unresolved. Issues of anticolonial violence and gender identity embedded within this anticolonial vernacular also produced lingering tensions within the party. Though women often appeared in Panther iconography of the period, including striking pictures of figures such as Kathleen Cleaver as well as more abstract depictions of women warriors modeled on revolutionary art of the Third World, they generally did so in the context of a heteronormative and patriarchal framework for understanding female agency. As scholar Robeson Taj Frazier observed more generally of radical black discourse in this period, "Race, the Third World, and radical Afro-Asian partnership were often depicted through language, imagery, and symbols that privileged male intellectual production and agency over that of women . . . the heteronormative male was thus frequently treated as the anchor and stimulus of international revolutionary struggle."[3]

"Philosophical Hydrogen Bombs": Cleaver, Douglas, and the Revolutionary Arts

In forming the Black Panther Party for Self Defense in October 1966, Huey Newton and Bobby Seale had fused anticolonial ideology with urban Black Power activism into a form of direct action aimed at capturing the hearts and minds of local Oakland residents. The next step in the BPP's evolution owed much to Eldridge Cleaver and Emory Douglas, both of whom joined the party in early 1967, shortly before the crisis caused by the Mulford Act. These two men shared with the founders of the BPP a set of influences ranging from Malcolm X and Robert F. Williams to Mao Zedong and Frantz Fanon. Cleaver and Douglas, however, brought with them a set of experiences and talents that helped to subtly shift the direction of Panthers' anticolonialism at a crucial moment in the party's history.

Born in 1935 in Arkansas, as a child Cleaver was part of the World War II era exodus of American Americans out of the South. His father moved the family west in search of new job opportunities in the mid-1940s, eventually settling in Los Angeles. By Cleaver's own account, he had little in the way of political awareness in his early years. As a teenager he drifted into petty

crime that ranged from bicycle theft to a 1954 felony charge for possess-
ing a "shopping bag full of marijuana" that sent him to Soledad for three
years.[4] Released on parole in 1957, he returned to prison the following
year on an assault conviction stemming from a series of rapes. It was during
his incarceration at San Quentin, Folsom, and Soledad from 1958 to 1966
that Cleaver honed the anticolonial analysis of urban black America that
underlay his post-prison activism as part of the BPP. The Nation of Islam
played the most important role in Cleaver's transformation from nihilistic
young man who celebrated raping white women as an "insurrectionary
act" to an anticolonial intellectual.[5] "From 1959 to 1963," Cleaver declared,
"the Black Muslims dropped philosophical hydrogen bombs on the terrain
of the American Negro brain." This was particularly true for the NOI's
converts behind bars, where Elijah Muhammad found a receptive audience
for his message of black pride and self-improvement coupled with a condemnation of "white devils" and their institutions.[6]

Unlike Newton and Seale, who had only passing involvement with the
NOI, Cleaver became a full-fledged member, and by 1963 he had been
promoted to head of the San Quentin mosque after its previous leader
(and Cleaver's cellmate) was shot and killed by a prison guard. Through
his involvement with the NOI, Cleaver was drawn into an international
analysis of U.S. race relations that continued to evolve long after he broke
with the organization.[7] He also came into contact with the AAA during this time, as al-Mansour worked with Cleaver and other inmates at
San Quentin in defense of their right to practice their faith behind bars.[8]
Malcolm X, however, was the single most important figure in Cleaver's
political awakening. The charismatic NOI minister's "style, fearlessness, and
mental prowess" appealed to Cleaver, as did the fact that "[l]ike me, he had
been a gangster . . . ruthless and gun-toting."[9] More significant in terms of
Cleaver's ideological development was Malcolm's brief but eventful career
following his break with the NOI. In the internecine feud that gripped the
NOI in 1964–65, Cleaver stood firmly behind Malcolm, embracing both
his practical efforts at internationalizing the black freedom struggle and his
willingness to consider coalitions that transcended race and religion.[10]

Following the assassination of Malcolm X in February 1965, Cleaver
threw himself into formulating his own vision of black anticolonialism.
No longer at home in the NOI and lacking alternative organizations or
institutions in which to pursue his evolving interest in exploring links
between black Americans, the Cold War, and the Third World, Cleaver
focused his energies on writing. Encouraged by his lawyer, Beverly

Axelrod, with whom he began an impassioned correspondence, Cleaver wrote a series of essays from behind bars. His prison writings, many of which were later collected and published as the critically acclaimed *Soul on Ice*, reflected an attempt to graft a critique of capitalism and imperialism onto the framework of black internationalism that he had inherited from Malcolm X and the NOI. Untroubled by theoretical heterodoxy, he eagerly devoured works by Mikhail Bakunin, Vladimir Lenin, Mao Zedong, Fidel Castro, and Che Guevara as well as Marxist-influenced American historians Herbert Aptheker and William Appleman Williams.[11] Like the founders of the BPP, Cleaver was also strongly influenced by Third World anticolonial struggles. Cleaver closely followed news from the Third World, and "[t]he rise of China, Cuba, the Congo, [and] Vietnam" was a consistent theme in his prison notebooks. Though he lacked direct access to these distant events, his prison reading list included works ranging from Frantz Fanon to Ghana's Kwame Nkrumah.[12] His understanding of Third World anticolonialism was deeply gendered in its linking of self-determination to manhood, as he described Algerian leader Ben Bella, for example, as "one of my machos."[13] And while he nominally disavowed the sexual violence against women that had landed him behind bars, his writings from this period were imbued with heteropatriarchal sentiments that were strident even in the larger context of a society deeply imbued with those values.[14]

While Cleaver's self-taught jailhouse education mirrored that which Newton and Seale received at Merritt and through participating in groups such as the AAA, SSAC, and RAM, his vision of how to put it into practice differed in significant ways from that of the Panthers' founders. Locked behind bars, Cleaver had no hope of directly participating in community organizing, much less the kind of dramatic armed patrols that marked the first six months of the BPP's existence. Indeed, while Cleaver hailed Third World guerrilla movements and celebrated the spontaneous violence of the 1965 Watts uprising, he also expressed doubts about the ultimate effectiveness of armed struggle as a tool for minority groups seeking to enact social change in the United States.[15] In what turned out to be a prescient analysis, he warned that such resistance would almost certainly be crushed:

> If you resist their sticks, they draw their guns. If you resist their guns, they call for reinforcements with bigger guns. Eventually they will come in tanks, in jets, in ships. They will not rest until you surrender or are killed. The policeman and the soldier will have the last word.

In light of the ability of the state to deploy "unlimited firepower," as well as his own inability to take place in such direct actions, Cleaver's prison-era writings explored alternative methods for decolonizing black America.[16]

One solution to the power imbalance facing black Americans in the United States was to seek external allies. Building on the pioneering work of Malcolm X and Robert F. Williams, Cleaver stressed the importance of allying with the emerging states of the Third World. This emphasis on international solidarity was the logical conclusion of using the model of internal colonialism to understand the black experience in the United States. While the material circumstances of the "black colony" in the United States might differ from those prevailing among Third World people, all shared an ongoing history as victims of capitalism, imperialism, and white supremacy. From the genocidal conquest of the Americas, African slavery, and formal colonialism to more subtle contemporary practices, including the neo-colonialist economic exploitation of the Third Word and the domestic reliance on people of color as a low-paid, disposable labor force, the prosperity of the West was made possible by "a system of foreign and domestic exploitation, rooted in the myth of white supremacy and the manifest destiny of the white race."[17] Thus rather than marching on Washington or petitioning the federal government, black Americans urgently needed "to gain organizational unity and communication with their brothers and allies around the world, on an international basis."[18]

If affiliating with a global majority of color offered African Americans a powerful set of potential allies, it left unresolved more practical questions about how to leverage that support to enact revolutionary change within the United States. Cleaver's solution was to work in parallel with a new generation of white radicals in order to wrest control of the country from the inside while simultaneously reaching out to the Third World for external support. Following from his jail cell the developing unrest among American young people, who were disenchanted with the war in Vietnam as well as white supremacy at home, Cleaver hailed a "new generation of whites, appalled by the sanguine and despicable record carved over the face of the globe by their race in the last five hundred years, [who] are rejecting the panoply of white heroes, whose heroism consisted in erecting the inglorious edifice of colonialism and imperialism." In an illustration of the links between foreign and domestic coalition building that would mark his tenure with the BPP, Cleaver saw the rise of revolutionary anticolonialism in the Third World as pivotal in cementing the relationship between African Americans and white radicals in the United States. "[J]ust as world revolution has prompted the oppressed to re-evaluate their self-image in terms of the changing conditions, to slough off the servile attitudes inculcated by long years of subordination," he argued, "white youth are repudiating their heritage of blood and taking people of color as their heroes and models."

> For today the heroes of the initiative are people not usually thought of as white: Fidel Castro, Che Guevara, Kwame Nkrumah, Mao Tse-tung, Gamal Abdel Nasser, Robert F. Williams, Malcolm X, Ben Bella, John Lewis, Martin Luther King Jr., Robert Parris Moses, Ho Chi Minh, Stokely Carmichael, W.E.B. Du Bois, James Forman, Chou En-lai.[19]

For Cleaver, one of the most important consequences of decolonization, and particularly of the radical turn in Third World independence movements during the 1960s, was how it aided the building of bridges between white and black activists in the United States while linking both groups to allies overseas.

In a significant departure from most Black Power advocates, Cleaver identified the emerging counterculture as both another link between black and white youths and a lever by which they could collectively undermine the U.S. empire from within. Picking up on a theme that Norman Mailer had championed in his controversial 1957 essay "The White Negro," Cleaver argued that since African Americans had little investment in the mythologies of white America, black culture had an inherently subversive quality. As young whites became disillusioned with the world created by their elders, they were increasingly rejecting not only the political system but also the cultural apparatus that propped it up. In its place, they turned to black culture and its white interpreters ("soul by proxy"), such as the Beatles, who were, Cleaver wrote, "injecting Negritude by the ton into the whites, in this post-Elvis Presley-beatnik era of ferment."[20] The revolution that Cleaver prophesied in *Soul on Ice* and his other prison writings did not come out of the barrel of a gun so much as from the poetry of Allen Ginsberg, the brutal, balletic grace of Muhammad Ali's boxing, the music of Bob Dylan, and the frenzied movements of the Watusi and the Twist. As Cleaver described it, the Twist was "a guided missile, launched from the ghetto into the very heart of suburbia. The Twist succeeded, as politics, religion, and the law could never do, in writing in the heart and soul what the Supreme Court could only write on the books."[21] This was, in essence, a modified version of Harold Cruse's call for a cultural revolution as the prelude to

Cultural Revolution

remaking U.S. society as a whole, though with far more emphasis on the possibility of cooperation with at least some white Americans.

As with Cruse's calls for a "cultural revolution," there remained unresolved questions in Cleaver's prison writing about how, precisely, to translate aesthetic challenges to mainstream white culture into political or economic revolution. If nothing else, however, Cleaver's essays helped win his own freedom. With Axelrod's aid, several of his works were smuggled out of prison and published in *Ramparts*, a Catholic literary magazine headquartered in San Francisco that had become the leading voice of New Left journalism under the editorship of Warren Hinckle and Robert Scheer in the mid-1960s.[22] Cleaver's growing status as a literary icon undoubtedly aided his release on parole in December 1966. It also shaped his immediate post-prison approach to activism. Though he had considered forming an all-black political organization modeled on Malcolm X's Organization of Afro-American Unity (OAAU), upon his release Cleaver instead focused his energies on working for change through various cultural institutions. As a staff writer for *Ramparts*, Cleaver built connections with white youth while making good on his vow to "[blaze] a new pathfinder's trail through the stymied upbeat brain of the New Left." With poet and playwright Marvin X, he cofounded the Black House, a San Francisco venue that became "the center of non-Establishment black culture throughout the Bay Area" and provided a home for both local artists and visiting Black Arts Movement luminaries from the East Coast, including Amiri Baraka, Sonia Sanchez, and Askia Touré.[23]

It was via the Black House that Cleaver was introduced to Emory Douglas, who would go on to play a crucial role in crafting a visual identity for the BPP. Douglas was born in Grand Rapids, Michigan, in 1943, but as with many other early Panther members, he moved west as a child, settling in San Francisco with his mother in 1951. Like Cleaver, Douglas had early run-ins with the law, including several stints in juvenile detention for charges ranging from truancy to gambling, fighting, and burglary. A nine-month sentence at the Log Cabin Ranch, a rural facility for juvenile offenders in the mountains outside Santa Cruz, California, saw Douglas assigned to care for and clean up after the camp's pigs, an experience that would later surface in unexpected fashion in his work as a revolutionary artist. After throwing bottles at a police car, Douglas was sent away again, serving a fifteen-month sentence at the Youth Training School in Ontario, California, adjacent to the men's prison at Chino. In part as a result of working in the print shop while serving his sentence, Douglas enrolled in San Francisco's City College in 1964 with plans to become a commercial artist.[24]

Though not as known so much as Merritt College in its role as an incubator of Black Power and black internationalism, City College played host to a similar mixture of community and educational activism. Involvement with the college's Black Student Association (which was linked to San Francisco State's Black Student Union) and the arrival of Amiri Baraka in San Francisco helped to radicalize Douglas in 1966–67. Inspired by both the Black Arts Movement and, as he later explained it, "the revolutionary art of the world that was coming in, from Viet Nam, the work out of Cuba, the Middle East," Douglas began to experiment with blending graphic design techniques borrowed from advertising and contemporary commercial art with black aesthetics and proletarian internationalism.[25] The result in visual terms was similar in many ways to the fusion that Cleaver produced in his prison writings. The two men met after Douglas volunteered to be the resident set designer for the Black Communications Project, a radical theater company that Baraka helped to create during his West Coast stay. Many of the company's productions were staged at the Black House, and it was there that Cleaver and Douglas established a relationship with each other and with the nascent BPP, which provided security for several of Baraka's performances.[26]

The jumbled mix of art, politics, and activism at the Black House, including both local figures and representatives from the East Coast Black Arts Movement, was illustrative of the cosmopolitan nature of Black Power in the Bay Area. While many of those in the orbit of the Black House would eventually line up in separate, sometimes warring, factions of the black freedom struggle, in 1966 and early 1967 the differences between cultural nationalism and revolutionary nationalism had yet to harden into firm divisions. Nor was it certain that Douglas and Cleaver would end up aligning themselves with the BPP and its particular brand of community-centered direct action. Although they admired Newton and Seale's organizing efforts in the East Bay, Douglas and Cleaver were initially content working primarily within the artistic wing of the black freedom struggle. Cleaver's willingness to dabble in Marxism and work with the predominantly white New Left, as well as his romantic relationship with his white lawyer, led to tensions with Marvin X and others in the Black House, who were more attuned to pan-Africanism and developing a purely black aesthetic.[27] But as a successful writer with a book contract and a regular job, Cleaver had little reason to risk his parole status by aligning himself with the BPP and their tactics of armed provocation. It took a dramatic encounter at the *Ramparts* offices to push both Cleaver and Douglas to embrace a more direct approach to anticolonial activism.

In February 1967, a number of local black organizations, including the nascent BPP, banded together to promote a ceremony marking the second anniversary of Malcolm X's assassination. *Ramparts* provided meeting space for the event's planning, and when Newton, Seale, and a small cadre of Panthers clad in black leather jackets and armed with shotguns arrived at the offices escorting Betty Shabazz, Malcolm's widow, they created an immediate sensation. At this point in their history, the Panthers were still heavily reliant on armed displays of resistance as a way of both attracting supporters and distinguishing themselves from rival organizations. Leaving the *Ramparts* building after the meeting, Newton became embroiled in a confrontation with San Francisco police. With a shotgun in his hand, he jacked a round into the chamber and taunted an SFPD officer, daring him to draw his gun. After a tense moment, the policeman backed down and walked away. The incident inspired both Douglas and Cleaver—the latter declared Newton to be "the baddest motherfucker I've ever seen!"[28] Shortly afterward, both men joined the BPP (although Cleaver's membership remained secret at first to avoid attracting undue attention from his parole officer). Together they helped chart a new course for the party that paved the way for its expansion into a national and ultimately international organization.

"When I Say Motherfucker": A New Vocabulary for Black Anticolonialism

When Newton dispatched the Panthers to Sacramento on May 2, 1967, to protest the Mulford Act, Cleaver and Douglas were both present. Unlike Seale and the rest of the contingent, however, Cleaver was armed with nothing more than a camera, a pen, and a notepad. Though Cleaver's status as an unarmed observer was largely dictated by the terms of his parole, it was also illustrative of the new strategy that he would help to implement as the BPP's minister of information. In the aftermath of the Mulford Act, the Panthers abandoned the armed patrols that had won them notoriety in the streets of Oakland. Instead they leveraged the heightened visibility they had gained as a result of the Sacramento demonstration to expand their appeal beyond the neighborhood. Central to this approach was the creative use of an anticolonial vernacular that drew on the party's local roots and history of armed theatricality while simultaneously shifting the primary theater and mode of action. Though the BPP continued to operate in Oakland and inspired others to found chapters of the organization in communities across the United States, arguably its most important contribution in 1967–68 was to bring the struggle from the streets back to the realm of ideas, ideology, and culture.

The Black Panther Party's anticolonial vernacular was born in response to a particular set of circumstances in 1967–68, including the dilemma posed by the Mulford Act and the fallout from the Sacramento demonstration. It was the organic creation of talented individuals including Douglas, Cleaver, and Tarika Lewis (who published her drawings under the pen name Matilaba), combined with the dramatic sensibilities of Newton and Seale's early operations in Oakland. But while closely associated with a handful of Panther artists and writers, it had no single author, and it was not confined solely to speeches, images, or the printed word. In songs and chants ("The revolution has come! / Off the pigs! / Time to pick up the gun!"), with their eye-catching paramilitary uniforms, and in renaming public spaces after fallen Panthers (transforming West Oakland's DeFremery Park into Bobby Hutton Memorial Park, for example), the BPP found multiple ways to express complex ideas about colonialism, violence, self-determination, and internationalism in sharp and concise fashion.[29] But while these diverse forms of anticolonial discourse—and their various local manifestations outside the party's national headquarters in Oakland—remain a topic worthy of further investigation, the *Black Panther* newspaper provided the most enduring and far-reaching expression of the BPP's anticolonial vernacular. Well after its halting beginnings, the paper played a crucial role in defining the Panthers' identity both inside and outside the party.

The four-page inaugural issue of the *Black Panther Community News Service*, produced in April 1967 under Cleaver's direction, featured hand-lettered headlines and was entirely focused on a single local incident (the police killing of Denzil Dowell in Richmond). By the start of 1968, the *Black Panther* had grown into a professionally produced and lavishly illustrated weekly that mixed local news and commentary with coverage of national and international developments. From Douglas's and Lewis's striking illustrations to Cleaver's characterization of American hegemony as "the international pig power structure," the *Black Panther* offered a critique of capitalism, white supremacy, and imperialism that melded a global analysis with local issues and idioms.[30] The paper provided a way for the BPP to reach beyond its limited membership in Oakland to a wider audience not only among African Americans, but also other communities of color as well as white radicals. As the party began to expand to include chapters outside Oakland, the *Black Panther* provided an ideological touchstone and a common vocabulary that helped to unite its dispersed membership. It also served a more practical role in party building. Selling the paper became a central activity around which chapters could be organized, and the proceeds (from an estimated weekly circulation of somewhere between 139,000 to 200,000 by the end of the 1960s) were the single most important source of the party's funds.[31]

Building on a premise previously explored by Harold Cruse and RAM, the Panthers' anticolonial vernacular was premised on the notion that African Americans were not citizens denied their rights but a "black colony" imprisoned in ghettos within the heart of what Cleaver dubbed the "white mother country." As such, black Americans from Oakland to Harlem were linked to the Third World by a history of racialized colonialism. "In the aftermath of Watts, and all the other uprisings that have set the ghettos of America ablaze," Cleaver declared, "it is obvious that there is very little difference in the way oppressed people feel and react, whether they are oppressed in Algeria by the French, in Kenya by the British, in Angola by the Portuguese, or in Los Angeles by Yankee Doodle."[32] The *Black Panther* was by no means the first black publication to feature coverage of international events or promote solidarity with the Third World. From mainstream outlets like the *Chicago Defender* to Paul Robeson's *Freedom* newspaper and its successor *Freedomways* to 1960s publications such as the *Guardian, Black America, On Guard, Black World, Muhammad Speaks,* and *Soulbook,* the black press had long devoted attention to decolonization and its links to the struggle against white supremacy inside the United States. What distinguished the *Black Panther* were the ways it articulated connections between black Americans and the Third World.

The most immediately striking feature of the *Black Panther* was its use of language and imagery as a way of bridging the gap between anticolonial theory and the lived experience of the community from which it sprung. Elaine Brown, who would eventually ascend to lead the party in the 1970s, described the paper as "dedicated ... to reporting news and information in words the People could understand."[33] Much more so than its contemporaries and predecessors, the Panther newspaper self-consciously employed a specific form of urban African American vernacular in its words and visual presentation. Drawing on the party's origins as a vehicle for organizing the "brothers on the block," the artists and writers who contributed to the paper in its early years often presented their vision of black anticolonialism in what BPP chief of staff David Hilliard dubbed "the language that was born out of oppression." Hilliard expressed the logic behind this concept in colorful terms:

> When I say motherfucker everybody in here recognizes that it's legitimate. The only motherfuckers that don't recognize it and don't like it are the motherfuckers that's in behalf of fucking up the people's freedom. . . . So fuck them, fuck them, fuck them.[34]

Cleaver was notorious for leading crowds in chants of "fuck Ronald Reagan" while Bobby Seale devoted several pages in his 1971 autobiography to the etymology of the word "motherfucker," asserting that "the racism and oppression of black people, from history to this very day . . . has caused this word . . . to be part of the vernacular of the ghetto."[35]

Newton later expressed reservations about the use of profanity, and by the early 1970s the Panthers began to move away from it in both speeches and the newspaper.[36] Scholars have often downplayed it as well, presumably under the assumption that it might undermine efforts to have the BPP taken seriously as a subject of academic study. But what BPP minister of education Raymond "Masai" Hewitt dubbed "the vernacular . . . of rebellion and revolution" was a crucial part of the party's attempts to spread its anticolonial message beyond traditional activist circles while distinguishing itself from both the liberal civil rights movement and revolutionary groups such as RAM and PL that skewed toward a college-educated and often middle-class audience.[37] The result was, in the words of Aaron Dixon, who headed the party's Seattle chapter, "blunt, hardcore," and "[u]nlike any other paper I had seen."[38]

In their use of profanity, the Panthers drew from African American verbal folk traditions including toasts, signifying, and word games such as the dozens, as well as the work of Black Arts Movement figures such as Amiri Baraka with his ringing declaration that "[t]he magic words are: Up against the wall mother fucker."[39] It also fit into a long tradition of working-class and lumpenproletariat groups that employed salty language as a way of indicating their alienation from the "polite" world of the bosses and the bourgeoisie. "[O]bscenity," remarked West German activist and Panther ally Karl Dietrich Wolff in 1969, "was always one of the weapons of the oppressed."[40] As scholar Benedict Anderson observed, "the most important thing about language is its capacity for generating imagined communities, building in effect *particular solidarities*."[41] In this respect, the language used by the BPP signified the group's rejection of working within the existing U.S. social and political system in the late 1960s. Blacks were not citizens denied their rights but rather, as Hewitt phrased it, the "victims of American Democracy for over 400 years." As such, they should not be bound by "any verbal Marquis of Queensbury Rules as to what we should say about the oppressor or how we should say it. . . . If we want to call him a motherfucker, then he's a motherfucker."[42] Some fifty years later, scholar Steven Salaita echoed those sentiments, declaring, "Insofar as 'civil' is profoundly racialized and has a long history of demanding conformity to the ethos of imperialism and colonization, I frequently choose incivility as a form of communication."[43] Thus when Eldridge Cleaver called for "a coalition with every people in the world who has been fucked over by another people," the very way in which he expressed the proposition was indicative of his rejection of both conventional American politics and traditional conceptions of international relations based on government-level interactions between nation-states.[44] Sharp, simple, and rooted in a culturally particular urban African American folk vernacular, "motherfucker" was a verbal marker of the Panthers' embrace of their status as what historian David Roediger termed "anticitizens." It also fit with Fanon's analysis of decolonization as "not a rational confrontation of viewpoints. It is not a discourse on the universal, but the impassioned claim by the colonized that their world is fundamentally different."[45] What better way to express this difference than by calling a motherfucker a motherfucker?

Profanity was not the only distinguishing characteristic of the BPP's anticolonial vernacular. In speeches and the pages of the *Black Panther*, party leaders employed a colorful vocabulary that acted as verbal shorthand for their ideological challenge to colonialism, militarism, and white supremacy in their neighborhoods, the United States, and around the world. Cleaver, for example, frequently referred to the United States as "Babylon," signifying its status as a decadent and declining empire, and he delighted in taunting California governor Ronald Reagan as "a punk, a sissy and a coward."[46] Perhaps the most famous example, however, was party's use of the epithet "pig." The BPP's popularization of the term dated to May 1967, as its leaders were seeking alternate ways to confront the police at a time when armed patrols were no longer a viable option. As Seale described it:

Huey said, just before we went to press with the second issue of the newspaper, "We have to have some terms that adequately define the police and fascist bigots who commit murder, brutalize, and violate people's constitutional rights." I told him we already called those who actually do this "fascists" and "swine." Huey said, "Yeah, but black people aren't picking it up. It's not simply enough so that they'll understand it. Children, teenagers, and older people, everybody." Then Huey, walking around the room thinking, said, "Swine . . . pig . . . swine" and Eldridge sat down at the typewriter and typed out the definition.[47]

Cleaver's definition of a pig as "a low natured beast that has no regard for the law, justice, or the rights of the people . . . usually found masquerading as a victim of an unprovoked attack" served to cast the police, rather than the Panthers, as the true threat to peace and justice in Oakland. Douglas, reaching back to his experiences taking care of the pig pen while serving as a juvenile offender, illustrated the term with the first of his many pig drawings, which appeared in the second issue of the Panther paper under the caption "Support your local police."[48]

These drawings mixed potent political symbolism with humor to challenge the moral and practical policing powers of the state. Amiri Baraka recalled that "just looking at [Douglas's pig illustrations] would crack you up in a mixture of merriment and contempt!"[49]

While the Panthers initially employed "pig" in the specific context of police brutality in Oakland, its use quickly blossomed to express a wider national and international critique of U.S. hegemony. By 1968 the Panthers were employing the term in reference to the U.S. government and its puppets and allies around the world. "Internationally," Cleaver insisted, "we have to place ourselves in the Third World, with the oppressed people of the world against the pigs, the international pig power structure."[50] Ideologically, this construction served to emphasize the commonalities between oppressed groups around the world struggling against the U.S. government and its allies to win the right to self-determination. Echoing Che Guevara's insistence that "[s]olidarity among peoples does not now come from religion, customs, tastes, racial affinity or its lack. . . . [but] from a similarity in economic social conditions and from a similarity in desire for progress and recuperation," Cleaver sought to define opposition to "the international pig power structure" as the determining factor in the party's coalition building. At the same time as they sought to elide differences between themselves and their allies in the Third World, the Panthers' use of terms such as "pig" and "motherfucker" rhetorically grounded them in the specific milieu of the urban, African American community that had birthed the organization in October 1966. In essence, by doing so the BPP offered a preemptive answer to the question later posed by postcolonial scholar Homi K. Bhabha,

WHAT IS A PIG?

"A low natured beast that has no regard for law, justice, or the rights of people; a creature that bites the hand that feeds it; a foul depraved traducer, usually found masquerading as the victim of an unprovoked attack."

BATTLE FATIGUE

Figure 3. December 20, 1967. Photo courtesy of Emory Douglas/Art Resource, NY.

Figure 4. May 31, 1970. Photo courtesy of Emory Douglas/Art Resource, NY.

who pondered whether it was "possible to be 'culturally particularist' with-out being patriotic? Committed to the specificity of event and yet linked to a transhistorical memory and solidarity?"[51] New York Panther Assata Shakur was blunter in her assessment that "Panthers don't try to sound all intellectual, talking about the national bourgeoisie, the military-industrial complex, the reactionary ruling class. They simply called a pig a pig."[52]

Illustrations by Emory Douglas and Tarika Lewis, published regularly in the *Black Panther* and often turned into posters and other forms of public art, used a visual vocabulary to similarly demonstrate links between the Panthers' local struggles and other movements around the world resisting white supremacy, capitalism, and U.S. militarism. In an illustration headed "It's All the Same," published in March 1968, Douglas used three panels to depict identically clothed pigs armed with guns, napalm, and mace, labeled "local police," "national guard," and "marines."[53]

By the end of 1968, Douglas was using caricatures of pigs to represent not only soldiers and police officers but also figures ranging from San Francisco mayor Joseph Alioto, California governor Ronald Reagan, national political figures such as Lyndon Johnson, Richard Nixon, and George Wallace, and even Santa Claus.

Opposed to these tools of racialized colonialism in the United States and around the world was a diverse group that was bound together by having a common enemy and a common goal of self-determination. In September 1968, Douglas juxtaposed a quote from Mao Zedong, declaring that "war can only be abolished through war," with illustrations of an armed black freedom fighter standing alongside Vietnamese and Afro-Cuban guerrillas, a Mexican revolutionary, and a Native American warrior with a flaming hatchet.[54] As evidenced by this and other illustrations, Douglas was entirely

Figure 5. September 28, 1968. Photo courtesy of Emory Douglas/Art Resource, NY.

"WE ARE ADVOCATES OF THE ABOLITION OF WAR . . . WE DO NOT WANT WAR; BUT WAR CAN ONLY BE ABOLISHED THROUGH WAR AND IN ORDER TO GET RID OF THE GUN IT IS NECESSARY TO TAKE UP THE GUN."

Chairman Mao

Figure 6. September 28, 1968. Photo courtesy of Emory Douglas/Art Resource, NY.

comfortable working with a transnational and transhistorical vocabulary. His work for the BPP was heavily influenced by the art of Third World revolutionary movements, particularly those in Cuba and Vietnam, and he directly collaborated with the Organización de Solidaridad con los Pueblos de Asia, África y América Latina (OSPAAAL) in 1968 to produce posters celebrating international solidarity with the African American people.[55] At the same time, however, Douglas remained closely linked to the verbal and visual vernacular that characterized the origins of the Panthers in the East Bay's urban African American community. Amiri Baraka characterized Douglas's work as "a combination of expressionist agitprop and homeboy familiarity," which "come[s] on like drawings, straight out of the hood."[56]

An illustration from March 1968 depicting Lyndon Johnson, Robert F. Kennedy, Secretary of Defense Robert McNamara, and Secretary of State Dean Rusk as pigs with broken necks, for example, was paired with words "on landscape art": "It is good only when it shows the oppressor hanging from a tree by his mother f—kin neck."[57]

The very layout of the *Black Panther* reinforced links between local issues facing African Americans and broader international developments,

Figure 7. Anticolonial vernacular at work: Emory Douglas comments on the U.S. political establishment (focusing on Secretary of State Dean Rusk, Secretary of Defense Robert S. McNamara, President Lyndon B. Johnson, and Senator Robert F. Kennedy). March 16, 1968. Photo courtesy of Emory Douglas/Art Resource, NY.

particularly in the Third World. The October 26, 1968 edition, to take one typical example, featured a front-page article by Cleaver urging the paper's readers to "look outside the borders of the United States in order to relate to the present balance of revolutionary forces in the world." Accompanying this injunction was the iconic photograph of U.S. athletes Tommie Smith and John Carlos giving the Black Power salute following their first-place and third-place finish in the two-hundred-meter race at the Mexico City Olympic Games. Inside were stories from Laos, Vietnam, Mexico, Brazil, Cuba, and Iraq in addition to coverage of local and national news relating to African Americans.[58] Following the example of *Soulbook*, the *Black Panther* initially had no dedicated "international" section. Rather, local, national, and global appeared side by side in its pages. An approving comment on China's first test of a thermonuclear weapon in July 1967, for example, was sandwiched between short items dealing with grassroots organizing in Atlanta and Los Angeles, all of which appeared under the heading "The World of Black People."[59] As with their predecessors in RAM, the Panthers' definition of blackness in this period was expansive, with color serving not as a fixed cultural or biological construct but rather as a marker of struggle against white supremacy and colonialism.

"Off the Pig": Symbolic Violence in the Panthers' Anticolonial Vernacular

Depictions of violence provided another crucial element of the Panthers' anticolonial vernacular, one that built upon international referents while also drawing on the history and contemporary lived experience of black people in the United States. Accounts of Fanon's contributions to the evolution of the black freedom struggle in the United States have generally empha-sized his role in legitimating violence as a both a practical and psychologi-cal necessity in resisting colonialism. Equally, important, however, was his description of the routinized violence that lay at the heart of the colonial system itself. The crumbling infrastructure, poverty, and human misery of the ghetto were, in Fanon's description, the inevitable consequence of "the violence which governed the ordering of the colonial world." The police, whose task was to "ensure the colonized are kept under close scrutiny, and contained by rifle butts and napalm," were the most visible agents of this violence, but it extended to include virtually all of the institutions that structured life for the colonized.[60] Exposing the ways in which the exercise of state violence shaped the daily life of Oakland residents, and of urban black America more broadly, was a crucial element in the BPP's program from the formation of the party in October 1966. While the party's armed patrols initially served this purpose with respect to police brutality, by mid-1967 the task of dramatizing this violence increasingly moved from the streets of Oakland to the pages of the *Black Panther*.

The first issue of the paper highlighted the killing of Denzil Dowell in North Richmond as evidence of a larger pattern of police misconduct in black communities and championed armed self-defense as necessary to "free our communities from this brutal form of oppression."[61] Subsequent issues published in the aftermath of the Sacramento demonstration widened the scope of analysis, linking local acts of police brutality to a larger pattern of colonial violence directed at people of color by the U.S. government and its agencies both at home and abroad. In a column written for the second issue of the newspaper, Newton argued that "[t]here is a great similarity between the occupying army in Southeast Asia and the occupation of our communities by the racist police."[62] The BPP subsequently expanded on this comparison with both words and images, striving to communicate these links to a rank-and-file audience that knew little about the geopolitics of Vietnam or the nuances Fanon's work but could easily relate to being brutalized and intimidated by local police. Whereas in "fascist America," insisted New Haven BPP member Rory Hithe, "they use the thin blue line, fascist dog policemen, national guardsmen, cynical F.B.I. agents and traitorous, bootlicking civil rights leaders" to oppress people of color, externally the United States relied on "sadistic C.I.A. agents, the mercenary U.S. armed services, and running dog treaty organizations such as the North Atlantic Treaty Organization (NATO), the Organization of American States (OAS), the Southeast Asia Treaty Organization (SEATO), the Central Treaty Organization (CENTO), and the Association of Southeast Asian Nations (ASEAN)."[63] While the tools and venues varied, in each of these cases the U.S. government employed organized violence to oppress and exploit people of color. As scholar Cynthia B. Young observed in her larger study of the U.S. Third World Left, activists in this period "used a focus on state violence and the internal colony to provide the ideological glue connecting U.S. minorities and Third World majorities."[64]

Illustrations in the pages of the *Black Panther* provided one of the most powerful tools in the BPP's efforts to convey the impact of colonial violence on daily life in the black ghetto and its links to U.S. imperialism overseas. Emory Douglas's depictions of snarling, armed pigs terrorizing the black community easily paired with similar illustrations depicting violence inflicted against the Vietnamese and other Third World peoples struggling for self-determination. Tarika Lewis contributed similarly themed drawings of police violence and intimidation featuring hideous pigs dressed in police uniforms and terrorizing black youth.[65] By the end of the 1960s, Douglas had begun experimenting with ways to illustrate the more subtle ways in which white colonial control of the ghetto inflicted violence and suffering on black people. One of his iconic images depicted an armed black woman sitting in wait for a greedy landlord, while beside her a baby is eyed by oversized rats.

Later (starting in 1971 after Cleaver and Newton split), Douglas expanded upon this effort in drawings dramatizing the way in which poverty, hunger, ill health, and dilapidated schools and housing constituted a form of routinized and institutionalized violence.[66] Whether it was through caricatures of police officers and soldiers or his realistic drawings of, in the words of Philadelphia BPP member Mumia Abu-Jamal, "people in the ghetto, sisters with their hair in braids, with frayed sleeves and worn shoes," Douglas provided a vivid and easily accessible way to illustrate the racialized colonial violence that linked African Americans to people of color around the world.[67]

Another key element of the Panthers' anticolonial vernacular was the assertion that any serious attempt to overturn white colonial control of the ghetto would require a willingness on the part of the colonized to confront it with force. In "patrolling the pigs," the Panthers had not only dramatized the violence of the police but also, in openly bearing arms and demonstrating a willingness to use them, showed the residents of West Oakland that it was both necessary and possible for black people to rid themselves of the passivity and inferiority complex that Fanon had identified as a consequence of colonialism. The Mulford Act deprived the Panthers of this option, and Newton recognized that the BPP was not prepared to initiate guerrilla warfare without first building a broader base of support in the black community and perhaps beyond. Thus, while the party quietly continued to amass weapons, one of the major challenges facing the Panthers in mid-1967 was finding a way to convincingly advocate for the psychological and practical role of violence in black liberation in the United States without running afoul of the law or prematurely entering into an open, armed struggle that would have surely doomed the party. It was partly in response to this dilemma that Cleaver, Douglas, Lewis, and others in 1967–68 turned to embedding anticolonial violence in the party's visual, written, and spoken vernacular.

vernacular- site of violent images as it became more chally; to legals carry guns

Figure 8. September 12, 1970. Photo courtesy of Emory Douglas/Art Resource, NY.

Stripped of the ability to dramatically embody anticolonial violence, or at least potential violence, in the form of armed patrols, the BPP's rhetoric grew increasingly bold in response. Rhetorically, at least, "picking up the gun" morphed from self-defense against local incidents of police brutality to a form of revolutionary violence directed against the entire white colonial system. Cleaver was typically blunt in exhorting black Americans to "get some guns, organize, and square off to deal with this honkie."[68] BPP minister of education George Murray offered a similarly concise summary of the role of violence in black liberation: "Change. Freedom everywhere. Dynamite! Black Power. Use the gun. Kill the pig everywhere." Chicago BPP leader Fred Hampton agreed, declaring, "Kill a few and get a little satisfaction. Kill some more and you get some more satisfaction. Kill em all and you get complete satisfaction."[69] While usually employed as part of a blanket attack on colonial systems that controlled black people, sometimes this language was directed at more specific targets. In an open letter to Los Angeles police chief Thomas Reddin published in the *Black Panther* in November 1968, John Huggins of the L.A. chapter of the BPP declared that "[a]s a closing message to you we'd like to say UP AGAINST THE WALL MOTHERFUCKER!" Black leaders deemed to be "bootlickers" or "Uncle Toms" as well as specific police officers "Wanted Dead for Murder" were also singled out by the Panthers for at least rhetorical violence. Perhaps most famously, David Hilliard attracted notoriety and legal attention for announcing in a 1969 speech, "We will kill Richard Nixon. We will kill any motherfucker that stands in the way of our freedom."[70]

As with the party's efforts to illustrate the links between the black ghetto and the Third World, visual imagery played arguably the most important role in conveying the BPP's willingness to use arms. Images of guns, including carbines, M16s, and the iconic shotgun wielded by Newton were ubiquitous in the *Black Panther* in 1967–68. Douglas and Lewis also frequently contributed drawings of armed black people proudly carrying guns, ammunition, and explosives, often styled after similar depictions of Cuban and Vietnamese guerrillas. While black men featured most heavily in these visual representations, both Lewis and Douglas made a point of showing women and children handling firearms, again echoing examples from Third World guerrilla struggles. One of Lewis's iconic pieces showed a mother teaching her young child how to shoot. In a drawing published in December 1968, Douglas depicted a young boy asking his approving father for a machine gun, shotgun, dynamite, hand grenades, and matches as a Christmas gift. Around the borders of the drawing were slogans including

Figure 9. January 3, 1970. Photo courtesy of Emory Douglas/Art Resource, NY.

"Off the Pig," "Blow Oink Away," and "Snipe the Hogs!"[71] Both artists also frequently portrayed black men and women directly employing anticolonial violence against their enemies. In 1968 the pages of the *Black Panther* regularly featured drawings of pigs being stabbed, shot, strangled, set on fire, hung from trees, blown to pieces, splashed with acid, dropped on spikes, crushed under a boot, and carried away in coffins.

While Douglas often depicted this violence in outlandish and cartoonish fashion, Lewis's pieces tended to feature more realistic depictions of armed black men ambushing police paired with injunctions on proper guerrilla tactics ("No More Riots . . . Twos and Threes").[72]

The increasing visual and rhetorical emphasis on violence served a number of purposes for the party in 1967–68. As with the previous armed police patrols, one of the central goals of the BPP's anticolonial vernacular was to communicate its ideas and call to action men and women who might not have attended college, read Fanon, Mao, and Che Guevara, or participated in covert groups such as RAM. This meant that even as the *Black Panther* opened a broader channel of communications for the BPP, one that transcended the streets of the Bay Area, its editors and writers consciously attempted to pitch their message in terms drawn from the milieu of the party's founding and early operations. As Douglas explained it in May 1968:

> We, the Black Panther artists, draw deadly pictures of the enemy—pictures that show him at his death door or dead—his bridges are blown up in our

pictures—his institutions destroyed—and in the end he is lifeless. We try to create an atmosphere for the vast majority of black people—who aren't readers but activists—through their observation of our work, they feel they have the right to destroy the enemy.[73]

Similarly, Lewis's striking drawing of a black guerrilla fighter standing before the backdrop of a flaming city, with the caption "Before we talk reconstruction, let's accomplish the ruins," was a simple and direct way of communicating Fanon's assertion that "[d]ecolonization is always a violent event."[74]

The verbal and visual emphasis on anticolonial violence in the pages of the *Black Panther* and elsewhere also served to served create transhistorical and transnational links between the BPP and individuals, groups, and nations that fought for self-determination against colonialism and white supremacy. In arguably the most famous photo of Newton—first appearing in the *Black Panther* in June 1967 and repeatedly reprinted in the newspaper as well as on posters—the BPP's minister of defense was pictured sitting in a large wicker throne, with a modern M1 rifle in one hand and a spear in the other, personally embodying a kind of "imagined community" (to use Benedict Anderson's phrase) that linked black Americans to their African ancestors as well as contemporary resistance to white supremacy and colonialism.[75] The increasingly prominent role of Mao Zedong in the Panthers' visual and verbal lexicon was also symptomatic of a larger shift in the way the party expressed its connections to the Third World. Whereas previously the BPP had used the Red Book primarily as a tool to raise money within white radical circles, Mao's assertions that that "political power grows out of the barrel of a gun" and that "in order to get rid of the gun it is necessary to take up the gun" featured heavily in the pages of the *Black Panther* and in the speeches of Panther leaders in 1967–68. By 1969, Bobby Seale could stand in front of a large, multi-ethnic rally outside the San Francisco Federal Building and exhort the crowd to "[h]old your Red Books up and tell the brothers where we getting some new ideology from."[76]

During this period, Mao joined a host of other Third World figures as additional referents that came to define the party's public image within the black community and beyond. In a May 1968 essay, Minister of Education George Murray invoked Fanon in asserting that "[w]e can create a black world, a black nation. . . . The way we can make this happen is through violence. . . . When we take out a policeman, major businessman or senator . . . we are educating ourselves and people like us." The rhetoric of anticolonial violence simultaneously linked the Panthers to both the

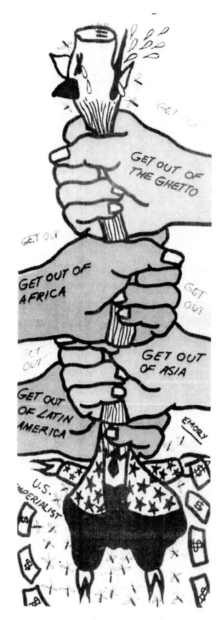

Figure 10. October 19, 1968. Photo courtesy of Emory Douglas/Art Resource, NY.

black past (via the history of slave rebellions) and the revolutionary Third World of the present. Such actions, Murray declared, would be "in the spirit of Malcolm X, Huey P. Newton, Nat Turner, Denmark Vesey, the Viet Cong, and black guerillas in Southern Rhodesia."[77] When Emory Douglas drew armed Panthers flanked by Cuban guerrillas and Native American warriors or a figure of a pig labeled "U.S. Imperialism"—with its neck being wrung by black and brown hands labeled "Get out of the ghetto, Get out of Africa, Get out of Asia, Get out of Latin America"—it conveyed in simple and direct terms that the local struggle waged by the BPP in Oakland was linked to a long history of global struggle against white supremacy and colonialism.[78]

"Righteous and for Real Peoples' Power": Evaluating the BPP's Anticolonial Vernacular

The most obvious accomplishment of the BPP's anticolonial vernacular was to create a vocabulary that helped to bind the party to an identity that was neither entirely national nor entirely diasporic. Though prose, speeches, art, dress, and even music the Panthers built on their early operations in the East Bay in 1967–68, forging links based on transnational and transhistorical notions of blackness while remaining firmly rooted in the local circumstances of urban African American life. In doing so, they identified themselves as part of an imagined community of antiracist, anticapitalist, anticolonialist freedom fighters without becoming too closely entangled with any particular nation, government, or political-economic system or losing sight of their local roots. Among other advantages, this approach allowed the Panthers to avoid the "land hang-up" that had historically frustrated black nationalist ventures. As Cleaver observed, the long history of injustices perpetrated against black people in the United States had produced a "feeling of alienation and dissociation" powerful enough that they "long ago would have readily identified themselves with another sovereignty had a viable one existed."[79] This was complicated, however, by the unique position of black Americans as a colonized people with deep roots and a long history living inside a First World superpower. The solution, he suggested, was for black people to embrace this liminal position as neither a nation-state in the traditional sense (since they were dispersed and lacked land) nor full citizens of the United States (an impossibility given that the nation was founded and maintained by a system of white supremacy):

> Black Power must be viewed as a projection of sovereignty, an embry-
> onic sovereignty that black people can focus on and through which they
> can make distinctions between themselves and others, between them-
> selves and their enemies—in short, between the white mother country
> of America and the black colony dispersed throughout the continent on
> absentee-owned land, making Afro-America a decentralized colony. Black
> Power says to black people that it is possible for them to build a national
> organization on somebody else's land.[80]

The Panthers' anticolonial vernacular facilitated this "embryonic sovereignty" by linking black Americans to Third World nations and other groups
seeking self-determination while acknowledging the realities of daily life
in U.S. ghettos and celebrating African American culture. As such, it was
highly influential not only within the party but also in the development of
what Cynthia Young identified as key trends in the "interstitial approach" of
the U.S. Third World Left, with its emphasis on "interpolating and signaling
a community with certain shared interests: the commitment to eradicating
colonialism, imperialism, racism, class exploitation, and, in some admittedly
rare instances, homophobia and misogyny."[81]

Another major accomplishment of the party's populist anticolonial
discourse was to call attention to the links between capitalism and white
supremacy without becoming trapped in sterile academic debates over
which of those two world historical forces was more important in producing the oppression of black people. Thus, while Cleaver argued that capitalism and the desire of the West to expropriate labor and resources from
people of color had historically fueled the growth of white supremacy, he
noted that "[p]eople who confront this situation daily, and who haven't had
time to do elaborate studies of the situation, don't have time to distinguish
between the economics and the racism." Newton expressed similar sentiments, suggesting that the most important thing was not to untangle this
complicated historical relationship theoretically but to "develop a power
that will make it non-profitable for racist[s] to go on oppressing us."[82] Similarly the party's anticolonial vernacular drew on Marxism and its variants
without becoming too deeply involved in theoretical nuances of Marxism.
In lambasting "the avaricious businessman, the racist, decadent, demagogic
politicians of the world, and the pig police forces, be they in the Black

community or in Vietnam" and calling for "righteous and for real people's power," Panther leaders advanced a collectivist critique of capitalism in terms designed to appeal to a working class and lumpenproletariat who experienced its negative effects on a daily basis but had little interest in a seminar on Marxist-Leninist theory. Indeed, for all the favorable references to Mao, Che Guevara, Ho Chi Minh, and other Marx-inspired revolutionaries, the *Black Panther* did not hew to anything approaching a party line in 1967–68. Some on the Left, then and now, have criticized the Panthers for their heterodoxy and theoretical laxness. But by keeping the focus on a simple demand for "land, bread [and] housing" the BPP was able to articulate anticapitalist sentiments to a large audience without becoming mired in Marxist dogma or the doctrinal infighting that had often characterized groups such as the CPUSA and PL.[83]

By mixing a critique of white supremacy, capitalism, and militarism, the Panthers' anticolonial vernacular also opened up the possibility of alliances with white radicals involved in the antiwar movement. In 1968, Cleaver led the BPP in forging an alliance with the Peace and Freedom Party (PFP), which had its roots in the predominantly white antiwar movement in the San Francisco Bay Area. The immediate origins of this collaboration lay in expediency—the PFP sought black votes in the upcoming election, while the BPP wanted publicity for its campaign to "Free Huey" following Newton's October 1967 arrest (detailed in chapter 4). But emphasizing the colonial situation facing African Americans as an economic as well as racial process that had direct links to the Vietnam War and other U.S. imperial endeavors overseas helped prepare a sometimes skeptical Panther membership for working tactically with "mother country radicals" in the PFP. The BPP's anticolonial vernacular was also potentially attractive to many white antiwar activists as it allowed them to connect their efforts to end the war in Vietnam to the Panthers' struggles to take control of their own communities. Cleaver's personal affinity for the emerging counterculture in the San Francisco Bay Area, his position at *Ramparts*, and the admiration he expressed for the younger generation of white radicals in *Soul on Ice* helped cement this relationship.[84]

The broad-based anticolonial ideology expressed by Cleaver, Douglas, and other Panther activists and artists also facilitated connections with a growing Third World Left in the United States that related to the Panthers' urban-centric critique of white supremacy, capitalism, and imperialism. Anticipating notions of polyculturalism later expressed by scholar Vijay Prashad, the BPP's anticolonial vernacular allowed for a shared set of ideas about colonialism and self-determination among people of color in the United States while simultaneously leaving room for different groups to offer variations based on their own experiences and expressed in their own culturally and geographically particular terms.[85] Thus, groups such as the Red Guards (based in San Francisco's Chinatown), the Young Lords (a Puerto Rican nationalist group with a strong following in Chicago and New York), and the Brown Berets (a Los Angeles–based Chicano group) offered their own versions of the Panthers' ten-point program, but in doing so they modified it to include demands such as treatment for tuberculosis sufferers in Chinatown, freedom for Puerto Rico, and respect for Spanish-language speakers in the United States.[86] More directly, the Panthers provided assistance to groups looking to emulate the party's success in using the *Black Panther* as both an organizational tool and ideological touchstone. When a nascent Chicano/a group based in the Mission District of San Francisco dubbed Los Siete de la Raza (named after seven Chicano youth charged with killing a white policeman) sought to publish its own newspaper, the BPP initially provided space in the *Black Panther*, while Emory Douglas helped train artists who would go on to produce the independent publication *Basta Ya!*[87]

For all its strengths, the anticolonial vernacular developed by the Panthers in 1967–68 also contained a number of ambiguities and contradictions that contributed to the party's growing pains as it expanded beyond its initial base in Oakland. Most obviously, the increasingly heavy reliance on rhetorical violence masked a growing divide between those who saw it as a symbolic substitute for armed revolution and those who took it more literally. Newton, Seale, and Hilliard argued that the party's calls to "off the pigs" and "kill any motherfucker that stands in the way of our freedom" did not signify a fundamental change in the party's initial caution and respect for the law regarding the handling of firearms. While leaving open the possibility of an eventual escalation to guerrilla warfare (and quietly amassing an arsenal in preparation), they were careful to ensure that the BPP's day-to-day operations remained legal and aboveground for the indefinite future. Thus, Newton continued to insist in 1968 that the Panthers would only use guns in self-defense and that "we're not advocating violence." Seale, meanwhile, explained that when used as part of the Panthers' vernacular, phrases such as "off the pig" and "kill" did not mean "commit murder" but rather were a "a reaction to someone . . . that is about to unjustly attack."[88] Whatever the intent of the party's founders, however, the rhetoric of anticolonial violence once unleashed was not always easy to contain to the realms of symbolism or self-defense. As detailed in the chapters that follow, the question of how to interpret the role of violence in the BPP's daily operations would eventually contribute to a catastrophic split within the party.

The nature of the relationship between black Americans and the governments and peoples of the Third World was another point of ambiguity in the Panther's anticolonial discourse that would eventually pose complications for the party. In the *Black Panther* and elsewhere, the party championed Third World solidarity in broad strokes without dwelling on the specific situations of these nations or on the many potential conflicts in their relationships with each other or with black Americans. Scholars have sometimes criticized these types of rhetorical comparisons as both oversimplifying the diverse and contested nature of the Third World and ignoring the many differences that separated black Americans living in a First World superpower from the colonial and postcolonial subjects in Africa, Asia, and Latin America the Panthers so frequently invoked. Whatever the scholarly validity of such comparisons, as an organizing device to build a constituency among black Americans and other people of color within the United States this kind of rhetoric was tremendously effective for the BPP in 1967–68. The notion of an imagined and idealized community that linked people of color around the world in a battle against white supremacy, colonialism, and capitalism allowed the Panthers to organize locally while claiming links to a larger movement that transcended race and geography. Where it fell short, however, was in preparing the party and its members for building working relationships with governments and movements in the Third World.

As Malcolm X had discovered in the early 1960s, notions of a unified Third World standing shoulder to shoulder in a struggle for freedom with black Americans quickly vanished when confronted with the complex realities of nationalism and Cold War geopolitics. If the Panthers wanted to move beyond symbolism to forge actual alliances with the Third World, they would need to directly confront the question of what, specifically, these nations could do to help black Americans and vice versa. For the most part, the BPP's anticolonial vernacular simply ignored this difficult question in favor of sweeping rhetorical and visual statements of solidarity. To the extent that they did address it, BPP leaders in 1967–68 tended to indulge in the same notions of African American exceptionalism that had marked RAM's approach to the subject. Echoing Robert F. Williams, Muhammad Ahmad, Donald Freeman, and other RAM theorists, Newton insisted that "black people in America are the only people who can free the world, loosen the [yoke] of colonialism and destroy the war machine." Working from the assumption that "[w]e are the driving shaft . . . in such a strategic position in this machinery that once we become dislocated the functioning of the remainder of the machinery breaks down," Newton posited that black anticolonialism in the United States was inherently internationalist and that black Americans were in a unique position to "destroy the machinery that's enslaving the world."[89] One result of this particular vision of African American exceptionalism was that, like RAM, the BPP's leaders had little incentive to engage in the difficult and complicated task of building links across borders, languages, and cultures. While it had no effect on their ability to build a coalition in the United States, as the Panthers began to explore overseas links in 1968 this attitude would pose serious problems for the party.

For all its success at fueling the growth of the party at home, the BPP's anticolonial vernacular also alienated some potential supporters in the African American community. Newton eventually ordered the Panthers to drop their use of profanity as it was likely to preemptively turn off some older and more socially conservative members of the community who might otherwise be receptive to the party's message. The Panthers' emphasis on building cross-racial coalitions and their attention to the economic aspects of colonialism also created tensions with groups and individuals, such as Maulana Karenga's Los Angeles-based US Organization, that identified primarily on ethno-cultural lines.[90]

The party's discourse also often clashed with its avowed commitment to gender equality. Women, including Tarıka Lewis, Kathleen Neal Cleaver, and Judy Juanita, were involved in the party from early on and made important contributions to the development of the *Black Panther*. But while images of female warriors were not uncommon, the party's anticolonial vernacular simultaneously reinforced notions of patriarchy while frequently relegating women to supporting roles in the revolution. The armed women who appeared in party-sanctioned art could easily slide into what scholar Anne McClintock referred to as Fanon's "eroticized image of militarized sexuality" that "masculinizes the female militant, turning her into a phallic substitute, detached from the male body but remaining, still, the man's 'woman-arsenal.'"[91] As Robeson Taj Frazier noted in his study of radical black internationalism during this period, even in the most revolutionary "representations and articulations, female agency and femininity conformed to male standards; subversive women were dominantly framed in hegemonic masculine and heteronormative terms."[92]

Figure 11. 1969. Photo courtesy of Emory Douglas/Art Resource, NY.

In November 1967, to give one example, Eldridge Cleaver wrote an editorial in the Panther newspaper denouncing beauty pageants such as Miss America as "a racist ritual" that served to "perpetuate racism and stereotypes." But rather than concluding that such exhibitions inherently demeaned women, his solution was to propose a "humanized Miss Third World Contest" to more properly judge the "beautiful world of Blackness."[93] Cleaver's celebration of "pussy power," with the corresponding assertion that "revolutionary power grows out of the lips of a pussy," was based on a similarly sexist notion that women's most important contribution to the struggle was to give or withhold sex in order to encourage "these males who call themselves men" to take up the gun. Nor were such sentiments confined to Eldridge Cleaver (who also frequently peppered his speeches and writings with homophobic slurs such as "punk").[94] In a nuanced analysis of the party's aesthetics and iconography, with a particular emphasis of the role played by Emory Douglas, scholar Erika Doss concluded that by "reconfiguring and romanticizing black men as the very embodiment of revolutionary rage, defiance, and misogyny," the party "reinscribed the most egregious forms of patriarchal privilege and domination, from machismo and misogyny to violence and aggression."[95] As the BPP expanded beyond its original base in Oakland in largely decentralized fashion, with local chapters enjoying a great deal of autonomy, the anticolonial vernacular found in the pages of the *Black Panther* and elsewhere provided a common vocabulary as important as the gun or the iconic uniform of the black beret, powder-blue shirt, and black leather jacket in cementing the party's identity. The party's growth, however, also tested the ability of its leaders to contain the ambiguities and contradictions imbedded in this discourse.

Chapter 4

"I Prefer Panthers to Pigs"

Transnational and International Connections, 1968–1969

As the BPP reached its one-year anniversary in October 1967, the party was, in the estimation of David Hilliard, "almost dead." With only a dozen members (at least one of whom, Earl Anthony, turned out to be an FBI informant), no active community service programs, and struggling to pay rent on its small storefront office in Oakland, the Panthers had virtually ceased to exist as a grassroots organization.[1] The FBI, which kept close tabs on the party through both internal and external surveillance, concluded that "the BPPSD ceased to be active as an organization in late August, 1967" and that by October the Panthers "had no headquarters and was no longer conducting membership meetings."[2] Eldridge Cleaver and Emory Douglas were working to revitalize and reinvent the party by developing the *Black Panther* as an organizing tool, but the Panthers' anticolonial vernacular took time to establish and propagate. With the BPP short on both money and members, the newspaper appeared sporadically, and it was unclear if the party would survive long enough to reach a larger audience with its unique blend of anticolonial theory and streetwise presentation. One of the only encouraging developments for the Panthers in late 1967 was that Huey Newton's probation period, the result of an earlier felony assault conviction, expired on October 27, allowing him to play a more active role in the party without having to regularly report to his probation officer.

On the day his probation expired, Newton attended a paid speaking engagement at San Francisco State University (SFSU), where he promoted the BPP to members of the Black Student Union (BSU). The BSU was an important player in the Bay Area's cosmopolitan Black Power scene, but by late 1967 there were already cracks forming between the activists who had once intermingled at places like SFSU, Merritt College, and the Black House. Many in the BSU were skeptical of the Panthers' willingness to work in coalition with white radicals, a policy that stemmed from the party's commitment to revolutionary nationalism as well as Cleaver's personal contacts with the New Left. Newton described the ensuing discussion at SFSU as "challenging," but the $500 speaking fee represented a desperately needed infusion of resources.[3] As they drove back across the Bay Bridge, Newton and Hilliard hit upon the idea of using the money raised at SFSU to host a gambling party from which they would take a percentage of the winnings and sell matchboxes of marijuana on the side to raise additional funds. That this seemed an attractive option for financing the continued operations of the party speaks volumes about its dire organizational predicament in the fall of 1967.[4]

Newton spent the evening celebrating his freedom at a variety of local establishments before joining the gambling party at two o'clock on the morning of October 28. Upon leaving several hours later, Newton and his companion, Gene McKinney, were pulled over by Oakland police officer John Frey. Frey, who recognized the license plate from a list of Panther vehicles, called for backup and was soon joined by a second officer, Herbert Heanes. Despite three criminal trials that would stretch into 1971, what exactly transpired next remains an unresolved source of controversy. All accounts agree, however, that the traffic stop concluded violently, with Frey fatally shot, Heanes wounded, and Newton suffering a critical gunshot wound in the stomach. Newton stumbled bloody and dazed into Hilliard's house in the aftermath of the shooting, and the BPP chief of staff drove him to the nearby Kaiser hospital. Police arrived shortly afterward and handcuffed Newton to his hospital gurney as he writhed in pain. Arrested and charged with first-degree murder, Newton recovered in police custody before being taken to the Alameda County Jail to await trial.[5]

With a wounded Newton behind bars and possibly facing the death penalty, Bobby Seale still serving a six-month prison sentence for his role in the Sacramento demonstration, and Eldridge Cleaver shackled by the terms of his own parole, the Panthers appeared on the brink of extinction. Instead, the high-profile trial of Newton that began in July 1968 revitalized the party by bringing it national attention. The publicity surrounding the trial would have meant little, however, had the Panthers not been prepared to take advantage of the opportunity. By providing a colorful, compelling, and easy-to-grasp template linking white radicals, urban communities of color, and allies in the Third World, the anticolonial vernacular pioneered by Cleaver, Douglas, and others within the BPP facilitated the party's efforts to raise support from a diverse set of allies as part of the "Free Huey" movement. Among the major developments that accompanied the prosecution of Newton were the creation of a formal alliance between the Panthers and white radicals in the Bay Area (most notably the nascent Peace and Freedom Party) and as well as the geographic expansion of the BPP itself through the creation of chapters outside the Bay Area, beginning in Los Angeles and soon spreading to Seattle, New York, and beyond, ultimately including as many as sixty-eight local branches.[6]

The sometimes-tense relations between the BPP and its white allies and the rich and varied history of the party's local chapters outside of Oakland are complicated subjects that have been well-chronicled elsewhere.[7] The party's efforts to leverage its anticolonial vernacular and local connections into alliances with other Third World–oriented groups in the United States, including the Young Lords, the Brown Berets, and the San Francisco-based Red Guards and Los Siete de la Raza, as well as its involvement in the Third World student strikes at San Francisco State University and the University of California, Berkeley, have also received significant attention.[8] Less well understood by historians, however, are the Panthers' efforts to forge international and transnational connections as part of the "Free Huey" campaign. Following in the footsteps of Malcolm X, Robert F. Williams, and Kwame Ture, Panthers traveled to Japan, Mexico, Cuba, Montreal, and Scandinavia and appealed to the UN in 1968 and early 1969. These efforts to cultivate alliances with foreign governments, international organizations, and transnational groups not only won support for Newton's defense but also laid the groundwork for more lasting relationships that would transcend the ad hoc personal diplomacy practiced by the BPP's predecessors and contemporaries. Yet for all the strides that the Panthers made in transforming their rhetoric into something more tangible, complications would beset their ongoing efforts to cultivate support outside the borders of the United States.

As the Black Power pioneers of the early 1960s had discovered, relations between minority groups in the United States and the foreign governments or international organizations to which they appealed were seldom conducted on equal terms. While the mushrooming growth of the BPP as a national organization in 1968 gave the party more leverage than Malcolm X or Williams had enjoyed as individuals, the Panthers still interacted with their potential state-level partners as supplicants rather than as equals. Transnational connections with non-state groups outside the United States avoided this power imbalance but came with their own set of potential complications. The ad hoc, person-to-person diplomacy that formed the foundation of these relationships often revealed ideological schisms both within the party and between the BPP and its potential allies. Moreover, as with foreign governments, transnational partners often had their own preconceptions and interests that did not always align with those of the Panthers. None of this is to downplay the tremendous strides that the BPP made internationally in 1968–69. But even as the party laid the foundations for an institutionalized presence outside the United States, the challenges and dilemmas it faced in this period foreshadowed the difficulties that the Panthers would encounter as they navigated the tumultuous waters of the Cold War and the Third World in the early 1970s.

"Free Huey" at the United Nations

The United Nations provided the venue for the BPP's first official foray into foreign affairs. On July 24, 1968, a group of Black Panthers including Bobby Seale, Eldridge Cleaver, Emory Douglas, and members of the party's newly founded New York City chapter arrived at the UN building in Manhattan. After meeting with representatives from the Tanzanian and Cuban governments and filing an application requesting official recognition as a nongovernmental organization, they marched outside to hold a press conference. Dressed in their signature black leather jackets despite the summer heat, the Panthers addressed their reasons for visiting the UN. Their most urgent goal was to draw international attention to the Newton trial, transforming it from a local issue of crime and punishment into an international referendum on white supremacy and colonialism. "Because Huey P. Newton stood up to oppose and denounce the imperialist aggression of the United States in international affairs and the vicious oppression of Black people in the domestic areas," they declared, "he has been singled out for silencing by the power structure." In response, the Panthers called for "the oppressed and colonized people, to organize demonstrations before the embassies, consulates, and property of the imperialist exploiters of the United States." Drawing on their colonial analysis of black America, they also requested "the stationing of UN Observer Teams throughout the cities of America wherein Black people are cooped up and concentrated in wretched ghettos."[9]

From its creation at the San Francisco Conference in June 1945, African American activists had seen the UN as a venue to which they could appeal for aid in combating white supremacy within the United States. During the 1940s and 1950s, groups ranging from the left-leaning National Negro Congress (NNC) and the Civil Rights Congress (CRC) to the NAACP had petitioned the organization to address the treatment of black Americans as a human rights issue. These early efforts to make use of the UN as a venue for the black freedom struggle foundered due to a combination of Cold War geopolitics and domination of the organization by a handful of great powers, many of which still held colonies of their own.[10] This came to a head in 1961, when black activists in New York staged a raucous demonstration at the UN to protest the organization's complicity in the removal and execution of Prime Minister Patrice Lumumba in the Republic of the Congo. Several developments, however, combined to make the UN once again a potentially relevant venue by the mid-1960s. The rapid spread of decolonization significantly changed the face of the organization as new nations composed of formerly colonized people of color joined in the wake of their independence. The Tanzanian delegation with whom the BPP met in July 1968 was one of thirty-six member states that had joined since 1960.[11] Meanwhile, U.S. interventions in Cuba, Vietnam, and the Dominican Republic and support for Israel during the 1967 war with its Arab neighbors served to mobilize anti-American and anticolonial sentiment at the UN. By 1964, Malcolm X, who had earlier previously offered tacit support for the pro-Lumumba and anti-UN demonstrations, declared that the time had come to "[e]xpand the civil-rights struggle to the level of human rights, take it into the United Nations."[12]

Panther leaders explicitly cited Malcolm X's injunction as they turned to the UN in mid-1968.[13] In appealing to United Nations, however, they were not only motivated by the legacy of Malcolm and the need to gain publicity for the "Free Huey" campaign but also by ideological developments inside the party itself. In 1968, as the BPP began to expand nationwide, the Panthers embraced the UN as a way to deal with the so-called "land question" that had long bedeviled black nationalist groups in the United States. Did black nationalism require a separate black nation-state?

If so, how were black people, dispersed across the interior of a First World superpower, to gain the land needed to assert their independence? For revolutionary nationalists like the Panthers, an additional question revolved around how to locate black nationalism in an international context and reconcile it with the larger goals of Third World anticolonialism and world-wide socialist revolution. Part of the BPP leaders' response to this dilemma was to create what Cleaver dubbed an "embryonic sovereignty" through the party's anticolonial vernacular, one that symbolically located black people as part of a global anticolonial majority while acknowledging their unique position within the United States.[14] But as the BPP expanded through the creation of decentralized local chapters, it raised anew the question of how to respond to the "land question."

It was Cleaver who first broached the notion of using the United Nations in order to bridge the gap between local community activism and formal nationhood. As black people successfully combated "community imperialism" at the local level, they would simultaneously take part in a "UN supervised plebiscite throughout the colony," in which they would decide whether they wanted to seek formal separation from the United States. The very process of implementing the plebiscite, Cleaver postulated, "would correspond to the role of the first or the key political campaign that happened in all countries emerging from colonial bondage":

> In Guinea the political focus was provided by the campaign against De Gaulle's Constitution. In Ghana it was the national election that placed Kwame Nkrumah at the head of the government. The campaign leading to the Plebiscite would be the means of solidly organizing Afro-America along national lines.[15]

Moreover, by situating black nationalism within the framework of the UN, Newton declared that the Panthers would "demonstrate our internationalist as well as nationalist position to the people; we simultaneously educate them and put pressure on the U.S. Government in the eyes of the world." Newton was sufficiently impressed with this idea to modify the BPP's ten-point program in mid-1968 to add Cleaver's call for a UN-supervised plebiscite "for the purpose of determining the will of black people as to their national destiny."[16]

For all its appeal as both a publicity tool in the "Free Huey" campaign and as a venue in which to explore black nationalism in an international context, dealing with the UN proved to be as challenging for the BPP as it had for the party's predecessors in the black freedom struggle. Though decolonization had broadened the UN's membership, it remained firmly rooted in individual nation-states, the vast majority of which were reluctant to directly challenge the United States on behalf of the BPP or set the precedent of intervening in the internal affairs of member nations. On a practical level, the Oakland-based Panther leaders had no contacts with member delegations at the UN, complicating potential efforts to bring their case before the organization. Prior to the July visit to New York, BPP leaders attempted to address this issue by working through allies in SNCC. The Panthers had tapped SNCC leaders Stokely Carmichael and James Foreman in 1968, appointing them prime minister and minister of foreign affairs respectively, as prelude to a potential merger between SNCC and the BPP.[17] Both men had developed relationships with representatives of foreign governments during their international travels, and the hope was that their connections within the UN would not only allow the BPP to gain entrance but also provide an opportunity for Seale and Cleaver to address the General Assembly. Shortly after arriving in New York, however, this ambitious plan was scuttled by tensions between SNCC and the BPP.

The roots of the BPP-SNCC split were both ideological and practical. As a result of their sometimes-troubled history of working with white volunteers, SNCC leaders had come to distrust such alliances and were skeptical of the BPP's willingness to explore coalitions with groups such as the primarily white Peace and Freedom Party.[18] Carmichael, meanwhile, had come to reject Marxism as a useful tool for understanding the black experience, turning instead to a more essentialist pan-Africanism that clashed with Panthers' revolutionary nationalism. Behind the scenes, he clashed with Foreman over the direction of SNCC, further complicating efforts to coordinate with the BPP. Relations between the two organizations were also frayed by tensions between experienced SNCC leaders who had spent years organizing the black freedom struggle and the brash and often younger BPP members who had vaulted from relative obscurity into icons of the Black Power movement.[19] A tinderbox exacerbated by the FBI's COINTELPRO efforts ignited when Oakland-based Panthers arrived in New York in July. Following an explosive meeting, which according to some accounts ended with the Panthers confronting Foreman with a gun, the BPP-SNCC alliance effectively ended, leaving the party without the necessary contacts to gain entrance to the UN.[20]

It took a last-minute appeal from Cleaver to "Queen Mother" Audley Moore, a former CPUSA member who had helped to mentor RAM members earlier in the decade, to secure an invitation for the BPP to meet with members the Tanzanian delegation.[21] Moore's intervention helped salvage the Panthers' inaugural attempt at international diplomacy. While they were unable to address the General Assembly or convince a member state to introduce a resolution supporting the party's plan for a black plebiscite, BPP leaders did make valuable contacts with the Tanzanian and Cuban governments, and they were able to parlay their UN visit into additional publicity for the "Free Huey" movement. For a group that less than a year earlier had been on the verge of extinction and little known outside the San Francisco Bay Area, this was a major accomplishment. The struggle to gain access to the UN, however, was a harsh reminder of the difficulty that non-state groups, particularly those representing oppressed minority populations, faced in dealing with nation-states and the international bodies in which they were represented. The cruel irony of using the UN as a venue in which to explore the "land question" was that without a formal state of their own, black Americans would never be effectively represented in that body. In the wake of their UN trip, BPP leaders pursued two separate tracks designed to give them the kind of international leverage that they had struggled to achieve while in New York. One track involved following up on the contacts with the Cuban government to create a more formal alliance with a sympathetic partner in the Third World. However, given the challenge of dealing even with friendly foreign governments, the BPP's leadership also began to explore transnational connections that would bypass nation-states entirely while creating global solidarity networks.

Tokyo and Montreal: Early Efforts at Transnational Movement Building

While the BPP identified most strongly with the revolutionary Third World, the party's initial efforts at transnational organizing in 1968–69 were most successful in western Europe and Japan. Though they attempted some sporadic contacts with Mexican students and activists in 1968, the only lasting transnational connections built in this period were rooted in Scandinavia and West Germany.[22] In retrospect, this should not be surprising. The Third World nations and people with whom BPP leaders believed they shared natural affinities tended to be represented by independent governments, most of which jealously guarded their independence and were not keen on diplomacy taking place outside their control. Those Third World groups that were not under the direct control of national governments, such as the various guerrillas fighting against Portuguese colonialism and white supremacy in sub-Saharan Africa, tended to be too far away and too deeply immersed in their own struggles to engage with a new and relatively unknown organization such as the BPP. Meanwhile, 1968 marked the ascendency of a global New Left movement that swept across most of the industrialized, noncommunist First World. While the outlook and agenda of these groups varied from country to country (indeed, even within individual countries), they tended to share opposition to the Vietnam War and U.S. imperialism more broadly, admiration for Third World anticolonialism, and a hunger for an alternative to Soviet communism and U.S. capitalism.[23] In theory, at least, the Panthers and their anticolonial vernacular were well suited to alliances with the kaleidoscope of New Left groups that sprang up around the world in the late 1960s. In practice, transnational diplomacy proved to be alternatively frustrating and rewarding for the BPP.

One month after their UN visit, Panther leaders embarked on an inaugural effort at transnational diplomacy. This venture was the result of an overture in the summer of 1968 from a coalition of Japanese artists, activists, students, and intellectuals. Founded in April 1965, Beheiren (Citizens' Alliance for Peace in Vietnam) was an umbrella organization that encompassed a wide range of viewpoints and backgrounds, all united by opposition to the U.S. war in Vietnam and their own government's complicity in the U.S. aggression. Nominally led by novelist and social critic Makoto Oda, in practice Beheiren was a loosely knit organization that eventually encompassed over three hundred local chapters throughout Japan.[24] From the beginning, the group's leaders had sought to build transnational connections not only with peace activists and New Left groups in the United States but also with representatives of the civil rights and Black Power movements. The group was, in the words of historian Yuichiro Onishi, "committed to promoting internationalism and solidarity with people mobilizing against the rampant pursuit of wealth, whiteness, and imperialist interests."[25] Beheiren leaders, including Oda and Tsurumi Yoshiyuki, made direct contact with Carmichael and other figures in SNCC prior to reaching out to the Panthers. In August 1966, the group hosted a Japan-U.S. Citizens' Conference for Peace in Vietnam that included SNCC representative Ralph Featherstone.[26]

The high-profile anti–Vietnam War stance taken by both SNCC and the BPP was one obvious point of connection with Beheiren. But as noted by historian Simon Andrew Avenell, so too were the efforts by Black Power activists in the United States to theorize the relationship between colonialism, white supremacy, and U.S. militarism. For Oda, Yoshiyuki, and other Beheiren activists, the notion that white supremacy underlay not only anti-black racism in the United States but also U.S. imperialist aggression in Vietnam and a neo-colonialist relationship with its Japanese client state was a crucial innovation. Much as the Panthers' anticolonial vernacular offered a way to overcome their minority status in the United States, this brand of Third World anticolonialism allowed Beheiren to separate itself from Japan's imperialist past and complicity in Washington's war in Vietnam by identifying as fellow victims—and opponents—of U.S. policy. And while Beheiren remained firmly committed to nonviolent tactics in its demonstrations in Japan, it supported the right of other groups to win their freedom through armed struggle when necessary.[27]

In August 1968, Beheiren leaders extended an invitation to Eldridge and Kathleen Cleaver to visit Japan as part an international conference dealing with the Vietnam War, the U.S.-Japan Security Treaty, and the status of Okinawa. Eldridge was prevented from attending by the terms of his parole, so Earl Anthony, the Los Angeles Panther who was a mole for the FBI, unbeknown to the party leaders, took his place. The two BPP emissaries traveled first to Hawaii, where they encountered last-minute trouble getting a visa for entry into Japan, likely as a result of high-level government concerns over their visit. Although demonstrations by activists in Tokyo pressured the Japanese government into issuing the visa, Kathleen Cleaver decided to forego the trip, leaving Anthony alone to represent the party.[28] Anthony's visit to Japan in August 1968 was the first time a BPP member had traveled overseas in pursuit of transnational alliances and as such was a watershed moment in the party's history. Ultimately, however, the trip yielded few positive results and illustrated many of the challenges posed by efforts to build such transnational connections.

Left to represent the BPP by himself, Anthony departed from the party's established line to offer a more essentialist take on the problems facing black Americans and people of color around the world. Rejecting both Marxism and the possibility of working with white activists, he insisted that "racism was *the* dominant problem for Afro-Americans, and a major one for other Third World people."[29] Anthony's position was not only a departure from the BPP's revolutionary nationalism, which stressed the inherent links between white supremacy and capitalism as systems of oppression, but also a repudiation of the party's ongoing cooperation with the primarily white Peace and Freedom Party. It was also an odd choice of message when addressing Japanese groups that had made a concerted effort to forge links across both geographic and racial lines. Like the BPP, Beheiren actively worked with whites of the U.S. New Left (including SDS members and, later, Jane Fonda's "FTA" antiwar tour of U.S. bases in the Pacific).[30] Whether the result of deliberate sabotage at the behest of the FBI or, as Anthony claimed, a spur-of-the-moment "personal decision," the result was to turn the party's first foray into transnational diplomacy into a something of a debacle.[31] BPP leaders were not pleased when they received word of Anthony's speeches, and instead of promoting further collaboration with Beheiren they buried any mention of the entire affair. Collaboration with Japanese groups did not resume for over a year, until Deputy Minister of Information Elbert "Big Man" Howard visited in the fall of 1969 to meet with members of the Tokyo-area Sanya Liberation Committee.[32] Anthony, meanwhile, was placed under house arrest by Chairman Hilliard after returning to the United States, effectively ending his tenure with the party.[33]

Chance played a major element in the disappointing results from the BPP's first effort at forging a transnational alliance. If Eldridge or Kathleen Cleaver had managed to make the trip to Japan, Anthony would not have had the opportunity to single-handedly wreck the venture. But even under more ideal circumstances, forging connections with Beheiren or other such groups was a fraught endeavor. Anthony was surprised upon his arrival to discover that, much like the Panthers, Beheiren did not speak with one voice. As he toured Japan and Okinawa meeting Beheiren's many member organizations, he found that "[t]here were pro-Maoists, anti-Maoists, Trotskyites, Stalinists, and numerous other groups. . . . The sponsoring faction would always ask me leading questions, which were geared to bring a response from me that would be an ideological attack upon other factions."[34] While the extremely loosely knit nature of Beheiren as an organization made it somewhat exceptional in this regard, the very nature of transnational "citizen's diplomacy" involved interacting with a wide spectrum of individuals and groups that often had only the loosest of connections.

The BPP got a second chance at transnational diplomacy in late November 1968 when the party was invited to attend the Hemispheric Conference to End the War in Vietnam, held in Montreal. The three-day conference gathered sixteen hundred delegates from twenty-five countries, including Chilean senator Salvador Allende (head of the Latin American Solidarity Organization) and North Vietnamese minister of culture Hoang Minh Giam. Most of the attendees, however, were not government officials but representatives of various antiwar groups from the United States,

Canada, and elsewhere.[35] Unlike during the ill-fated Japan venture, the BPP was represented at Montreal by its senior leaders, including Seale and Hilliard. In a speech before the assembled delegates, Seale drew on the party's anticolonial vernacular in attacking "the avaricious businessman, the racist, decadent, demagogic politicians of the world, and the pig police forces, be they in the Black community or in Vietnam." Drawing on comparisons offered in a different context to domestic audiences, Seale linked the founding of the BPP to Newton's realization that the police terrorizing West Oakland were essentially the same as the "pig forces committing murder and genocide right in front of our faces in Vietnam." This background of oppression created natural links between U.S. people of color, Vietnamese, and the revolutionary Third World. "It's time," Seale concluded, "that we begin to stand up in some form of unity" and apply "people's power" in order to "make this racist tyrant, the U.S. aggressor[,] act in a desired manner."[36]

The Montreal gathering was the first attempt by BPP leaders to apply their anticolonial vernacular to building a transnational coalition against U.S. imperialism at home and abroad. Seale's speech was said to have been greeted with "thunderous applause," and although the BPP delegation was small, it managed to attract a disproportionate amount of attention from both attendees and the media. On the closing day of the conference, the crowd chanted "Panther Power to the Vanguard!" amid a bonfire of burning draft cards, while the North Vietnamese culture minister exclaimed, "You are Black Panthers, we are Yellow Panthers!"[37] As with the UN venture, this was an impressive accomplishment given that a little over year earlier the Panthers had been a small, Oakland-based group with no national or international support and perhaps no more than a dozen members. But the Montreal gathering also illustrated some fundamental weaknesses in the BPP's strategy of transnational coalition building.

The Panthers had inherited from RAM a framework that posited black Americans as the natural vanguard of the worldwide anticolonial struggle by virtue of their strategic location within the heart of the United States. As Newton posited in 1967, "Black people in America are the only people who can free the world, loosen the [yoke] of colonialism and destroy the war machine."[38] While this thesis helped to empower small numbers of motivated BPP members to take on the seemingly impossible task of opposing the U.S. government, it could also sometimes slide over into a paternalistic attitude toward Third World people that complicated the party's efforts at international and transnational collaboration. While Seale was careful to praise the Vietnamese in his speech at Montreal, coverage of the event in the *Black Panther* reflected the most negative aspects of the party's claim to vanguard status. "The BLACK PANTHER PARTY did not attend the Hemispheric Conference," declared Raymond Lewis, "The BLACK PANTHER PARTY dominated it." Lewis went on to insist that "[l]iterally no one objected to the PANTHERS leadership of the conference," with both the Vietnamese and white delegates taking direction from the party. "At any other conference called to 'End the War in Viet Nam,'" he declared, "the dominant figures would naturally be the ones the war is all about—Hanoi and Viet Cong delegation. But not at this conference.... PANTHER POWER prevailed." While Lewis was certainly exaggerating the extent to which the Panthers dominated the conference, contemporary reports indicate that were was friction between the BPP and other delegates. The *New York Times* reported that "a flurry of fighting, pushing and shoving" broke out on the conference floor as a result of a dispute between the BPP and the organizers. Ideological debates also divided the delegates, and some activists returned home from Montreal disappointed with "another fiasco of left division and petty-factionalism."[39] Ultimately, while the conference helped to further raise the Panthers' international profile, it did not lead to lasting relationships or institutional links between the party and the other assembled groups and revealed blind spots caused by the party's ideological commitment to its own vanguard status.

Scandinavia and Germany: The Panther in Western Europe

The BPP's most successful transnational efforts in 1968–69, and the only ones that left a lasting institutional legacy, were in western Europe. The combination of the high-profile trial of Huey Newton in Oakland and the broad reach of the *Black Panther* brought the party to the attention of a number of European New Left parties and groups in the late 1960s. Activists in Scandinavia, particularly Denmark and Sweden, provided some of the strongest support for the Panthers and the "Free Huey" campaign during this period. This seemingly odd pairing, matching Oakland-based Black Panthers with blond, blue-eyed activists in snowy Scandinavia, was somewhat serendipitous but also rooted in larger international and national developments.

As was the case across much of the noncommunist, industrialized world in the 1960s, the Left in Sweden and Denmark was in a state of turmoil.

As historian Thomas Elman Jørgensen has chronicled, the combination of the post-Stalin revelations of Soviet tyranny, the grim reality of life in the neighboring "people's democracies" of eastern Europe, and the increasingly conservative role played by the working classes in western Europe led to a crisis among Scandinavian leftists who had once looked to Marxism for inspiration. At the same time, the spread of decolonization and the polarizing effects of U.S. interventions in the Third World, particularly in Vietnam, led many to embrace the revolutionary movements of the global South. The result was the growth of an anticapitalist, noncommunist, and pro-Third World outlook that, while shaped by local conditions, had much in common with New Left politics elsewhere in western Europe as well as in the United States and Japan.[40] In such an environment, the BPP's anticolonial vernacular and its status as a Third World–oriented group within the heart of U.S. imperialism made it particularly appealing to a new generation of Scandinavian activists.

SNCC representatives, in this case Stokely Carmichael, helped lay the groundwork for collaboration between Scandinavian activists and the black freedom struggle in the United States. In November 1967, Carmichael made a series of appearances in Sweden, Norway, and Denmark that included an interview on Swedish television. His visit raised the profile of the U.S. Black Power movement and led to lasting interest that soon transcended a single figure or organization.[41] It is doubtful, however, that this attention would have amounted to significant transnational collaborations with the BPP without the fortuitous intervention of a young, Jamaican-born resident of Denmark. Connie Matthews, who worked for the United Nations Educational, Scientific, and Cultural Organization (UNESCO) in Copenhagen, was inspired by what she read of the Panthers during the Newton trial and used her contacts among the European Left to raise awareness of the party and its struggles in the United States. As part of this process, she arranged for Bobby Seale, David Hilliard, and Raymond "Masai" Hewitt to undertake a Scandinavian tour in March 1969.[42] The result was the most successful of the party's early efforts at ad hoc transnational diplomacy.

The Panthers' trip, which included stops in Sweden, Denmark, Norway, and Finland, ran into initial difficulties as they were confronted by the widespread assumption, even among many potentially friendly activists, that the BPP was a narrowly nationalist, even racist organization. This impression was in part due to media coverage of the party but also owed much to recent visits by Carmichael, who would move to Guinea in 1969 and later change his name to Kwame Ture. While still nominally affiliated with the BPP in early 1969, Carmichael had rejected Marxism and alliances with white radicals in favor of a more essentialist pan-Africanism. Thus, as Hewitt explained it, the BPP representatives in March 1969 found themselves in the difficult position of having to respond to Carmichael's "deviations from the Party line, blowing at rampant racism and cultural nationalism," which had been "especially confusing to the representatives of the various revolutionary groups represented in Scandinavian countries."[43]

In addition to relying on the inclusive language embedded in the party's anticolonial vernacular, BPP representatives employed two specific strategies in their Scandinavian tour to facilitate transnational alliances with Scandinavian activists. First, Seale and the rest of the delegation emphasized the party's commitment to a non-doctrinaire socialism and anti-imperialism that provided natural links to European New Left groups. Declaring the need for a global "stand against capitalism" rooted in "the people, not the governments," Seale also reassured his audience that "we don't fight racism with more racism," an implicit rejection of Carmichael's approach. They also made a strategic nod to local concerns by declaring that "we don't fight imperialism with more imperialism, such as the way the Russians [are] using imperialistic tactics in Czechoslovakia, etc."[44] The crushing of the Prague Spring by Soviet tanks in August 1968 was a fresh and painful memory, particularly for those nations for whom the Red Army was close and ever-present. The Panthers presented themselves to their Scandinavian hosts as a vibrant and open alternative to both Carmichael's essentialist pan-Africanism and the grim tyranny of Soviet communism with its stodgy version of Marxism.

In addition to employing a form of revolutionary triangulation, the Panthers also offered a more nuanced version of their vanguard thesis as part of the Scandinavian excursion. While the notion of black Americans as *the* vanguard of the world revolution was empowering for a minority group living within a First World superpower, as demonstrated by events at Montreal it could complicate relations with other groups. In speaking to audiences in Scandinavia, Seale stressed that the BPP was one of many vanguards among "all the revolutionary peoples and revolutionary fronts throughout Asia, Africa and Latin America." In Asia, it was the revolutionary governments of China and Vietnam that played the lead role, while in Africa it was the freedom fighters in Mozambique, Angola, and South Africa. In Latin America, the "Cuban brothers" were at the vanguard, along with revolutionaries in Venezuela and elsewhere. Even in the United States,

Seale placed black Americans amid a number of other groups, including radical whites:

> The Black-American peoples . . . standing in solidarity with Mexican-American class brothers, standing in solidarity with the Chinese brothers, and the vanguard organizations of these particular groups, the Indian-Americans, and of course along with the progressive white revolutionaries, who the Black Panther Party really considers the true vanguard within the ethnic group of white people . . . [are] getting things going.[45]

Seale did not explicitly address Europe in his roll call of vanguards, but the message to his Scandinavian audiences was clear: any group of people who shared the party's commitment to revolutionary actions against the linked forces of capitalism and white supremacy could claim membership in this movement and even leadership within their own regional context. This savvy spin on the party's vanguard thesis brought it in line with the inclusive rhetoric of the BPP's anticolonial vernacular and its emphasis on honoring local circumstances while building transnational links among activists.

While geographic factors limited the kind of practical support that Scandinavian activists could offer to the BPP fund-raising and awareness campaigns, the brief European visit showed that, with the right approach and the local contacts, the party could spread its influence and message outside the United States with a minimal investment of time and resources. Matthews was rewarded for her role in organizing the Scandinavian trip and overseeing the ensuing solidarity committees with an appointment as the BPP's international coordinator. She was subsequently summoned to Oakland for consultation with the party's leaders and gave a number of speeches before returning to continue her organizing work.[46] Matthews eventually married New York Panther Michael Cetewayo Tabor, and the two went on to join the international section of the BPP in Algeria (discussed in the next chapter) in the early 1970s.[47] Meanwhile, the example set by the Scandinavian solidarity committees was repeated by young activists in West Germany in 1969.

As in Japan and Scandinavia, transnational links to the Panthers in the Federal Republic of Germany originated in a combination of local and international factors. The Sozialistischer Deutscher Studentenbund (German Socialist Student League, usually referred to by its German-language initials, SDS) provided the initial point of contact between young Germans and the Panthers. The German SDS began life as the youth arm of the established Social Democratic Party (SDP), but it was expelled in 1962 as its members embraced New Left politics similar to those of their U.S. counterparts in Students for a Democratic Society.[48] In the latter half of the 1960s, the German SDS, and particularly the influential Berlin chapter headed by Rudi Dutschke, began to identify with both Third World anti-colonial struggles and the Black Power movement in the United States. As with New Left groups elsewhere around the world, the German SDS's focus on the Third World reflected outrage at the escalating war in Vietnam, frustration with the inability of both U.S. capitalism and Soviet communism to create truly democratic and egalitarian societies, and optimism in the ability of states and groups in the global South to offer alternatives to the grim Cold War nuclear standoff. Black Power, meanwhile, was attractive because it offered, in the words of historian Martin Klimke, "a case of an anti-imperialist movement in a highly industrialized country that was seen as the motherland of imperialist aggression."[49] For the young Germans in the SDS, Black Power showed that resistance was possible even for those living within the heart of the First World. Again, as in both Japan and Scandinavia, connections between the German New Left and the BPP were facilitated by the pioneering efforts of activists in SNCC. German SDS leaders who attended the July 1967 Dialectics of Liberation conference in London were favorably impressed by Stokely Carmichael's appearance, and that same year the organization officially endorsed the U.S. Black Power movement, including violent resistance if necessary, at its national conference. The following year, SNCC representative Dale Smith spoke at an anti–Vietnam War event organized by the German SDS in West Berlin.[50]

Factors more specific to the German past and present also influenced the German SDS and its engagement with Black Power and the Third World. The legacy of Nazism, particularly the Holocaust, hung heavily over postwar Germany. Young Germans, in particular, had to grapple with the failure of their parents' generation to prevent the rise of Hitler or to mount effective resistance to his regime once in power. Having been "educated by German history" with respect to the need to resist "the fascist murderous gang," as German SDS member Christian Semler explained in a letter to the BPP, young activists were keen to prevent such calamities in the future.[51] To those in the SDS, the German government's alliance with the United States, which including hosting facilities that supported the U.S. war effort in Southeast Asia, constituted complicity in the ongoing genocide in Vietnam. This tragedy presented an opportunity, indeed a responsibility, for young Germans to succeed where their parents had failed in standing up to aggression and genocide. As a result, German SDS members embraced the anti–Vietnam War campaign with a fervor that belied the geographic and historical distance that separated them from that conflict.[52] Moreover, U.S. military bases in West Germany were home to a large number of black GIs, many of whom chafed at the racism they experienced both within the armed forces and from some aspects of German society. A number of these GIs ended up identifying with the Black Power movement, either through formal membership in one of the U.S.-based organizations or through informal local networks on base. While activists in Scandinavia had to rely on media coverage and occasional visits from figures such as Carmichael, Seale, and Hilliard, the young Germans in the SDS had ready access to potential allies in the U.S. black freedom and antiwar struggles from within the very heart of the war machine that they jointly opposed.[53]

For all the practical and ideological links between German activists and the U.S. Black Power movements, it took the intervention of Karl Dietrich Wolff to create a more formal network of support linking German activists and the BPP. Wolff had become involved in the German SDS while a student and eventually rose to serve as the organization's national chairman in 1967–68.[54] After stepping down, he embarked on a tour of the United States at the invitation of the American SDS, Students for a Democratic Society. Among the highlights of Wolff's visit was a comical appearance before a U.S. Senate subcommittee on the Internal Security Act, which had subpoenaed the German activist to question him about his associations with American radicals. In a farcical session that saw Wolff dancing rhetorical circles around his would-be interrogators (while simultaneously claiming not to be fluent in English), he infuriated the committee's acting chair, arch-segregationist Strom Thurmond of South Carolina, and brought raucous approval from the gallery by playfully declaring "I prefer panthers to pigs."[55] Of more direct import to future transnational relations, however, was his meeting with BPP leaders in Oakland in March 1969. Introduced to the Panthers by antiwar activist Tom Hayden while visiting the Bay Area, Wolff quickly latched on to the party and its struggles against both U.S. imperialism and the U.S. justice system.[56] After returning to Germany, Wolff worked with Connie Matthews and visiting BPP deputy minister of information Elbert Howard to form a Black Panther Solidarity Committee in Frankfurt. The committee not only raised funds for the party but also staged a number of public demonstrations in support of jailed BPP members, hosted visiting Panthers such as Howard and Kathleen Cleaver, and used translated BPP writings to educate young Germans about the party's struggles in the United States.[57] While the Solidarity Committee's work was initially limited to rhetorical and financial support, in the early 1970s elements of the German Left sought even more direct, and violent, solidarity with the Panthers (a subject chronicled in chapter 6).

The BPP's alliances with western European activists in 1968–69 represented a promising beginning of a transnational coalition that linked the global New Left with communities of color in the United States and revolutionaries in the Third Word. This coalition was rooted not simply in opposition to the war in Vietnam, but also in a shared understanding that linked that conflict to capitalism, imperialism, and white supremacy. This notion was not new for black activists in the United States or anticolonial leaders among the "darker nations," who had been offering variations on this thesis since the early twentieth century. This particular formation, however, had an appeal that crossed over to include a wide network of white New Left activists around the world. By bypassing national governments, the Panthers were able to achieve substantial gains with a minimal investment of time and other resources and little in the way of compromises or entangling relationships that might limit their freedom of action. The most successful of these ventures were largely autonomous in their daily operations, with the most extreme of these being the British Black Panthers, a group not covered here since they were an independent entity that was inspired by the Oakland-based BPP and shared the party's name and sensibility but operated entirely independently in pursuit of their own agenda.[58] For those groups that did share more direct links to the party, the combination of occasional visits by BPP leaders with the work of local activists such as Matthews and Wolff and the long reach of the anticolonial vernacular (in both English and in translation) allowed the Panthers to leverage the power of educated and materially comfortable young European activists. This in turned allowed the latter to influence their home societies while raising awareness of the situation facing black Americans. Unlike state governments, these activists were happy to ally with the BPP while demanding little if anything in return. Indeed, many eagerly deferred to the party's self-proclaimed vanguard status, particularly when couched in the modified form proposed by Seale during his Scandinavian visit.

These relationships were not without complications, however. European activists' fascination with the Panthers sometimes slid into an Orientalist exoticization of black Americans in general and the BPP in particular. French novelist, playwright, and activist Jean Genet illustrated this temptation in declaring during a U.S. visit that "America's Blacks, and especially the Black Panthers are the only thing that glows, that shines intensely, even burns and fascinates in this sadly boring country."[59] Historians Maria Höhn and Martin Klimke observed that for young German activists, "Black Panther GIs presented novel forms of masculinity and a revolutionary authenticity that their own privileged middle-class upbringing could not provide them." But while these face-to-face encounters might "make abstract ideas such as international class and race solidarity immediate and real," they did so in part by creating a shallow and glamorized understanding of blackness.[60] This same problem plagued the Panthers' relationship with white radicals in the United States, but in Europe and Japan it was further complicated by the mediating role that the party came to play in the conflicting feelings aroused by American popular culture. Around the industrialized world in the 1960s, American music, movies, and fashion were immensely appealing, particularly to a younger generation that could use these imported cultural forms as a way of distinguishing themselves from their parents' generation. However, many of these same young people were also deeply troubled by America's hegemonic status as well the U.S. government's policies in Vietnam and elsewhere. The Panthers and their anticolonial vernacular were perfectly placed to exploit this dichotomy by marrying the attractively subversive elements of American popular culture—from black leather jackets to rock and funk music and colorful slang—to an unquestionably "authentic" anti-imperialist politics.[61] The downside of this appeal, however, was that it facilitated shallow, self-serving identification with the BPP in lieu of a more nuanced and committed commitment to the party's principles and struggle. This is not to imply that all European activists (or all white American allies of the party) fell victim to such a glamorized understanding of the Panthers and what they represented. Nevertheless, navigating the gap between well-off European activists and the BPP was as challenging in its own way as relations with Third World governments and peoples.

"Molasses and Blood, Machetes and Screams": The Cuban Connection

Even when successful, transnational alliances came with inherent limitations. Without formal borders and armed forces to protect them, transnational groups couldn't offer lasting sanctuary to the BPP or even a reliable venue for hosting visiting Panthers. This was particularly true of partners located in states that had important trade or military alliances with the

United States. The troubles that party members had with visas and local law enforcement in their visits to places such as Japan, Germany, and Mexico illustrated the natural limits of relying on organizations and activists based in states locked within Washington's Cold War orbit. Moreover, the various revolutionary models that the Panthers sought to emulate—from Algeria to Cuba, China, and Vietnam—had all defined their revolutions in national terms.[62] Thus, for all the potential promises of transnational support networks and all the drawbacks and challenges of dealing with foreign governments on highly unequal terms, the BPP could not entirely forsake attempts to cultivate more formal international alliances to supplement their fledgling transnational solidarity network.

While Mao, his Red Book, and the People's Republic of China played the most prominent public role in the BPP's anticolonial vernacular, it was Cuba that the party turned to in its first attempt at state-level diplomacy in 1968–69. The island and its government under Fidel Castro was an attractive partner for the BPP in part because of its previously expressed commitment to support black radicals ranging from Amiri Baraka to Robert F. Williams and Stokely Carmichael, who made a triumphant state visit in July–August 1967 during the inaugural conference of the Organización Latinoamericana de Solidaridad. Although after leaving Cuba both Williams and Carmichael offered thinly veiled criticism of Castro's regime and its attitude toward issues of race and revolution, the island retained an important place in the black radical imagination.[63] In recounting his attitude toward Cuba on the eve of his own exile there in December 1968, Cleaver declared, "Like every other Babylonian, I had watched the Cuban Revolution from beginning to end. . . . The very name, Cuba, was full of molasses and blood, machetes and screams."[64] This romanticized understanding of Cuba and its revolution was further reinforced by the creation of OSPAAAL as part of the 1966 Tricontinental Conference. Headquartered in Havana, OSPAAAL published journals, newsletters, and posters celebrating anticolonial revolutions around the world while implicitly or explicitly naming Cuba as a champion of these struggles.[65]

More immediate practical factors also stimulated the BPP's decision to pursue contacts with Cuba in 1968. Its location ninety miles from U.S. shores made the island a more convenient spot for the Panthers to conduct their nascent international diplomacy than distant venues such as China or Algeria. This was particularly relevant for those within the party who had visions of building an external base that would allow the Panthers to train and equip fighters who could then slip back into the country undetected.

Cleaver apparently broached this subject with the Cuban mission in New York during the July trip to the UN and received assurances, later writing that "if I came to Cuba they would give me a facility for training some men and they would help us reenter the United States."[66] Prior to testing this commitment, the BPP took advantage of an offer from the Cuban government to send representatives to visit the island as part of an OSPAAAL celebration of "Solidarity with the Struggle of the Afro-American People" timed to correspond with the third anniversary of the Watts uprising in August 1968. An initial attempt to send BPP representatives to Cuba was foiled when Chief of Staff Hilliard, Minister of Education George Murray, and Field Marshall Landon R. Williams were detained and then deported by Mexican police while attempting to transit through the country. A second attempt succeeded, and in late August, Murray and Joudon Ford of the New York BPP chapter toured the island and gave speeches as part of the OSPAAAL-sponsored event.[67]

The Murray-Ford trip represented the BPP's first attempt at conducting state-level diplomacy outside the United States. While on the island they met not only with Cuban government representatives but also with other OSPAAAL members, including delegates from North Korea and Guinea (home of the revolutionary government of Sékou Touré and his honorary co-president Kwame Nkrumah). In appealing to their Cuban hosts and other potential allies, Ford and Murray drew heavily on the BPP's evolving anticolonial vernacular while linking the "Free Huey" campaign to Third World anticolonialism. Identifying as "a colony within the imperialist domains of North America," Murray vowed that the Panthers would "not . . . put down our guns or stop making Molotov cocktails until colonialized Africans, Asians and Latin Americans in the United States and throughout the world have become free." While embracing a form of African American exceptionalism in stressing the "the historic duty of Black people in the United States to bring about the complete, absolute and unconditional end of racism and neo-colonialism," Murray was also careful to note that in doing so "we will follow the example of Che Guevara, the Cuban people" and other Third World revolutionaries. Murray also took an explicitly Marxist line in attacking the concept of private property and blaming Newton's imprisonment on "the capitalist beasts that make up the power structure of the USA."[68]

The BPP's efforts to cultivate support from the Cuban government and OSPAAAL in July and August 1968 paid some immediate short-term dividends in the form of international publicity for the party and its efforts to free Newton. Granma, the official Cuban news agency, reprinted Murray's speech as well as an article hailing Newton's contributions to the revolution.[69] Speaking for the Cuban Communist Party, Luis Lara declared that "Cuban revolutionaries are prepared to give their lives for the cause of the Afro-Americans, which is the cause of the peoples of the world." The OSPAAAL Executive Secretariat expressed similar support, calling "upon all its members . . . all revolutionary and progressive forces of the world and the North America people to celebrate this day in a combative way, by denouncing the plots for the physical elimination of Huey Newton, encouraging his . . . example and by expressing with concrete actions and solidarity messages their acknowledgment and support of the revolutionary struggle of the Afro-Americans."[70] The vocal support for Newton from OSPAAAL and the Cuban government was a major achievement for the party. Less than a year earlier, the Panthers had struggled to reach over a dozen members and were barely managing to survive as a local organization in Oakland. By the summer of 1968, however, they were hailed as revolutionary heroes in Havana and directly compared to Malcolm X. The party reciprocated with statements of support for "the brothers and sisters in Cuba" while Emory Douglas contributed artwork for OSPAAAL posters.[71]

The support of OSPAAAL and the Cuban government was a boon to the "Free Huey" movement and a testament to the ability of the party's anti-colonial vernacular to help build bridges to the revolutionary Third World. When combined with the transnational solidarity networks in Europe, the Cuban connection offered the party a diversified set of alliances outside the borders of the United States, which provided everything from publicity and fund-raising to perhaps a base for guerrilla training and staging. It remained unclear, however, whether the Cuban government was truly willing to go beyond rhetorical support and make good on the promises that Cleaver believed he had secured while in New York. It was also uncertain whether or how foreign-supported guerrilla warfare operations fit into the BPP's rapidly evolving strategy within the United States. Those questions would be answered in dramatic fashion by the end of 1969, with Eldridge Cleaver taking center stage as the foremost Panther advocate of both guerrilla warfare and Cold War–inspired internationalism.

Chapter 5

"Juche, Baby, All the Way"

Cuba, Algeria, and the Asian Strategy, 1969–1970

Within two years of its founding in October 1966, the Black Panther Party experienced three watershed moments. The first was the Sacramento demonstration and the subsequent passage of the Mulford Act, which led the party to abandon armed patrols and turn to alternative forms of activism to advance its anticolonial agenda. The second was the arrest and trial of Huey Newton on murder charges and the ensuing national and international growth of the party as part of the "Free Huey" movement. The third took place on April 6, 1968, two days after the assassination of Dr. Martin Luther King, Jr. While civil disturbances erupted in cities across the nation in the wake of King's murder, Oakland remained outwardly quiet. On the night of April 6, however, Eldridge Cleaver led a small group of BPP members in what he later called "a military action against the Oakland Police Department." Armed with an AR-15 rifle and other firearms that he had accumulated over the previous months, Cleaver and a small caravan of Panthers drove through Oakland looking to ambush police officers as retaliation for the killing of King. "All we wanted was pig blood," Cleaver recounted, "A dead pig."[1] What followed was a confused engagement that ended with Cleaver wounded and another Panther, seventeen-year-old Bobby Hutton, shot and killed by police while trying to surrender.

The April 6 shootout had both immediate and long-term consequences for the BPP. Arrested in the wake of the action, Cleaver waged a legal battle to avoid returning to prison on parole violations. But when the California Supreme Court eventually ordered him to surrender into the custody of the California Adult Authority at the end of November, Cleaver instead slipped out of the country. After a brief stay in Canada, he traveled via boat to Cuba, arriving in Havana on Christmas Day.[2] Thus began a seven-year exile that forced Cleaver into a direct engagement with both the Third World and the Cold War. In addition to visiting Cuba, North Korea, China, and North Vietnam, Eldridge, in partnership with Kathleen Cleaver, established the international section of the Black Panther Party in Algeria in September 1970. At first glance, these efforts to carve out an international power base for the BPP appear to be the logical extension of the Panthers' efforts at overseas outreach that began with the "Free Huey" movement in 1968 and had roots as far back as the party's origins with Newton's and Seale's reading of Mao and Fanon. A closer examination, however, reveals that Cleaver precipitated a major practical and ideological shift in the BPP's international engagement in 1969–70. His brief and frustrating stay in Cuba offered a vivid demonstration of the challenges associated with translating rhetorical invocations of Third World anticolonialism and proletarian internationalism into something more concrete. Forced out of Cuba in May 1969, Cleaver embraced an alternative strategy from his new base in Algiers, one rooted not in informal transnational solidarity networks but rather in direct connections with revolutionary governments in Asia. The BPP's "Asian strategy" was a calculated gamble that saw the party stake its international reputation on a direct connection to Cold War geopolitics rather than on the more diffuse rhetorical invocations of Third World solidarity imbedded in its anticolonial vernacular.

While the April 6 action and the ensuing fallout helped to inadvertently launch a new phase in the BPP's internationalism, it also highlighted emerging divisions within the party. As Cleaver and his allies embraced guerrilla warfare, Cold War–inspired alliances with foreign governments, and an increasingly doctrinaire Marxism-Leninism, an opposing faction, initially led by Chairman David Hilliard and later by Newton himself upon his release from prison in August 1970, rejected both state-level diplomacy and what Hilliard dubbed "an orgy of wishful adventuristic militarism" in favor of local community service programs supplemented by informal transnational solidarity networks.[3] For a time, these two approaches coexisted uneasily as the strident rhetoric of the anticolonial vernacular helped cover fundamental differences over the direction of the party. Questions over the role of anticolonial violence and the nature of the party's international engagements, however, fed growing intra-party tensions that left the Panthers vulnerable to both government repression and changes in the larger Cold War landscape.

Anticolonial Violence and Cleaver's Road to Exile

From the beginning, the BPP walked a fine line with respect to the use of violence. The party's colonial analysis of black America and its embrace of the examples provided by Frantz Fanon, Che Guevara, and the NLF distinguished it from the more narrow emphasis on self-defense offered by groups such as the Deacons for Defense and Justice or Robert F. Williams's NAACP chapter in Monroe, North Carolina. The Panthers' armed patrols constituted both a practical and symbolic challenge to the daily operation of police forces that "occupy our black communities like a foreign troop occupies territory."[4] After the Mulford Act, the party stopped the patrols but stepped up its rhetorical commitment to anticolonial violence. Even at their most provocative in 1966–67, however, Newton insisted that the Panthers' use of firearms conform to state and local laws. And for all the calls to "off the pigs" and "kill any motherfucker that stands in the way of our freedom," the BPP publicly disarmed in response to the Mulford Act rather than embark on a campaign of guerrilla warfare.[5] The rhetorical violence embedded in the party's anticolonial vernacular could be interpreted as a prelude to armed revolution, but it could just as easily be seen as a substitute for the real thing. Cleaver carried no weapons in his early days with the party (so as not to jeopardizing his parole status), and his prison writings cast doubt on the utility of violence as a tool of struggle against a state apparatus that was capable of mustering "unlimited firepower."[6]

The ambiguity in the BPP founding leaders' approach to anticolonial violence could be confusing to rank-and-file members and leaders outside of Oakland. Aaron Dixon, head of the Seattle chapter, recalled that "[a]lthough the party often invoked guerrilla warfare in articles and pictures in the party paper and on posters depicting armed men and women, the chairman [Seale] had never once informed me that I was to lead guerrilla attacks against police forces. At the time [1968] I did not realize that new chapters and branches all over the country were grappling with this same dilemma—to attack or not to attack." Even among the upper echelons,

David Hilliard later recalled, "Everybody in the Party wrestles with the issue of armed struggle."[7] Two developments combined to eventually lead elements within the BPP's Oakland-based leadership to resolve this ambiguity in favor of a direct assault on the Oakland Police Department. The first was Newton's arrest on charges of killing one Oakland police officer and badly wounding another in October 1967. While Newton vehemently proclaimed his innocence, others within the party interpreted the shootings as the opening salvo in a war of liberation for black America. In the *Black Panther,* Cleaver hailed Newton for "outshooting two pigs," while an unsigned editorial in the same issue evoked Karl Marx in declaring that "[t]he weapon of criticism will never equal the criticism of weapons." Emory Douglas celebrated "Minister of Defense Huey P. Newton defending the black community—two pigs down[,] two less to go."[8]

Cleaver used the royalties from *Soul on Ice* to begin assembling a small arsenal, while questioning his own courage to follow what he believed to be Newton's example of revolutionary violence. In raising his gun against the OPD, Cleaver asserted, Newton had made the most important statement "by a black man in Babylon since Nat Turner took his quota of heads in Virginia."[9] Newton continued to profess his innocence and urged caution, resisting suggestions to stage a jailbreak in favor of mounting a more traditional legal defense, while instructing the party to avoid spontaneous violence. But with Newton behind bars, Cleaver increasingly dominated the day-to-day running of the party and became its most visible public face. Convinced that Newton had "upped the ante" by "having offed the pig," Cleaver clearly felt pressure to make a similarly dramatic contribution to the revolution. "After Huey offed pig officer John Frey," he later wrote, "I slowly began to hold myself in contempt."[10]

A second, and likely decisive, factor in pushing some Panthers from anticolonial rhetoric to anticolonial violence was the increasing state repression directed at the party in 1968. The Panthers' decision to publicly disarm in response to the passage of the Mulford Act had not lessened tensions with local law enforcement, and Newton's alleged role in killing an OPD officer only heightened police hostility. In Oakland and in the new chapters in Seattle, Los Angeles, New York, and elsewhere, party members experienced frequent confrontations with police. In early 1968, Bay Area law enforcement officials stepped up their campaign against the Panthers by targeting their leaders for harassment. At 3:30 a.m. on January 16, heavily armed officers from the San Francisco Police Tactical Squad raided Cleaver's home, kicking down the door and threatening Eldridge, Kathleen, and their guest Emory Douglas before departing without making any arrests. A little over a month later, Berkeley police officers burst into Bobby Seale's house and dragged him and his wife away on weapons charges, which were subsequently dropped.[11] Dozens of party members were brought up on charges in February and March 1968, and though most were eventually dropped, the effect was to give the impression that the police had declared open season on the Panthers. In response, Newton issued a communiqué from behind bars declaring that the assaults had brought the BPP to "a critical situation" and ordering all party members to "acquire the technical equipment to defend their homes" and be prepared to use it against police intrusions.[12]

Police actions against the Panthers in early 1968 culminated on April 3, when shotgun-wielding officers of the OPD invaded a party meeting at St. Augustine's Episcopal Church. The church's pastor, Father Earl A. Neil, was sympathetic to the Panthers, and the following day he held a press conference blasting the actions of the police.[13] The press conference, however, was overshadowed by news that Martin Luther King, Jr., had been assassinated by a sniper in Memphis. King had received relatively little attention from the BPP, even as his views on Vietnam and the plight of the inner city had begun to echo those voiced by the Panthers. His assassination, however, was a shock even to those who consistently highlighted the role of violence in perpetuating white supremacy. In a tape recording made just prior to leading the attack on Oakland police on April 6, Cleaver declared that King's death signaled "the end of an era and the beginning of a terrible and bloody chapter."

> [T]he war has begun. The violent phase of the black liberation struggle is here, and it will spread. From that shot, from that blood. America will be painted red. Dead bodies will litter the streets and the scenes will be reminiscent of the disgusting, terrifying, nightmarish news reports coming out of Algeria during the height of the general violence right before the final breakdown of the French colonial regime.[14]

King's assassination was clearly an important catalyst, but it needs to be understood against the background of escalating police actions against the Panthers in the preceding months as well as the anticolonial analysis of black America that Cleaver invoked in his declaration of war. In this context, the death of King was not an isolated national tragedy but rather part of the routine violence required to hold black Americans in colonial domination. As efforts to organize within the law had clearly proved inadequate, whether through King's nonviolence, the BPP's anticolonial vernacular, or the legal defense of Newton, "[a]ction is all that counts now," Cleaver asserted.[15]

In an early sign of the split that would later divide the party, Cleaver's decision to engage "openly in a war for the national liberation of Afro-America from colonial bondage to the white mother country" led to impassioned debate behind the scenes in the days after King's murder.[16] Although Chairman Hilliard embraced the rhetoric of anticolonial violence, he voiced strong opposition to Cleaver's planned ambush. Hilliard objected to the action as contrary to Newton's explicit directives, which promoted self-defense against police intrusions but also called for avoiding spontaneous acts of violence until the community was sufficiently organized for a proper revolutionary struggle. In the wake of King's assassination, Newton restated these sentiments in private communications from behind bars, sentiments that he planned to share publicly by having his words read at a fund-raising event scheduled for Oakland's DeFremery Park on April 7.[17] In addition to this seemingly clear instruction from the party's cofounder and minister of defense, Hilliard also had more practical concerns about Cleaver's plan. "We're not trained guerrilla fighters," he argued. "Half of these guys don't know how to hit the broad side of a barn." After a climactic debate on the afternoon of April 6, Cleaver persuaded a majority of the assembled Panthers to take part in the action, and Hilliard reluctantly accepted the decision and agreed to accompany them.[18] The ensuing "battle," however, confirmed all of his fears and helped to divide the party permanently.

Cleaver later admitted, "We had no illusions that the fourteen of us who undertook this task were capable of defeating the Oakland Police Department or any other police department that night." Rather, in a gendered reading of violence that owed much to Fanon, Cleaver hoped "to stand up as black men inside of Babylon and to give the pigs a taste of that which they had been issuing out to black people for four hundred years. A taste of their own medicine, specifically hot lead."[19] Even by this more modest measure, the action was a disaster. While accounts of the shootout vary, all agree that it began inauspiciously for the Panthers when, rather than executing a guerrilla ambush, Cleaver was surprised by two police officers after stopping the caravan of Panther cars to urinate in an alleyway.[20] As Hilliard had predicted, the OPD had much of West Oakland staked out in anticipation of trouble and easily recognized the Panther cars as they cruised the neighborhood in search of targets. After an inconclusive exchange of fire, the BPP raiding party separated and fled. Cleaver and Hutton, the youngest member of the party at age seventeen, were trapped in a basement of a nearby house and subject to police gunfire and tear gas. Unable to breathe, the pair surrendered their weapons and emerged with their hands up. Police, however, fatally shot the unarmed Hutton before taking a wounded Cleaver into custody.[21]

The California Adult Authority immediately revoked Cleaver's parole, and following a brief stay in an Oakland hospital he was sent to the state prison in Vacaville. After two months behind bars, however, a superior court judge granted Cleaver's petition of habeas corpus, finding that, "[t]he peril to his parole status stemmed from no failure of personal rehabilitation, but from his undue eloquence in pursuing political goals ... which were offensive to many of his contemporaries."[22] Free on bail pending charges stemming from the recent shootout (and the state's appeal of the superior court's decision), Cleaver embarked on a whirlwind series of speaking engagements in which he launched furious attacks on California governor Ronald Reagan—"[t]hat jive punk—the dickless motherfucker"—while promising "a guerrilla resistance movement that will amount to a second Civil War." Revisiting the notion that insurrection at home would create opportunities for allies in the Third World, he trumpeted plans for domestic unrest so powerful that "the enemies of America can come in here and pick the gold out of the teeth of the Babylonians."[23] In many ways, the minister of information's rhetorical fusillades upon his release from Vacaville represented a return to his early efforts on behalf of the BPP, which relied more on the charisma and eloquence that the superior court judge had cited than on his marksmanship. For all his talk of armed revolution, Cleaver was clearly more comfortable and effective leading college students in chants of "Fuck Ronald Reagan!" than he was planning and executing guerrilla ambushes.

Had he been allowed to remain free pending trial, Cleaver might have confined himself to a strategy of rhetorical confrontation. But when the California Supreme Court overruled the lower court and ordered his return to custody on November 27, Cleaver decided that he would rather be an exiled (or martyred) guerrilla fighter than an imprisoned intellectual. He initially planned a dramatic last stand at Merritt College, but Newton vetoed this plan from behind bars, sending a message instructing the minister of information to flee the country instead. This time Cleaver followed Newton's directions. With the aid of the San Francisco Mime Troup, he disguised himself as an elderly man and slipped out of the Bay Area undetected the day before he was scheduled to surrender to the California Adult Authority. After a brief stop in Canada, Cleaver made his way to Cuba by boat. His aim upon reaching Havana on December 25, 1968, was nothing less than organizing a guerrilla army with which to take the fight back to the country that he called Babylon.[24] Cleaver quickly discovered, however, that for all the Panthers' success in building an organization with a national membership and international reach, dealing with even the most revolutionary of states provided challenges that rivaled in many ways those the party faced in the United States.

Cuba Libre? The Trials and Tribulations of Radical Internationalism

Arriving in Cuba was a dream come true for the budding American guerrilla warrior. Shortly arriving, Cleaver recalled, "I had an audience with Fidel Castro, shook his big hand. I thought everything was going to be wonderful."[25] Cuba had inspired Cleaver well before he had joined the Panthers. After seeing a television report while still in prison, he wrote to his lawyer Beverly Axelrod to enthuse, "How beautiful the Cuban Revolution is! The triumphant spirit of the people seemed to leap from the glass eye of the T.V. set, and Fidel was banging on the rostrum and blowing his soul to the people." But it was more than a romantic attachment that brought Cleaver to exile in Cuba. Connections between Cuban officials and Cleaver's editor at *Ramparts* (Robert Scheer), initial contacts the BPP had made with Cubans during the July 1968 visit to the UN, and the subsequent tour of the island by Panther representatives in August had led him to believe that Castro's government was ready to support the party with more than words.[26] Indeed, Cleaver's ambitions upon reaching Havana transcended mere exile and protection from extradition. In addition to using the island as a base to "be able to print stuff and use their radio to broadcast to the United States," he believed that he had reached an understanding with the Cuban government that "if I came to Cuba they would give me a facility for training some men and they would help us reenter the United States."[27] Far from arriving as a supplicant, Cleaver saw himself as a fellow revolutionary who was helping the Cubans by promoting guerilla warfare within the heart of the U.S. empire. "It wasn't as though we went there begging," he later recalled. "We went there to get what was ours." This understanding, however, was based on what Cleaver himself later characterized as a "very naïve" reading of Cuban internal politics and Cuba's position within the complicated calculus of the Cold War.[28]

Without access to the relevant Cuban documents, it is impossible to definitively reconstruct the evolving attitude of Castro's government toward the U.S. Black Power movement in general and the BPP in particular. Nevertheless, the available evidence points to two underlying sources of tension between black militants and their sometimes-reluctant ally in the late 1960s. The first was Cuba's shifting position in the international socialist bloc, which had both practical and ideological implications for its approach to groups such as the Panthers. Although Cuba in the radical imagination stood as a beacon of communist defiance ninety miles from U.S. shores, the reality was more complicated. In addition to facing U.S. hostility, including invasion and repeated assassination attempts, Castro's government also had to negotiate its position with respect to the twin titans of the communist world. As with other nations in the Third World, the Sino-Soviet split of the early 1960s provided Cuba with challenges and opportunities. In the best case, nations looking for aid could play Moscow and Beijing against one another while maintaining their own independence. As Sino-Soviet hostilities sharpened in the second half of the decade, however, it became more difficult for smaller nations to successfully maintain this balancing act. Siding with one communist power or the other had not only practical consequences in terms of receiving aid, but also ideological implications for thinking about the conduct of revolutionary foreign policy. The Soviet Union and its Warsaw Pact satellites emphasized a long-term view of worldwide revolution that downplayed immediate conflict with the United States. China in the 1960s, however, maintained a more militant approach toward confrontation with the "paper tiger" of U.S. imperialism, particularly in the Third World.[29] Cleaver was broadly aware of the Sino-Soviet split when he arrived in Havana in December 1968, but he had little notion of how it might affect his own efforts in exile. He would soon find that dealing with the politics of the socialist world could be as confusing and frustrating as those back home.

Working from interviews and publicly available sources, historian Ruth Reitan has concluded that Cuban support for the Panthers fell victim to that nation's changing national security policy and the need to take a side in the Sino-Soviet split. By the mid-1960s, Che Guevara's policy of aggressively supporting revolutionary movements in both the First and Third Worlds, which closely corresponded to that of Mao's China, had been defeated by a faction that was more closely aligned with the Soviet Union and shared

Moscow's belief that Cuban security demanded a cautious approach to relations with the United States.[30] Robert F. Williams noted this shift firsthand from his exile in Havana, observing that by 1965, "[t]he Moscow-oriented elements in Cuba [had] gained the ascendency and the new party line was to curse everybody and everything that smelled even faintly Chinese."[31] Williams, who had formed cordial relations with the Chinese during a series of visits in 1963–64, was increasingly uncomfortable with the changing winds of Cuban politics and relocated to Beijing in July 1966. By this point, the new direction in Cuban foreign policy had already surfaced publicly at the January 1966 Tricontinental Conference in Havana, when Castro publicly attacked the Chinese government, accusing them of siding with the United States and of "senility."[32]

Cleaver had picked up on some of the internal shifts in Cuban policy while still behind bars. Watching a television report on a Cuban rally at the time of the Tricontinental Conference in 1966, he noted the conspicuous absence of Che Guevara. "I wonder about what became of Che," Cleaver pondered in a letter to his lawyer. "He was ultimate on the Left . . . and it is said that a revolution devours its own children and who can deny that?"[33] Guevara's death as part of a failed Bolivian operation in 1967 coupled with a sustained economic crisis that left Cuba increasingly dependent on Soviet aid further entrenched the advocates of a conservative policy with respect to the United States.[34] Cleaver, however, was unaware of the degree to which changes in Cuban national security policy and Cuba's increasingly close ties to the Soviet Union would impact his own plans for a guerrilla base ninety miles from U.S. soil. Soon after arriving, however, it became clear that Castro's government had little interest in further antagonizing the United States on his behalf. The Cubans agreed to shelter Cleaver but were unwilling to publicly announce his presence on the island, much less provide him a propaganda outlet similar to that they had once afforded Williams or a base with which to train Panther exiles for a guerrilla army. Though not privy to the high-level decision making that doomed his plans, Cleaver, like Williams before him, could sense the effects of the changing international landscape on his fortunes in Cuba. "[T]he point that had me more uptight than any other," he recounted, "was that it was kind of clear that Cuba had sided with the Soviet Union against China in the internal struggle in the world socialist movement."[35]

Kathleen Cleaver later recalled, "The Cubans . . . at that point with their Soviet mindset . . . they weren't dealing with the issue of Blackness, they didn't want to hear about it. To them, blackness was subversive."[36] The subversive nature of blackness in this context was not simply related to the Soviet desire to downplay race in favor of class when it came to building revolutionary coalitions. It was also related to the complicated history of Cuban race relations. In facing the world, Castro's government presented itself as a vocal champion of antiracism, with a particular emphasis on support for the struggles of African Americans in the United States and liberation movements in Africa. Within Cuba, however, the situation was more complicated. Prior to the revolution, the island had been sharply divided by skin color, with light-skinned Cubans atop the political, economic, and social structure and dark-skinned Afro-Cubans and their descendants at the bottom. Though seldom expressed with the same legal clarity as Jim Crow laws in the United States, white supremacy was deeply woven into the fabric of Cuban life.[37] From 1959 to 1961, the revolutionary government under Castro took important steps to combat this history of discrimination. In addition to publicly condemning anti-black racism and repealing legal impediments to full participation for dark-skinned Cubans, the revolution's sweeping social measures, including land reform and various health, education, and literacy campaigns, brought tremendous gains to an Afro-Cuban population that tended to cluster in poorer and more rural areas.[38]

Despite early progress, three factors combined to limit the Cuban government's willingness to engage with issues of race domestically after 1961, ultimately complicating relations with Cleaver and other African American exiles who sought to use the island as a base. The first was the persistence of pre-revolution racial ideology among the Cuban elite. It is hardly surprising that the mostly light-skinned Cubans who dominated the new government were unable to completely shed centuries of deeply ingrained notions of white supremacy upon taking power. Robert F. Williams complained that while "many Cuban officials . . . claim to be Socialist, they still have some of the same attitudes, and that is that blacks are to be discriminated against, and power should be in hands of whites."[39] By many accounts, Castro himself viewed black Cubans in paternalistic terms, seeing them as clients to be aided by the revolution rather than as partners in making their own liberation.[40] This tendency was reinforced by the ideology of the revolution, which promoted a color-blind Marxism as the solution to the island's history of discrimination and rejected racially based solutions as theoretically unsound and practically divisive. The government's tilt toward the Soviet Union and its rigid interpretation of Marxism-Leninism only accentuated this tendency to downplay the salience of race, as opposed to the more flexible Maoist model that recognized racial nationalism as part of the larger

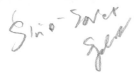 Sino-Soviet

struggle against capitalism and imperialism.[41] Williams found that these various factors combined in Cuba, such that "[a]nyone who is Pro-Chinese or black nationalist is considered counterrevolutionary."[42]

Concerns over internal security were the final blow to the revolution's early efforts to engage with race in a domestic context. In the aftermath of the abortive U.S.-sponsored Bay of Pigs invasion in 1961, Castro's government moved to shore up its control over Cuban society by eliminating potential domestic threats. Among the major targets of the post-invasion crackdown were independent black political, economic, and social organizations. The Second Declaration of Havana, presented by Castro in February 1962, declared the issue of racism "eradicated" within the Cuban context, thus ending official debate on the matter and rendering those who raised the issue open to charges of aiding the island's enemies.[43] In the wake of economic troubles in the late 1960s, the government again targeted black intellectuals and activists, and Cleaver arrived in Cuba at arguably the height of anti-black hysteria in official circles.[44] As a result, he was quickly forced to confront the contradiction between the Castro government's outward-facing antiracism and its reluctance to acknowledge, much less deal with, the legacy of white supremacy in Cuba.

Although the visiting BPP delegation in August 1968 had been assured that "Cuban revolutionaries are prepared to give their lives for the cause of the Afro-Americans, which is the cause of the peoples of the world," that commitment did not necessarily extend to black Americans within Cuba itself.[45] African American exiles were tolerated, even publicly welcomed in many cases, so long as they were willing to keep to the script laid out by the Cuban government. Specifically, exiles were to keep the focus on U.S. racism while avoiding any comment or meddling in domestic racial affairs.[46] Cleaver, however, was not so easily contained. Having already been warned by Stokely Carmichael that "the white Cubans were racists," he quickly picked up on the government's double standard with respect to race and repeatedly raised awkward questions of his hosts.[47] His demand to train a black guerrilla army on Cuban soil at a time when the government was in the midst of a crackdown on Afro-Cuban organizing surely set off alarms in Havana. Even if aimed at a return to the United States, the notion of black men with guns parading around the island was likely as threatening to Castro's government in Cuba as it was to Ronald Reagan's in California.

Denied the base he believed he had been promised by Cuban representatives in New York, Cleaver took up informal organizing among African American exiles in Cuban. Havana was the preferred destination of the 154

U.S. commercial airline hijackers between 1968 and 1972, and the majority of those who ended up receiving political asylum in Cuba were African Americans.[48] Motivated by factors ranging from political attachment to the Cuban revolution to a desire to escape local criminal charges, the skyjackers were an embarrassment to the United States but also something of a headache for Castro's government. Unsure what to do with the high-profile refugees, Cuba officially welcomed most hijackers as guests. Privately, however, Cuban officials suspected many hijackers of either mental illness or being U.S. agents. Instead of the hero's welcome they expected, most hijackers ended up in Cuban prisons, work camps, and, if they were lucky, halfway houses.[49] Raymond Johnson, a hijacker from Louisiana who claimed to be affiliated with the BPP, implied that he was speaking for Cleaver when he sought out and complained to an Associated Press reporter in June 1969 that "[t]he Panthers have not been received in a revolutionary fashion." Johnson also complained of "a peculiar kind of racial discrimination," saying that "white Cubans "have a subconscious conspiracy to maintain control of the island." While Seale and the Oakland-based BPP disavowed any connection with Johnson, his complaints mirrored those voiced in private by Cleaver.[50] Some of the more politicized among the hijacker community in Cuba, including several who knew Cleaver from his time in prison, sought out the Panthers' minister of information to complain of their treatment. Cleaver's Havana penthouse apartment became known informally as *la casa de las panteras*, and it was soon home to a rag-tag network of hijackers, some of whom had run away from Cuban labor camps.[51]

Out of contact with his comrades in the United States and constantly watched by government minders, Cleaver came to see Cuba as "sort of a San Quentin with palm trees, an Alcatraz with sugar cane." His attempt to organize African American hijackers only served to heighten tensions with his reluctant hosts. Cleaver later recalled that "the Cubans were trying to decide what they were going to do about us, since we had some guns in the pad—a pistol and two AK-47s. We were in that siege frame of mind, that Afro-American, 'Custer's Last Stand' frame of mind.'"[52] An American reporter finally broke the story of Cleaver's presence in Cuba in May 1969, perhaps with his blessing as a way of ensuring that his hosts did not quietly jail or otherwise dispose of him. In the wake of this public revelation, and with Angela Davis scheduled to make a high-profile visit to the island, the Cuban government abruptly cut ties with Cleaver, hustling him onto a plane bound for Algeria.[53] Cold War dynamics within the socialist camp, Cuban racial politics, the disruptive effects of global skyjacking, and his inability to negotiate with his hosts on equal terms had all combined to doom Cleaver's ambitious plans to establish a base for the Panthers in Cuba.

Panthers in the Casbah: Algeria and the Pan-African Cultural Festival

Joined by a heavily pregnant Kathleen Cleaver shortly after his unexpected arrival in Algiers, Eldridge found himself marooned without contacts, institutional support, or a source of income. (The U.S. government had declared him to be a Cuban national, thus preventing payment of royalties from *Soul on Ice*).[54] Cleaver's knowledge of his new host country was almost entirely based on his reading of Fanon. "At that time," he later admitted, "I didn't know anything about Algeria."[55] Algiers hosted a number of prominent resistance groups, ranging from the Palestinian Fatah party to representatives of the South Vietnamese NLF, the African National Congress (ANC), and a variety of other sub-Saharan African groups dedicated to combating colonialism and white supremacist governments in their home countries. The Algerian government under Houari Boumédiène had broken relations with Washington in 1967 in protest against U.S. support for Israel during the Six-Day War and was bound by no extradition treaties with respect to U.S. fugitives. But while the adopted home of Frantz Fanon and oft-described "Mecca of the revolutionaries" seemed an ideal destination for a budding guerrilla warrior, Algeria posed its own complications for Cleaver.[56]

Cuban-Algerian relations had cooled after Boumédiène had replaced Algeria's revolutionary hero and first independent president, Ahmed Ben Bella, in a 1965 military coup.[57] Whether for this reason or because they were simply eager to wash their hands of the whole situation, the Cuban government apparently made no effort to even inform the Algerian government of Cleaver's arrival, much less provide him with contacts or support in his new home. And while Boumédiène remained committed to continuing his predecessor's material and rhetorical support for anticolonial rebels around the world, his domestic plans involved an expansion of Algerian natural gas production and exporting that would greatly benefit from improved relations with the United States. In the wake of the 1965 coup, CIA officials welcomed the leadership change, describing Boumédiène as "warm, open, and attentive to US officials."[58] U.S. support of Israel in the 1967 war and the ensuing occupation of Palestinian territory in the West Bank and Gaza temporarily set back relations with Algiers. Economic factors, however, continued to push the two countries toward rapprochement in the late 1960s and early 1970s. As Kathleen Cleaver recalled, at the time she and Eldridge arrived in Algiers, "American technicians were working in Algerian oil fields, American oil companies had invested in the natural gas industry, and an American company was computerizing the operation of SONATRAC, the government oil corporation."[59] Thus, while safe from immediate extradition to the United States, Cleaver had to worry not only about his tenuous legal status within Algeria upon arrival, but also about whether the Boumediene government's commitment to supporting anticolonial revolutionaries was strong enough to risk upsetting the increasingly close economic connections with U.S. companies by harboring a high-profile Black Panther fugitive.

As with the BPP's transnational ventures in Europe, it took the timely intervention of a well-placed local contact to secure Cleaver's entrée into the world of Algeria politics and diplomacy. Elaine Klein, an American-born sympathizer with the Algerian revolution and a former associate of Fanon, held a job in the Algerian Foreign Ministry at the time of Cleaver's arrival. Upon finding out that Cleaver had been essentially dumped in Algeria by the Cubans, she was able to temporarily normalize his status in the country by securing him an invitation to attend the 1969 Pan-African Cultural Festival in Algiers as part of a larger BPP delegation.[60] Eldridge and Kathleen lived in spartan, state-provided accommodations while awaiting the arrival of the Panther delegation from the United States prior to the opening of the conference on July 21, 1969. For the Cleavers, it was not only a family reunion but also a chance for Eldridge to live openly after six months of silence and invisibility. He would be able to reconnect with comrades from the struggle in the United States while building on the work done in Europe and elsewhere to raise the BPP's international profile.

The First Pan-African Cultural Festival, the result of planning by the OAU begun two years earlier in Congo, opened on the same day that American Neil Armstrong became the first human to walk on the surface of the moon. Cleaver dismissed the significance of the Apollo 11 mission, telling a U.S. reporter, "I don't see what benefit mankind will have from two astronauts landing on the moon while people are being murdered in Vietnam and suffering from hunger even in the United States."[61] Keeping their focus firmly on earthbound events, the BPP used the conference as a venue for their anticolonial vernacular on a world stage and a practical opportunity for transnational and international alliance building. Thanks to Klein's intervention, the Panther delegation, which included Cleaver as well Chief of Staff Hilliard, Minister of Education Hewitt, and Minister of Culture Douglas, was allowed to set up a public headquarters at the Afro American Information Center in downtown Algiers. With Douglas's cartoons and posters adorning the walls and Panther leaders holding court in the heart of the Algerian capital, the BPP had a prominent public role at the festival.[62] In an appearance alongside officials from Fatah, a confident Cleaver was greeted with chants of "Power to the People" and an outpouring of support from local residents who thronged to the center.[63]

Not only did the BPP delegation garner significant public and media attention, in Algiers they also had an opportunity to follow up on the transnational organizing efforts already begun in Europe by connecting directly for the first time with the leaders of popular resistance movements from across Africa and around the Third World. The Afro American Information Center was close to Fatah's Algerian headquarters, and Cleaver struck up a warm relationship with the Palestinian resistance group and its leader Yasser Arafat.[64] Prior to arriving in Algiers, Cleaver had expressed relatively little interest in the Israeli-Palestinian conflict. When asked in July 1968 about tensions in the region, the normally opinionated minister of information was at a loss for words, finally concluding, "I do not know what the solution to that problem is." During his time in prison, Cleaver had claimed to be attending Jewish religious services and expressed significant interest in Theodor Herzl and Zionism.[65] African American interest in Judaism was not unusual, however, particularly prior to 1967. As scholar Alex Lubin observes, "To many black radicals, Jewish diasporic politics, including the politics of Zionism, have been useful frames for understanding the politics of black nationalism."[66]

Cleaver's shift to embrace Arafat and the Palestinian cause was likely motivated both by genuine respect for fellow anticolonial fighters as well as by more pragmatic calculations. Israel's dramatic victory over its Arab neighbors in the June 1967 Six-Day War and the ensuing occupation of the Gaza Strip and the West Bank led a number of black activists to see that nation less as a plucky underdog and more as an aggressive colonial power.[67] It also inflamed popular and government opinion in much of the Arab world. American support for Israel had long produced tensions in the region, and Algeria, which cut diplomatic relations with the United States in the wake of the 1967 war, was a particularly strong supporter of the PLO. "Living in Algeria," Cleaver later recalled, "we were very conscious of the Arab position in support of the Palestinians."[68] The fact that Mao's China, to which the Panthers had long looked for support and inspiration, also provided significant rhetorical and material support to the PLO in this period may have helped push the Panthers in this direction as well.[69] As a result of the connections made in Algiers, Fatah and the BPP established close ties that were soon visible in the pages of the *Black Panther* as well as in Cleaver's operations in exile. By September 1970, Cleaver stood should-to-shoulder with Arafat while proclaiming, "The Black Panther Party unequivocally supports the Palestinian people and their Vanguard forces in their struggle against the Zionist aggressor and the Hussein reactionaries who have combined with the US Imperialist aggressors to drown in blood the glorious march of the Palestinian people to freedom, liberty, independence, and peace."[70] International section member Donald Cox traveled to Kuwait at the invitation of Fatah in order to attend a Palestinian student conference in February 1971. Addressing the assembled delegates, he reaffirmed the party's commitment to Palestinian liberation, declaring, "The young fedayeen being trained in the camps, on the battlefields, held captive, these are our revolutionary brothers. The young brothers in the ghettos of the U.S. are our fedayeen."[71]

The festival provided further opportunities for Cleaver and the rest of the delegation to make direct connections with groups they had once invoked only in rhetoric and images. In a lively dinner held in a courtyard of the former headquarters of the FLN in the Casbah, the Panther delegation met with revolutionaries from Haiti, Angola, Mozambique, and Zimbabwe to discuss anticolonial violence and the role of revolutionary culture in the global struggle against white supremacy.[72] While the rhetoric employed by the Panther delegation in Algiers, stressing Third World solidarity, anticolonialism, and opposition to white supremacy, was consistent with that promoted in the pages of the *Black Panther* and elsewhere since 1967, Cleaver seized the opportunity at the festival to advocate moving beyond words. His time in exile had further convinced him that black Americans were analogous to colonized people in the Third World and that in both cases anticolonial violence was the only appropriate response. "We know that it is possible for us to overthrow the capitalist system, and to rid the earth of capitalism, imperialism, and neo-colonialism and also all forms of oppression entirely," he declared. "It is our job to continue our struggle no matter what the resistance from the pigs might be."[73] Though frustrated in his initial attempts to bring the battle from a base in Cuba, Cleaver's mingling with guerrilla leaders while in Algiers reinforced his revolutionary fervor. Asked by an Algerian interviewer what means the BPP would use to achieve its goals in the United States, Cleaver responded curtly: "Guns,

guns."When asked what additional tools he might consider, he added,"And bombs. Guns. Just like you had to do it here."[74] Though recognizing that the Panthers in the United States were up against "a highly industrialized, a highly mechanized, and mobile military establishment that has communications that we cannot hope to match," he insisted that the Panthers were "perfectly willing to continue to the bitter end, whatever that might be."[75] Nor was Cleaver's rhetoric confined to vague pronouncements. In an interview with journalist Lee Lockwood he offered both specific strategies ("Simple things like the fact that all the lights should be broken out in Babylon") as well as the prediction "that by 1972 we will have a military *coup* in the United States and a military dictatorship, because by that time there will be a full-scale war going on in the United States."[76]

Cleaver's increasingly fervent commitment to anticolonial violence needs to be understood not only against the background of domestic events leading up to the botched April 6 action in Oakland and his interactions with guerrilla leaders while in exile. It also needs to be viewed with respect to the larger debate over the relationship between culture and revolution at the Pan-African Cultural Festival as well as developments within Algeria and the BPP. In a firsthand report on the festival in the *Black Scholar*, black studies pioneer Nathan Hare identified two major issues that divided the participants. The first was the debate between advocates of negritude, a philosophy espousing a common black culture linking the nations of Africa and the diaspora (a notion mostly common associated with Senegalese politician, poet, and intellectual Léopold Senghor), and those who followed Fanon's line in rejecting cultural or racial essentialism as a distraction from revolutionary struggles for freedom.[77] The second, a related though more narrow debate, was between black Americans at the conference who supported the BPP's broad-based formulation of revolutionary nationalism and those who identified with a more essentialist pan-Africanism. Stokely Carmichael, who had moved to Guinea and would become known as Kwame Ture, was the most prominent advocate of the latter position in Algiers. Carmichael had publicly resigned from the Panthers in February 1969, citing among other things the party's commitment to Marxism-Leninism as being incompatible with his more Afrocentric vision of black liberation. Cleaver blasted Carmichael in an open letter from exile, and the two men had a tense confrontation at the festival."The victims of Imperialism, Racism, Colonialism and Neo-colonialism come in all colors," Cleaver insisted, "and . . . they need a unity based on revolutionary principles rather than skin color."[78]

Against this backdrop, Cleaver's public statements in Algiers need to be understood as part of an effort to position the Panthers within the revolutionary nationalist camp inside the United States and as disciples of Fanon on the world stage. Rejecting negritude, the BPP in Algiers joined those embracing a broadly based revolutionary culture that stressed solidarity among the oppressed and a commitment to action rather than celebrating the past glories of Africa or extolling the essential virtues of blackness. As "Masai" Hewitt explained it, "Our interest in culture is only in the caliber of the culture, whether it be a .308 Winchester or a .357 Magnum."[79] In stressing their willingness to match revolutionary words with actions, the Panthers were also undoubtedly trying to justify their high profile at the festival and establish parity with more the more established revolutionary groups represented in Algiers. This was particularly important for Cleaver, who needed to burnish his credibility as a guerrilla spokesman in order to help win the support, or at least tolerance, of the Boumédiène government. In making the case for his relevance on the world stage while in Algiers, Cleaver often fell back on notions of African American exceptionalism that the BPP had inherited from RAM and continued to promote in its anticolonial vernacular. In conversation with fellow revolutionaries from the Third World, he stressed the unique and strategic position of black Americans within the belly of U.S. imperialism. Other revolutionary groups, he insisted, "have an interest in any amount of pressure that we can put on that government because, if we can just slow it down and force it to have to deal with us, then the other people would be able to liberate themselves and then in return we would expect them to come to our rescue."[80]

Cleaver's militant statements were also likely motivated by the need to stake out a position in the emerging split within the BPP over the role of anticolonial violence in the black liberation struggle. While the party, at least nationally, remained firmly committed to revolutionary nationalism, the internal debate over the timing and means by which to carry out that revolution had only grown sharper in the wake of the disastrous April 6 shoot-out and Cleaver's subsequent exile. As Cleaver tried to organize a guerrilla army in Cuba, the Oakland-based BPP moved in a very different direction. The BPP initiated the first of its "survival programs" in January 1969 by offering free breakfasts to Oakland schoolchildren. The breakfast program was subsequently expanded to include a wide range of community services in chapters around the country, including sickle cell anemia testing, busing of relatives of prisoners to visit their loved ones, and starting an innovative school for children in Oakland. Though the BPP leaders stressed that these programs were not liberal social reforms but rather about "survival pending revolution," they nevertheless represented a significant shift away from the more confrontational approach that marked the party's origins and early operations.[81] Even as the pages of the *Black Panther* continued to celebrate anticolonial violence both at home and in the Third World, U.S.-based Panther leaders including Newton, Hilliard, Seale, Ericka Huggins, and Elaine Brown had learned hard lessons from two years of brutal confrontation with the federal government and local police. While Cleaver could confidently declare from exile that "[r]epression strengthens our party," those left behind to bear the brunt of that repression drew a different conclusion.[82] With scores of Panthers dead or behind bars and the party's coffers drained by constant battles with the legal system, armed revolution would have to wait until the BPP had not only recovered its strength, but also built strong enough support in the community to withstand the battering inflicted by agents of the state.

The survival programs and the approach they represented were in direct contrast to the more aggressive line pursued by Cleaver from exile, largely isolated from the changes taking place back home in Oakland and elsewhere in the first half of 1969. The arrival of Hilliard and the BPP delegation in Algiers undoubtedly brought to the surface larger debates over the future of the party that dated back to Hilliard and Cleaver's dispute before the April 6, 1968, action. While Cleaver offered some tepid public support for the survival programs, in an interview from Algiers with filmmaker William Klein he insisted that "[w]e have a breakfast for children program ... but that's not what the Black Panther Party is all about." What was needed, he declared, was not simply survival programs but "some liberated territory in Babylon that we are willing and prepared to defend, so that all the exiles, fugitives, draft-dodgers, and runaway slaves can return to help finish the job." Privately he lamented the new direction of the party, which he ascribed primarily to Hilliard's influence.[83] There was almost certainly a gendered aspect to Cleaver's rejection of these programs as his preferred means of effecting change was "to stand up as black men inside of Babylon and to give the pigs a taste of ... hot lead."[84] In his public embrace of Fatah and other guerrilla movements as well as his increasingly bellicose statements about armed revolution, Cleaver was clearly seeking to combat what he saw as the reformist drift of the BPP and stake his claim to leadership of the party from exile.

Despite tensions behind the scenes and the public feud with Carmichael, the BPP's appearance at the Pan-African Cultural Festival was

undeniably successful in terms of international and transnational engagement. As with the Panthers' other overseas ventures, it is important not
to lose sight of the tremendous leap that the Panthers made from a small,
local group on the verge of extinction in late 1967 to an internationally
recognized organization that held its own, at least publicly, with established
groups such as Fatah and the ANC. The festival and the Panthers' presence
at the Afro American Information Center not only represented a public
relations triumph, it also provided the party's first genuine links to Third
World guerrilla groups. Combined with the growing network of supporters
in western Europe and the United States, the contacts made by the BPP
in Algiers provided the basis for an extraordinarily broad coalition that
promised to put flesh on the bones of the party's anticolonial vernacular.
For Eldridge and Kathleen Cleaver, however, the transnational links built
during the event were encouraging but not sufficient. While the rest of the
Panther delegation could declare victory in Algiers and return home, the
minister of information remained an exile dependent on the goodwill of
the Algerian government for his continued protection. During the course
of the festival, several hijackers with whom Cleaver had associated in Cuba,
including Byron Booth, Clinton Smith, and James Patterson and his family,
arrived in Algeria hoping to find a more welcoming reception than they
had received in Havana.[85] While swelling the ranks of his nascent Panther
cell, the new arrivals also increased the pressure on Cleaver to win official
recognition and secure funding for his operations in Algiers.

Beyond the need for a safe place for his family and comrades to
live, Cleaver also retained a genuine commitment to make good on his
oft-delayed plans for assembling an army of guerrilla warriors with which
to bring the battle back to the United States. In interviews from Algiers, he
made clear that he had no desire to die in exile. "I have to return to Babylon,
to live or die in Babylon," he declared, "but to fight, as it is only human to
do."[86] Making good on this promise, however, would require the kind of
support that only nation-states were capable of offering. However exciting
it might be to brush shoulders with African and Arab guerrilla movements,
these groups were still struggling to liberate their own countries and could
not provide the logistical and financial assistance that Cleaver needed if he
wanted to mobilize his own revolutionary army. Indeed, one of the few
points of agreement between Cleaver and Carmichael in 1969 was that
any successful black revolution in the United States would require practical
alliances with sympathetic national governments.[87] But while Carmichael
sought this support from African nations on the basis of racial and cultural

affinity, Cleaver pursued an alternative strategy that leveraged the Cold War in Asia to facilitate his efforts to build a base of operations for his revolutionary army in Algiers.

The DPRK, Vietnam, and the Asian Strategy

The period from mid-1969 through early 1971 constituted a second act for both Cleaver and BPP internationalism, one more closely rooted in the nuances of Cold War geopolitics and Asian variations of Marxism-Leninist theory than in the sweeping rhetoric of the party's anticolonial vernacular. Scholars including Judy Wu, Robin Kelley, Fred Ho, Bill V. Mullen, Robeson Taj Frazier, and Betsy Esch have detailed the intellectual and ideological appeal of Asian socialist nations to black radicals in the 1960s.[88] In the case of the BPP's Asian strategy, however, the underlying motivation had as much to do with the practical dilemmas that Cleaver confronted in exile as it did with idealized notions of "the revolutionary hope of the East."[89] In a series of ad hoc efforts to carve out an international power base for both himself and the BPP, Cleaver abandoned the notion of nonalignment or an alternative Third World approach to international relations in favor of a more direct engagement with the Cold War in Asia. He also moved away from informal transnational coalitions in favor of more direct ties to nation-states. "We find our most efficacious and useful alliances," he declared in December 1970, "are with those people who are directly confronted with the aggression by the U.S. imperialist government."[90] In practice, the NLF, the Provisional Revolutionary Government of South Vietnam (PRG), and the governments of North Vietnam and North Korea were Cleaver's most important allies during this period. Unlike the Cuban and Algerian governments, none of these entities were concerned with antagonizing the United States, and they welcomed support from American dissidents of all stripes. These Cold War–inspired alliances not only facilitated high-profile public events for Cleaver in Asia, they also afforded him leverage in his negotiations with the Algerian government in pursuit of a more permanent base of operations inside that country while simultaneously bolstering his position inside an increasingly divided BPP leadership structure.

It was the Democratic People's Republic of Korea (DPRK)—North Korea—that provided the initial opening for Cleaver's new strategy. In the midst of the Pan-African Cultural Festival in July 1969, the North Korean embassy requested an audience with Cleaver, with Elaine Klein acting as an intermediary.[91] Without access to the North Korean diplomatic archives, it is impossible to know for certain what prompted the DPRK to reach out to Cleaver and the BPP. Given the degree to which Kim Il-sung had consolidated control over the country's political and security apparatus by the mid-1960s, however, it seems unlikely that the embassy in Algiers acted without consulting Pyongyang first. At the ensuing meeting, the North Korean ambassador extended an invitation to Cleaver to attend the "International Conference of Journalists of the Whole World in the Fight Against U.S. Imperialist Aggression," which was to be held in Pyongyang in September.[92] Cleaver accepted, thus beginning a relationship that would have important practical and ideological consequences for the development of the BPP and its international strategy over the next three years.

To twenty-first-century observers accustomed to thinking of the DPRK as a paranoid, isolated regime ruled by an eccentric dynasty of dictators unable to feed their own people, Kim Il-sung's North Korea might seem a strange choice of allies for the freewheeling Cleaver and the BPP. In the late 1960s, however, this pairing made a good deal of sense for both parties. Belying its reputation as a hermit kingdom, North Korea aggressively pursued leadership in the Third World in the 1960s, positioning itself as a small, formerly colonized country that had successfully fought off the United States while maintaining its independence from both Moscow and Beijing. To outside observers, throughout much of the 1960s North Korea contrasted favorably in many ways with South Korea, with its sputtering economy and corrupt military dictatorship propped up by U.S. aid. South Korea was still occupied by American troops. The DPRK, meanwhile, appeared to have succeeded not only in rebuilding but also vastly expanding its industrial base in the wake of the Korean War while avoiding vast disparities of wealth and providing its citizens with all the basic consumer necessities.[93] Internationally, North Korea flexed its diplomatic muscles by bidding farewell to Chinese "volunteer" troops in 1958, opening relations with dozens of new governments in the Third World in the early 1960s, and providing direct aid to revolutionary movements. Kim personally traveled to Indonesia in 1965 to address a summit marking the tenth anniversary of the Bandung Conference as part of a larger bid to exercise North Korean leadership in the Third World.[94] His government undoubtedly saw these alliances as a way to cement the DPRK's international position and stake out its independence from its Soviet and Chinese patrons. In this context, reaching out to the BPP was a logical extension of efforts to cultivate goodwill in the Third World. Not only would it provide a propaganda opportunity against the United States, it also helped to showcase North Korea's leading role in supporting revolutionaries around the world struggling against the legacy of both capitalism and white supremacy.

Cleaver's decision to accept the invitation to the Pyongyang conference of radical journalists had as much to do with a pragmatic assessment of his current situation in Algiers as it did with the specific appeal of the DPRK's ideology and foreign policy. With the end of the Pan African Cultural Festival, the Cleavers and the small group of Panther exiles living in Algiers were at loose ends and in need of any support they could get. The invitation offered not only a chance to cultivate goodwill with the DPRK but also to make other connections that might prove useful in building his international power base in Algiers.[95] Accompanied by Byron Booth, one of several hijackers who followed Cleaver from Cuba to Algeria, the Panthers' minister of information arrived in Pyongyang on September 11, 1969. Once again, however, the Sino-Soviet split served to confuse and frustrate Cleaver as he worked to expand the BPP's international influence. Upon arrival, he found that Chinese, who were still engaged in a border conflict with the Soviet Union that dated back to March 1969, were not in attendance at the conference. The Soviet participants, meanwhile, frustrated Cleaver by seeking "to water down the positions that were being taken." In his notebook he wrote, "[T]o me ... it was disgusting especially to watch the so-called Marxist-Leninists from the first Socialist country in the world ... reduced to abject reactionaries." He likewise privately lamented that "[t]he contradiction between the Soviet position and the Chinese position has resulted in a stalemate of stultifying confusion in the international Proletarian World Revolution," and he wondered how he would be able to explain to comrades in the United States "why the Russians and Chinese are killing each other and why the Chinese are not at the Conference."[96]

In the midst of the confusion and infighting of the Sino-Soviet split, the position taken by the DPRK was a refreshing change for the small BPP delegation. Not only was Kim's government unbendingly hostile to the United States and its allies, it also appeared to have avoided the infighting that was gripping much of the socialist world in the late 1960s. Cleaver declared the DPRK to be "beautiful, clean, honest, free, and totally revolutionary" and celebrated Kim's role in developing an indigenous Third World variation of Marxism that had helped his country remain independent in the face of both U.S. aggression and Sino-Soviet confusion and duplicity.[97] Booth hailed his visit as "like catching glimpses of the future ... seeing what unity and the correct revolutionary program can create for those intent upon putting an end to oppression and the exploitation of man by man."[98] Undoubtedly, Cleaver's and Booth's opinions of the DPRK were shaped by the carefully controlled nature of their visit, which included tours of "the schools and the co-operatives where production exceeds the hideous dreams of the pig capitalists," somber war museums and memorials, and an opportunity to confront U.S. troops at the armistice line at Panmunjom.[99]

While Cleaver and Booth were certainly naïve about the degree to which average North Koreans were "free," the appeal of the DPRK for the Panther delegation transcended mere propaganda. After having experienced firsthand the ripple effects of the Sino-Soviet split in Havana, Algiers, and Pyongyang, Cleaver appreciated the fact that "[t]he Koreans don't bite their tongues at all, they tell it like it is and they take a very revolutionary attitude, an anti-imperialist attitude and I can say they are serious."[100] His hosts also apparently endorsed and encouraged Cleaver's plans for urban guerrilla warfare in the United States—which he developed in great lengths in his notebooks during the course of the conference—offering him the opportunity to engage in target shooting in addition to the more theoretical work associated with the conference.[101] "These people really relate to the gun on a deep level," he enthused, "and what they want to do is off Yankees and that's—there ain't no bull shit about that."[102] Moved by what appears to have been a combination of genuine enthusiasm for the DPRK's aggressive blend of communism and nationalism as well as a desire to secure practical support for his fledging operations in Algiers, Cleaver stayed on for several weeks after the conference to tour the country and receive additional political instruction. He and Booth returned to Algeria fired up with enthusiasm for Juche—Kim Il-sung's unique contribution to the development of Marxism-Leninism.

Loosely translated as meaning self-reliance, Juche was first promulgated by Kim in 1955 and subsequently developed over the next two decades into an increasingly elaborate state ideology. Combining elements of Marxism-Leninism, Maoism, Confucianism, and Korean nationalism, Kim sought to adopt communism for the unique circumstances of the DPRK while simultaneously serving notice that the North was not beholden, ideologically or otherwise, to its more powerful patrons in Moscow and Beijing. As explained by Kim in an article reprinted in the *Black Panther*, "The establishment of Juche means holding fast to the principle of solving for oneself all the problems of the revolution and construction in conformity with the actual conditions at home, and mainly by one's own efforts . . . applying the universal truth of Marxism-Leninism and the experiences the international revolutionary movement to one's country in conformity with its historical conditions and national peculiarities."[103] For Cleaver and other admirers outside of North Korea, the ideological appeal of Juche was similar to that of Maoism, with its emphasis on making nationalism compatible with Marxism-Leninism. By the late 1960s, however, the clarity of China's revolutionary message was muddied by the complications of Sino-Soviet infighting and the internal chaos unleashed by the Great Proletarian Cultural Revolution. The DPRK, meanwhile, offered an example of a much smaller nation that seemed to have forged a revolutionary path independent of both the capitalist West and the two giants of the socialist world. As such, Juche-era North Korea offered an appealing model to both revolutionary states in the Third World and to groups such as the Black Panthers that sought to meld nationalism with a form of proletarian internationalism while maintaining their own freedom of action. As Cleaver explained, "[I]t's a concept of self-reliance that justifies the independent existence of each party and gives it some ideological defenses against the type of domination that is traditional in the Socialist movement."[104] Booth was blunter in advocating replacing that "Maoist type . . . shit going on now in the United States [with] Kim Il Sung because we have got to build a consciousness to this cat, to the Korean situation, to his writings, etc."[105]

"Juche, baby, all the way," was a message that quickly spread from Cleaver's notebooks into the speeches of other Panther leaders as well as the pages of the *Black Panther* as the minister of information helped introduce Kim's gospel to the United States by way of Algiers.[106] In the six months after Cleaver's visit, the Panther paper regularly featured articles explaining and celebrating Juche as well as the "heroic leader Kim Il Sung" and the "beautiful people, so vigorously mobilized, so efficiently organized, moving with the harmony of one man"—the people over whom he presided. In March 1970 the *Black Panther* featured a special seven-page supplement focused on the DPRK, with an introduction by Cleaver that linked the detention of pro–North Korean activists in South Korea to "the railroading of Huey P. Newton, Bobby Seale, the Chicago Seven . . . through the pig courts of Babylon."[107] The North Korean government reciprocated with statements of support and further opportunities for travel and international exposure. DPRK state media made numerous favorable mentions of the Panthers, and in January 1970 Kim addressed a New Year's telegram to the BPP, celebrating "the militant ties between the Korean people and the progressive black people of America . . . in the battle against U.S. imperialism[,] our common enemy."[108] Cleaver was personally rewarded for his efforts on behalf of the DPRK with an invitation to return to Pyongyang as head of his own delegation in 1970.[109] The U.S. People's Anti-Imperialist Delegation (covered in more detail in the next chapter) would be the high-water mark of the Panthers' international engagement and was made possible in large part by Cleaver's willingness to directly engage with the Cold War in Asia.

If the DPRK played the most important role in facilitating Cleaver's access to travel and publicity while in exile, it was the NLF and the Provisional Revolutionary Government of South Vietnam (PRG) that helped to secure his place within Algeria. As was the case with the DPRK, Cleaver was introduced to the NLF in Algiers by Elaine Klein. At the Pan-African Cultural Festival, Cleaver stood beside NLF representatives, declaring that they faced the same enemy and that "we need each and we love each other." The Vietnamese, in turn, hailed him with a Black Power salute and presented Cleaver with a ring made from the scrap metal of downed American bombers (which he dubbed "the first good use I've ever seen those war materials put to").[110] Cleaver was invited to attend a memorial ceremony for Ho Chi Minh at the NLF's Algerian headquarters shortly before leaving on his first Korean trip, and while in the DPRK he made contact with both the NLF and government representatives from North Vietnam.[111]

Cleaver had multiple reasons for embracing connections to the Vietnamese. Like RAM and SNCC before it, the BPP had long championed the cause of the South Vietnamese resistance while linking it directly to their own struggles against "community imperialism" and police brutality in urban black neighborhoods. More practically, public affiliation with the NLF would not only raise the profile of the BPP in the socialist world, it would also improve the Panthers' position in Algeria and the Third World more broadly. Opposition to the U.S. war in Vietnam was one of the few factors that united the diverse group of states outside the orbit of the United States.[112] Forging a high-profile connection with the Vietnamese thus offered Cleaver an opportunity to simultaneously build support for his base of operations in Algiers and win further international attention. It also undoubtedly helped to bolster his position within the BPP at a time when the combination of exile and internal splits within the party left him increasingly isolated from the movement in the United States.

The NLF and the government of North Vietnam had reasons of their own for seeking a public alliance with the BPP in 1969. Support from U.S.

dissidents and antiwar activists was always welcome, but it was particularly important in the period from 1968 to 1971. As historian Lien-Hang T. Nguyen detailed in her pioneering study *Hanoi's War*, the decision by the Vietnamese Workers Party (VWP), and particularly General Secretary Le Duan, to embark on an ambitious plan to win military victory in the South with the 1968 Tet Offensive had important repercussions for Vietnamese military and diplomatic efforts. While Tet was a political success to the extent that it turned many Americans against what appeared to be an endless war, it was a military disaster for both the NLF and North Vietnam. Forced to abandon dreams of military victory in the South, at least for the three years following Tet, the VWP and its allies in the South shifted to diplomacy as a way of buying time and following up on the offensive's political successes. The most obvious sign of this strategy was the informal diplomatic talks held with U.S. representatives in Paris starting in May 1968. In addition, however, the VWP and NLF both actively courted the U.S. antiwar movement during this period as a useful diplomatic lever at a time of military deadlock. While further work remains to be done in Vietnamese archival sources on the specific nature of these connections, the NLF's approach to Cleaver and the BPP was a logical extension of the diplomatic strategy of the Vietnamese revolution during this time.[113]

Cleaver and his fledgling diplomatic mission in Algiers reaped numerous benefits from his association with the Vietnamese. Cleaver's People's Anti-Imperialist Delegation would eventually be invited to Hanoi in August 1970, where his public appearances burnished the BPP's revolutionary credentials in both the United States and the Third World. More important from a day-to-day perspective was the role that Vietnamese representatives in Algiers played in the development of what would eventually become the international section of the BPP. "It was only through the successful promotion and sponsorship of the Vietcong," Cleaver acknowledged, "which soon became the Provisional Government of Vietnam [PRG], that we broke through to any recognition or status."[114] Not only did the NLF and PRG vouch for Cleaver in meetings with Boumédiène, they also ended up providing him with a new and prestigious venue for his Algerian operations. When the Algerian government formally recognized the PRG as the government of South Vietnam and accorded them an embassy in 1970, Cleaver and his crew of exiles was allowed to occupy the NLF's former headquarters, a two-story villa in the El Biar section of the Algiers.[115] While the Algerian government provided the building and an accompanying stipend for the international section (primarily due to the intervention of Mohammed Yazid), it was the ongoing endorsement of the NLF and PRG that facilitated this arrangement. The Vietnamese "not only lent credibility to my overseas operations," Cleaver explained, "but intervened on our behalf when the Algerians clamped down."[116] More broadly, the government of North Vietnam gave the BPP a propaganda coup by offering to release a number of U.S. POWs in exchange for the freedom of Bobby Seale and Huey Newton.[117] In return, Cleaver contributed to propaganda broadcasts for both the NLF and the government of North Vietnam and passed on material for publication in the Black Panther.[118]

While the BPP's Asian strategy, of which Cleaver was the primary author, maintained the Panthers' earlier focus on the Third World, the terms of that engagement changed significantly. Cleaver's efforts in this period were characterized by direct, government-level contacts with representatives of North Korea and North Vietnam (as well as with the NLF and PRG) rather than the broad symbolic and rhetorical gestures that had marked the BPP's engagement with the Third World in 1967–68 or the transnational organizing efforts of 1968–69. Although not entirely incompatible with the broadly defined Third World solidarity of the party's anticolonial vernacular, this new approach mandated a more narrowly focused emphasis on the geopolitics of the Cold War in Asia. Where the Black Panther had once featured an analysis of foreign developments filtered through the lens and expressed in the language of the urban black experience in the United States, in 1969–70 it increasingly served as a venue for reprinting state-generated propaganda pieces from the party's new Asian allies. To this extent, the party's anticolonial vernacular eroded as a result of its direct engagement with the Cold War, supplemented but not entirely replaced by a more narrow state-level discourse that often had little direct connection to the daily lives of the party's rank-and-file members and supporters in the United States.

The era of the Asian strategy also coincided with a refinement of the BPP's previously scattershot and impressionistic Marxism. The attention given to Juche by the Panthers during this period did not extend to the formulation of any kind of formal party line, but it did result in the Panthers giving considerably more attention to the doctrinal nuances of Marxism-Leninism. The origins of this shift predated Cleaver's Asian trip and coincided with the BPP's escalating feud with various cultural nationalist groups, most notably Maulana Karenga's US Organization in Los Angeles. In July 1969, as tensions increased between the Panthers, US and pan-Africanists such as Carmichael, the party amended its ten-point program to replace references to "white men" with "capitalists."[119] Cleaver, however, increased the BPP's explicit engagement with Marxism-Leninism in the aftermath of his first trip to the DPRK in the fall of 1969. During the course of that visit, he developed a detailed critique of the BPP's original ten-point program, declaring that it was "limited to the contradictions of the Black colony" and "not based firmly upon Marxism-Leninism." Having "outgrown present program," he concluded, "[w]e must issue [a] new expanded party program"—one that moved away from the narrow focus on black America to "attack complete system."[120] Though careful not to voice such blunt criticisms of the party in public, Cleaver subtly pushed for a greater engagement with class struggle in a June 1970 pamphlet that was later reprinted in the *Black Panther.* The time had come, he suggested, to adapt "the classical principles of scientific socialism" to the specific historical experience of African Americans. In the process, he hailed both Mao and Kim Il-sung for their selective application of Marxism-Leninism to fit the conditions in their own countries and identified Huey Newton as having picked up their mantle by providing "the ideology and methodology for organizing the Black Urban Lumpenproletariat."[121] This embrace of the finer points of revolutionary doctrine was not limited to Cleaver. Despite the tensions between the two men, David Hilliard joined Cleaver in November 1969 in declaring that "[t]he ideology of the Black Panther Party is the historical experiences of Black people in America translated through Marxism-Leninism."[122] Although the BPP remained ideologically diverse, particularly at the local level, during the Cleaver-led engagement with the Cold War in Asia the party came as close as it ever would to formalizing its commitment to Marxism-Leninism.

The new international approach promoted by Cleaver in 1969–70 yielded some initially impressive results. When he arrived in Algiers in June 1969, Cleaver's fortunes had been at low ebb. Cut off from his comrades in the United States and unceremoniously ejected from Castro's Cuba, Cleaver was operating in a foreign city without contacts, funds, or even legal permission to be in the country. A little more than a year later, he was not only well established in Algeria but also on the verge on embarking on a foreign tour that would see him feted by generals and heads of state in Pyongyang, Hanoi, and Beijing. Upon his return, he would preside over the formal opening of the BPP's international section in what had been the Algerian headquarters of the NLF, symbolism that Cleaver surely appreciated. None of these accomplishments would have been possible without Cleaver's willingness to directly engage with the Cold War in Asia. The

Asian strategy, however, also came with risks and costs. In forging direct alliances with foreign governments, Cleaver left himself increasingly dependent on the whims of his new allies and highly sensitive to changes in the Cold War environment. Moreover, his engagement with the geopolitics of the Cold War while in exile sometimes served to distance him from the issues that had initially inspired his engagement with the black freedom struggle. As Cleaver prepared to fly off for a three-month Asian tour in July 1970, events in Oakland, Washington D.C., and Beijing were conspiring to undermine the BPP's international strategy just as it appeared poised to enter the spotlight on the world stage.

engagement w. CW in Asia

Chapter 6

"Gangster Cigarettes" and "Revolutionary Intercommunalism"

Diverging Directions in Oakland and Algiers, 1970–1971

August 1970 marked a triumphant period in the brief and turbulent history of the Black Panther Party. On August 5, after almost three years behind bars, BPP cofounder and minister of defense Huey Newton was released from prison after a California appellate court threw out his manslaughter conviction. Free on a $50,000 bail bond pending a new trial, Newton stood on top of a parked car to address thousands of admirers outside the Alameda County Courthouse.[1] In the days that followed, he began to reassert control over the party, sending a letter to the government of North Vietnam offering BPP members as soldiers in the fight to liberate the South and propounding a new doctrine he dubbed "intercommunalism" that sought to make sense of the party's place in an increasingly interconnected world. As Newton celebrated his freedom in Oakland, Minister of Information Eldridge Cleaver was in the midst of leading the People's Anti-Imperialist Delegation on a high-profile tour of Asia that saw the delegation received by generals and government officials in North Korea, China, and North Vietnam. The Cleaver delegation returned to Algiers in early September to preside over the formal opening of the international section of the Black Panther Party in a renovated villa formerly occupied by the NLF. The international section served, in the words of Kathleen Cleaver, as an "embassy of the American revolution."[2]

After halting efforts in 1968–69, the BPP's international and transnational strategies matured dramatically in 1970–71. Thanks to the Cleavers, Connie Matthews, Elaine Klein, and a host of local activists and solidarity committees, the BPP could boast not only a base in Algiers and diplomatic recognition from the Algerian government but also alliances with revolutionary states in Asia and continuing transnational support from groups in Germany, Scandinavia, and Japan. The party also inspired the formation of similarly named and themed groups in places ranging from Great Britain to Israel, Canada, India, and New Zealand by the early 1970s.[3] In Newton's intercommunalism, meanwhile, the party offered an innovative analysis that looked beyond the Cold War to examine the ways in which the power of globalized capitalism married to a technological and communications revolution had effectively rendered nation-states obsolete, replacing them with a "global village." In response, Newton advocated creating informal transnational networks linking dispersed communities around the world in ways that would ultimately result in "some universal identity that extends beyond family, tribe, or nation—an identity that is essentially human and does not depend upon people thinking that others are something less than they are."[4]

The growth of the BPP's engagement with the world outside the United States was undeniably messy and hard to categorize by the start of the 1970s. Formal state-level contacts rooted in Cold War geopolitics coexisted uneasily with informal transnational efforts that sought to transcend the nation-state altogether. These divergent directions were on full display in the pages of the *Black Panther*, where the party's earthy anticolonial vernacular brushed up against stilted propaganda proclamations reprinted from Pyongyang and Beijing and where discussions of guerrilla warfare tactics shared space with a celebration of feeding schoolchildren and aiding the elderly. But while it is easy to find fault with the BPP's cafeteria-style internationalism, the diverse nature of the party's foreign connections was not necessarily a flaw. National governments, after all, are routinely engaged in a wide variety of foreign relations that seldom fit neatly into a single, easy-to-define or one-size-fits-all policy. And while the BPP had internal divisions over anticolonial violence and its relationship to the Cold War, the same could be said of many successful national liberation movements during the second half of the twentieth century. Indeed, few but the most unreconstructed political scientists would insist that states are themselves unitary actors in the realm of foreign relations. The differences between Huey Newton and Eldridge Cleaver on the question of international strategy were quite sharp at times but no more so than those between U.S. national security advisor Henry Kissinger and Secretary of State William P. Rogers in the same period.[5] Up until early 1971, the Black Panther Party maintained a sometimes-precarious balance between its U.S.-based leadership and its foreign wing in Algiers, with their alternative approaches to black liberation and international (or transnational) relations.

The People's Anti-Imperialist Delegation and the International Section

The U.S. People's Anti-Imperialist Delegation, which arrived in Pyongyang in July 1970, represented the culmination of Cleaver's strategy of domestic and international alliance building. Cleaver was the head of the eleven-person group, which also included Elaine Brown, an L.A. Panther who had ascended to the inner circle of the national party, as well as members of other organizations, including the San Francisco–based Red Guards, the Peace and Freedom Party, the Movement for a Democratic Military, *Ramparts* magazine, and New York Newsreel.[6] After a brief stop in the Soviet Union, Cleaver led this diverse collection of activists on a two-and-half month journey that began in North Korea and continued on to North Vietnam and the People's Republic of China.

The delegation returned to Algiers in September to preside over the formal opening of the international section of the Black Panther Party. In a poem written upon his return, titled "Gangster Cigarettes" (slang meaning marijuana joints), Cleaver offered "a Guinness Book of Records boast":

> That I'm the first to blast
> From the same bag of goods
>> In Moscow
>> In Pyongyang
>> In Hanoi
>> And two in Peking
> Just another untamed vato,
> From Rose Hill, East L.A.[7]

In this wry reflection on his international travels in service of the revolution, Cleaver captured both the strengths and weaknesses of the People's Anti-Imperialist Delegation and its approach to "people's diplomacy" in revolutionary Asia.

Figure 12. Eldridge Cleaver and unidentified Vietnamese women in the Democratic Republic of Vietnam (DRV) as part of the tour of the People's Anti-Imperialist Delegation, August 1970. Eldridge Cleaver Papers, Bancroft Library, University of California, Berkeley.

The most obvious accomplishment of the delegation was to attract international attention to the Panthers while positioning them as the vanguard of the U.S. Left. In his incisive analysis of the BPP's domestic operations, Nikhil Pal Singh suggested that "we should understand them as being the practitioners of an insurgent form of visibility, a literal-minded and deadly serious guerrilla theater in which militant sloganeering, bodily display, and spectacular action simultaneously signified their possession and real lack of power."[8] The Cleaver-led delegation brought a similar form of "insurgent visibility" to the world stage as the swaggering "untamed vato" from L.A. shook hands with generals and dignitaries while exuding disdain for institutions of traditional diplomacy. In public statements and appearances in Pyongyang, Hanoi, and Beijing, Cleaver and other members of the delegation married the sweeping rhetoric of Third World solidarity and anti-imperialism to the geopolitics of the Cold War in Asia. "We have come to understand," declared the delegates in a statement released on their way to Pyongyang, "that Black people in the United States are treated as an internal colony, and are subject to the same genocidal aggression by U.S. imperialism as are the peoples of Asia." As a result, "[u]nderstanding the Korean people's struggle, and communicating this to the American movement is a crucial step in developing this internationalist perspective."[9] Statements such as these linked the BPP's anticolonial vernacular and analysis of the domestic situation of people of color in the United States to the new diplomatic direction initiated by Cleaver as part of the "Asian strategy" of Cold War–inflected international alliances.

The People's Anti-Imperialist Delegation succeeded in garnering significant attention from both the mainstream and alternative press as well as wary interest from the security apparatus of the U.S. government, which closely tracked its movements.[10] In mid-August, the North Vietnamese government held a public ceremony marking the International Day of Solidarity with the Afro-American People (an event that had its origins in the OSPAAAL celebration of the Watts uprising), at which the delegation took center stage. While it was ideologically and racially diverse, with a female majority of delegates, Cleaver positioned himself as its leader and public face. The trip and the ensuing international media coverage bolstered his position in the party and burnished his credentials as a diplomatic representative of the black freedom struggle in the United States. It also positioned the Panthers as leaders of an alliance between the antiwar movement and the emerging force of the U.S. Third World Left. In a gesture acknowledging the BPP's key role in the antiwar struggle, North Vietnamese officials gave the delegation a packet of over three hundred letters written by American POWs to be taken back to the United States.[11]

In addition to its symbolic value, the delegation's travel also allowed Cleaver to expand upon the ties with the revolutionary governments in Asia that he had begun to cultivate in Algiers and during his first trip to the DPRK in September 1969. In North Korea, the delegation was greeted by Kang Ryang-uk, vice president of the Presidium of the Supreme People's Assembly, as well as Kim Il-sung's uncle and close adviser, who hailed "[t]he struggle of the Black Panther Party and the Black people in America against the cursed policy of racial discrimination of the U.S. imperialists" while specifically calling for the release of Bobby Seale and other Panthers behind bars.[12] Members of the group also met with North Vietnamese premier Pham Van Dong and famed military leader Võ Nguyên Giáp as well as exiled Prince Norodom Sihanouk of Cambodia and numerous lower-level officials from their socialist hosts.[13] There were clear limits on the diplomatic status accorded to Cleaver and the delegation. They were not granted access to the highest-level officials in Pyongyang, Hanoi, or Beijing, and most of the meetings they did have were largely pro forma publicity opportunities. Nevertheless, receiving official recognition from state-level actors was significant not only as a symbolic nod to the BPP's rising international status but also to keep Cleaver's operations in Algiers afloat on a daily basis. In return, the anti-imperialist delegation contributed to propaganda efforts on behalf of their hosts. In addition to continuing to forward Vietnamese, North Korean, and Chinese material back to Oakland to be published in the *Black Panther*, Cleaver made a broadcast from Hanoi aimed at encouraging African American soldiers to "start ripping off the uncle toms and those pigs who're giving you order[s] to kill the Vietnamese people. . . . Throw those hand grenades at them, and put that dynamite up under their houses, up under their jeeps."[14] As historian Judy Wu observed, broadcasts such as these not only served as part of the DRV's public diplomacy on the international front, they also bolstered morale among a war-weary North Vietnamese population by highlighting divisions and weakness within the camp of their superpower opponent.[15]

Even as the delegation enjoyed its welcome in revolutionary Asia, there were already signs of the internal disputes that would contribution to the fracturing and eventual dissolution of the party. In a private account of the trip written upon her return to the United States, Elaine Brown described bitter divisions behind the scenes, with Cleaver blasting the Oakland-based leadership, David Hilliard in particular, as the "'right wing' of the Black Panther Party" for their embrace of the survival programs and rejection of armed struggle. Lamenting that the Panthers in the United States had become "a 'Breakfast-for-Children' Party," Cleaver apparently went so far as to call for the murder of David Hilliard and his brother June Hilliard while on the trip.[16] Brown also reported that Cleaver and *Ramparts* editor Robert Scheer exercised dictatorial control over the delegation, particularly its female members. Eldridge, in Brown's account, threatened her life, publicly humiliated his wife Kathleen, physically abused Connie Matthews, and saw the female members of the delegation as there to meet his sexual needs. Judy Wu, who interviewed several members of the delegation, concluded that the power dynamics within the traveling party were highly patriarchal, with Cleaver exercising "authoritarian control" and targeting "members of his own delegation for humiliation and hostility." Kathleen Cleaver and other women in the international section have denied having problems with Eldridge on the basis of gender. And as Wu observed, both Cleaver's actions while heading the delegation and Brown's post facto accounts of the trip must be understood against the backdrop of the contest for leadership within the BPP as well as the external pressures on the party.[17] Nevertheless, the patriarchal and misogynistic elements of Cleaver's leadership in the party are well documented, including his embrace of "pussy power," in which he defined women's role in the revolution as providing (or withholding) sex in order to encourage men to be proper revolutionaries.[18]

The external relations of the People's Anti-Imperialist Delegation also illustrated a fundamental problem that had vexed the BPP's efforts at foreign alliances from the very beginning. For all its success in attracting public attention, the delegation was often caught in an awkward position between transnational and international diplomacy. In Judy Wu's description, the delegation "[appropriated] President Eisenhower's concept of 'people's diplomacy . . .' [and] challenged the ability of the U.S. government to represent their interests. Instead, they sought direct, people-to-people contact with socialist Asia."[19] This effort at building transnational connections was undermined, however, not only by the troubled internal dynamics of the delegation but also by the nature of their contacts in the DPRK, North Vietnam, and China. As was invariably the case with foreign visitors to these countries, the delegation's travels were closely circumscribed and monitored by their host governments. While the groups with whom they met, such the Korean Democratic Women's Union or the central committee of the Vietnam Women's Unions, were often nominally independent actors, the nature and context of these meetings sharply limited the opportunity for genuine people-to-people diplomacy. As historian Lien-Hang Nguyen concluded, "Although these people's diplomats were drawn from mass organizations and other non-state entities, the Communist Party directed their campaigns. In others words, there's no removing the state (or the nation) from this transnational history of non-state actors."[20] The strict control exercised by the hosts in revolutionary Asia complicated opportunities for meaningful transnational connections. It placed the People's Anti-Imperialist Delegation in the position of interacting with national governments that tended to view them, not inaccurately, as clients rather than as equals in the struggle against U.S. imperialism. While they received a warm welcome and were accorded many of the public courtesies of state-level visitors, these gestures did nothing to alter the fundamental power imbalance between a sometimes-fractious group of U.S. citizens and the revolutionary states that hosted them. This imbalance was an inescapable element of the BPP's "Asian strategy," which traded some measure of the party's autonomy in seeking support from more powerful nation-states for their struggles within the United States.

The compromises required of the party in cultivating its international alliances in Asia were most visible in the delegation's fawning public comments with regard to their host governments. Upon her return, Elaine Brown bragged that that North Korean people "have nothing to envy anybody in the world" and that China, then in the grips of the chaos of the Cultural Revolution, was a place where "where human beings respond to each other as human beings for the first time in history."[21] This praise was certainly sincere to a point—the combination of what Wu identified as a form of romanticized "radical orientalism" with the carefully staged nature of their tour undoubtedly predisposed the members of the delegation to respond favorably to their hosts.[22] So too did the fact that the delegation shared many points of genuine commonality with revolutionary governments in their opposition to white supremacy, capitalism, and the U.S. role in Asia. But the BPP members of the delegation, and Cleaver particularly, given his delicate position in Algiers, were also aware that their partnerships with China, the DPRK, and the Vietnamese were not equal ones and that the support they received was conditioned on agreeing to serve as outlets for state propaganda. Liberal civil rights activists and organizations in the United States that aligned with the federal government during the Cold War, most notably the NAACP, did so at the cost of acquiescing to a vastly narrowed debate on issues of race and inequality. They also had to at least tacitly endorse the oppressive measures used by the U.S. government to silence individuals who refused to accept those limits. But in attempting a mirror image of the accommodationist strategy by casting their lot with America's Cold War adversaries, the Panthers and the People's Anti-Imperialist Delegation also had to sacrifice a degree of autonomy in exchange for state-level support.

Despite these many internal and external challenges, the People's Anti-Imperialist Delegation could boast of both real and symbolic accomplishments upon its return. At a time when the party was on defensive against police and FBI pressure in the United States, the delegation allowed the Panthers the opportunity to go on the offensive internationally, flouting the U.S. ban on travel to communist nations and burnishing the party's internationalist credentials for both a foreign and domestic audience. The trip also deeply affected many of the individuals involved. For all the problems she faced in dealing with Cleaver, Elaine Brown celebrated the voyage as "the first time in . . . our own lives we were treated as human beings and as respected members of the human race."[23] Although Brown's enthusiasm was undoubtedly influenced by the need to portray the party's new allies in a positive light, Judy Wu's interviews confirmed that many members of the delegation found the trip to genuinely emotionally and intellectually fulfilling, inspiring them to return dedicated to continuing service in pursuit of an American revolution that they believed to be imminent.[24] Cleaver and the BPP also derived more tangible benefits from the trip, most notably in shoring up support for Panther operations in Algeria. Nowhere was this clearer than in the formal opening of the headquarters of the international section of the Black Panther Party in Algiers upon the return of the delegation. At a reception on September 13, 1970, held in a whitewashed, two-story villa in the El Biar neighborhood that had formerly belonged to the NLF, delegates from the embassies of the DPRK, China, and the PRG joined dignitaries from several African nations and high-ranking members of the Algerian government to toast Cleaver and the Panthers. Along with the building came official recognition as a resistance movement from the Algerian government, a regular stipend for expenses, entrance and exit visas for party members, identity cards, and access to telexes and telephones for international communication with both the BPP headquarters in Oakland and the party's allies in Asia and Europe.[25] Cleaver's Asian strategy and the alliances he had forged on his two international trips were instrumental in facilitating this accomplishment and vital in ensuring the international section's continued operations in Algiers.

The establishment of the international section of the BPP as an officially accredited revolutionary movement in Algiers was a major milestone, not only in the development of the Panthers but also in the history of African American internationalism. For all the efforts of U.S.-based activists from Martin R. Delany to W.E.B. Du Bois, Marcus Garvey, Vicki Garvin, Malcolm X, and Stokely Carmichael, the international section was the first time that black American activists had established an independent, officially recognized, institutional presence outside the United States. Recognition from the Algerian government was not only symbolically important but also facilitated Cleaver's efforts to build connections with other governments and movements while supporting the growing contingent of Panther exiles in Algiers. As law enforcement in the United States continued to crack down on BPP chapters across the country, a number of party members fled to join Cleaver's operation. Field Marshall Donald Cox, Pete and Charlotte O'Neal from the Kansas City BPP chapter, and Larry Mack, Sekou Odinga, Michael Tabor, and Richard Moore (later Dhoruba bin Wahad) from the New York branch, along with several of their family members, joined the international section in 1970–71. Eventually the group grew to encompass almost thirty people spread across the headquarters villa and several apartments throughout the city.[26]

As the international section continued to grow in 1970–71, maintaining and supporting its operations proved to be as challenging as the path to formal recognition. Though willing to grant the section the diplomatic courtesies it accorded to other resistance movements, the government of President Boumédiène balked at providing the military training facilities that Cleaver had long sought in order to build a guerrilla army to take the fight back to Babylon.[27] Moreover, the Panthers with their (in Cleaver's words) "fast cars, Russian machine guns, and plenty of fresh-air macho," consistently tested the patience of the Algerian government and its secret police force. Factors ranging from drug use to the style of dress preferred by some female members of the delegation and the international section's high telex bills led to friction with local authorities. This was exacerbated by the fact that the stipend provided by the government was insufficient to support the daily needs of Cleaver's ambitious operations in exile. As a result, party members in Algiers resorted to "hustling," including fencing stolen passports, visas, and even cars in order to make ends meet, activities that did little to endear the Panthers to their sometimes reluctant host.[28] With the ever-present threat that the Algerian government might ditch the Panthers in order to facilitate economic connections with the United States, the international section remained reliant on continued interventions by its Asian allies. Cleaver later reflected that "the Algerian government in its crooked dagger style of rubbing people out, very nearly reached us, and would have, had it not been for the Vietnamese and the North Koreans."[29] While leveraging the support of revolutionary governments in Asia to pressure the revolutionary government in Algiers worked in the short term, it left Cleaver and the international section dependent on allies over whom they had no control and highly vulnerable to changes in the Cold War environment.

At the same time as he had to contend with the Algerian government and maintain the favor of his allies in the DPRK and Vietnam, Cleaver also struggled with problems inside the international section and the BPP. Nothing in his experience as author, activist, and revolutionary had prepared him for the day-to-day logistical challenges of housing, feeding, and caring for over twenty people, including several young children, while simultaneously carrying out delicate international diplomacy and plotting guerrilla war. At times Cleaver sounded like a frustrated middle manager as he lamented the messy state of the headquarters villa and the failure to empty trash cans in a timely fashion, musing, "Maybe we need a suggestion box in this motherfucker, maybe that'll solve the problem."[30] Not surprisingly, given the hothouse atmosphere of exile in Algiers, maintaining party discipline was more challenging than taking out the trash. There were persistent though never proven rumors that Eldridge had murdered one of the members of the international section, Clinton Rahim Smith, after discovering that he had had an affair with Kathleen Cleaver.[31] Both Cleavers denied these allegations, but privately Kathleen blasted her husband for his own extramarital activities as well as for physically abusing her on multiple occasions.[32]

Problems in maintaining internal cohesion grew even worse with the arrival of individuals with little direct connection to the BPP and sometimes a tenuous grasp of reality. LSD guru Timothy Leary had been serving a time at a minimum-security prison for drug offenses when he escaped in September 1970 and subsequently made his way to Algeria with help from allies in the Weather Underground. The international section agreed (with Huey Newton's approval) to house Leary and his wife Rosemary in exile, but the impish "pope of dope" was a poor fit for the Panthers and their nascent international organization.[33] Leary's insistence on proselytizing the joys of acid while in Algiers, aided by a stash of over one thousand tabs of "Orange Sunshine" smuggled over by supporters from the United States, brought additional unwanted attention from local authorities. The last straw was apparently his efforts to dose members of the Algerian secret police, whom he had invited to a party. Cleaver responded by placing Leary and his wife under house arrest, an action he described as a "revolutionary bust," while publicly decrying the negative impact of drug culture on the revolution.[34] These internal problems in Algiers, which would later grow with the arrival of hijackers who had only tenuous connections to the BPP, were compounded by increasing tension with the leaders of the Oakland-based Panthers.

Huey Newton and "Revolutionary Intercommunalism"

While the minister of information and his crew of exiles pursued state-level allies in Asia and plotted urban guerrilla warfare in the United States, the Oakland Panthers and many of the other U.S. chapters moved away from violent confrontations and Cold War politics in favor of local community service programs in 1969–70. The roots of this growing divide went back as far as the internal dispute over Cleaver's botched ambush of the OPD in April 1968. The differences grew in the wake of Cleaver's flight from the United States, as those left behind struggled to deal with the daily challenges posed by police repression and the party's mounting legal woes. Prior to 1971, several factors prevented the Oakland and Algiers contingents from formally splitting. The first was that Panther leaders in the United States had yet to develop an ideological alternative to the Cold War internationalism that Cleaver pushed as part of his Asian strategy. Although the community-focused work of the U.S. party increasingly clashed with the international section's emphasis on guerrilla warfare and the nuances of Juche and Korean reunification, those running the party in Oakland struggled to formulate a way to incorporate this new approach into a coherent ideological vision for black liberation. Newton and Seale had drawn heavily on the anticolonial analysis and militant rhetoric of Fanon, Mao, and Che Guevara in founding the party, and the Panthers had identified with the Vietnamese struggle from the very beginning. Ideologically repositioning the party as a domestic community service organization was a delicate task, even without Cleaver waving the banner of revolution and international proletarian solidarity from Algiers. This challenge was compounded by the fact that both Newton and Seale (convicted of charges stemming from his role in the demonstrations at the 1968 Democratic National Convention in Chicago) were imprisoned for much of 1969–70. In their absence, there was no BPP leader with the stature to publicly challenge Cleaver. As the ranking Panther leader in the United States not behind bars, Chief of Staff David Hilliard had his hands full managing the party's daily operations and was ill prepared to take on the high-profile Cleaver and his new allies. The result was an uneasy truce between Oakland and Algiers, with the two factions moving in different directions while publicly maintaining a unified front.

Huey Newton's release from prison on August 5, 1970, radically shifted the balance of power within the party's wings. Newton initially appeared to endorse Cleaver's strategy of Cold War internationalism and anticolonial violence. On the day of his release he held a press conference at which he offered Black Panther volunteers to the resistance forces in South Vietnam. Shortly afterward he formalized this offer in a letter to the NLF and PRG, promising "an undetermined number of troops to assist you in your fight against American imperialism." In offering Panthers to fight in Vietnam, he invoked "the spirit of international revolutionary solidarity" as well as the party's "obligation to . . . advance Marxism-Leninism." Although the Vietnamese politely declined, Newton's decision to "offer these troops in recognition of the necessity for international alliances to deal with this problem [of U.S. imperialism]," seemed a straightforward endorsement of Cleaver's strategy of Cold War alliance building in Asia.[35] In an interview a week after his release, Newton followed up these statements by reasserting that "[o]ur program is armed struggle" and that "[w]e have hooked up with the people who are rising up all over the world with arms, because we feel that only with the power of the gun will the bourgeoisie be destroyed and the world transformed." Asked about the BPP's influences, he followed Cleaver in invoking "Fidel and Che, Ho Chi Minh and Mao and Kim Il Sung, but also all the guerrilla bands that have been operating in Mozambique and Angola, and the Palestinian guerrillas who are fighting for a socialist world."[36] Newton also bolstered his revolutionary credentials by winning the support of George Jackson, a California convict who had become politicized behind bars and who declared that "[t]he people of the U.S. are held in the throes of a form of colonialism" and that "[t]here is no case of successful liberation without violence."[37] Jackson's case attracted even greater attention when his younger brother Jonathan was killed in a shootout at the Marin County Courthouse in August 1970 in a failed bid to win his freedom. Vowing to continue the struggle from jail, George Jackson aligned himself with the BPP and founded the San Quentin branch of the party. At a time when the national leadership of the party was moving toward less confrontational approaches centered around community service, the alliance with Jackson and his followers helped inoculate Newton against charges that the Panthers had abandoned their commitment to revolution by any means necessary.[38]

Even as he publicly supported Jackson, Cleaver, the international section, and the Asian strategy, Newton was already in the process of steering the Panthers in a new direction at the time of his release from prison. While still behind bars, Newton had privately worried that the attention accorded to Cleaver's Asian allies in the *Black Panther* was alienating the party from its core supporters in the United States. "Who are we selling papers to?" he complained in a tape sent from prison to Hilliard, "the black community, or the Chinese or the Koreans?" At Newton's behest, the Panther newspaper changed its format in November 1969, consigning international news to a separate section at the end of the paper.[39] This seemingly cosmetic change was in fact quite significant, signaling a retreat from Cleaver's emphasis on intertwining Third World internationalism and Cold War geopolitics with the daily struggles of urban black America. International developments were repositioned as related to, but separate from, the party's work in the United States. At the same time, Newton endorsed a series of practical measures that gradually repositioned the Panthers as more locally focused and reform-oriented. In addition to the various survival programs, the party organized a series of dispersed National Committees to Combat Fascism (NCCF) to lobby for community control of the police. This initiative was consistent with the BPP's increasing emphasis on tackling practical issues such as police brutality through community action at the local level rather than waiting for a revolution that might never come or depending on international allies thousands of miles away.[40] As early as September 1970, a month after Newton's release from prison, a CIA report on Newton's address to the Revolutionary People's Constitutional Convention (RPCC) in Philadelphia observed that "the Panther's undisputed No. 1 leader and martyr, was considerable more moderate in his address, to the gathering."[41] The biggest changes, however, came in the fall of 1970 as Newton went public with a new vision for the Panthers that directly challenged Cleaver's Cold War internationalism and emphasis on anticolonial violence.

During an address at Boston College on November 18, 1970, Newton introduced his concept of intercommunalism. While he had briefly alluded to this new analysis of the party's international relations at a speech in September, the Boston College appearance represented the first time that the party's cofounder and newly dubbed "supreme commander" explained it in depth to a public audience.[42] The central precept, which Newton continued to expand upon in the months that followed, was that the United States was not only an empire but also one so powerful and far-reaching that it had fundamentally changed everything. The difference between the contemporary U.S. empire and previous empires, such as that of the Romans, was "that other nations were able to exist external to and independent of the Roman Empire because their means of exploration, conquest, and control were all relatively limited." In the second half of the twentieth century, however, the combination of technology, particularly in transportation and mass media, with the unprecedented military and financial power wielded by the United States on behalf of corporate capitalism had so permeated the

Newton & US empire

rest of the world that it had undermined the very notion of the nation-state. Thus, "when we say 'empire' today, we mean precisely what we say. An empire is a nation-state that has transformed itself into a power controlling *all* the world's lands and people."[43] The result was that for the rest of the world "nationhood did not exist, because they did not have the criteria for nationhood. Because their self-determination was destroyed, because their economic determination was destroyed, because their cultural determination was transformed."[44] In place of a collection of jostling nation-states was a single, hegemonic world system controlled directly or indirectly by powerful capitalist interests in the United States.

Following from Newton's suppositions about the nature of the U.S. empire were several prescriptions for those movements seeking to resist it. First, he concluded that traditional anticolonialism, which aimed at the restoration of nation-states free from imperial domination, was no longer a viable strategy. "If a people is colonized," Newton explained, "it must be possible for them to decolonize and become what they formerly were."

> But what happens when the raw materials are extracted and labor is exploited within a territory dispersed over the entire globe? When the riches of the whole earth are depleted and used to feed a gigantic industrial machine in the imperialist's home? Then the people and the economy are so integrated into the imperialist empire that it's impossible to 'decolonize,' to return to the former conditions of existence.[45]

The BPP leader was frank in acknowledging that this new thesis required overturning some of the fundamental assumptions upon which the party had been built. In announcing intercommunalism, he simultaneously renounced the colonial analysis of black America that had its roots in the writings of Harold Cruse, had been further developed by RAM in the early 1960s, and had been a foundational element of the BPP's philosophy in the latter half of that decade. Acknowledging that "[w]e used to call ourselves before we became conscious, a dispersed collection of colonies here in North America," Newton conceded that the party's critics had been correct all along in asserting that "you're not a nation, you're a community." And if it no longer made sense to think of black Americans as a colonized people or a "nation within a nation," it was equally futile to pursue international alliances premised on the primacy of the nation-state as the foundational unit of world politics. "We are no longer internationalists," Newton declared in his Boston College speech. "We're not afraid about that."[46]

In place of anticolonial internationalism, Newton offered "revolution-ary intercommunalism" to meet the changed circumstances confronting oppressed people in the late twentieth century. In a dialectical analysis drawing on Marx and Hegel, Newton suggested that just as capitalism had replaced feudalism, "the communications revolution, combined with the expansive domination of the American empire," had replaced the old sys-tem of nation-states with a "global village."[47] It was no more possible—or desirable—to return to the days of isolated nation-states than it was to return to feudalism. Rather, the goal of any revolutionary movement should be to replace "reactionary Intercommunalism," which ordered the world system around the principle of profit for a handful of corporate enterprises, with a similarly globalized system "that would allow the people of the world to develop a culture that is essentially human and would nurture those things that would allow the people to resolve contradictions in a way that would not cause the mutual slaughter of all of us."[48] Just as capital-ism had created the possibility of socialism, the material and technological developments that made possible "reactionary Intercommunalism" created the opportunity for a more utopian "revolutionary Intercommunalism" that avoided the worst feature of both nationalism and capitalism by binding the world's people together regardless of color, creed, culture, or nationality. In striving to reach this goal, the central organizing unit was not the nation (or proto-nation) but the community: "a small unit with a comprehensive collection of institutions that exist to serve a small group of people."[49] As each community, whether it be black Americans, Asian Americans, or those struggling for freedom in the nations of the Third World, achieved control over its own local institutions it would improve the lives of its residents while laying the groundwork for a "universal identity that extends beyond family, tribe, or nation."[50]

Newton's intercommunalism posed obvious questions about the future operations of the BPP. If the Panthers were "no longer internationalists" and no longer committed to a guerrilla war for national liberation (as such a venture was no longer tenable in light of the end of nation-states as effective units), what was to be the party's role going forward? Newton provided two answers to this question. First, the BPP, as a vanguard organization, would educate the masses about the new realities of reactionary intercommunal-ism and the nature of the U.S. empire in order to prepare them for the struggles to come. "The primary concern of the Black Panther Party," he declared, "is to lift the level of consciousness of the people through theory and practice to the point where they will see exactly what is controlling them and what is oppressing them, and therefore see exactly what has to be done—or at least what the first step is."[51] Second, while promoting the growth of a mass consciousness in opposition to empire, the BPP would ensure the survival of the black community in the United States through its various service programs. If the world was, as Newton posited, a collection of dispersed communities rather than discrete nations, then it made sense to focus the party's efforts on its own local community while preparing to link with others around the world engaging in similar efforts. "[U]ntil such time that we can achieve . . . total transformation," Newton declared, "we must exist. In order to exist, we must survive, so, therefore, we need a survival kit." Building on the party's existing community programs, he repositioned the notion of self-defense as something more than "patrolling the pigs" or plotting guerrilla warfare:

> The violence of the aggressor comes in many forms. The vicious service-revolver of the police is only one manifestation of violence. But it is equally violent for the State and the small ruling circle to deprive the people of housing, of medical care, of food, of clothing, those acts are acts of aggression, when we live in such an affluent society. The Black Panther Party views those acts as very violent ones.[52]

In this analysis, the act of feeding schoolchildren or providing free health care to senior citizens was just as revolutionary and infinitely more practical and effective than standing up to the OPD with a loaded shotgun. "The gun itself is not necessarily revolutionary," as Newton explained, "because the fascists carry guns—in fact they have more guns."[53]

As an intellectual contribution to understanding transnational capitalism and its discontents in the late twentieth century, intercommunalism has attracted praise from a number of scholars.[54] While Newton undoubtedly exaggerated the extent to which transnational capitalism had entirely replaced nationalism as the driving force in world affairs, his analysis was prescient in looking beyond both the Cold War and decolonization while anticipating the rise of neoliberal globalization in the decades to come. President Richard Nixon's dramatic bid to open relations with China, the rise of Soviet-American détente, the crisis of the U.S.-led Bretton Woods international monetary system in the early 1970s, the neoliberal turn of the 1980s, and the decline of the Third World as an effective political construct all seemed to conform to Newton's predictions about the shifting nature of the world system. In adapting Marxism to fit the changed circumstances of late-twentieth-century U.S. hegemony, he anticipated the works of scholars such as Michael Hardt and Antonio Negri, whose 2000 book *Empire* shared much in common with Newton's intercommunalism. "We can't go back to our mother's womb, nor can we go back to 1917," Newton declared. Intercommunalism was a creative attempt to apply the practical lessons he had learned with the BPP to a searching analysis that retained the dialectical spirit of Marxism while acknowledging its limitations in grappling with a world fundamentally remade by capitalism in the nearly one hundred years since Marx's death.[55] In its focus on transnational organizing at the community level, intercommunalism also offered the possibility of organizing for liberation free from entanglements with either a hopelessly corrupt U.S. state apparatus or foreign governments that, however well meaning, had little understanding of the history and circumstances facing black Americans.

Intercommunalism was also a tactical masterstroke in its ability to provide an ideological justification for the shift in party operations to play to the Panthers' practical strengths while steering away from activities that had proved for the most part counterproductive, at least in the United States. The BPP had always excelled in its ability to convey complicated concepts such as colonialism, institutionalized white supremacy, and Third World internationalism in a fashion accessible to the brothers and sisters on the block, whether in the form of the party's early armed patrols or in the anticolonial vernacular on display in the artwork of Emory Douglas and in the pages of the *Black Panther*. And while of more recent vintage, the BPP's survival programs had proven to be popular and effective at the local level.[56] The party's sporadic (and Pyrrhic) attempts at guerrilla action, meanwhile, had showed no signs of precipitating a revolution that would unseat the U.S. government. As Newton explained it, "we'll reach the shore when the people reach the level of consciousness to change the society, and therefore change the world. Until that time. . . . it is very necessary to stop just talking about revolution, because you might not be able to participate; you might not be able to participate, if you are wiped out beforehand."[57] Similarly, while Cleaver's international alliances had brought publicity to the Panthers and help underwrite the existence of the international section in Algiers, they had had little tangible impact on the day-to-day operations of the party in the United States. Whatever one made of the "genius" of Kim Il-sung, from the perspective of the Oakland-based leadership neither the Koreans nor any of Cleaver's Asian allies were in an immediate position to protect the Panthers from police harassment or improve the daily life of black Americans.

For all of its theoretical and practical merits, intercommunalism suffered from a number of problems and contradictions at its inception. The biggest unanswered questions centered on its practical implantation. Specifically, given the tremendous economic and military power wielded by the U.S. empire, how could a loosely bound collection of dispersed communities ever hope to overthrow it in order to advance to the utopian vision of revolutionary intercommunalism outlined by Newton? Cleaver's North American Liberation Front had the virtue of at least offering a clear plan for affecting change: urban guerrilla warfare against the supposed soft underbelly of U.S. capitalism, followed by the overthrow of the federal government with aid from sympathetic foreign government and fellow guerrillas around the world. Newton, in contrast, focused on education and community survival programs in part as a way of deferring the difficult question of how, exactly, to enact large-scale, revolutionary change in the face of such powerful resistance. Even if successful at the local level, what good would it do to control a single community, whether in Oakland or Vietnam, so long as the United States maintained a hegemonic grip over the world system through a combination of military and financial might? As Newton himself noted, "A community evolves around a greater structure that we usually call the state and the state has certain control over the community."[58] This was a problem that had long vexed black nationalist movements in the United States, and Newton had little to offer in response other than vague notions of cooperation between these dispersed communities to undermine reactionary intercommunalism from within. Newton's vision of a decentralized, transnational anti-imperialist movement rooted in local grassroots activism was attractive to the extent that it avoided the kind of compromising entanglements and power imbalances that characterized Cleaver's Cold War internationalism. In the short term, however, intercommunalism entailed turning away from the tenuous but nevertheless real alliances that the party had built in Asia with little in the way of a practical replacement. As New York Panther Assata Shakur remarked, "The problem [with intercommunalism] was that somebody had forgotten to tell these oppressed communities that they were no longer nations."[59]

The theoretical challenges posed by intercommunalism were compounded by Newton's difficulties in explaining this new theory to an often confused and reluctant rank and file. Unlike figures such as Cleaver, Bobby Seale, or Elaine Brown, Newton had never been a particularly dynamic or comfortable public speaker. His leadership in the early days of the party had relied instead on individual acts of bravery and his ability to work

well in small group situations to rally a select core of members.[60] Upon his
release from prison, Newton confronted the daunting task of repositioning
a party that had dozens of chapters spread around the United States as well
as legions of supporters not directly affiliated with the Panthers, many of
whom saw the minister of defense as a one-dimensional icon of black manhood and anticolonial violence. Even staunch party loyalists were shocked
when Newton took the stage to deliver, in a reedy voice, dense addresses
that were short on rhetorical bombast and long on dialectical material-
ism. Shakur recalled that "almost no one understood Huey's long speeches
explaining intercommunalism," saying that "he had a kind of high-pitched
monotonous voice and his rambling for three hours about the negation of
the negation was sheer disaster."[61] Philadelphia Panther Mumia Abu-Jamal
agreed, writing, "Huey, [who] we all would have died for in a heartbeat, was
not a good public speaker."[62] It did not help that his message of abandoning
traditional anticolonialism and international alliances clashed dramatically
with long-held BPP positions. Newton struggled mightily to try to convey
the complexities of intercommunalism, admitting ruefully in 1971, "So far
I haven't been able to do it well enough to keep from being booed off the
stage."[63] Given that education was one of the pillars of his new strategy,
Newton's inability to convince his own closest allies was troubling. Hilliard
observed that party members were "impatient and dismissive of Huey's new
theory," and even sympathetic scholars have agreed that intercommunalism
was generally ignored or rejected by the Panther rank and file.[64]

In prioritizing education and the survival programs while downplaying
talk of immediate revolution and alliances with nation-states, Newton's
intercommunalism provided the ideological basis for a break with Cleaver
and his operations in Algeria. Tied to this shift were more subtle changes in
the way that party leaders understood and articulated gender and sexuality,
which in turn paved the way for an alternative approach to both domestic
and international operations. Shortly after his release from prison, Newton published an article in the *Black Panther* calling on party members to
embrace feminism and gay rights. Acknowledging the existence of patriarchy, misogyny, and homophobia within party, Newton observed that "we
want to hit a homosexual in the mouth because we are afraid we might be
homosexual; and we want to hit the woman or shut her up because we are
afraid that she might castrate us, or take the nuts that we might not have
to start with." The time had come, however, to give up these "insecurities"
and "hang-ups" in order to establish a "revolutionary value system." In practice this meant forming "a working coalition with the gay liberation and

women's liberation movements." It also required changing the way party members thought and behaved, including forsaking the use of homophobic slur such as "faggot" and "punk" (the latter term being one oft-employed by Cleaver).[65] Within the party itself, Panther women, including Ericka Huggins and Elaine Brown, occupied increasingly important roles within the national leadership in the early 1970s. When combined with intercommunalism and its emphasis on transnational community building, the BPP's new position on gender and sexuality constituted a direct challenge to the link between national liberation, armed struggle, and manhood that characterized the early years of the party and continued to dominate Cleaver's operations in exile. While Cleaver sought "to stand up as black men inside of Babylon and to give the pigs ... [a] taste of their own medicine," the U.S.-based Panthers were beginning to explore alternate notions of liberation and transnational cooperation less rooted in the male politics of violence.[66]

The Split in the Party

Ironically, given intercommunalism's emphasis on an interconnected global village, the distance between Algiers and Oakland and the difficulty of coordinating activities via sporadic long-distance phone calls initially helped prevent a direct clash between Newton and Cleaver and their increasingly divergent approaches to black liberation. Cleaver publicly endorsed the party's new approach by renaming his operation the "Intercommunal Section" in deference to Newton's wishes.[67] Privately, however, the Algiers contingent found intercommunalism to be "gibberish" fueled by Newton's "cult of personality." Kathleen Cleaver told me that "we changed [the name] to be disciplined and accepting but it was very awkward."

> It was incoherent particularly if you are part of a socialist-world that practices, or at least gives lip-service to, international proletarian solidarity. . . . And solidarity is how we are able to live there and stay [in Algeria].[68]

In practice, Cleaver continued to pursue the same combination of state-level Cold War alliances and commitment to guerrilla warfare that had marked his operations in Algiers prior to Newton's release. Free from outside interference, it is conceivable that the domestic and international wings of the BPP could have worked out a way to coexist or even operate in complementary fashion despite their many differences. The PLO, with whom

Cleaver regularly interacted in Algiers, offered an example of a contemporary liberation group with a dispersed base that often disagreed on both tactical and strategic matters but remained functional in spite of this. Any hopes of replicating this example, however, were doomed by the efforts of the U.S. government.

With a network of informants within the party and telephone taps intercepting communications between Oakland and Algiers, the FBI (with help from the CIA's MH/CHAOS program) was well positioned to exploit the divide between the Newton-led Panthers in the United States and the Cleaver's international section.[69] Beginning in March 1970, FBI agents forged letters designed to widen the rift between Newton and Cleaver and convince each man that the other was plotting against him. After dispatching these letters to their intended targets, FBI agents then eavesdropped on the ensuing communications within the party that they provoked, observing with pleasure on February 25, 1971, that "the fortunes of the BPP are at a low ebb."[70] Kathleen Cleaver later recalled that upon receiving the letters, "We did not know who to believe about what, so the general effect, not only of the letter but the whole situation in which the letters were part was creating uncertainty. It was a very bizarre feeling."[71] The differences between Oakland and Algiers were real and might well have eventually led to a break even without outside intervention. The FBI's efforts, however, forced the issue and escalated the stakes such that when the split did finally take place it spilled over into violence between the two factions.

Privately Cleaver lamented in a December 1970 letter to Newton that "we are being blocked, by you, because of your refusal or failure to [communicate] with us[,] to inform us," pleading with Newton to continue printing material from his revolutionary Asian allies.[72] The breaking point finally arrived on February 26, one day after the FBI's gleeful report on the BPP's internal problems. The precipitating factor was Newton's decision to purge some of the party's most militant advocates of guerrilla warfare. Purges were not new, as the dramatic rise in membership and the creation of local branches across the United States starting in 1968 had forced Panthers leaders to periodically expel members for offenses such as being drunk on duty or on suspicion of being an informant.[73] In early 1971, however, Newton specifically targeted Panthers either involved with or advocating for underground guerrilla campaigns. In January he expelled Geronimo Pratt (later ji-Jaga), a decorated Vietnam veteran who had put his military training to use in organizing the defense of the Los Angeles chapter of the Panthers against attacks by the LAPD. In the wake of a December 1969 gun battle with police who were attempting to raid the Panthers' L.A. headquarters, Pratt went underground on instructions from the BPP's Central Committee. Sent to the American South, his primary task was to work with other members of the underground to organize a military force that would serve as the clandestine military wing of the BPP.[74] By 1971, however, this operation no longer fit into Newton's vision for the Panthers and threatened his efforts to reposition the party. Given the paranoia deliberately stoked by COINTELPRO, Newton was also likely concerned about the existence within the BPP of an underground army over which he had little control.

After Pratt was arrested in Dallas in 1970 and charged with a 1968 murder in Santa Monica, Newton publicly purged him and several of his closest comrades from the party, effectively cutting off the nascent underground operation. One month later, Newton expelled the so-called Panther 21, a group of New York City BPP members who were on trial for conspiracy to bomb several New York City Police Department stations. Though the national party had initially defended the Panther 21, their public endorsement of the Weather Underground's bombing campaign, combined with an implicit criticism of the more reformist direction coming out of Oakland, brought Newton's ire down upon the New York chapter. When several of the Panther 21 skipped bail and went underground in early February rather than facing trial, Newton responded by publicly purging the entire group.[75] Pratt and many of the New York Panthers had been close to Cleaver and shared his conviction that armed struggle in the United States was both necessary and inevitable. Cleaver had also corresponded privately with members of the Weather Underground and defended them publicly, declaring that "the criticism of the Weathermen that has come to my attention seems to me to be reactionary, invalid and valuable only to the enemy." This was accompanied by a pointed injunction—"Fuck all those who block the revolution with rhetoric—revolutionary rhetoric or counterrevolutionary rhetoric"—which constituted a thinly veiled attack on the more reformist elements within the BPP. Cleaver was thus undoubtedly unnerved by Newton's decision to purge the Panther 21 for voicing similar sentiments.[76]

Combined with the differing ideological visions coming out of Oakland and Algeria and the intra-party paranoia stoked by the FBI's covert letter-writing campaign, the purge tipped the delicate balance that held together the national and international wings of the BPP. In an ill-fated attempt to demonstrate party unity, Newton and Cleaver talked live by telephone on a local Bay Area morning television program on February 26, 1971. Cleaver surprised the Panther leader by using the venue to attack the recent purge, demand the dismissal of David Hilliard, and lament that the BPP was "falling apart."[77] After the tense on-air conversation concluded, a furious Newton stormed out of the studio and placed a private call to Algiers in which he formally expelled Cleaver and the entire international section from the BPP. In the weeks that followed, the *Black Panther*, which remained under Newton's control, published a series of articles attacking Eldridge and claiming that he was holding Kathleen Cleaver prisoner in Algiers. Newton followed with a long essay in April lamenting that Cleaver's fixation on the gun and guerrilla warfare had "influenced us to isolate ourselves from the Black community, so that it was war between the oppressor and the Black Panther Party, not war between the oppressor and the oppressed community." With Cleaver gone, however, "we are now free to move toward the building of a community structure which will become a true voice of the people, promoting their interests in many ways."[78]

Behind the scenes, Newton sought to neutralize Cleaver's operation in Algeria. Recognizing that Cleaver was dependent on the continued support of his nation-state partners, particularly those in Asia, Newton warned the exiled minister of information, "I'm going to write the Koreans, I'm going to write the Chinese, and the Algerians to kick you out of our embassy."[79] The U.S. Panther leadership soon followed up on this threat with letters to Fidel Castro, Kim Il-sung, Prince Norodom Sihanouk, Pham Van Dong, and others, condemning "the dangerously infantile leftist practices of Mr. Eldridge Cleaver" and warning that he and his allies in Algeria "no longer represent the Black Panther Party."[80] The most immediate consequences of the split, however, were felt within the United States, as Panther members and chapters were forced to pick sides between the Newton and Cleaver factions. While the national leadership of the BPP maintained control over the party's infrastructure, most notably the *Black Panther*, as well as retaining at least nominal oversight of the remaining local chapters, Cleaver and the international section maintained a strong base of support among Panthers in New York, New Jersey, San Francisco, and Los Angeles.[81]

Partisans on each side engaged in rhetorical as well as real violence in the months after the split, including at least two murders (Robert Webb of the Cleaver-aligned New York City Panthers and Robert Napier, distribution manager for the *Black Panther*).[82] "For a period," recalled San Francisco Panther (and Cleaver supporter) Nuh Washington, "our attention was taken away from the people as we concentrated on former comrades who were viewed as more serious threats than our enemies."

"Off the Pig" was replaced in New York with "Off Huey Newton." In San Francisco, paranoia was rampant as comrades struggled whether to strike first rather than wait for "hit squads." These so-called "hit squads" were seen as mindless robots doing the bidding of "the Servant" (Newton). Consequently, comrades holed up in safe houses, snuck in and out of San Francisco and Los Angeles for meetings, played whist, cooked communal meals and drank "bitterdog." Such living divorces one from the people, and induces fear that paralyzes or makes one reckless.[83]

Even more destructive to the long-term future of the party than sporadic violence unleashed by the split was the widespread sense of fear and disillusionment among the rank and file that followed. As one Panther member put it, "The ideological split between Huey and Eldridge scared me more than the police ever could."[84] Philadelphia Panther Mumia Abu-Jamal was blunter, declaring:

> Cleaver was an idol to me; Newton whom I had once served as a bodyguard, a hero. The prospect of us fighting one another sickened me. "I didn't join the BPP to get in a goddamn gang war!' I thought angrily to myself. "Shit! I could've stayed in North Philly for this dumb shit!"[85]

As sectarian strife roiled the BPP in the months that followed, many Panthers drifted away from the party, and by some accounts as many as 40 percent of members left.[86] Some founded their own local organizations, such as the Black United Liberation Front (BULF) in Philadelphia and the Sons of Malcolm in Kansas City, while others joined existing community groups or new organizations such as the Republic of New Afrika (RNA), entered into mainstream politics, or simply returned to "civilian" life.[87]

Amidst the chaos unleashed by the BPP's fragmentation and the ongoing FBI and police efforts to finish off the Panthers, three groups offering contrasting interpretations of the party's original mandate stood out as challengers on the national and international stage during the early 1970s. Under Newton and then Elaine Brown, the BPP kept its name but closed its regional chapters and consolidated the remaining members as part of a "Base of Operations" strategy to seize political and economic control over the city of Oakland. Although Newton traveled to China, Cuba, and the Middle East in the ensuing decade, the post-1971 BPP downplayed international alliances in favor of building one spoke of a larger transnational hub through its local operations in the Bay Area. Cleaver and the remnants of the international section, meanwhile, pursued an array of international and transnational strategies for keeping alive their dream of a revolution that would overthrow the government of the United States. After exploring connections with socialist governments in Africa, Cleaver eventually embraced the example set by Palestinian Black September guerrillas and their strategy of transnational anticolonial violence. A third group, the Black Liberation Army (BLA) emerged from the remnants of the BPP's underground wing in the United States. Although the BLA shared Cleaver's commitment to revolutionary violence and at times collaborated with the exiles in Algiers, in practice its small, clandestine cells focused more on directly applying the lessons of figures such as Carlos Marighella (a Brazilian revolutionary and author of the *Mini-Manual of the Urban Guerrilla*) in the United States rather than working on cultivating international or transnational connections.

For all the disastrous human consequences that followed in its wake, one positive result of the split was that it afforded the opportunity for the resulting splinter groups to formulate their approaches to black liberation free from the burden of having to balance the loosely wound coalition that had characterized the party prior to the break. While Newton challenged Cleaver by declaring that "we'll battle like two bulls, we'll lock horns," the 1970s saw many Panthers and ex-Panthers moving beyond the macho posturing and male-dominated leadership that characterized much of the party's early history.[88] Both the BPP and the BLA featured women in important leadership positions during this period, while Kathleen Cleaver and Denise Oliver played crucial roles in keeping what was left of the international section and its operations afloat. Although in retrospect it seems clear that the BPP and its splinter groups were doomed and would not last out the decade, the years following the Newton-Cleaver break saw leaders in Algiers, Oakland, and the black underground offering innovative practical and ideological improvisations as they attempted to grapple with the consequences of the split, ongoing government repression, and the changing international and domestic climate of the détente era.

Chapter 7

"Cosmopolitan Guerrillas"

The International Section and the RPCN, 1971–1973

In a tense private phone conversation following their televised argument on February 26, 1971, Huey Newton warned Eldridge Cleaver in Algiers, saying, "I'd like a battle, brother. We'll battle it out." Deflecting Cleaver's attempts at conciliation, the BPP's cofounder terminated the conversation by expelling the international section and yelling, "You're a punk!"[1] When the two hung up, the Black Panther Party as it had existed since its inception in October 1966 was essentially dead. In the wake of the split, Cleaver raged against "the conniving scheming designing treacherous jackanapes, who have been . . . plotting behind their backs to destroy . . . righteous revolutionaries, motherfuckers who have righteously put their lives on the line and gotten down, the napes have stabbed them in the back."[2] In practice, however, Newton's expulsion of the international section had little immediate effect on day-to-day operations in Algiers. Communications with Oakland had been tenuous even at the best of times, and the international section's existence depended far more on the favor of the Algerian government and Cleaver's Asian allies than it did on Newton, Brown, Hilliard or anyone else within the U.S.-based BPP. Newton attempted to disrupt these relationships by dispatching letters repudiating Cleaver to his foreign allies and publishing warnings in the pages of the

Black Panther.[3] The exiles in Algiers, however, countered by collaborating with former Panthers in New York and allies in West Germany to construct an alternative leadership structure and publish newspapers (*Right On!*, *Babylon*, and *Voice of the Lumpen*) that would contest Newton's control of the BPP in the United States and provide institutional legitimacy to the international section in its dealings with other governments.[4]

Ironically, the most dramatic blow to the international section came not from Cleaver's rivals in the BPP, whom he derisively referred to as the "Peralta Street Gang," but rather from one of his putative Asian allies.[5] Nixon's bid to open relations with Mao's China in 1971–72 dramatically disrupted the Cold War dynamics in Asia that had facilitated the ongoing operations of the international section. Not yet ready to give up the fight, Cleaver and his fellow exiles instead sought to reorient their operations in response to changing domestic and international conditions. Initially hopeful of moving his base of operations to the People's Republic of the Congo, Cleaver ultimately embraced a strategy for transnational anticolonial violence that was in many ways the mirror image of Newton's intercommunalism. Fueled by new technology (particularly Sony handheld video recorders) and the tireless efforts of Kathleen Cleaver, the Revolutionary People's Communications Network (RPCN) served as the aboveground apparatus connecting the exiles in Algiers with former Panthers and allies around the world. The ultimate goal, however, remained not simply communications but revolution. Inspired by the German Red Army Faction and the Palestinian Black September guerrilla group, Cleaver hoped that the RPCN would facilitate his own vision of "Cosmopolitan Guerrillas" who would exploit "the landscape of technology, the channels and circuits of our environment," in order to strike across borders against "all pigs and pig structures."[6]

"Pig Nixon," Sino-American Rapprochement, and a Turn to Africa

In October 1971, six months after their expulsion from the BPP, the members of the international section watched in horror as the secret efforts at Sino-American rapprochement that had begun shortly after Richard Nixon took office exploded into public view. "When the news came that Henry Kissinger was in Peking making arrangements for Richard Nixon to go to China," Cleaver recalled, "it fell like an atomic bomb in Algeria."[7] China had never figured as prominently in Cleaver's ad hoc diplomacy as

Nixon

Vietnam and North Korea had. Nevertheless, the revelation that Mao was prepared to negotiate with "Pig Nixon" was a bitterly disillusioning experience. "As long as there was Mao and his Red Book proclaiming war and the people's struggle," Cleaver lamented, "there was something to look toward."

> There was some standard even though it was shaky and somewhat suspicious. There was still a way of defining even the Soviet Union, for instance, as revisionists because the Chinese were there and they were still pure. But when you see Nixon shaking hands with Mao and you know what Nixon is about, then the whole system just disintegrates. And since all of this happened to us and wasn't in History books it's not surprising that we were traumatized because our whole (ideological) mental structures collapsed and well, they just have to be rebuilt, you know.[8]

Cleaver, however, would have neither the time nor the space to rebuild as the ideological shock of Nixon's overture to China signaled a fundamental shift in the Cold War environment in the early 1970s.

Historian Jeremi Suri has argued that U.S., Chinese, and Soviet leaders embraced détente in part out of a shared desire to contain the domestic unrest that roiled the industrialized world in the late 1960s.[9] Nixon's overture to Beijing was obviously motivated by more than a desire to undercut the Black Panthers, but the administration was certainly aware of the BPP and its foreign operations as it undertook preparations for the meeting. Kissinger had been among the recipients of FBI and CIA reports on Cleaver's operation in Algiers, and the secretary of state invoked Huey Newton by name in an offhand remark about the terms of a proposed Sino-American agreement during his secret negotiations with Zhou Enlai in 1971.[10] Whether by design or happenstance, Nixon's engagement with China, combined with the gradual U.S. withdrawal from Vietnam, proved devastating to Cleaver's operation in exile. The Nixon-Mao summit, he noted bitterly, "started a whole stampede throughout the Third World and Socialist World for establishing a diplomatic relationship with the United States."[11] Most foreign governments, he wrote, "don't want to fuck with Uncle Sam" to begin with, and in the changing international climate of the early 1970s even those handful of revolutionary nations "who have related to [the Panthers' struggle] at a stage when it seemed to be something romantic and not involving very much . . . now are beginning to get up-tight because the pressure is getting stronger and the situation is heating-up."[12]

Nixon's foreign policy initiatives had particularly dramatic effects on smaller nations that had looked to the PRC for inspiration and support, including Cleaver's two closest Asian allies, North Vietnam and the DPRK. "Various countries, which we thought were our friends and allies to the end," he lamented, "are now making a separate peace with our sworn enemy, the fascist imperialist U.S. government and ruling class."[13] In the aftermath of the Nixon-Mao meeting, Kim Il-sung began to reposition the DPRK internationally. While still engaged in the Third World, Kim's government reacted to the changing international environment and its own increasingly strained domestic situation by building economic relationships with avowed capitalist enemies, including Japan and countries in western Europe (most notably France), and opening negotiations with South Korea.[14] In a sign of the shifting currents unleashed by Nixon's diplomacy, when Cleaver warned that Sino-American rapprochement would undercut efforts to internationalize the black freedom struggle, the North Koreans rebuked him, accusing the exiled former Panther of engaging in the cardinal sin of "revisionism."[15] North Vietnam and the PRG continued to court public support from antiwar elements in the United States and elsewhere as leverage for the ongoing peace negotiations in Paris. But as the end of the war loomed, the leadership of a soon-to-be united Vietnam was more interested in rebuilding and dealing with regional rivals than in cultivating an anticolonial coalition that included groups such as the BPP or the international section.[16] Cleaver's canny exploitation of Cold War geopolitics in revolutionary Asia had made possible the founding and continued existence of the international section in Algeria. His inability to control those developments, however, was dramatically demonstrated when, in Cleaver's words, "Richard Nixon and Henry Kissinger went to China and stole Mao Tse-Tung away from us."[17] There was no single, dramatic break between Cleaver and his Vietnamese and North Korean patrons. Rather, the combination of his expulsion from the BPP and the larger shifts brought about by détente, Sino-American rapprochement, and the winding down of the Vietnam War led to a gradual disengagement that left the international section to fend for itself in Algeria.

Diplomatically outmaneuvered by "Pig Nixon" and forcibly confronted with the limits of relying on state-level partners in Asia over whom he had little or no leverage, Cleaver and the international section cast about for new alternatives. Shortly after being expelled from the BPP, the exiles received an invitation to attend the International Conference of Solidarity with the People Under Portuguese Domination held in Brazzaville, the capital of the People's Republic of the Congo. Eldridge and Kathleen Cleaver, along with former New York Panthers Denise Oliver (who was also a member of the Young Lords) and Michael Tabor, traveled to Brazzaville in April 1971, staying several weeks after the conference to attend May Day celebrations, tour training camps for fighters from the Popular Movement for the Liberation of Angola (MPLA), and meet with Congolese military and civilian leaders, including President Marien Ngouabi.[18] Although this trip predated the public revelation of Kissinger's visit to China, Cleaver was already eager to seek additional allies given his perpetually precarious situation in Algiers. In this context, Ngouabi's Marxist-Leninist government seemed to offer all of the ideological affinities of states such as China, the DPRK, and North Vietnam while also sharing unique cultural and historical connections to black Americans that these revolutionary Asian states lacked. Upon his return to Algiers, Cleaver proclaimed that the People's Republic of Congo represented a "synthesis between the cultural aspects of our African connectedness and the revolutionary aspects" and as such was an ideal partner for black Americans looking for allies in their struggle against the U.S. government.[19] To promote this notion, Cleaver approved the release of documentary footage of the trip shot by a photographer, William Stevens, who had accompanied the Panther delegation. The Algerian exiles also collaborated with editors at *Right On!* and *Voice of the Lumpen* to publish a collection of essays extolling the virtues of the Congolese revolution. Among the messages included was the flattering assertion of First Secretary of the Congolese Workers Party Claude-Ernest Ndalla that "the blows that we strike against American imperialism in the Congo, in Vietnam, in Laos, in Cambodia, or in Chile, these blows cannot have the same impact that the blows that the Afro-American people can strike against American imperialism on its own soil."[20]

As a veteran of the struggles between revolutionary nationalists and cultural nationalists in the United States and head of an anticolonial exile group that depended on increasingly tenuous relationships with nation-state allies in Asia, it is hardly surprising that Cleaver embraced the People's Republic of Congo in the aftermath of the delegation's visit in spring 1971. By situating Marxism-Leninism in the context of an indigenous African government, Cleaver suggested such an alliance would "unite the Afro-American liberation struggle stronger that it has even been united before."[21] Specifically, he hailed Ngouabi's government for making concrete the combination of black nationalism, anticolonialism, and proletarian internationalism that Malcolm X had tentatively begun to explore just before his assassination.[22]

As an indigenous African example of Marxism-Leninism, Congo could appeal to black Americans' sense of cultural and racial pride without falling into the trap of narrow ethnic nationalism that might foreclose alliances with revolutionary states and groups outside of Africa. "What the Soviet Union meant to Europe, what China meant to Asia, and what Cuba meant to Latin America," Cleaver declared, "the Peoples' [*sic*] Republic of the Congo means to Africa and to black people everywhere."[23]

Unstated but implicit in these paeans to Congo was the hope that the same sense of cultural affinity that attracted black American support would also bind Ngouabi's government, making it a more reliable partner than allies in Asia, Europe, or elsewhere. This was a need that became ever more pressing in the aftermath of Mao's betrayal. Amid an increasingly precarious situation in Algiers, Cleaver petitioned the People's Republic of Congo to host the international section.[24] As Malcolm X had discovered, however, even friendly African nations had their own needs of state that often trumped ideological, cultural, or racial affinities with black Americans. Cleaver's petition to Ngouabi's government never received a response. This likely stemmed in part from distractions and internal turmoil in Brazzaville and the fact that the needs of a small group of American exiles were simply a low priority for the revolutionary government as it sought to ensure its viability in an increasingly challenging international environment. It certainly did not help that upon hearing of Cleaver's visit, Newton wrote directly to Ngouabi warning that "the Hidden Traitor Renegade Scab Eldridge Cleaver, who presently occupies the Black Panther Embassy in Algiers, Algeria neither represented the Black Panther Party nor any organized Black movement within the United States."[25] Cleaver continued to seek support on the African continent, but his efforts to arrange an audience with exiled Ghanaian leader Kwame Nkrumah were also frustrated, unsurprisingly given that the former president was closely associated with Stokely Carmichael, with whom Cleaver had frequently and publicly feuded.[26]

The RCPN and "Voodoo"

As they searched for a new home for the international section, Eldridge and Kathleen Cleaver also explored ways to continue the revolution without the need for constant state-level support from foreign allies. For all his ideological differences with the leadership of the U.S.-based BPP, the strain of relying on the whims of the Algerian government compounded by Mao's dramatic reversal eventually led them to embrace elements of Newton's intercommunalism. Specifically, they began to look beyond alliances rooted in Cold War internationalism to explore transnational strategies for black liberation in the age of neoliberal hegemony. In 1971, the Cleavers established the Revolutionary People's Communications Network, "an international apparatus for exchange of information among revolutionary peoples and organizations engaged in the international anti-imperialist struggle."[27] Kathleen Cleaver, who played arguably the most important role in building the new organization, declared in an October 1971 press conference that "it's very relevant that . . . revolutionary people have access to their own sources of news about revolutionary activities, not only in this country, with each other, but around the world." This need was particularly pressing given the confusion inspired by the BPP split and the changes in the Cold War environment. It was vital, she declared, "to inform other people of the true strengths and the true weaknesses of the revolutionary movement, so that we may build on the basis of correct information and advance our struggle on the basis of real facts."[28] While building the basis for a transnational revolutionary movement that could survive in the era of détente, the RPCN would also serve the more short-term goal of reconnecting the former-Panther exiles in Algiers with supporters around the world. The transnational solidarity networks that had supported the BPP from 1968 to 1970 had been shaken by the split within the party and the increasingly domestic-focused and reformist drift of the Newton-led Panthers. RCPN publications provided some linkage. The newspaper *Babylon* featured correspondents in Algiers (the Cleavers and Denise Oliver), New York (Janet Cyril), Philadelphia (Mumia Abu-Jamal), San Francisco (J. Frank Lin), and Detroit (Paulette Frye).[29] Meanwhile, Kathleen Cleaver, who was not a fugitive and retained her U.S. passport, traveled extensively in an attempt to rebuild connections with groups around the world that had once sympathized with the Panthers.

The RPCN had its strongest support in New York, home to a number of former Panthers who sympathized with Cleaver and the international section, and in West Germany, where students and activists worked with radical American GIs stationed in Germany who considered themselves a "Black Panther Task Squad."[30] Former German SDS leader Karl Dietrich Wolff, who had helped link that group to the BPP starting in 1969, provided the crucial organizational link between German activists, radical GIs, and the Panther exiles in Algiers. Starting in November 1970, Wolff's small press helped to publish *Voice of the Lumpen*, a newspaper staffed by dissident black soldiers based in Germany. Heavily influenced by the *Black Panther* and its anticolonial vernacular and primarily aimed at U.S. soldiers stationed in Germany, it also served as a link to German activists. Working with radical black GIs and supporting the Panthers offered a chance for Germans disillusioned by the crushing of revolutionary forces in Europe in 1968 and the dissolution of SDS to continue the struggle.[31] At the same time, the stresses placed on the U.S. Seventh Army in Germany by the war in Vietnam, which lead to a drain on its ranks and thinly stretched resources, and ongoing racial tension as a result of institutionalized white supremacy in both the army and German society, made it fertile recruiting ground for self-identified Black Panthers on U.S. bases in the late 1960s and early 1970s.[32] The Cleavers, who already had strong connections to the West German Left, quickly seized on this possibility as they sought to rebuild after the split. The first issue of the RPCN's *Information Bulletin* identified prisons and the military as the two best locations for future organizing and recruiting as both offered highly centralized populations of disaffected black Americans. "[A]ll the righteous, the vast majority, the hard core, the cream of the crop," Eldridge Cleaver declared, are "jacked up, in the prisons and in the pig's military."[33]

An incident in southwestern Germany in late 1970 helped to cement the alliance between elements of the German Left, radical black GIs, and the Cleavers' operations in exile. On November 19, two discharged black soldiers and contributors to *Voice of the Lumpen*, William Burrell and Edward Lawrence Jackson, attempted to enter Ramstein Airbase in order to put up posters promoting a planned visit to Germany by Kathleen Cleaver. Upon being denied entry, Burrell and Jackson were involved in a shooting incident that resulted in injuries to one of the base sentries. The two were subsequently arrested by German police and put on trial in a German courtroom.[34] Although the split of the BPP several months after the shooting incident discouraged many of the Panther support committees, the trial of the so-called Ramstein 2, which began in Zweibrücken in April 1971, provided renewed opportunities for cooperation. At a time when the U.S.-based BPP was moving away from alliances with radical whites in the United States and Europe to focus on local black activism in Oakland, the international section continued to cultivate ties to both German radicals and disaffected GIs. In July, Kathleen Cleaver spoke at the University of Frankfurt in support of the Ramstein 2 and in the process laid the groundwork for transnational links with German activists to replace those that had been damaged following the split.[35] At the conclusion of the trial in August 1971, Burrell was found not guilty and put on a plane to Algeria, where he joined Cleaver and the international section.[36] By October 1971, the *Voice of the Lumpen* had become an official organ of the RCPN, joining *Right On!* and *Babylon* as an alternative to the post-split *Black Panther* newspaper. That same month, Kathleen Cleaver traveled to New York with Elaine Klein and Jessica Scott, who had worked on the *Voice of the Lumpen* in Germany, to help link the fledgling transnational group to former BPP members and their supporters in the United States.[37]

An improvisational creation in the aftermath of the BPP split and the dramatic international changes inaugurated by Nixon's visit to China, the RPCN was an innovative effort at transnational organizing in the era of détente. At a time when both domestic and international trends were turning against the tide of radicalism that had washed over much of the industrialized world in the 1960s, the RPCN sought to develop a support system that would allow activists to continue the fight against the U.S. empire in the challenging circumstances of the 1970s. Whereas Huey Newton's response to these developments was to emphasize a return to locally focused organizing while deferring a battle against "reactionary Intercommunalism" on the world stage to an unspecified future date, the RPCN was necessarily transnational in orientation from its inception. Among the most innovative tactics employed by the group was the use of emerging technologies to facilitate connections between dispersed and persecuted radicals who were increasingly forced to go underground in the 1970s. Most of the exiles in Algiers were without valid passports and subject to arrest or deportation if they attempted to travel outside of the country. Even Kathleen Cleaver, who retained a passport and was not wanted on any criminal charges, found that diplomatic pressure from the United States often made it difficult to gain entrance visas (as happened at least once in her attempted travel to Germany).[38] Printed materials such as *Voice of the Lumpen* provided one means of connecting activists. Ultimately, however, the logistics and cost of running a large-circulation newspaper with global reach were prohibitive for a small, decentralized group such as the RPCN that lacked the substantial aboveground base enjoyed by the BPP.

The RPCN used what Eldridge Cleaver dubbed "voodoo" to confront the dilemma posed by isolation, limited resources, and ongoing state repression. With portable personal video cameras and players, RCPN activists could quickly produce propaganda films (voodoo) that could be easily transported across borders and shown to audiences large and small. This new video activism freed the RPCN from having to rely on unwieldy print distribution networks or the more centralized and expensive production associated with traditional filmmaking. Cleaver had been experimenting with this "voodoo" at least since March 1971, when he demonstrated it to ambassadors from the PRG and Cambodia along with representatives from the DPRK and North Vietnam, who were apparently impressed.[39] The BPP delegation took their portable Sony video camera when they toured the People's Republic of the Congo. William Stevens subsequently cut the resulting footage into a film with editing assistance (via long-distance telephone) from French director Chris Marker.[40] As the Cleavers and their allies in Algeria and elsewhere sought to rebuild radical networks via the RPCN, grassroots video played a crucial role. Donald Cox, one of Cleavers' most important lieutenants in Algiers, explained,

> The filming of videos became the means for bridging the distance between the International Section and comrades in particular and the rest of the American people in general. Thanks to friends in Algiers, the personnel of Air France, and people that received and distributed them in the states, like William and Miriam Seidler in Philadelphia, we would film a video and it would be showing inside the United States within twenty-four hours.[41]

In an ironic commentary on the unintended effects of technology and globalization, a cartoon in the pages of *Babylon* depicted RCPN activists using Sony video recorders and televisions to outwit "the pigs" and educate the masses.[42]

The combination of video voodoo, printed matter, and the travels of Kathleen Cleaver, Denise Oliver, and others provided the sinews connecting the activists associated with the RCPN. Mere communication, however, was not Eldridge Cleaver's goal. In spite of the immense challenges posed by the party's split and ensuing disintegration of the black radical movement in the United States, Sino-American rapprochement, and the larger shifts in the Cold War environment in the early 1970s, Cleaver remained as committed as ever to his vision of overthrowing of the U.S. government. "The American Revolution has progressed to the phase of a violent peoples revolution," he declared, promising that "[w]e are moving now for the seizure of power."[43] The body that would lead this fight in the United States, which he dubbed the "Afro-American People's Army," "must come into being through combat, fighting from its inception for its right to be."[44] The ultimate goal of the RPCN was to provide a support and communications network in service of this larger goal. "[T]he Revolutionary Peoples Communications Network," proclaimed a September 1971 communiqué, "was initiated to provide the above ground information apparatus to the revolutionary forces[,] many of which are underground in Babylon."[45]

Free from the moderating hand of Newton, Hilliard, and the Oakland-based BPP, Cleaver could now pursue his goal of initiating guerrilla warfare in Babylon, at least in theory. In practice, he still faced the difficult question of how to recruit, organize, equip, and lead his army to victory against the overwhelming firepower of the U.S. state. The most obvious solution was to turn to disaffected Panthers in the United States who shared Cleaver's belief in revolutionary violence and were willing to go underground in order to put this tactic into practice. Initially Cleaver planned to employ the Black Liberation Army (BLA) as the military wing of his revolution inside the United States. The BLA (covered in more depth in the next chapter) had grown out of the underground wing of the BPP and attracted a number of more militant former Panthers, particularly on the East Coast, in the aftermath of the party's split. Following the suspected involvement of BLA members in two attacks on New York City police officers in May 1971, however, the group went deep underground, making communications with Algiers and the RPCN difficult if not impossible. Moreover, BLA members apparently grew wary of accepting advice or taking orders from a man exiled thousands of miles away, a person who had little direct knowledge of conditions they faced on the ground in the United States. Fortuitously, however, the loosening of ties to the BLA was accompanied by the rise of two new groups, both of which had at least indirect ties to Cleaver and his operations in Algiers, that offered new models for conducting guerrilla warfare on the changing global terrain of the early 1970s.

The RAF, Black September, and "Cosmopolitan Guerrillas"

Many involved with the German New Left in the 1960s drifted away in the aftermath of the dissolution of the German SDS and the government's decision to offer amnesty for activists convicted of minor crimes.[46] Some stayed active in the various solidarity committees linked to the BPP, the international section, Angela Davis, and the Ramstein 2. A small number, however, chose to go underground to begin a war against the West German state and U.S. installations there. The Red Army Faction (Rote Armee Fraktion), sometimes referred to as the Baader-Meinhof Gang after two of its founders, Andreas Baader and Ulrike Meinhof, had its roots in the radical German Left and anarchist movements of the late 1960s, including several individuals involved with the firebombing of Frankfurt department stores in 1968 "in protest against people's indifference to the murder of the Vietnamese."[47] In the aftermath of a May 1970 jailbreak, in which Meinhof and several associates freed Baader from custody (stemming from his conviction in the Frankfurt bombings), the nascent underground cell traveled to Jordan, where they received guerrilla training in PLO camps.[48] In June 1970 they announced themselves as the Red Army Faction in the pages of the radical German newspaper *Agit 883*, declaring that the time had come to "START THE ARMED STRUGGLE."[49] The RAF followed this with a series of bombings and shootings targeting German police, U.S. military facilities, and the right-wing Axel Springer media corporation. Support for these operations, which later expanded to including kidnapping and hijacking, came from aboveground sympathizers as well as from bank robberies aimed at acquiring the funds necessary to arm and equip the group's guerrilla cells.[50]

At least one RAF member spent time in Algiers, where she had direct contact with Cleaver and the growing collection of hijackers connected to the former international section, and historian Martin Klimke has suggested that Panther-affiliated GIs in Germany may have been involved in providing weapons for the group.[51] More broadly, the BPP in general and Cleaver in particular were influential in shaping the group's approach to anticolonial violence. From the Panthers, the RAF took the notion that armed struggle in the metropole could play a crucial role in winning a global battle against colonialism and white supremacy. The best way for those in the heart of the capitalist West to support those fighting for their freedom in places such as Vietnam was to strike directly at the U.S. empire and its "lackeys" in West Germany. Invoking the birthplace of the BPP in their declaration of war against the German state, Meinhof asserted that "what is beginning to happen here has been going on for a long time in Vietnam, in Palestine, in Guatemala, in Oakland, and Watts, in Cuba and China, in Angola and in New York."[52] As historians Maria Höhn and Klimke concluded, "In the eyes of the RAF, the Black Panthers became both a role model and a partner in what they conceived as an international revolutionary struggle."[53] In a graphic demonstration of the party's influence, the RAF's first communiqué concluded with the injunction "*die rote-armee Aufbauen!*" ("Build the Red Army!") superimposed over a drawing of the iconic panther employed by the BPP. The RAF also directly tapped the Panthers' anticolonial vernacular, including the use of the word "pig" to describe German police.[54]

As the BPP's most vocal public advocate of urban guerrilla warfare, Cleaver played a particularly influential role in shaping the way West German guerrillas saw their role in the struggle. Prior to the formation of the RAF, Cleaver had urged European activists to take up the gun, and the group's April 1971 manifesto "The Urban Guerrilla Concept" directly invoked the BPP's former minister of information.[55] This crucial early document was, according to RAF member Margrit Schiller, deeply informed by discussions among the group's members about the lessons to be learned from the Panthers.[56] Specifically, RAF leaders identified the BPP's attempt to simultaneously operate aboveground and underground wings as a tactical mistake in light of the repressive powers of the state. Echoing Cleaver's cry to "intensify the struggle," the RAF argued that the time had come to embrace "illegality as an offensive position for revolutionary intervention."[57] The RAF failed in its goal of bringing about a revolution in West Germany, and it did not bring down U.S. imperialism. But despite an intense domestic security campaign by the German state that surpassed that mounted against the BPP in the United States, and waves of arrests that several times appeared to have broken the back of the RAF, the group survived and even grew during the 1970s, remaining in operation until its remaining members voluntarily disbanded in 1998.[58]

In its persistence, the RAF joined the BLA in demonstrating that Cleaver's notion of an urban guerrilla force operating within the heart of the First World was not as implausible as it may have first appeared. But the group that most directly inspired Cleaver in the early 1970s as he grappled with the changing international landscape was one that had roots closer to his own Algerian headquarters. Black September was a Palestinian guerrilla organization that arose out of divisions within Yasser Arafat's Fatah. Although the circumstances and context differed in many ways, the struggles within Fatah during the late 1960s and early 1970s over the role and scope of anticolonial violence shared similarities to those that split the BPP during the same time period. Fatah was united in its opposition to the Israeli colonization of Palestinian land, and it was committed to engaging in guerrilla operations against the occupying forces. But there were sharp differences within Fatah, and the Palestinian resistance more broadly, over both tactics and targets. Arafat led a faction within Fatah and the larger PLO umbrella organization that sought to balance military operations with a longer term diplomatic strategy aimed at securing international recognition and support for the Palestinian cause. Others within Fatah, however, were more concerned with delivering vengeance not only against Israel, but also against Arab leaders who failed to support their cause. Led by Salah Khalaf, the militant faction within Fatah took its name from events in September 1970, when King Hussein of Jordan ordered a bloody assault on Palestinian refugee and training camps in his country as part of the battle for control of the kingdom between the monarchy and exiled Palestinian fighters. In response, Black September mobilized militants from Fatah and other Palestinian resistance groups to launch a wide-ranging campaign of anticolonial violence.[59]

The most notable aspect of Black September's operations, which included assassinations, hijackings, bombings, sabotage, and, most dramatically, the kidnapping of Israeli athletes at the 1972 Summer Olympics in Munich, was the degree to which they exploited vulnerabilities within an increasingly globalized and interconnected world to operate across borders. While groups such as the RAF, the BLA, and the Weather Underground largely confined their operations to their respective home soils, Black September struck at targets in Africa, the Middle East, and Europe as well as international air travel in a series of dramatic hijackings in the early 1970s.[60] The group also explicitly tailored its actions in an attempt to win support from other militants sympathetic to the Palestinian cause. Among the demands of the Black September guerrillas who staged the assault at the Munich Olympics was the release of German RAF prisoners. In the aftermath of the raid, which resulted in fourteen deaths when German police attempted to free the hostages by force, the RAF issued a statement praising the Palestinian fighters.[61] Although the two groups never formally collaborated, the Munich action raised the specter of what historian Paul Thomas Chamberlin dubbed a "global offensive" in which "small states and guerrilla groups sought to exploit a proliferating array of transnational connections . . . using a revolutionary set of tactics and strategies never before seen in history."[62]

Observing the operations of the RAF and Black September from Algiers, Cleaver became enamored with the notion of stateless, transnational anticolonial violence as a new template for resisting the American Empire and its clients at a time when Nixon's diplomacy was rapidly neutralizing revolutionary anticolonialism in both the socialist bloc and the Third World. Although he had long supported strikes against the American Empire and liberation for Palestine while condemning both Israel and "the dyed-in-the-wool lackey clique of Amman, headed by arch-puppet King

Hussein," the tactics employed by the RAF and Black September appealed to Cleaver as much as their ideology.[63] Hailing those he dubbed "Cosmopolitan Guerrillas," Cleaver observed that "the instantaneity of communication and transportation, along with the elaborate nature of technology, and the world market, the complex interconnected nature of the world economy, has created a unity on the planet for which our narrow nationalist perspectives and analogies do not prepare us to deal with." While this analysis of the death of the nation-state echoed Newton's intercommunalism, Cleaver was less interested in transnational community building than he was in exploiting "the landscape of technology, the channels and circuits of our environment," in order to strike at "all pigs and pig structures" around the world.[64] He was particularly impressed with Munich and with Black September's hijacking operations, which illustrated the vulnerability of advanced Western capitalist states to small groups of dedicated guerrillas operating across national frontiers. Asserting that "[w]e who are waging struggles in the metropolis of the international empire of Babylon, can not retreat into the Sierra Maestra [mountains of Cuba]," Cleaver hailed Black September for turning the technology of globalization against its masters, attacking not just individual targets but also the very notion of borders and frontiers with its shadowy transnational operations in the heart of the industrialized West.[65]

Given the increasingly tenuous state of his base in Algiers and his difficulties in maintaining connections with potential underground comrades in the BLA, it is hardly surprising that Black September's model of a loosely organized, transnational anticolonial violence appealed to Cleaver. There were some obvious potential problems, however, as Cleaver contemplated applying this strategy to black liberation in the United States. Most fundamentally, it remained entirely unclear how such a guerrilla force could hope to actually overthrow the U.S. government or affect meaningful change. Although the BLA, the Weather Underground, the RAF, and Black September had shown it was possible for guerrillas to conduct sustained operations, none of these groups had succeeded in their ambitious goals. In fact, Black September, the group that most inspired Cleaver's plans for an army of "Cosmopolitan Guerrillas," was effectively brought to heel by Fatah and the PLO by the end of 1973 after it became apparent that its operations were doing more harm than good to the Palestinian cause.[66] In the United States and Germany, bombings, sabotage, and the killing of police officers appeared to have accomplished little outside of building public support for increasingly militarized government actions against those labeled as domestic terrorists. As Harold Cruse had warned in the mid–1960s, there was little reason to believe that domestic bombings would be any more effective than wartime strategic bombing in effecting revolutionary change, "for the capitalist owners simply rebuilt their property and proceeded to exploit it as before, under the same system."[67]

Cleaver acknowledged that many were skeptical of the prospects for armed rebellion in the United States. In extolling the need for an Afro-American people's army in the pages of *Babylon*, he conceded, "There are those, I know, who feel let down at this point, because here I go again talking about guns."[68] For Cleaver, however, the failure of the various 1960s movements to bring about revolution, along with the ascendency of Nixon and the conservative counterreaction, left little choice. Whereas some would-be revolutionaries had embraced the notion of urban insurgency with a sense of optimism in the 1960s, with Robert F. Williams famously proclaiming the prospect of a ninety-day war bringing the government to its knees, Cleaver seems to have clung to it with a sense of desperation in the early 1970s.[69] In the wake of détente and the neutralization of the socialist bloc, it was clear, he believed, that "[t]he ruling class of the United States is unfolding a plan to carve up the planet in such a way that when the deal goes down the Afro-American people will find themselves trapped inside and at the mercy of a white racist empire." Seeing no way to combat these developments at the level of national politics or international diplomacy, the only choice was to "organize ourselves into a powerful, deadly, invincible block inside the United States" and ally with "all the other oppressed people inside Babylon and the world who have not made their separate peace with the enemy and continue to struggle for their human rights." Making no promises of an easy or inevitable victory, Cleaver insisted only that "[t]here is a world of difference between 30 million unarmed niggers and 30 million niggers armed to the gills."[70]

Beyond the question of long-term goals and efficacy, Cleaver's dream of a Black September–style guerrilla group operating in and out of the United States faced many practical hurdles. Stripped of support from both the BPP and his Asian allies, on uneasy terms with the Algerian government, and unable to locate a new home for the international section, Cleaver was struggling to keep the RPCN afloat, much less engage in an ambitious campaign of transnational revolutionary violence. Kathleen Cleaver carried the brunt of the burden of raising funds and gaining support to keep the RPCN functioning during her trips to the United States and Europe. She later recalled, however, that "[w]hile attracting considerable interest, the

RPCN was never able to provide substantial organizational cohesion to the scattered newspapers, groups, and individuals it sought to link together. Apathy and defeat seemed generalized in the movement in America, and the fear and confusion generated by the split in the Panther Party posed a major obstacle to anything connected with Eldridge Cleaver."[71] Even a light and lean transnational guerrilla group needed some means of supporting itself. It was fitting, then, that the apparent solution to this dilemma arrived literally out of the blue in the summer of 1972.

Hijacking, Natural Gas, and the Dissolution of the International Section

On June 2, 1972, Willie Roger Holder and Catherine Marie Kerkow hijacked Western Airlines Flight 701 from Los Angeles. Holder, a troubled Vietnam veteran with a history of petty crimes, had no previous involvement with the Black Panthers or any other activist groups. His somewhat erratic plan involved ransoming the passengers in exchange for the freedom of Angela Davis (then awaiting a verdict in her trial in San Jose, California), $500,000, and transit to North Vietnam for himself and Kerkow. Unable to secure freedom for Davis and informed that the plane lacked the range to reach Hanoi, the hijackers instead took the ransom payment and directed the pilot to land in Algiers, where they planned to seek asylum with Cleaver and his fellow band of exiles. Though Cleaver had no advance knowledge of the hijacking, when news arrived via a call from the Algerian government, he rushed to the airport to greet them and inquire about the ransom.[72] Starved for funds to continue the operations of the RCPN, support the exiles nominally under his leadership, and perhaps begin his long-delayed guerrilla warfare campaign, the $500,000 that arrived along with Holder and Kerkow was a tantalizing prize. Having embraced hijacking as one of the tools of the cosmopolitan guerrilla, he and his organization now stood to directly gain from its application. Instead, echoing lessons from his earlier dealing with the governments of Cuba and his Asian allies, Cleaver was forcibly reminded that nation-states retained significant power even in this supposed age of transnational insurgency.

When the hijacked Western Airlines flight touched down in Algiers in June 1972, the government of President Boumédiène was deeply involved in negotiations for the state oil company Sonatrach to export natural gas to a Texas-based U.S. company. This contract, valued at potentially $1.2 billion, would raise badly needed funds for Algeria's economic development. While still publicly committed to Algeria's revolutionary heritage and opposed to the U.S. war in Vietnam and support for Israel, Boumédiène was loath to jeopardize the potential windfall from natural gas exports, particularly in service of those who seemed more like bandits than legitimate liberation movements.[73] Much to Cleaver's frustration, the Algerian government returned the $500,000 ransom payment along with the plane rather than turning it over to the hijackers or the international section. Holder and Kerkow were granted asylum and released into Cleaver's custody, but this too proved a mixed blessing. Hopes of selling the hijackers' story to the U.S. press in order to raise at least some money failed to materialize and soon they became simply another burden on the already overstretched operations of the international section and RCPN in Algiers.[74]

Compounding the series of setbacks they had suffered internationally and in dealing with Boumédiène, the tensions of daily life in exile had taken a tremendous toll on the group even prior to the arrival of the hijackers. "Those conditions that stimulated the intense momentum of the Panther movement in the United States," Kathleen Cleaver later observed, "did not exist, and the cultural isolation of the Panthers attenuated their sense of belonging to a genuine community." At the time, she privately lamented the "stagnation, chaos, disinterest, disgust, [and] perversity," that characterized "the life of the marooned exiles in Algiers":

> Shit is getting so thick; so fucked up, so intolerably disorganized and lackadaisical—everyone seems to have been turned inside out[,] and claim to sanity, much less sociability, can hardly be made by anyone.[75]

Timothy Leary, who fled his virtual imprisonment at the hands of Cleaver in early 1971, offered a predictably more colorful assessment, describing life in the international section as "a Graham Greene horror story, complete with exotic North African locale, sexual intrigue, personal disintegration, and a cast of exiles caught in webs of counter-intelligence, revolutionary conspiracy, treachery, bravery, and melodrama."[76]

Beset by internal and external turmoil, the final act of the international section came in August 1972 in response to another hijacking drama. The hijackers of Delta Airlines Flight 841 were, in the words of Kathleen Cleaver, "an odd assortment of friends who had shared a house together in Detroit."[77] A group of five adults and two children, the hijackers had been living in a Detroit commune prior to executing their plan to seize a plane, demand a ransom, and fly to Algeria. Although two of the commune's members, Melvin and Jean McNair, had previously considered joining the Panthers in Detroit, none had any real connections or experience with the BPP or other activist organizations. When the hijackers were eventually questioned in Algiers after being released into the custody of the international section, Kathleen Cleaver found that they had "little political consciousness" but instead "strange spiritist beliefs and vaguely pan-African convictions."[78] What they also had, however, was a $1 million ransom that they received in exchange for freeing the crew and passengers of the plane upon reaching Algeria on August 1, 1972. Mindful of the government's confiscation of the previous ransom, Cleaver and Sekou Odinga reportedly followed the vehicle transporting the hijackers from the airport and shouted out the window "Don't give up the bread! Don't give up the bread!" before being halted at gunpoint by Algerian police. The money, however, was already gone. Once again Boumédiène's government choose to return both the ransom and the plane in order to avoid further antagonizing the United States and jeopardizing the proposed natural gas deal.[79]

Tensions between the Panthers and the Algerian government had been mounting well before the hijackings in the summer of 1972. Eldridge Cleaver acknowledged that the exiled Panthers, with their "fast cars, Russian machine guns, and plenty of fresh-air macho," had tested the patience of their hosts from the very beginning.[80] So long as Cleaver and his associates confined their activities to issuing propaganda and engaging in dubious hustling operations in Algiers, they were a nuisance that could be tolerated in the name of revolutionary solidarity. The hijackings, however, escalated matters by thrusting the international section, which was nominally recognized and supported by the Algerian government, into the public spotlight amid a global upswing in air piracy. Before Delta Airlines Flight 841 had even landed in Algiers, the representative of the Algerian Interests Section in Washington, Abdel Kader Bousselham, was summoned to the State Department. There he was warned by the assistant secretary of state for African affairs, who said that "he could not over-emphasize the seriousness with which this second incident is viewed at the highest level of the USG [US Government] nor the effect that its outcome will have on the progress of our relations." U.S. officials explicitly cited statements by the Panthers in Algeria as encouraging the hijackings and warned that this constituted "a direct intervention" into U.S. domestic affairs. Bousselham responded by quickly and emphatically disowning Cleaver and his contingent of exiles:

It was a statement made by an irresponsible person [Cleaver] and Algeria could not be made to assume responsibility for it. How could anyone pretend to SPEAK for GOA [Government of Algeria] and pretend to make such appeals in its name. He wished to denounce this statement as a falsehood if it had been made in the name of GOA. He attached absolutely no value to it and rejected the responsibility of its author.[81]

As had been the case in Cuba, the tensions hijacking exposed in Algeria were symptoms of a larger divergence in aims between Cleaver and his hosts. Changing Cold War dynamics ushered in by détente combined with the weight of U.S. economic power to render the Panthers no longer worth protecting.

Though not privy to the high-level discussions in which the Algerians denounced Eldridge Cleaver to U.S. officials, the Panther exiles were acutely aware of the change brought about by the hijackings. In the aftermath of the second hijacking, Kathleen Cleaver recalled, "The hostility towards the Panthers among Algerians, from the lowest policeman to the highest official, became blatant."[82] Long frustrated by the meager support from the Algerian government, which was unable to cover the day-to-day costs of the growing delegation, much less provide the kind of arms and training that Eldridge Cleaver had long desired, he responded to the increasing pressure with a desperate gamble. On August 2, he released an open letter to Boumédiène to the press in Algiers, which was picked up by *Le Monde* and other newspapers, asking for the return of the $1 million ransom to which he believed the Panthers were entitled. Warning that "without money to organize and support the struggle, there will be no freedom, and those who deprive us of this are depriving us of our freedom," he suggested that failure to turn over the money to the Panthers would be tantamount to the "the Algerian government . . . [fighting] the battles of the American government for the fascist imperialist ruling circles that are oppressing the whole American people."[83]

Cleaver's brazen public bid to pressure Boumédiène into releasing the ransom was the last straw so far as the Algerian government was concerned. It was bad enough that the hijackings were jeopardizing potentially lucrative economic arrangements with the United States. Cleaver's outburst not only called further attention to this fact but also constituted a public attack on Boumédiène's government and its revolutionary credibility. In response, the Algerian police raided the international section's villa on August 10, seized their telephone and telex equipment, and put the entire delegation under house arrest.[84] In the aftermath, Cleaver was summoned to the office of Salah Hidjeb (also known as Si Salah), the head of the Algerian Sécurité Militaire. The Algerian official was blunt, according to Cleaver's account of their meeting, declaring that it was widely believed "that we [the Panther exiles] don't do anything. We are nothing but Palace Revolutionaries." The official went on to confront the international section's remaining members with a laundry list of complaints, ranging from encouraging hijacking to drug offenses, kidnapping, and death threats. Cleaver replied by urging his hosts not give in to American pressure to evict the Panthers in order to facilitate the pending natural gas deal. In a clear demonstration that national self-interest trumped any remaining ideological affinity for the exiled former Panthers, Salah curtly replied, "This is Algeria's gas, and we can sell it to who[m]ever we like—capitalist, communist, it doesn't make any difference."[85] Privately, Algerian foreign minister Abdelaziz Bouteflika assured U.S. secretary of state William P. Rogers that his government was "interested in developing its relations with U.S." and added that the Black Panther exiles "do not make any effective contribution to Algeria from [a] revolutionary, ideological, or moral standpoint."[86]

The Legacy of the International Section and the RPCN

In the aftermath of the hijackings, the Algerian government lost all remaining patience for what was left of the international section. A September 5, 1972, intelligence report by the CIA, which continued to keep close tabs on the Panther contingent in Algiers, reported that "[l]ast week, the villa was empty and Cleaver was gone."[87] By the end of 1972, the vast majority of the exiles had fled for other destinations. Pete and Charlotte O'Neal left for Cairo in September 1972 and from there traveled to Tanzania, where they took up farming and eventually engaged in a very different brand of transnational activism, founding the United African American Community Center in the village of Imabaseni and hosting visiting young people from their hometown of Kansas City. Connie and Michael Tabor settled in Zambia, while others, including Sekou Odinga, quietly returned to the United States.[88] Cleaver had nominally turned over the international section to Pete O'Neal, who was apparently on better terms with the Algerian government, in January 1972. With O'Neal's departure, formal control of the organization devolved to hijackers Willie Roger Holder and George Brown, neither of whom had any real connections to the domestic or internationally based black freedom struggle.[89] What had once been a thirty-person "embassy of the American revolution," with connections to liberation movements in Algiers, activists in Europe and the United States, and powerful state-level allies in Asia, was reduced to a skeleton crew consisting of the Cleaver family and a handful of hijackers with no place else to go. In January 1973, Eldridge and Kathleen secretly traveled to France, effectively ending their three-and-half-year effort to institutionalize an international base for the African American freedom struggle.

The rise and fall of the Panthers' international section highlighted both the perils and opportunities of the evolving Cold War for the black freedom struggle in the 1960s and 1970s. By embracing and exploiting Cold War dynamics in Asia, Cleaver and his fellow exiles were able to build an institutional base that did not depend on the U.S. government for support or legitimacy. Canny triangulation between Algiers, Asian allies, and supporters in Europe and elsewhere helped to keep the international section (and later the RPCN) afloat for almost two years after its members were expelled from the BPP. The fate of the international section in the era of détente, however, drives home the point that during the Cold War there was no such thing as a free lunch. Not only did these alliances leave Cleaver dependent on his new allies and vulnerable to unexpected shifts in the Cold War environment, they also led him to tailor his message to appeal to governments and movements that in most cases had only superficial knowledge of and concern for African Americans living in the United States. As Huey Newton had observed from his jail cell, paeans to the genius of Kim Il-sung might serve Cleaver's needs in exile, but they did little to endear the party to its core base of supporters in urban black America. Diplomacy almost invariably involves choosing between imperfect options. For all the drawbacks, given the position in which he found himself and the aims he sought to achieve, Cleaver's alliances with revolutionary Asia were almost certainly the best available option at the time. That the international section was able to operate from 1970 to 1973 in spite of the unrelenting hostility of the U.S. government, concerted FBI and CIA efforts to undermine the Panthers from within, the reluctance of its Algerian hosts, eventual excommunication from the BPP, and the logistical challenges of holding together a fractious group of exiles is a testament to the efficacy of the "Asian strategy."

Similarly, Cleaver's embrace of the model provided by Black September in the early 1970s was prescient in identifying the ability of stateless groups to exploit the vulnerabilities that came along with the rise of an increasingly high-tech and interconnected world economy. A larger and harder to resolve question involves the appropriateness of these kind of tactics for the black freedom struggle in the United States. The experiences of the BLA, Weather Underground, and the RAF in Germany validated the notion that urban guerrillas could operate for prolonged periods in the heart of the capitalist West. The results produced by these groups, however, were not encouraging for those who saw revolutionary violence as a tool for social change in the First World. The notion that a black guerrilla army, whether it was supported by Kim Il-sung or by a dispersed transnational network, could seize and hold power in the United States remained as far-fetched in the early 1970s as it been when Robert F. Williams had promised a ninety-day victory in the previous decade. But if the government of the United States was, in the words of Martin Luther King, Jr., "the *greatest purveyor of violence* in the world today," fighting a genocidal war in Southeast Asia, maintaining an empire of military bases around the world, and subjecting people of color inside its borders to institutionalized poverty and police brutality, then anticolonial counter-violence could plausibly be seen as not only a just response but a necessary one.[90] Given the foundational role of white supremacy in the United States and a centuries-long history of war and repression against people of color at home and abroad, including under a succession of avowedly liberal presidents, reform from within the system was no more likely to bring justice to people of color than was anticolonial violence. Romanticized and gendered notions of violence as a way to "stand up as black men inside of Babylon" undoubtedly fueled the obsession of Cleaver and others within the movement with taking power by force.[91] But this strategy was also rooted in a nuanced understanding of the relationship between white supremacy, capitalism, and the violence that supported them. "[W]hether we like it or not," Cleaver observed, "the world that we live in is controlled with guns, organized and controlled by those who rule. This is the basic fact that we have to deal with. Those who cannot move beyond that point—I don't know what to say to them."[92] The international section, the RPCN, and the "Cosmopolitan Guerrillas" ultimately and perhaps predictably failed in their efforts to remake America through revolutionary violence. It does not necessarily follow, however, that their goals and tactics were as irrational as suggested by their detractors.

The failure of the international section and its offshoots had much to do with forces beyond the control of its members, from the corrosive effects of COINTELPRO through the calculations of national interest in Algiers, Beijing, Pyongyang, and Hanoi that ultimately undermined the foundations of its foreign support. Internal flaws and weaknesses also played a role in its dissolution, however. Some of these were likely unavoidable: holding together a diverse community of exiles living far from home under conditions of constant uncertainty, with a number of them likely suffering from some form of post-traumatic stress disorder as a result of their violent encounters with police and the stresses of Panther life, was a challenging task even under the best of circumstances. "[W]orking on that level was new to most of us," recalled Charlotte O'Neal decades later, "and I think maybe diplomacy wasn't uppermost in everybody's minds."[93] The leadership structure of the international section, however, almost certainly exacerbated both its internal and external problems. Running an ambitious and precarious operation an exile was inevitably a cooperative endeavor, with responsibilities that included everything from child care and cooking to high-level international diplomacy and weapons training. Leadership, however, was centralized in the person of Eldridge Cleaver. Cleaver was, by his own admission, unprepared for the responsibility of coordinating daily living for as many as thirty people while also trying to carry out his ambitious plans for revolution in the United States.[94] This was further complicated by his tendency to treat the female members of the group dismissively and sometimes violently. Women, including Kathleen Cleaver, Elaine Klein, Denise Oliver, Charlotte O'Neal, and Connie Matthews Tabor, played a crucial role in creating and maintaining the international section. Elements of the RPCN also attempted to draw attention to the importance of gender and the precarious situation of black women as victims of white supremacy, capitalism, *and* patriarchy.[95] But from his autocratic and patriarchal control over the People's Anti-Imperialist Delegation to his treatment of Kathleen, Eldridge Cleaver appears to have advanced little from his earlier conception of "pussy power" in which women were subservient sex objects rather than full equals in the revolution. While attempting to keep the RCPN above water in late 1971 amid "all the petty ridiculous bullshit," Kathleen Cleaver privately lamented, "Unfortunately, Eldridge seem to feel there is some sexual problem—I have more or less lost interest in that since I do not understand how fucking will lead to freedom."[96]

Chapter 8

The Panthers in Winter, 1971–1981

Few chroniclers of the Black Panther Party have been as dedicated as the
security apparatus of the U.S. government. From the BPP's entrance into
the FBI's "Security Index" in April 1967 through the party's dissolution at
the start of the 1980s, the Panthers were the object of constant government
scrutiny via the likes of wiretaps, informants, and visual surveillance.
Although the resulting reports, which on occasion went all the way up
to the White House, were inevitably warped by the ideological, political,
and personal biases of the government observers and analysts, they also
offered a unique perspective on the Panthers' development. In some cases,
the government, with its web of informants and sophisticated surveillance
technology, was in a better position than the party's own leaders to observe
the shape of the BPP's operations. On September 5, 1972, a classified CIA
report remarked on the diverging fortunes of the Oakland-based Panthers
and Eldridge Cleaver's operation in exile. "The militant faction of the
Black Panther Party appears to be decaying," the report noted in reference
to Cleaver, "while the non-militant Newton-Seale faction undergoes a
rebirth.... [and is] enjoying renewed popularity with the black community."

Their political activity is indicative of a major change in the policy and
direction of the national Black Panther Party. BPP reports from two dozen

cities show that the Newton-Seale faction, the dominant faction in the BPP, has put down the gun and picked up the ballot as its new weapon.

The report went on to warn that BPP's new "image of respectability" and emphasis on community service programs likely concealed "the birth of Mafia-type activities designed to gain control of the black ghetto communities where sanctuaries for long-range revolutionary activities would be assured."[1] For once, the CIA was at least half right.

The BPP split in February 1971 resulted in a number of organizations claiming the mantle. The Oakland-based leadership under Huey Newton was by far the largest and most capable of these. While worthy of a history in its own right, the under-examined story of the post-1971 Panthers is relatively clear in its broad outlines. Accelerating a trend that had begun with the advent of the program serving free breakfast for schoolchildren, the BPP underwent a dramatic transformation in the 1970s. Downplaying revolution, anticolonial violence, and Cold War influences, leaders including Newton, Elaine Brown, Ericka Huggins, and Bobby Seale steered the party toward mainstream electoral politics while expanding the Panthers' existing community service programs. As part of Newton's "Base of Operations" strategy, chapters around the country were ordered to close local offices and move to Oakland in order to concentrate on winning control of the city's political landscape. Although the long-term goal nominally remained some form of revolution, the effect was to reposition the Panthers as a conventional local political and community organization. In the process, the BPP largely disengaged from the international and transnational alliances that had marked the party's peak in the late 1960s. The party also rejected the strategy of urban guerrilla warfare advocated by Cleaver and others prior to the split. The Panthers retained a small, well-armed military wing in the 1970s, but instead of preparing to overthrow the U.S. government, members of Newton's "Buddha Samurai" (as he called it) were focused on the black community of Oakland "to maintain the party's influence over the wild streets of the East Bay."[2]

The Oakland-based Panthers under Newton, and then Elaine Brown from 1975 to 1977, were not the only claimants to the party's legacy. The Black Liberation Army (BLA) was born out of the ashes of the BPP's original underground military wing, a unit that Newton had disowned as he pivoted the party toward more mainstream political activity in 1970–71. A loose-knit, dispersed organization, the BLA had its strongest base of support among former New York City Panthers. While Bobby Seale and Elaine

Brown ran for political office in Oakland, figures affiliated with the BLA embarked on a guerrilla campaign that included bank robberies, bombings, and assassinations of police officers. But without an aboveground political apparatus and the international contacts that Cleaver had once enjoyed, the BLA had little ability to leverage its sporadic acts of violence into something even vaguely approaching a revolution. By the end of 1973, police had killed or captured most of the key BLA leadership, although the organization soldiered on throughout the decade before being briefly reborn under somewhat different circumstances in the latter half of the decade.

Back to Oakland: The "Base of Operation" Plan

Huey Newton beat Richard Nixon to China by five months, but the race to shape the Cold War in Asia was already over by the time that the Panthers' cofounder touched down in Beijing. Taking advantage of an invitation proffered shortly after his release from prison, Newton, Elaine Brown, and a small delegation of Panthers arrived in China for a ten-day tour in September 1971.[3] On the surface, Newton's visit, which included audiences with Premier Zhou Enlai, seemed to portend a return to the glory days of the Panthers' internationalism. In fact, however, the trip served largely as a form of revolutionary theater, as both the Chinese government and the Panthers publicly burnished their radical credentials in the midst of pivoting toward more accommodationist positions with respect to the United States. Newton was circumspect in revealing what he had discussed in his meetings with Chinese leaders, noting only, "Premier Chou En-Lai said many things to me . . . I will not comment on specifics."[4] Whatever was exchanged between the two men, the course that Newton and Brown charted for the Panthers in the aftermath of the trip made it clear that Cold War geopolitics and Third World anticolonialism were no longer important elements of the party's daily operations.

Whereas BPP leaders had once invoked Mao in support of "picking up the gun," in 1972 the Chinese leader and his nation served as a justification for entering into mainstream electoral politics. As Elaine Brown explained, "China's recent entrance into the U.N. was neither contradictory to China's goal of toppling U.S. imperialism nor an abnegation of revolutionary principles. . . . It was a tactic, Huey concluded, that offered us a great example. Those were the roots of Huey's new idea: to have Panthers run for political office."[5] Flores Alexander Forbes, a Southern California Panther who became a key member of the party's inner circle in the 1970s, recalled party leaders justifying the focus on local politics in Oakland as "a plan à la Mao's Long March" that would "rejuvenate our Party, which had suffered so much from being under attack by the U.S. government and local police agencies."[6] An article published in the *Black Panther* in April 1972 was even more explicit in declaring that foreign connections were no substitute for local political organizing. "We cannot blame the Communist Party of China and take our frustrations out on China," the author declared, "because we have been delinquent and negligent in carrying out our own revolution."

> We have only ourselves to blame. I think the problem is that too many revolutionaries have been living a vicarious revolution. . . . We must concern ourselves with the business at hand and stop complaining about other comrades in the socialist camp. They're taking care of business there. It's time we took care of business here. Chairman Mao isn't going to march victoriously into Washington. We are.[7]

Starting in June 1972, Newton and the Panthers unveiled a new strategy that put this logic into practice in the streets of Oakland.

Two elements informed the "Base of Operation" plan. The first was a directive to close down all Panther offices and chapters outside of Oakland. Those who remained loyal to the party were to pack up and move to California, where they would join the national leaders in building a single, powerful BPP organization in the East Bay. As would be expected, this directive was not always well received by the local Panther chapters that had sprung up around the country, and many chose to leave the party rather than move to Oakland.[8] For Newton, however, the benefits of centralization outweighed the loss of members. The BPP's cofounder had gone behind bars in October 1967 as leader of a small crew of trusted neighborhood friends and allies, many of whom he had known since grade school. He emerged in August 1970 as the nominal head of a sprawling national and international organization staffed by thousands of members he had never met. Newton had never been entirely comfortable overseeing such a large operation, and the internal strife unleashed by COINTELPRO and the split with Cleaver made him even more wary of depending on a dispersed base of supporters over whom he had no control. Ordering Panther members to move to Oakland would weed out the disloyal or unmotivated and concentrate those who remained in one location where party leaders could more easily oversee their operations. Increased efficiency would compensate for the loss in raw numbers, as the remaining loyalists would now be applying all of their energies to a single goal in Oakland. As Forbes described it, "[Newton] believed we would never be effective until we knew one another and worked around one another implementing a common program and agenda."[9]

As the birthplace of the Panthers, home to its national headquarters, and familiar turf for Newton, Oakland was an easy choice as the party's base of operations. However, party leaders also offered another set of explanations in explaining this decision to the rank and file. Unlike other cities where black activists had attempted to win control of municipal services, Oakland was not a once-great manufacturing city shattered by deindustrialization. As Brown explained it:

> This is not Gary, Indiana, or Newark, New Jersey, or Detroit, where so-called Blacks have taken over after people with money left the city and said "here, you have it, this junk we've left here, you can have this urban blighted area." Here we have the Port of Oakland which is the second largest containerized port in the world and the largest on the Pacific Ocean and that means there is money coming in here.[10]

The Port of Oakland, with its modern, containerized, and mechanized facilities, generated $6.5 million per year in revenue in 1970 and represented a rare bright economic bright spot in a region that increasingly saw its industries fleeing from inner cities to suburban areas or overseas. As historian Robert O. Self has chronicled, however, the nature of the port's financing and operations ensured that little or none of its revenues flowed back into the city of Oakland. The port's charter required that profits from its operations be reinvested into expansion of the port itself or used to service bonds held by financial institutions and individuals with no direct connection to the East Bay.[11] If a Panther-led coalition could seize control of Oakland and renegotiate the port's charter, it might produce a budget windfall that could bankroll a dramatic increase in city services. Winning local control over municipal facilities could also serve more revolutionary ends. Panther campaign documents declared that "Oakland is a military-industrial city" and noted that its port "was one of the main departure points for militarized cargo during the U.S. War in Vietnam."[12] Under Panther control, the port's revenues and its operations could be made to serve the people of Oakland rather than serve as profits for capitalists or facilitate the U.S. war machine. Aaron Dixon, a former Seattle Panther who made the journey to Oakland to take part in the new campaign, recalled that "[f]or years, cocaine had flowed freely into [the Port of] Oakland from South America. Now we could put an end to that. Elaine [Brown] used to joke that, instead, 'Now we'll have AK-47s coming in.'"[13]

The Oakland BPP's post-split strategy of withdrawing from the national scene and pursuing change at the local level was in some ways a return to its roots in 1966–67. The way in which the party went about that goal in the 1970s, however, represented a fundamental departure from its previous incarnation. In the early days of the Panthers, Newton and Seale had embraced a colonial model for understanding the position of black Americans. Based on their reading of Fanon and other anticolonial theorists, they concluded that the "brothers on the block" in West Oakland were not citizens denied their rights but colonial subjects whose continuing oppression was an inherent part of the system that governed not only Oakland but also the United States and its entire empire. Working from within that system at either the local or national level was pointless as its very nature was rooted in the infliction of violence on people of color. The confrontational tactic of "patrolling the pigs" was a perfect example of the BPP's early emphasis on confronting state violence from the outside in. Though Panther candidates had run for local and national offices in 1968, they had done so purely as protest candidates with no effort to actually turn out voters on Election Day. As late as April 1971, Newton declared that while the BPP might endorse candidates, "[w]e will never run for political office."[14] Two years later, however, Bobby Seale was running a serious and well-organized campaign for mayor of Oakland while Elaine Brown sought a seat on the city council.

The second major component of the "Base of Operations" strategy was to abandon direct confrontations with the system in favor of trying to win elections and change it from within. In her memoir, Brown suggested that it was China's entrance into the United Nations that had inspired Newton to shift the BPP's effort to working within the U.S. political system.[15] The roots of this change, however, well predated Newton's visit to China. The advent of the "survival programs" in early 1969 in the wake of Cleaver's botched police ambush and flight to Cuba were indicative of a gradual realization among Panther leaders that the strategy of directly confronting the armed might of the U.S. state was simply untenable for the party in its current state. Although it took another four years to move from community service to electoral politics, this was a logical progression of the party's evolution in the face of state repression. Having deemed armed revolution to be impractical, if not downright suicidal, but still committed to affect-ing social change, the BPP's remaining leaders eventually concluded that engaging with the political system was the only practical course open to the party if it wished to survive and stay relevant. In campaign appear-ances Brown and Seale directly addressed this issue, acknowledging that the party's past commitment to revolutionary anticolonialism modeled on the struggles of Algeria, Cuba, and Vietnam might lead critics to ask, "What does this [electoral campaign] have to do with guerrilla warfare? And is it true that the Black Panther Party is saying that we don't have to fight?" In response, Brown bluntly declared that "[t]here's a practical problem, when you talk about liberating territory, or establishing a provisional revolution-ary government."

> Think about those issues when you start talking about implementing a revolutionary process in the United States of America, with its super-technological weapons, where they do not have to commit a troop to take out the whole city, because they have "smart" bombs, helicopters, and all kinds of things so that it doesn't even require the entrance of one troop. Think about that. We have to start talking about how to win, not how to get killed. We can begin by talking about voting in the city of Oakland, the Oakland elections, in April 1973, for Bobby Seale, for Elaine Brown.

In light of the fact that "[t]he Oakland Police Department has got all the guns," the only viable course of action for "implementing people's power in just one city" was to do so at the ballot box.[16]

Nominally, at least, the BPP leaders portrayed the 1973 electoral cam-paign (and a subsequent run for city council by Brown in 1975) as part of a long-term strategy for revolution across the United States. The party's ten-point platform, revised in March 1972, remained a radical call for fun-damental political and economic change.[17] The local focus of the Oakland campaign was explained to the rank and file as the first step in a larger plan. As Forbes later recalled, "The final phase, once Oakland was taken, was to relaunch the revolution and replicate the Oakland success in other major U.S. cities."[18] The way in which the party ran the campaign, however, was indicative of a major practical and ideological shift that made the Panthers look more like the left wing of the Democratic Party than the vanguard of the revolution. A Seale-Brown campaign leaflet was blunt in exhorting voters to "Elect Two Democrats" while claiming that, in Oakland, at least,

"It's Not a Race Problem: It's a Jobs Problem."[19] The duo's fourteen-point platform, while undeniably progressive, was centered almost entirely on taxation, spending, and job creation policies that were well in line with the liberal wing of the Democratic Party. Even their intended requirement that Oakland police and fire officers live within city limits, the sole and somewhat tenuous link to the BPP's initial efforts to rein in the OPD's history of abusive treatment of black residents, was pitched in economic terms. The residency requirement, they argued, "would bring over $15 million back into the general economy of the city, and approximately $1 million into the city budget itself."[20]

No aspect of the Seale-Brown campaign was more indicative of the BPP's shifting agenda than their proposal for a "community-owned and operated Multi-Ethnic International Trade and Cultural Center." Whereas the party had once looked to the Third World for models of revolution and allies in their struggle to overthrow the U.S. government, the proposed trade center was a textbook example of neoliberal globalization. Its goal was not to promote revolutionary anticolonialism but "to greatly stimulate international trade and cultural exchange between Oakland and South American, Asian and African nations . . . which will produce more jobs as well as increase business." The notion of revolutionary solidarity among people of color that had once fueled the BPP's anticolonial vernacular was replaced with a consumerist internationalism that promised "[f]ood centers and restaurants [that] would provide foods from Third World countries, both for preparation at home and for consumption on the site." The primary enemy that the center would confront was not U.S. imperialism but rather Oakland's rival across the bay. Seale insisted that "such a Center in Oakland, in full swing, would rival San Francisco as a tourist attraction in the Bay Area and would draw visitors to the East Bay in great numbers."[21]

The BPP's pivot toward mainstream politics in 1973 was successful in some respects. Although they failed to win electoral office, Seale forced incumbent Oakland mayor John Reading into a run-off election, and Brown gained respectable vote totals in both her 1973 and 1975 campaigns.[22] With endorsement and help from farmworker organizer Cesar Chavez among others, they were able to mobilize significant popular support for what had at first appeared a quixotic quest.[23] While perhaps unable to win office on their own, the Panthers had demonstrated that they could be an important political player on the local scene with the ability to reliably turn out large numbers of black and progressive voters. The BPP, and Elaine Brown in particular, capitalized on this success by cultivating ties with the Democratic Party establishment in California, including Governor Jerry Brown and East Bay congressional representative Ron Dellums (who was given a weekly column in the Panther newspaper). In return for campaigning for California Democrats, they were rewarded with access to state and local leaders. In 1976, Elaine Brown was appointed to serve on the Oakland Council for Economic Development (OCED) and traveled to the Democratic National Convention as a delegate for Jerry Brown. This strategy culminated in 1977 when the BPP helped to elect Lionel Wilson as Oakland's first black mayor.[24] Newton also attempted to extend the party's influence nationally by cultivating ties to the emerging Congressional Black Caucus (CBC). No longer blasting black politicians as "Uncle Toms," Newton wrote to Congressman Robert N.C. Nix in 1972, declaring, "We know that Black elected officials, too, must endure a thousand assaults, from both the racist and so-called 'far-left' elements of our society." Though Newton received sympathetic letters from CBC members Charles B. Rangel and John Conyers, the small size and local focus of the Oakland Panthers limited their ability to cut deals with national politicians.[25]

The "Base of Operations" phase was appealing to many among the Panthers' battered rank and file. As Forbes explained, "To me, as one of the brothers in the trenches, what Huey wanted to do made a hell of a lot of sense; it made sense to stop fighting the police toe-to-toe. After thirty-plus dead Panthers in two years, shit, I [was] glad somebody up north realized that we could never win a shooting 'War of Liberation.'" In focusing on winning political power at the local level, the BPP leaders "outlined a tangible and viable program that I could really go for, and judging from the other comrade's [*sic*] responses, they could, too."[26] When combined with a greatly expanded suite of community service programs, which included everything from medical care to support for prisoners and their families, free clothes and food, cultural programs, and the highly successful Oakland Community School (OCS) under the direction of Ericka Huggins and Donna Howell, the BPP's new political program provided its members with the ability to make a concrete difference in the lives of local residents without having to fear constant clashes with police.[27] Newton even mended fences with the black church, an early target of BPP criticism, declaring that "the church is striving to come back into the favor of the community; so with the church the Black Panther Party will attempt this also.[28] "In effect," recalled Aaron Dixon, "we put our guns in the closet and instead drew upon the talents of our members to develop the programs and strategies for moving the community forward."[29]

Along with these practical changes came a gradual shift away from the gendered notions of violence and manhood that had often informed the party's operations from 1966 to 1970. The move from revolutionary violence and "standing up as a man inside Babylon" to local politics and community service opened up space for women to be more nearly equal contributors. During the period from 1972 to 1977, women played crucial roles not only in the rank and file, as they had from the beginning, but also in the leadership of the party. Brown was arguably the most visible and powerful Panther leader for much of the 1970s, editing the *Black Panther*, running the party while Newton was in exile, and acting as its chief liaison to local and national politicians. Gendered notions of leadership and violence within the party never entirely vanished. When Brown took charge she faced significant opposition and felt pressure to exert authority by performing a form of ritualized violence that had long been part of the Panther mystique. Appearing as party leader for the first time in August 1974, she was flanked by armed male bodyguards while declaring to the assembled members, "I have all the guns and all the money. I can withstand challenge from without and within." Like Newton, Brown relied on an all-male security force to back up these threats, sometimes delivering physical punishments to dissident members who threatened her authority.[30] Nevertheless, the increasing visibility of women within the BPP leadership ranks opened opportunities to shape policy that had not been available to grassroots female members in the early years of the party. By the end of this period, the BPP's Central Committee had six female members, a sharp contrast to the origins of that body when Kathleen Cleaver had been the only female member.

Long-time Panther Ericka Huggins exercised substantial power both as a member of the Central Committee and director of the Oakland Community School, while Joan Kelley, formerly of the party's L.A. chapter, oversaw the Oakland Community Learning Center (OCLC), which coordinated the Panthers' burgeoning social programs.[31] The party's move to distance itself from the heteropatriarchal foundations of its previous commitment to revolutionary violence was on full display in the 1973 electoral campaign, where Brown and Seale endorsed gay rights and produced leaflets explaining "Why Gay People Should Vote for Bobby Seale and Elaine Brown."[32] Emory Douglas's artwork in the *Black Panther* and elsewhere also underwent a major shift, replacing guns and violence as markers of anticolonial heroism with images of the everyday dignity of men, women, and children struggling to overcome poverty and improve their communities.[33]

Domestic Feuds and Decaying Internationalism

For all its apparent success in transitioning from a divided, battered, and besieged cadre of revolutionaries into an effective vehicle for local politics and social activism, the Black Panther Party of the 1970s had flaws that ultimately undermined its effectiveness as an agent for change. Most obviously, the shift in emphasis from revolutionary nationalism to mainstream electoral politics put sharp limits on the ability of the Panthers to attack the structural roots of poverty, white supremacy, and militarism. Taken at face value, the emphasis on creating jobs and improving city services that formed the heart of the 1973 Seale-Brown campaign made them complicit in the rhetoric and logic of liberalism, which portrayed the problems facing poor people and people of color in Oakland and elsewhere as susceptible to simple technocratic solutions rather than as endemic to the system of racialized capitalism. Even if this rhetoric was used to conceal the real intentions of the BPP's candidates, the fact that they felt the need to run on a liberal Democratic platform limited their ability to build a mandate for more sweeping social and political change. As historians Waldo Martin and Joshua Bloom concluded, "Unlike the Black Panther Party before the ideological split, the Oakland Black Panthers in the 1970s never provided a model for disrupting established relations of power."[34] The choice to focus on local politics in Oakland also sharply circumscribed the options that the Panther candidates could have considered even had they won office. As Self observed, "Municipalities like Oakland are poor instruments for either revolutionary or social-democratic projects. The property tax can never act as the primary leverage for redistributions because the very survival of the city's institutions depends on it—overtaxed employers and industries simply flee to cities that will not burden them with high taxes."[35]

Further complicating their efforts to achieve success in the mainstream political arena, the Oakland Panthers had generally poor relations with other black activists, many of whom they had once attacked as "pork chop nationalists" or "bootlickers" while asserting that the BPP was the true vanguard of the black revolution. As party members attempted to gather support for efforts to win office, they found relatively few allies outside Oakland. Nowhere was this clearer than at the landmark National Black Political Convention in March 1972. Held in Gary, Indiana, this historic event brought together a wide cross-section of black politicians and activists, ranging from Amiri Baraka to Jesse Jackson, Coretta Scott King, and Betty Shabazz, to consider ways to mobilize black political power in the

United States. Although the Panthers attended the conference, they were scheduled to speak away from the main hall during a musical interlude where Bobby Seale "was relegated to express the [BPP] program for voting in conjunction with the singing of Isaac Hayes." Though expressing no ill will toward "Brother Isaac Hayes," this slight further alienated the party from the growing national coalition of black political activists and elected officials gathered at Gary.[36]

The "Base of Operations" strategy also saw the Panthers moving away from the international and transnational alliances that had bolstered the party's fortunes in the late 1960s. For all of the complications and ambiguities that had accompanied them, these alliances (both real and metaphorical) had been instrumental in fueling the BPP's rise from a small, West Oakland neighborhood group into an internationally recognized force that received plaudits from Algiers, Beijing, Havana, Hanoi, and Pyongyang and anxious scrutiny from Washington. Beyond the practical assistance that foreign allies had provided, either in the form of fund-raising from transnational allies in Europe and Japan or state-level diplomatic pressure in support of the international section's operations, the notion of the Panthers as partners in a worldwide uprising against colonialism and white supremacy was a crucial element in the party's anticolonial vernacular. Third World anticolonialism served as a sort of force multiplier for the Panthers, allowing them to position themselves not as a helpless, persecuted minority but rather as a vital part of a worldwide majority of people of color helping to take down the American Empire from the inside. In refocusing on Oakland and on working within the U.S. political and economic system, the BPP deprived themselves of the ability to effectively imagine revolutionary change, much less carry it out.

It would be misleading to suggest that the Panthers of the 1970s entirely abandoned foreign connections or inspirations. In addition to Newton's travels, a second BPP delegation that included Emory Douglas and Raymond "Masai" Hewitt visited China in March 1972.[37] The *Black Panther* continued to feature extensive coverage of international events throughout the decade, from the anticolonial wars of liberation in sub-Saharan Africa to the battle against apartheid in South Africa, Palestinian resistance against Israeli occupation, the growth of the Third World bloc at the United Nations, and even the struggles of Irish Republican forces against British rule. Under the editorship of David Graham Du Bois (son of Shirley Graham and stepson of W.E.B. Du Bois) from 1973 to 1977, the Panther paper offered rich and cosmopolitan news coverage, with a particular focus on Africa and China.[38]

In both tone and practice, however, the BPP's relationship to other nations and groups shifted in subtle but important ways during this period. The party's earlier emphasis on a single, shared revolutionary struggle, perhaps best exemplified in the early art of Emory Douglas, was replaced by a more distant form of solidarity politics. At the heart of Newton's doctrine of inter-communalism was the notion that while all struggles against imperialism were ultimately linked, in the short term each group or nation would have to fight its own battle in its own way on its own home turf. While the Panthers strongly supported the efforts of the Popular Movement for the Liberation of Angola (MPLA) to liberate their country, for example, there was no sug-gestion that the tactics or the goals of the MPLA were applicable to the situ-ation of people of color in the United States. This new approach was more realistic about the capabilities of the BPP and the often tenuous nature of its connections to other anticolonial groups and nations around the world, but it effectively consigned the party to working within the existing U.S. politi-cal and economic system without outside aid or support. Having taken that step, there was little to distinguish the BPP from other mainstream American political groups that enjoyed larger bases of mainstream support and lacked the baggage that came along with having once been associated with Kim Il-Sung and having had leaders jailed on criminal charges.

The Panthers also retreated from the kind of practical alliances, both international and transnational, that figures such as Eldridge and Kathleen Cleaver, Connie Matthews, and Denise Oliver had forged during the late 1960s and early 1970s. Although Newton traveled to China, Sweden, Cuba, and the Middle East from 1972 to 1981, none of these visits resulted in the kind of ties that the Panthers had cultivated with foreign governments and support groups from 1968 to 1971. The European Panther solidarity committees gradually dissolved in the wake of the party's split and its shift toward a more domestic agenda in the United States. Newton's biggest concern with respect to the party's remaining foreign allies was apparently to ensure that they disowned Cleaver.[39] The *Black Panther* still published let-ters of support from individuals and groups around the world that had been inspired by the BPP, which by the mid-1970s included the Dalit Panthers in India, the Polynesian Panthers in New Zealand, and even a group of Mizrahi Jews who founded an Israeli Panthers group.[40] In practical terms, however, there were few connections between the Oakland-based party and its international supporters and imitators.

In their shift toward the "Base of Operations" strategy, Panther leaders also largely missed out on the surge of domestic and international alliance building centered around the resurgence of interest in African Liberation Day (ALD), inaugurated in 1958 at the first conference of Independent African States in Ghana, and the ongoing struggle against the apartheid regime in South Africa. The anti-apartheid campaign during the 1970s and 1980 served much the same function as the Vietnam War had for the Panthers in the 1960s by connecting black and white activists in the United States (particularly on college campuses) with allies in other countries in common opposition to white supremacy.[41] But while Panther leaders appeared at some ALD events and the party newspaper offered frequent coverage of the anti-apartheid battle, the BPP played only a marginal role in the movement, as its leaders sought to focus their limited resources on Oakland. In December 1973, the Panthers sharply criticized a proposed conference on African liberation for failing to address "actions aimed at organizing and unifying Black people around those very critical issues affecting their day-to-day survival." Though "hailing, supporting and publicizing the wide-ranging, militant struggles of the peoples of Africa for liberation," the party newspaper made clear that "the Black Panther Party understands that its first task, as a vanguard organization of Black people in America, is to carry forward, intensify and widen the struggle against the U.S. empire makers here at home!"[42] A private intra-party memo was more blunt, declaring that "[w]e do not support [the] African Liberation Day Support Committee, therefore we will not participate in African Liberation Day activities, scheduled for next month. Specifically, the A.L.D Committee has supported Stokely Carmichael and Eldridge Cleaver, but when they were asked to make it known that we were very instrumental in making the past African Liberation Day a success, they refused to acknowledge us. They were asked for an apology and refused to give it."[43] Although the Panthers eased this stance somewhat while Newton was in exile and eventually developed close ties to Pan Africanist Congress of Azania representative David Sibeko, the party remained largely on the fringes of the growing anti-apartheid coalition.[44]

"Illegitimate Capitalists" and Intra-party Violence

The BPP's changing relationship to violence was another important factor that undermined the party's effectiveness in the 1970s. By 1972, any vestiges of the Panthers' previous commitment to violence in support of an American revolution had been excised from the party's public presentation. The death of George Jackson at the hands of guards during a failed escape attempt from San Quentin State Prison in August 1971 had eliminated the last high-profile member of the party who spoke loudly in favor of anticolonial violence.[45] The *Black Panther* newspaper that had once printed not only images celebrating armed resistance but also practical guides to guerrilla warfare now discouraged such talk as suicidal and counterproductive. In an article headlined "Prospects for Revolutionary Intercommunal Warfare," Romaine Fitzgerald declared that "[l]iberated territory can only be established if the guerrilla forces can keep the enemy on the defensive and unable to amass for a sustained offensive."

> This cannot be the case in the U.S. because technology allows the pigs to destroy any area without even committing ground forces. We have no strategy for the enemy on this level. In the final analysis the strategy of protracted guerrilla warfare based on a dispersed peasant population is more absurd than Bolshevik spontaneity. Surely it will not break the back bone of the ruling-circle, the military forces.[46]

A review in the Panther paper of the 1973 film *The Spook Who Sat by the Door*, based on Sam Greenlee's novel about a black former CIA agent who organizes an urban uprising in the United States, savaged it for encouraging young black men to take up arms against the U.S. government. Such an action would "result in the wholesale slaughter of Black people" and be harmful to the cause as "the young, White dude in the uniform of the U.S. Army is not the enemy, even with his racism."[47] Newton publicly expressed regret for his past actions in encouraging such thinking, lamenting his August 1970 offer to send black troops to fight alongside the NLF in Vietnam as indicative of a "revolutionary cultist" period in the Panthers' history.[48]

As with the BPP's skepticism regarding foreign alliances in the 1970s, the turn away from anticolonial violence was rooted in a reasonable assessment of the party's capabilities. Although abandoning the notion of armed rebellion limited the Panthers' ability to advocate for truly revolutionary change, it is hard to begrudge or second-guess this decision in light of the tremendous sacrifices and limited gains that accompanied the more confrontational tactics favored by Cleaver and his allies. Had the party truly abandoned violence in favor of local social and political activism, it might have at least carved out a lasting place in the fabric of the East Bay even if the Panthers failed to achieve their lofty goal of remaking American society. Instead, however, violence remained crucial to the BPP's operations in the 1970s but was largely directed inward at the black community and its own members. While the BPP publicly disarmed, ditching both guns and their signature black-jacketed uniforms, it maintained a massive cache of weapons stored in safe houses across the Bay Area. Instead of being widely distributed to members, these weapons and their handling were turned over a small group of Newton's bodyguards (many of whom later went on to work under Elaine Brown during her tenure as party leader).[49]

Dubbed the Buddha Samurai by Newton, the armed wing of the 1970s Panthers differed substantially from the underground unit that Geronimo Pratt had led in the late 1960s prior to being expelled from the party.[50] This small, disciplined, and well-armed cadre was not intended to wage guerrilla warfare against the U.S. government or even to protect the BPP offices against assaults by local police. Instead, they served as personal bodyguards for Panther leaders, internal enforcers of party discipline, and, most importantly, as Newton's chief weapon in a crusade to establish control over Oakland's criminal underground. David Hilliard offered arguably the most positive interpretation of the Panthers' attempts to seize control of the East Bay's drug, prostitution, and after-hours nightclub enterprises in the 1970s. "We were approaching them in a way to make them part and parcel of our movement," he suggested, "serving the community they lived in, so that they might no longer be looked on as outcasts or as a predatory group."

> Their trade was still a byproduct of capitalism. A woman selling her body is still one of the world's oldest professions. But our thrust was to organize an illegitimate economic resource, connect it to our community programs, and put the money into our programs, with the end result being more respect for a segment of the community that had been historically criticized as a pariah.[51]

These operations, which Newton dubbed "taxing the illegitimate capitalists," provided badly needed income for a party that could no longer depend on consistent contributions from white supporters or sales of the *Black Panther* to finance its expanding political and community service operations in Oakland.[52] But they also took the BPP far from its revolutionary roots and made it complicit in the kind of violence within the black community that they had once attacked as counterrevolutionary. And for a party that was seeking to move away from the patriarchy and misogyny that often characterized its early history, the fact that these operations included profiting from prostitution was not encouraging. Newton himself was charged with murdering a young prostitute on the streets of Oakland in 1974, and Chief of Security Flores Forbes was sentenced for attempted murder following a failed attempt to assassinate one of the witnesses in the case.[53]

The CIA was perhaps unusually astute in observing in September 1972 that the BPP's operations in Oakland "faintly resemble the early days of the so-called American Mafia." But while government analysts believed that these "Mafia-type activities [were] designed to gain control of the black ghetto communities where sanctuaries for long-range revolutionary activities would be assured," the reality was that controlling the criminal underworld was becoming an end in itself for the Oakland Panthers rather than a springboard for revolution.[54] Increasingly running party operations out of the Lamp Post, an Oakland bar and nightclub, Newton traded the Little Red Book and *The Wretched of the Earth* for a new literary influence. "The Lamp Post," recalled Hilliard, "comes to symbolize a new influence guiding Huey: *The Godfather*."

> Before we've used Cuba, Algeria, and China as examples of revolutionary struggle. Now Mario Puzo's novel provides the organizational map, a patriarchal family, divided into military and political wings."[55]

Multiple Newton loyalists asserted that Puzo's novel and the 1972 film adaptation by Francis Ford Coppola were mandatory texts for party members as the Panthers waged their underground war to control the East Bay's "illegitimate capitalists."[56]

As with Puzo's fictional crime family, BPP members in the 1970s often found that the violence they used to control the local community was frequently turned inward on those suspected of disloyalty or insufficient devotion to Newton, Brown, or other party leaders. Such violence had never been entirely absent, and the BPP had long maintained a relatively rigid and hierarchical command structure at the national level. Previously, however, the dispersed nature of the party and the fact that access to firearms was relatively democratized, with weapons training in many cases mandatory for new members, had discouraged attempts by Panther leaders to routinely impose their will by force on the rank and file. But with the BPP centralized in Oakland and access to weapons restricted to an elite guard loyal only to the party leaders, harsh physical punishment for even minor infractions become much more common. Aaron Dixon, who was part of the BPP security squad in the 1970s, recalled that "[c]orporal punishment had never really been established as a party policy. It just seemed to grow out of our circumstances and our paramilitary ideology."

> In truth, this kind of physical discipline was something we could have done without. But our willingness to use it, and our acceptance of it, was symptomatic of deeper issues having little to do with revolution.[57]

This intra-party violence, combined with the BPP's ties to organized crime and Newton's increasingly heavy drug use, undermined the Panthers' efforts to establish a lasting presence even with their more limited and mainstream political and social agenda. By the mid-1970s, cofounder Bobby Seale and Chief of Staff David Hilliard had left, and Brown followed several years later, leaving a shrinking party in the hands of an increasingly erratic Newton and a handful of remaining loyalists. Dixon, who stayed on through the waning days of the party, recalled, "We were all trying to dull our senses, trying to deny what was happening, that our revolutionary family was coming to an end and we would all have to make a decision when to leave our slowly disintegrating revolutionary army."[58]

The Black Liberation Army and Guerrilla Warfare in the 1970s

While the Oakland-based Panthers pivoted toward mainstream political and social organizing supplemented with *Godfather*-style criminal activities, a handful of former BPP members across the country remained committed to carrying out the revolution by any means necessary. The origins and operations of the Black Liberation Army remain cloaked in mystery. As a small, underground network of revolutionary cells self-consciously engaged in illegal activities, the BLA kept little or no records of its operations and issued few public statements. It left no equivalent of the *Black Panther* newspaper that would allow historians to track its evolution on a weekly basis. Many of its surviving members are behind bars, and those who remain free, most notably Assata Shakur in exile in Cuba, have been reluctant to disclose details that might incriminate their former comrades in arms. The only extended scholarly work on the BLA remains an unpublished doctoral dissertation by Gaidi Faraj.[59] A number of journalists have written about the group, but these accounts have been warped by heavy reliance on police and FBI sources and a tendency to emphasize

the more sensationalistic aspects of the BLA's story while failing to grapple with the ideology that informed its origins and operation.[60] Although
a definitive account of the BLA is likely to remain elusive, a survey of
what is known about the organization is important in understanding the
legacy of the Panthers and their domestic and international agenda in
the 1970s.

As early as September 28, 1968, the published "Rules of the Black Panther Party" declared, "No party member can join any other army or force
other than the BLACK LIBERATION ARMY."[61] In 1968, however, the
BLA was almost certainly not a formal organization or even an unofficial
subsection of the party. Rather, it appears to have been a term used loosely
either as a synonym for the party itself or a blanket label for those committed to ending white supremacy in the United States by force if necessary.
As BPP (and later BLA) member Nuh Washington explained it, "Anyone
who desired freedom, to control their own destiny, is essentially a member
of the Black Liberation Army, in that sense."[62] A number of local BPP chapters apparently had underground or quasi-military wings in the late 1960s,
and BLA member Jalil Muntaqim later asserted that well prior to the 1970s
"the Black underground was becoming rich in experience in the tactics of
armed expropriations, sabotage, and ambush-assaults."[63] But it was developments within two specific BPP chapters, those in Los Angeles and New
York, that helped lay the foundations for the development of the BLA as a
distinct and ultimately separate unit.

The L.A. branch of the BPP was organized in 1968 under the leadership
of Alprentice "Bunchy" Carter. Carter had been an influential member of
the Slausons, an early L.A. street gang, before being sent to prison, where
he joined the Nation of Islam. In January 1966, Eldridge Cleaver was transferred to Soledad, where he met and befriended Carter, convincing him to
drop his affiliation with the NOI in favor of a more politicized approach
to black liberation. Upon his release, Carter renewed his acquaintance with
Cleaver, and in January 1968 he organized the L.A. Panther chapter, the first
branch of the party to operate outside of the Bay Area.[64] In forming the
chapter, Carter tapped a number of current and former Slausons to serve
under him. According to Faraj, in doing so he set up a two-tier structure
within the chapter. In addition to the public membership of the L.A. Panthers, Carter also recruited a small number of "Wolves," gang members who
were to serve as an "underground cadre" to carry out actions that could not
be traced directly back to the party and its leaders.[65] Though not ideologically or operationally distinct from the BPP in the way that the BLA would

eventually become, the notion of supplementing the party's aboveground operations with an underground military force can be traced directly back to the founding of the L.A. chapter under Carter's leadership.

Though other local chapters may have had similar quasi-underground arrangements, it was another L.A. Panther, Geronimo Pratt, who was responsible for bringing this innovation to the national stage. Pratt was a Vietnam veteran who had received multiple decorations while serving as a scout with the Eighty-Second Airborne. Rotated back to the States long enough to take part in crushing the 1967 Detroit rebellion, Pratt returned to Vietnam where he fought at Da Nang in the midst of the Tet Offensive. Disillusioned with the government that he had risked his life to serve, Pratt took an early discharge and traveled to the West Coast in the fall of 1968. While in L.A., Pratt met with Carter, and the two men struck up a close relationship while attending the High Potential program at the University of California, Los Angeles (UCLA).[66] Drawn into the world of the L.A. Panthers, Pratt put his military experience to use in fortifying party offices and training members in the care and use of various types of firearms and explosives. His talents also won him attention from the national headquarters in Oakland. While Newton was behind bars, Carter assumed many of the responsibilities of the minister of defense position, including traveling around the country to help prepare other chapters to resist police assaults. Following Carter's murder at the hands of a rival black nationalist group (the US Organization) in January 1969, an event directly precipitated by the FBI's COINTELPRO efforts, Pratt was appointed head of the L.A. chapter.[67]

On December 9, 1969, heavily armed officers from the newly created Special Weapons and Tactics (SWAT) branch of the LAPD staged a raid on the Panthers' headquarters at Forty-First and Central. A five-hour standoff and running gun battle ensued, and a police helicopter dropped dynamite on the roof of the building.[68] Although not in the office at the time, Pratt still faced charges stemming from the Central Avenue shootout. Skipping his L.A. court dates, he went underground in August 1970. With the approval of the BPP's Central Committee and Newton's blessing, Pratt set up a clandestine military training facility for party members in Texas. He also traveled across the South to share the tactics that he had pioneered while in Los Angeles.[69] Pratt's short-lived Texas training camp, which was terminated following his arrest on December 8, 1970, represented the first attempt to create a formal, underground military wing of the BPP. Its organization reflected Pratt's belief that the party would benefit from "a cell system, that empowered local leadership" rather than the centralized and hierarchical operations preferred by leaders in Oakland.[70] Both this leadership philosophy and the unit's emphasis on preparing for an underground war against the U.S. government were increasingly at odds with the direction taken by Newton upon his release from prison. Although the Panther cofounder had initially deferred to Pratt and his impressive military credentials, Pratt's arrest provided a convenient excuse for Newton to purge him and his more militant supporters from the party.[71]

A second impetus for the creation of the BLA came from within the New York City branch of the BPP. The New York chapter had roots in the city's rich black nationalist, pan-African, and Muslim movements, with members often taking African-inspired names and preferring dashikis to the standard West Coast Panther uniform of black leather jacket and beret. These trappings of cultural nationalism, as well as the fact that a number of New York party members were Sunni Muslims (in most cases inspired by Malcolm X's conversion after leaving the NOI), often led to tensions with national leaders in Oakland.[72] Additionally, by 1970 some New York party members had come to believe that Newton's emphasis on defending Panther homes and offices (outlined in his Executive Mandate #3) was misguided.[73] Standard guerrilla doctrine, as advocated by theorists such as Regis Debray and Carlos Marighella, was to avoid defending fixed objectives where insurgents could easily be located and overwhelmed by numerically superior police or military forces. As New York Panther and BLA member Assata Shakur explained it, "One of the basic laws of people's struggle is to retreat when the enemy is strong and to attack when the enemy is weak."

> As far as i was concerned, defending the office was suicidal. The pigs had the manpower, initiative, surprise, and gunpowder. We would just be sitting ducks. I felt that the Party was dealing from an emotional rather than rational basis. Just because you believe in self-defense doesn't mean you let yourself be sucked into defending yourself on the enemy's terms. One of the Party's major weaknesses, i thought, was the failure to clearly differentiate between aboveground political struggle and underground, clandestine military struggle.[74]

Shakur and others within the New York chapter preferred the guerrilla tactics pioneered by the Weather Underground in its secretive war against the U.S. government and military machine. An open letter to the Weather

Underground from the Panther 21—a group of New York party members charged (and eventually found not guilty) with planning an assault on NYPD stations and other targets—supported the Weather Underground bombing campaign, critiqued the BPP's leadership for failing to pursue similar efforts, and declared that "racism, colonialism, sexism, and all other pig 'isms' . . . can only be ended by . . . ARMED STRUGGLE."[75]

It was Newton's decision to purge Pratt and his allies and associates along with the Panther 21 in early 1971, followed shortly thereafter by the split with Cleaver, that led to the creation of the BLA as a distinct, if still inchoate, entity outside the structure of the BPP. In the beginning, at least, the BLA had no membership rolls or command structure. Washington recalled that in the wake of Cleaver-Newton feud, "[m]any were left out in the cold, but fortunately, other comrades who had gone underground were able to take them in."

> These comrades had been forced underground prior to the split, and had cut off communications with BPP National Headquarters in Oakland. This allowed for the creation of a haven for many disenchanted and expelled Panthers. Some expelled Panthers were even directed to the underground by Panthers still working for the Party.[76]

Early BLA cells organized in Los Angeles and San Francisco, but the largest unit was formed out of the ashes of the New York Panthers and included figures such as Lumumba Shakur, Zayd Malik Shakur, Assata Shakur, Sundiata Acoli, and Dhoruba bin Wahad. The New York wing of the BLA was initially in close contact with Cleaver in Algeria, who planned to use the group as the nucleus for his Afro-American People's Army. "To follow Algeria, that was the initial plan," recalled Dhoruba bin Wahad. "When the split went down, we were following instructions from Eldridge and D.C. [Donald Cox] in Algiers."[77] But disputes over tactics, compounded by the vast distance between New York and Algiers, soon led to tensions between Cleaver and the nascent BLA.

Safiya Bukhari, a New York Panther and BLA supporter, recoiled upon receiving a phone call from Cleaver demanding that they "escalate the struggle" by immediately launching guerrilla attacks. Although committed to liberation through violence if necessary, Bukhari found Cleaver's orders presumptive and ill-advised:

> I said "No!" I was not going to tell people to do that. I told Eldridge that the conditions were not right, and I was not going to encourage our people

to go out and take part in or become victims of a bloodbath. He told me that if I didn't do it there would be a second split in the Black Panther Party. I held firm because I truly believed I was right. Eldridge didn't know the objective conditions here. He was more than three thousand miles away in Algeria.[78]

Sekou Odinga, a former New York Panther who had fled to Algeria, was similarly dismissive, declaring in an interview that "[Cleaver] was not a military man; he only thought he was. . . . It may have looked like Cleaver was leading the BLA, but he wasn't. He just talked the talk."[79] After BLA soldiers did take the offensive with the assassination of two New York City police officers on May 19, 1971, the group's New York cells went deep underground, further compounding the existing communications problems. As Cleaver became immersed in his own struggles with the Algerian government and his erstwhile Asian allies, the two groups went their separate ways, leading to the de facto "second split" that Cleaver had prophesied. The only link between the two organizations was Odinga, who left Algeria in 1973 to join the BLA in New York and went on to become one of its longest serving members.[80]

One of the major weaknesses of most historical coverage of the BLA is the tendency to focus on the group's violent tactics without considering the ideology and goals that motivated its members. This focus on the group's criminality was facilitated by the BLA's tendency to eschew the frequent issuing of manifestos or party platforms in favor of direct action. Nevertheless, the group did make several attempts to explain its goals, strategy, and tactics during the 1970s. These statements must be treated with some care as the decentralized and secretive nature of the BLA makes it difficult to know how representative they were of the group as a whole. Nevertheless, a close reading of BLA memoirs and communiqués provides a relatively clear and consistent picture of the group's motivations. At its core the BLA was motivated by the same brand of revolutionary nationalism that had animated the formation and operations of the BPP from 1966 to 1971. Central to this proposition was that, in the words of BLA member Kuwasi Balagoon (Donald Weems), "[t]he ruling class of the United States and its Government colonizes the New Afrikan People; that is, Black people held within the confines of the present borders of the U.S."[81]

As had been the case in the early days of the BPP, two conclusions flowed from the BLA's colonial analysis of black America. The first was that anticolonial violence was a just and necessary response to the oppression that they faced. Balagoon, for example, compared the group to the PLO,

Irish Republican Army, African National Congress, and other anticolonial guerrillas in concluding that "[h]istorically and universally the counter to imperialist armies are liberation armies, the counter to colonial wars are wars of liberation, the counter to reactionary violence, revolutionary violence."[82] The second conclusion that flowed from the BLA's colonial analysis was that, in the words of Dhoruba bin Wahad, "[r]evolutionary nationalism . . . understood that there was a common solidarity between all people under the same economic and social political system. This oppression has its historical roots in the development of European hegemony and power in the world."[83] Thus while many BLA members were sympathetic to aspects of cultural and religious nationalism (and some shared membership in the separatist Republic of New Afrika), most retained a loosely Marxist conception that envisioned links between diverse peoples and nations created by the shared experience of racialized colonial occupation.

Declaring the BLA to be "anti-capitalist, anti-imperialist, anti-racist and anti-sexist," its leaders expressed goals nearly identical to those of the pre-split BPP, including "the institution of Socialistic relationships in which Black people have total and absolute control over their own destiny as a people." Like the BPP before them, BLA members also viewed their struggle within the United States as making a vital contribution to Third World liberation, "for in striving to liberate ourselves we must abolish a system that enslaves others throughout the world."[84] This analysis was on display in one of the organization's first public statements, a letter sent to the *New York Times* claiming responsibility for the killing of two NYPD officers in May 1971:

> The armed goons of this racist government will again meet the guns of oppressed Third World People as long as they occupy our community and murder our brothers and sisters in the name of American law and order; just as the fascist Marines and Army [that] occupy Vietnam in the name of democracy and murder Vietnamese people in the name of American imperialism are confronted with the guns of the Vietnamese Liberation Army, the domestic armed forces of racism and oppression will be confronted with the guns of the Black Liberation Army.[85]

In justifying their actions, the BLA closely echoed Newton's 1967 statement that "[t]here is a great similarity between the occupying army in Southeast Asia and the occupation of our communities by the racist police."[86] In doing so, they recapitulated not simply the rhetoric but also the ideology that had guided the early incarnation of the Black Panther Party.

Although rooted in a formulation of revolutionary nationalism that had its roots in the early to mid-1960s, the BLA and its members also had to account for the changing domestic and international circumstances of the 1970s. The birth and early growth of the Panthers had coincided with a rising tide of militant anticolonialism that seemed to have the United States and its allies on the defensive at home and around the world. Many party members in the late 1960s operated under the sincere belief that a revolution in the United States was as inevitable and imminent as the victory of the NLF in Vietnam. By the time the BLA emerged as a separate organization in 1971, however, it was clear that whatever success the Vietnamese might have would not be equaled by radicals in the United States any time in the near future. The election of Richard Nixon, the shattering blows dealt by COINTELPRO, the fragmentation of groups such as the BPP and SDS, and the ripple effects of détente complicated previous assumptions about the vulnerabilities of the American Empire. The BLA acknowledged these developments, and its calls for guerrilla warfare lacked the bravado of Robert F. Williams's prediction of a ninety-day victory in the first half of the 1960s. Muntaqim referred to the BLA's early operations as part of a "defensive-offensive" strategy intended not to overthrow the U.S. government but rather "to protect the interest of the aboveground political apparatus' aspiration to develop a mass movement towards national liberation."[87] In this conception, the BLA's military actions would draw the attention of the state away from allies operating aboveground, creating space for political mobilization while at the same time inspiring the masses and striking fear into the heart of the oppressors. It was essentially a holding action designed to allow larger domestic and international mobilization a chance to survive and recover in the hostile terrain of the early 1970s.

The "defensive-offensive" strategy had its origins in the period when the nascent BLA was still at least loosely connected to the BPP and its aboveground political apparatus. By May 1971, however, it was clear that the break with the Newton-led Panthers was irrevocable and that Cleaver's Algerian operation was not able to offer a viable replacement. This left the BLA in the position of being an underground unit without aboveground political partners. Nor did the group enjoy any significant international contacts that might provide shelter, arms, or even propaganda support. Despite lacking a viable means to translate their actions into a viable strategy for revolutionary change, BLA cells pushed ahead with their plans for guerrilla warfare in 1971–1973. These actions included assassinations (targeted killings of police officers), expropriations (robberies of banks and businesses to raise funds), and sabotage (bombings). Undoubtedly, the hasty move to armed action was stimulated by the paranoid, hothouse atmosphere of the early 1970s that saw BLA members fearing attacks from both the police and agents of the Newton-led BPP.[88]

Donald Cox privately critiqued the BLA's actions as impulsive and ill-timed in a letter sent to the New York cell from Algeria. Although supportive of armed struggle, Cox insisted that "[b]efore we commit ourselves we must build a foundation. . . . We can't do any building if we're running and hiding." He also took issue with the BLA's public communiqués as premature "until we have our foundation developed to the point where we can guarantee a continuity of actions" and warned, "I don't think it does us any good to talk about the fact that we have hand grenades when our enemy has hydrogen bombs."[89] Some BLA members later agreed that undertaking an offensive campaign against the state in the absence of community support, or at least a viable aboveground political unit, was a mistake. Odinga conceded that "[p]eople weren't ready for armed struggle."

> One of the things we now know, and should've known then, is we were way out in front of the people. A little more study would have made that clear. You can be in the vanguard of the struggle, but you have to have the people behind you, and they weren't.[90]

Mass support is not necessarily a prerequisite for a successful guerrilla campaign, but at the very least any such effort must be tied to some sort of political organization that can leverage the military actions of the underground into building such support. Divorced from the BPP and too busy plotting military action and running from the authorities to operate their own educational or propaganda wing, the BLA was unable to effectively connect their sporadic acts of violence to a larger political or ideological program.

Given the domestic and international climate of the early 1970s, it is highly unlikely that the BLA would have enjoyed meaningful success even with significant aboveground political support. But it would have allowed the group's members to contextualize their actions in such a way as to spur greater contemporary and historical discussion of their aims. The BPP's prolific and skillful public communications efforts, including the *Black Panther* newspaper and frequent speeches and interviews with party leaders, made it difficult to tar the party's members as simple criminals, despite the best efforts of the police, the FBI, the U.S. government, and large sections

of the media. In contrast, the secretive, underground tactics that characterized the BLA made it far easier for government officials, the press, and even
historians to casually dismiss them as "madmen" who "did it for nothing."[91]
Although the group's guerrilla efforts were ill-conceived and ultimately
counterproductive, they were motivated by a genuine set of grievances and
in service of an ideology, revolutionary nationalism, that offered a coherent
analysis and plan of action for battling colonialism, capitalism, and white
supremacy.

Taps for Revolutionaries and the Dawn of the Reagan Counterrevolution

By the end of 1973, police had killed or imprisoned a large percentage
of the BLA's membership. Muntaqim conceded that "[b]y 1974–1975,
the fighting capacity of the Black Liberation Army had been destroyed,"
although he argued that "the BLA as a politico-military organization had
not been destroyed."[92] With most of its surviving leaders behind bars, the
organization turned its efforts to prisons as a site of organization and political action. Arguably the most important legacy of the BLA was in its campaign for the reform or abolition of the U.S. prison system while bringing
attention to the plight of political prisoners and their treatment within the
United States.[93] Behind bars, ironically, BLA members were also able to
more coherently formulate and publicize the rational for the actions they
had undertaken earlier in the decade, most notably in the 1975 publication
Message to the Black Movement. Elements of the group did attempt a return
to guerrilla warfare in the latter half of the decade. Odinga returned to
the United States secretly in 1973 and avoided capture or detection. He
eventually teamed with Mutulu Shakur, a doctor at the radical Lincoln
Detox Clinic in New York City, other former BLA members (most notably
Kuwasi Balagoon), and several white radicals, including Kathy Boudin and
Marilyn Buck.[94] They scored a major coup by freeing Assata Shakur from
a New Jersey prison in November 1979 and assisting her subsequent flight
to Cuba. The primary focus of the revived group, however, was on so-called
expropriations, which largely took the form of a series of bank robberies
and stick-ups. The BLA–white radical alliance met its end in the aftermath
of a botched robbery of a Brink's truck in New York in October 1981.
Although captured members of the group tried to use the ensuing trial as
a forum for advancing their cause, this second iteration of the BLA shared

with its predecessor an inability to effectively tie its acts of violence to a larger political program.[95]

The BPP soldiered on in Oakland (with some regional offices reopening in the mid-1970s), where it was increasingly tied to the Democratic Party establishment. Newton's continuing problems with the law (including murder and assault charges), drug abuse, and erratic behavior hastened the demise of the Black Panthers as an effective force even at the local level. Mumia Abu-Jamal lamented Newton's fate: "Huey, a supreme commander without a command, a visionary with no outlet for his vision, a revolutionary bereft of a revolutionary party, retrogressed into the fascination of the street hustlers of his Oakland youth; the pimps, the players, the 'illegitimate capitalists' (as he called them) called him. It was, to be sure, a fatal attraction."[96] At best, the BPP in the latter half of the 1970s was a small but important player in California politics and community service in Oakland. At its worst, the party came to represent the kind of criminal organization that its opponents had long accused it of being. The last issue of the *Black Panther* newspaper appeared in September 1980, one month before former California governor and long-time Panther nemesis Ronald Wilson Reagan won election as the fortieth president of the United States. Newton continued to spiral into addiction and was murdered by a drug dealer outside an Oakland crack house on August 22, 1989.

Eldridge Cleaver experienced arguably the most colorful, if still ultimately tragic, post–BPP career. Cleaver withdrew from both the Cold War and the Third World in the aftermath of his departure from Algeria. Eldridge, Kathleen, and their two children (both born in exile) settled in Paris, where they lived clandestinely while appealing for asylum from the French government. Eldridge had tired of living in exile and was bitterly disillusioned by the collapse of the international section. "Face it," he told an interviewer who tracked him down in Paris, "people are Nationalists more than they are internationalist, and they use Internationalism in a very cynical way in order to further their own nationalist aspirations." As for the Third World, Cleaver declared it to be "an empty phrase," masking the "the many differences between the needs of the various countries involved."[97] Abandoned by both the BPP and his former international allies and unable to summon the creative powers that had fueled *Soul on Ice*, Cleaver decided to return to the United States to face trial in 1975.

While in an Alameda County, California, jail, Cleaver embraced evangelical Christianity. Upon his release on bail in August 1976, he underwent a whirlwind series of transformations as he attempted to reinvent himself as a born-again Christian minister while also exploring Mormonism, Sun Myung Moon's Unification Church, and a religion of his own creation that he dubbed "Christlam." The fact that he was also attempting to produce and market a new style of men's pants that featured a prominent external codpiece (or "penis sleeve") led some observers to doubt the sincerity of Cleaver's conversion(s). Entitling one of his sermons "The Golden Shower" also indicated a certain lack of commitment to his faith.[98] Politically, the former Panther swerved hard right, embracing his former nemesis Reagan's run for the presidency in 1980 and further reinventing himself as a fervent anticommunist in the pages of the *National Review*. In a 1981 interview, the erstwhile guerrilla leader invoked Booker T. Washington in urging black Americans to "cast down your bucket where you are" and declared that the United States "is the greatest country in the world. I really feel in my heart that America really needs to take control of the world."[99]

Cleaver's life in the late 1970s and early 1980s was a whirlwind that featured an appearance with Donald Rumsfeld at Vanderbilt University and at a benefit for cryonics featuring Wavy Gravy, Robert Anton Wilson, Paul Krassner, and Timothy Leary. While promoting his newfound embrace of American exceptionalism, he was hit in the face with an Oreo-cookie cream pie by the Anarchist Party of Canada (Groucho Marxist) and heckled by an audience in Oakland. Having been rejected for a job at a new Silicon Valley startup named Apple Computer in 1981, Cleaver found work as a tree surgeon in nearby San Jose, California.[100] By the 1990s, he had drifted back leftward, penning critiques of the first Gulf War and voicing support for the Million Man March organized by Nation of Islam minister Louis Farrakhan.[101] Cleaver died in 1998 in relative obscurity, a shadow of the "Cosmopolitan Guerrilla" who had once commanded international attention.

Ultimately, the hard-pressed leaders of the BPP, the international section and RPCN, and the BLA were unable to formulate an effective response to the changed international and domestic landscape that they confronted in the age of détente and late–Cold War stagnation. Not all members or former members met fates as tragic as those of Newton, Cleaver, and the imprisoned or killed soldiers of the BLA. A number of former Panthers went on to make productive contributions in community service, politics, and activism. But as Aaron Dixon lamented, most of the party's rank and file who returned to their communities battered and bruised from their confrontations with police repression and party infighting found that "there would be no cheering crowds, no open arms, no therapy, no counseling."[102]

Former New York City BPP member Afeni Shakur observed simply, "It was a war we lost."[103] The BPP and its various splinter groups undeniably failed to bring about the revolutionary remaking of American society that stood as their central goal. They efforts, however, left a rich and contested legacy that remains relevant in the twenty-first century at a time when white supremacy, colonialism, and the ongoing effects of neoliberalism and deindustrialization continue to haunt the world from Ferguson, Missouri, to occupied Palestine.

Epilogue

"Our Demand Is Simple: Stop Killing Us"

From Oakland to Ferguson

On August 9, 2014, Darren Wilson of the Ferguson, Missouri, Police Department (FPD) shot and killed Michael Brown, an eighteen-year-old African American man and recent high school graduate. Wilson fired twelve shots, at least six of which hit Brown, who was unarmed. The most serious crime of which Michael Brown was suspected at the time of his death was the theft of a box of cigarillos from a nearby convenience store.[1] In grand jury testimony, Wilson defended his use of deadly force, testifying that while the two men struggled, Brown "had the most intense aggressive face. The only way I can describe it, *it looks like a demon*." Wilson, who never faced criminal charges for the killing, went on to assert that the teenaged Brown "looked like he was almost bulking up to run through the shots, like it was making him mad that I'm shooting at him."[2] An investigation of the FPD by the U.S. Department of Justice (DOJ) in the months that followed determined that Wilson's behavior was far from an isolated incident. The DOJ "found substantial evidence of racial bias among police and court staff in Ferguson," concluding that "[t]he harms of Ferguson's police and court practices are borne disproportionately by African Americans, and there is evidence that this is due in part to intentional discrimination on the basis of race."[3]

In the days that followed Brown's death, protests in Ferguson, a pre-dominantly African American suburb of St. Louis, were met with a militarized response that featured police officers brandishing automatic weapons and equipped with gas masks, bulletproof vests, sniper scopes, night vision goggles, grenade launchers, and armored vehicles designed to withstand the impact of improvised explosive devices (IEDs). A FPD officer was caught on a CNN video taunting protesters by yelling, "Bring it, all you fucking animals! Bring it!"[4] An Iraq War veteran who had participated in the bloody counterinsurgency battle in Diyala province in 2005–6 observed, "In terms of its equipment, organization, and deployment methods, the Ferguson force looks more like an infantry or military police company in Iraq. Its police wear the same body armor; carry the same semi-automatic M4 carbines and semi-automatic pistols; patrol in similar fire-team and squad formations; and employ similarly aggressive tactics towards a population perceived to be hostile."[5] This link here was not entirely coincidental: many of the types of weapons brandished by the FPD were made available to domestic police departments as part of a Department of Defense program that transferred surplus from the Iraq and Afghanistan wars.[6]

In the crucible of the Ferguson protests, a movement was born that combined the traditional tactics of marches and demonstrations with new technology, most notably cell phone cameras and live-streaming video paired with social media such as Twitter. Largely decentralized and leader-less, the movement organized under the hashtag #BlackLivesMatter, a rallying cry created in 2013 by activists Alicia Garza, Patrisse Cullors and Opal Tometi in the wake of the shooting of Trayvon Martin, another unarmed, young African American male (Martin had just turned seventeen).[7] The Black Lives Matter movement spread across the country in the wake of Ferguson, with dramatic flashpoints in response to the deaths of unarmed African Americans at the hands of police officers, including Eric Garner in New York City, Tamir Rice in Cleveland, Walter Scott in South Carolina, and Freddie Gray in Baltimore. These protests called attention to the persistent inequities in police use of deadly force against people of color as well as the fact that the officers involved were seldom punished. Although the lack of consistent national statistics on police violence complicates a full understanding of the phenomenon, one recent study concluded that while people of color make up only 37.4 percent of the U.S. population, they account for close to half of those killed by police and over 60 percent of unarmed fatalities. Unarmed African Americans are twice as likely to be killed by police in such circumstances as whites.[8] More broadly, this movement, in the words of political scientist Fredrick C. Harris, "demanded that American society reconsider how it values black lives."[9]

The persistence of police violence directed against African Americans, enduring patterns of racialized economic inequality and de facto segregation, the militarization of U.S. policing and its links to wars in Afghanistan and Iraq, and the emergence of the Black Lives Matter movement raise the question of what relevance the Black Panther Party and its legacy have in the twenty-first century. The links between the BPP and these new, grassroots movements are for the most part indirect. While the Dallas-based New Black Panther Party (NBPP) and a related organization, the Huey P. Newton Gun Club, have sought to claim the legacy of the Panthers, these groups bear little resemblance to their supposed inspiration. Though nominally committed to "Revolutionary Black Nationalism/Pan Africanism," the NBPP's goals are more in line with the separatist black nationalism of the Nation of Islam.[10] Former Panthers, ranging from Bobby Seale, Elbert "Big Man" Howard, Elaine Brown, and the board of the Huey P. Newton Foundation to Dhoruba bin Wahad have denounced the NPBB. Seale has dismissed the organization as "a black racist hate group."[11] The NBPP has remained small and largely isolated since its foundation in 1989–90. It has few domestic or international allies and no real ties to the much larger and more active Black Lives Matter movement.

Times and conditions change, and it would be foolish to expect contemporary movements to manifest in exactly the same way as their predecessors. Nevertheless, the ideological and tactical innovations of the BPP as well as the party's successes and failures remain relevant to struggles against white supremacy, colonialism, and institutionalized violence against people of color in the twenty-first century. The Panthers' decision to build an organization that was international in both its analysis and connections was a major factor in facilitating the party's spectacular growth from its modest origins in a decaying West Oakland neighborhood to arguably the most iconic representative of the black freedom struggle in the late 1960s and early 1970s. Revolutionary nationalism allowed the Panthers to understand their struggle as simultaneously local, centered in urban black neighborhoods in the United States, and global, as part of a larger battle against racialized capitalism and imperialism. As chronicled in the preceding pages, both the BPP's anticolonial analysis of black America and its international and transnational alliances were fraught with tensions and contradictions. But for all the challenges that the party faced from within and without, it is impossible to imagine the Panthers achieving the success that they did in the absence of creative efforts to locate their struggle at the intersection of domestic and Third World anticolonialism.

Black Lives Matter and related groups are struggling with many of the same questions that animated the Panthers. Angela Davis, whose scholarly and activist career has spanned the eras of Black Power and Black Lives Matter, suggested in 2016 that "the demands of the BPP's Ten-Point Program are just as relevant—or perhaps even more relevant—as during the 1960s, when they were first formulated."[12] In identifying the problems facing the residents of places such as Ferguson as both systemic in nature and endemic to the everyday operation of the American state, these contemporary movements have embraced a version of the Panthers' domestic anticolonialism. In doing so, they have sought to avoid the patriarchal and hierarchical leadership structure that contributed to the downfall of the BPP while also downplaying the emphasis on anticolonial violence (either real or rhetorical) that characterized the early years of the party. Internationally, meanwhile, twenty-first-century activists face a far more challenging situation than that which confronted the Panthers. While the Internet and social media have made communications across borders far easier, contemporary movements must contend with an international environment that is far less conducive to the alliances of revolutionary states and groups that allowed the BPP to survive and even grow in the face of unrelenting hostility from the U.S. government.

"As Foreign Troops Occupy Territory": The Colonial Model in the Twenty-First Century

Perhaps the most important legacy of the BPP is the continuing salience of the colonial model to make sense of the situation of African Americans. The colonial analysis offered by Harold Cruse, subsequently adapted by RAM, and popularized by the Black Panther Party in the late 1960s and early 1970s, was never a perfect fit. As Cynthia B. Young observed in her broader analysis of the U.S. Third World Left, "The specific forms of oppression faced by national minorities who are legal citizens differ from that of colonized national subjects, though both were denied full citizenship rights. . . . [T]he collapsing of disparities implied in the use of the term ["Third World"] fails to acknowledge variation, hierarchies, and gradations within the Third World itself, or between it and the First World."[13] More recently, Keeanga-Yamahtta Taylor, though sympathetic to both the BPP and Black Lives Matter, has argued that is "inaccurate to describe Black Americans' relationship to the United States as colonial, despite [the] obvious similarities," particularly as the meager profits from the exploitation of the contemporary inner city are "not a motor of American capitalism compared to the cotton, rubber, sugar, and mineral extraction and trade that had fueled colonial empires for hundreds of years."[14]

For all of its limits, however, the colonial model as employed by the Panthers offers important insights into both the historical development of black America and the stubborn persistence of institutionalized inequalities along racial lines in the United States. From Oakland to Ferguson, these racialized inequalities are the result of systematic state policies with deep historical roots that have long benefited white people at the expense of people of color. They are the result of both white supremacy *and* capitalism and cannot be understood without reference to both. As Harold Cruse observed in the early 1960s, the enslavement of black people in the country that was to become the United States "coincided with the colonial expansion of European powers and was nothing but more or less than a condition of domestic colonialism. Instead of the United States establishing a colonial empire in Africa, it brought the colonial system home and installed it in the Southern states."[15] For over a century after the abolition of slavery, African Americans served as a cheap, disposable labor force on farms, factories, and in the homes of whites while remaining largely excluded from the body politic and segregated by law or custom. This colonial relationship is not as legible to modern observers in large part because at around the same time the BPP formed in the mid-1960s, the need for black labor that long fueled American capitalism was evaporating. It is undoubtedly true in the twenty-first century that there are few profits to be wrung from what Eldridge Cleaver once referred to as "the black colony" in the United States. And it is not a coincidence that this transition was accompanied not by decolonization or reparations but by the rise of a regime of mass incarceration that moved a significant number of the residents of that colony behind bars.[16] The legacy of colonialism, however, cannot be so simply removed from civic life.

The uprising in Ferguson in the summer of 2014 brought renewed attention to the lingering colonial aspects of black life in the United States. In response to the events in Ferguson, the Economic Policy Institute, a nonpartisan think tank, conducted a detailed study of how the St. Louis suburb was transformed over the course of several decades from an middle-class, white "sundown town" (where blacks were prohibited from entering after dark) to an effectively segregated municipality with a 67 percent African

American population, a 13 percent unemployment rate, and 25 percent of its residents living below the federal poverty line.[17] While devoid of the pointed language used by the BPP in reference to the "black colony" and "white mother country," the report systemically demolished the notion that the segregation, poverty, unemployment, and violence that characterized Ferguson were somehow accidental or the result of individual preferences or biases often lumped under the label "white flight." Rather, the report concluded that the most "powerful cause of metropolitan segregation in St. Louis and nationwide has been the explicit intents of federal, state, and local governments to create racially segregated metropolises."[18] Despite the abolition of legal segregation nationwide and the apparent triumph of the liberal civil rights movement in the 1960s, "[g]overnmental policies turned black neighborhoods into overcrowded slums" while "state-sponsored labor and employment discrimination reduced the income of African Americans relative to whites." Works by historians such as Thomas Sugrue and Robert O. Self buttress the report's contention that these policies were not confined to Missouri but rather were "duplicated in almost every metropolis nationwide."[19]

While the apparent triumph of the liberal civil rights movement won headlines, the deliberate underdevelopment of black America remained at the heart of U.S. public policy in the second half of the twentieth century. "Even as an officially sanctioned apartheid was being dismantled," observed scholar Nikhil Pal Singh, "new structures of racial inequality, rooted in a national racial geography of urban ghettoes and suburban idylls, and intractable disparities of Black and white wealth and employment were being established."[20] The result was that people of color who live in de facto segregated cities and suburbs suffer from both state-sanctioned violence in the form of a racialized policing and judicial system (as outlined by legal scholar Michelle Alexander in *The New Jim Crow*) as well as the less visible violence of state-sanctioned poverty and unemployment.[21] Even if there is little direct profit to be wrung from the "black colony" in the era of deindustrialization, its very exclusion and separation serves to enrich elements of the "white mother country" both materially and psychologically. The predominantly white St. Louis suburbs of Wildwood and Green Park, for example, have a poverty rate of less than 2 percent, while Ferguson's stands at almost 25 percent.[22] Understanding these disparities as the intentional product of governmental policies at the local, state, and federal level helps to explain why neither the crusading liberalism of Lyndon Johnson's Great Society nor the neoliberalism exemplified by Ronald

Reagan's administration and Bill Clinton's welfare reform efforts during the 1990s succeeded in reversing the racial inequalities that have characterized American life. "[T]he failure of the liberal state and liberalism as a political orientation to secure black equality and to lift impoverished African Americans into a stable working class" that Robert O. Self chronicled in his history of postwar Oakland is in fact endemic to its very nature as political ideology that serves the interests of white people at the expense of people of color.[23]

The colonial model also helps to explain the disproportionate police violence directed against people of color. The DOJ report on policing in Ferguson described a law enforcement culture that treated the black population "less as constituents to be protected than as potential offenders and sources of revenue."[24] In both their daily operations and, more visibly, in their militarized response to the 2014 protests, the FPD validated Huey Newton's assertion that "police are used to occupy our community just as foreign troops occupy territory."[25] The same state policies that fostered the unequal economic development of largely segregated neighborhoods and suburbs also contributed to the withdrawal of municipal services and encouraged a culture of policing that treats people of color as a threat to public order.[26] "What we have made of our police departments [in] America, what we have ordered them to do," wrote Ta-Nehisi Coates (son a former BPP member) in a December 2015 article in the *Atlantic*, "is a direct challenge to any usable definition of democracy. A state that allows its agents to kill, to beat, to tase, without any real sanction, has ceased to govern and has commenced to simply rule."[27] Fanon was more direct in observing that "[t]he colonial world is a world divided in two," where "the proximity and frequent, direct intervention by the police and the military ensure the colonized are kept under close scrutiny, and contained by rifle butts and napalm."[28] One does not have to accept a one-to-one relationship between French-occupied Algiers and the contemporary situation in Ferguson or other U.S. municipalities to grasp the continuing usefulness of the BPP's colonial model. In highlighting the linked forces of white supremacy, state violence, and economic exploitation of people of color as the direct result of state policies, rather than as the by-product of individual prejudice or sectional peculiarities, this analysis helps to explain why racial inequalities have persisted long after the nominal triumph of the liberal civil rights movement and continue even in a supposedly "post-racial" era under a black president. To use the parlance of the digital age, racialized inequality, economic exploitation, and violence are a feature, not a bug, in the American system, and to that it extent it shares something significant with more traditional forms of colonialism.

From "Off the Pigs" to "Hands Up, Don't Shoot": Twenty-First-Century U.S. Anticolonialism

Some of the tactics employed by the Panthers as part of their self-consciously anticolonial struggle have continuing relevance for Black Lives Matter and related groups, such as Black Youth Project 100 and We Charge Genocide, in the twenty-first century. Though employing cell phone cameras rather than guns, contemporary activists have embraced the BPP's strategy of "patrolling the pigs" by directly confronting the exercise and abuse of police power in the streets. In the midst of the Ferguson protests, activist Ashley Yates created iconic shirts featuring the slogan "Assata Taught Me" in reference to former BPP and BLA member Assata Shakur.[29] Though the Ferguson protesters and the larger Black Lives Matter movement have eschewed the calls for violent revolution associated with Shakur's more militant positions, they largely share the notion that oppressive systems and their agents are endemic in the daily lives of urban (and suburban) black Americans and must be confronted directly and publicly. Nor were these efforts solely confined to the issue of police violence. One of the more dramatic public demonstrations of contemporary black anticolonialism came on June 27, 2015, when activist Bree Newsome scaled a thirty-foot flagpole to forcibly haul down the Confederate battle flag that flew outside the state capitol building in Columbia, South Carolina. Newsome hardly fits the image of a Black Panther: when confronted by police, she peaceably submitted to arrest and quoted from the Bible rather than the ten-point program or the works of Chairman Mao.[30] But in explaining her actions, Newsome cited not simply the flag's ties to slavery and white supremacy but also the ongoing and institutionalized violence and oppression that continues to characterize African American life. Referencing unrest in response to police violence in Ferguson and Baltimore (which included the highly publicized burning of a CVS drug store), she decried media invocations of Martin Luther King, Jr., and calls for nonviolence:

> Our kids being shuffled from schools into prison is violence. Kids being hungry is violence. These are all—we live with violence every single day. The violence doesn't begin just when the CVS is burned.[31]

While Black Lives Matter is a broad movement encompassing a range of ideological and tactical perspectives, it holds in common with the BPP an analysis of white supremacy and racialized violence as institutionalized features of American life and a focus on exposing and confronting the exercise of state power through direct action.

Black Lives Matter and related groups and movements have also cultivated their own version of the anticolonial vernacular employed by the Panthers. Social networks such as Twitter and Tumblr have facilitated a form of activism that combines a cutting analysis of white supremacy, institutionalized inequality, and state violence against black people with humor, colorful language, images, and even emojis in a concise, easily accessible format that serves much the same function as Emory Douglas's and Tarika Lewis's artwork or Eldridge Cleaver's speeches did for the BPP. Even before Ferguson, "Black Twitter," an informal grouping of users of the microblogging service, frequently used hashtags not only as a way of affirming black identity but also to critique and undermine aspects of white supremacy. So-called "Blacktags" such as #onlyintheghetto, observed scholar Sanjay Sharma, "connote 'Black' vernacular expression in the form of humor and social commentary . . . expressive of everyday racialized issues and concerns."[32] When joined to #BlackLivesMatter, this form of expression has served as both a focal point for on-the-ground activism (by linking protesters and supporters) and a means of exposing and critiquing state violence and white supremacy for a wide audience outside traditional activist or intellectual circles. As journalist Jay Caspian King concluded in his profile of the movement for the *New York Times Magazine*, "Their innovation has been to marry the strengths of social media—the swift, morally blunt consensus that be created by hashtags; the personal connection that a charismatic online persona can make with followers; the broad networks that allow for the easy distribution of documentary photos and videos—with an effort to quickly mobilize protests in each new city where a police shooting occurs."[33] This format also facilitates transnational connections. In August and September 2014, for example, Palestinians who had recently experienced fifty-one days of warfare as a result of Israel's "Protective Edge" offensive in Gaza took to Twitter to share advice with Ferguson protesters on how to deal with tear gas.[34]

If the BPP's anticolonial analysis and vernacular remain salient in the twenty-first century, the party's struggles and failures also have relevance for contemporary activists. Although not nearly as intense as the COINTELPRO efforts unleashed against the Panthers, the FBI and Department of

Homeland Security have engaged in intensive surveillance of Black Lives Matter activists. Speaking to reporters in Cleveland, FBI deputy director Mark F. Giuliano stirred memories of the bureau's unsavory past by declaring, "It's outsiders who tend to stir the pot. If we have that intel we pass it directly on to the PD, we have worked with Ferguson. We've worked with Baltimore and we will work with the Cleveland PD on that very thing. That's what we bring to the game."[35] The hierarchical leadership structure of the BPP made the party vulnerable to police and government pressure as the arrest or defection of even a handful of key leaders could have dramatic effects of the party's operations. In adopting a decentralized structure, the Black Lives Matter movement is perhaps better positioned to withstand such external pressure. As Harris observed in his study of the movement, "They are rejecting the charismatic leadership model that has dominated black politics for the past half century." Instead they have "insisted on a group-centered model of leadership rooted in ideas of participatory democracy."[36] This is a model that owes much to the pioneering work of black feminist activists and theorists from Ella Baker to Angela Davis. As Davis recently observed, these "new generation organizations . . . have developed new models of leadership . . . that acknowledge how important Black feminist insights are to the development of viable twenty-first century radical Black movements."[37] While there are disputes over questions of gender and sexuality within the Black Lives Matter movement, the horizontal and more open nature of its organization and its origins in the activism of queer women of color provides much more of an opportunity for genuine dialog and change on these issues than did the male-dominated hierarchy of the BPP during its heyday in the late 1960s and early 1970s. The #SayHerName movement, for example, has pushed for equal attention to be given to police violence against black women.[38]

Exposing the routine exercise of state-sponsored violence against black Americans was a central goal of the BPP and is also a core element of the Black Lives Matter movement. More vexing, however, is the question of what role, if any, violence should play in bringing about larger structural changes. The Panthers remained united in exhorting self-defense against police attacks but eventually split over the question of whether to undertake anticolonial violence in order to bring about the revolution that they professed. While Eldridge Cleaver's faction, and later the BLA, took literally the call to "off the pigs," by the early 1970s the Newton-led BPP in Oakland abandoned the notion of direct confrontation in favor of electoral politics and community activism. Despite sensational charges that its members are encouraging terrorism or attacks against police, activists in Ferguson and elsewhere have eschewed the routine embrace of rhetorical violence employed by the BPP in its anticolonial vernacular, much less the open brandishing of weapons and calls to overthrow the U.S. government.[39] It is hard to imagine, for example, contemporary activists openly publishing and distributing the types of articles on urban guerrilla warfare tactics that were commonplace in the *Black Panther* during the late 1960s. The rallying cry of "hands up, don't shoot" (based on an accounts by some witnesses that Michael Brown had his hands up at the time of his killing) is indicative of the extent to which this contemporary movement against police violence differs from the more confrontational stance of the Panthers in the late 1960s and early 1970s. "Our demand is simple," said Black Lives Matter organizer Johnnetta Elzie: "Stop killing us."[40]

Given the price paid by the Panthers during the party's most militant period, the failure of the BLA's guerrilla efforts to affect any sort of meaningful change, and the overwhelming force that local, state, and federal governments are able to bring to bear, it is hardly surprising that few contemporary activists are willing to entertain even the rhetoric of anticolonial violence in service of black liberation in the United States. By the early 1970s, most of the surviving leadership and rank and file of the Panthers had already reached the conclusion that "we could never win a shooting 'War of Liberation.'"[41] A number of scholars, journalists, and former activists have expressed versions of this critique, citing the Panthers' flirtations with anticolonial violence prior to the Newton-Cleaver split as nihilistic and counterproductive. Historian Christopher B. Strain argued that "[t]he positive deeds of the Panthers—including the Free Breakfast Programs, Free Health Clinics, Clothing and Shoe Programs, and Busses-to-Prison Program—were often overshadowed by their violent rhetoric, and by the early 1970s, the scurrilous deeds of some Panthers had eclipsed whatever good the group had accomplished in Oakland."[42] But while it is easy to dismiss violence as an ineffective, if not immoral, tool in service of social change, this analysis leaves open the question of how the kind of revolutionary change sought by the BPP could take place without it.

Whatever one makes of Eldridge Cleaver's at times quixotic fixation with guerrilla warfare, he was not wrong when he observed that "whether we like it or not, the world that we live in is controlled with guns, organized and controlled by those who rule. This is the basic fact that we have to deal with. Those who cannot move beyond that point—I don't know what to say to them."[43] Having concluded on good evidence that the racialized violence that characterized both policing in Oakland and the war in Vietnam was inextricably linked to the fundamental political and economic institutions of the U.S. state, and was in fact closely identified with American liberalism, many Panthers saw little use in working within that system or appealing to the conscience of the American ruling class. "Nobody in the world, nobody in history," declared Assata Shakur, "has ever gotten their freedom by appealing to the moral sense of the people who were oppressing them."[44] And while African American political mobilization has succeeded in getting "black faces in high places," including the Oval Office, it has done little to address the underlying structural problems facing their constituents. "After forty years of this electoral strategy," observed Keeanga-Yamahtta Taylor, "Black elected officials' inability to alter the poverty, unemployment, and housing and food insecurity their Black constituents face casts significant doubt on the existing electoral system as a viable vehicle for Black liberation."[45]

In *The Wretched of the Earth*, Fanon famously declared that "[d]ecolonization is always a violent event."[46] Fanon's definition included not simply physical violence but also the symbolic and psychological violence that accompanied the dramatic changes that came with decolonization. The sweeping change sought by the Black Panthers in their ten-point program would have required at least the latter, and likely the former as well. Some of the more narrow goals sought by the Black Lives Matter movement with respect to curbing police violence could likely be accomplished through traditional channels of institutional reform. But in addressing the underlying structures of white supremacy, racialized violence, and economic inequality that has led to the systematic devaluing of black lives, the movement brushes up, however indirectly, against the larger and more revolutionary changes envisioned by the Panthers. In words that echo parts of the BPP's ten-point program, co-creator of #BlackLivesMatter Patrisse Cullors, speaking from Cuba, invoked the need for "new and radical demands that push for true public safety: Housing, jobs, and access to healthy food."[47] It remains unclear in the early decades of the twenty-first century if such changes are possible within an existing U.S. political and economic system that is itself upheld by the routine exercise of state violence.

International and Transnational Activism in a Neoliberal World

Even the most militant Panthers were not blind to the practical difficulties that they faced in putting revolutionary nationalism into practice as a minority population confronting the economic, political, and military might of the world's most powerful nation. A central focus of this book has been the BPP's attempt to resolve that dilemma by situating themselves as part of a larger majority of people of color struggling against white supremacy and capitalism on the world stage. Drawing on Malcolm X's injunction that "[t]he only kind of power that can help you and me is international power, not local power," the BPP leveraged their domestic anticolonialism into real and symbolic links to both the Third World and sympathetic audiences within other First World nations.[48] It is hard to imagine the Panthers achieving the success and notoriety that they did in the absence of these links, which not only provided material support, publicity, and refuge for party members beyond the reach of the U.S. government, but also contributed to a genuine belief among many activists that colonialism and white supremacy were on the retreat around the world. In addition to these practical benefits, international and transnational connections also helped to strengthen and refine the Panthers' domestic analysis of American society. These links also came with costs and drawbacks. The dramatic changes in the international environment that accompanied détente and the thawing of the Cold War were only the most dramatic example of the often-tenuous nature of some of the party's connections. Even at the height of the party's international success, during the era of the Cleaver-led "Asian strategy" in 1969–70, the BPP's state-level allies often treated the Panthers more as useful propaganda tools (for both domestic and foreign consumption) then as true partners. Transnational connections to activists in western Europe and Japan took place on more equal terms, but in addition to the complications of culture and language inherent in such exchanges, these relationships could not offer the same practical benefits as those with powerful, revolutionary nation-states.

If the internationalism of the BPP was fraught with both opportunities and dangers, contemporary activists in the United States face a more unambiguously bleak situation. The end of the Cold War, the rise of the neoliberal "Washington consensus" among international elites, and the fragmenting of the Third World political project leave those disenchanted with pursuing reforms through domestic channels in the United States few if any reliable state-level allies. Cuba and the DPRK remain revolutionary states but have been shorn of the power and allure that made them attractive to black activists in the 1960s. China has risen to become major world power but one guided more by state-driven capitalism and oligarchy then the revolutionary maxims of Chairman Mao. Despite the end of the Cold War, the United States retains a massive military deployed at bases around the world while conducting an uninterrupted string of military operations since 2001, including an ongoing drone war against suspected terrorist suspects that targets almost exclusively people of color in countries that would have once been classified as belonging to the Third World. Although there remain political parties and movements around the world critical of capitalism, settler colonialism, white supremacy, and the hegemonic role of the United States, there is nothing approaching the practical and ideological support for revolutionary movements that the Panthers enjoyed during the late 1960s and early 1970s.

International organizations such as the United Nations remain a potential venue for addressing the concerns of black Americans outside the confines of the nation-state. The parents of Michael Brown and Trayvon Martin as well as the Chicago-based group We Charge Genocide (which draws its name from a 1951 petition to the UN sponsored by the Civil Rights Congress) have brought their concerns about state violence inflicted against African Americans to various UN committees.[49] But as black organizations have found since the UN's founding, there are sharp limits to its ability to take any meaningful action on behalf of minority populations against its more powerful nation-state members. We Charge Genocide organizer Page May was frank in acknowledging this, saying that "[w]e knew the UN wasn't going to 'save us' in any shape or form," but held out hope that at the very least the experience of appearing before that body would empower black youth to look beyond the narrow confines of state-level discourse about policing.[50] Patrisse Cullors invoked the international precedent of the BPP in arguing that "anti-Black racism has global consequences" and thus "[i]t's essential that we center this conversation and also our practice in an international frame."[51]

Contemporary activists can take some solace in the way in which social networks have made transnational connections considerably easier than in the era of the BPP, at least for those with access to the Internet. In additional to informal transnational connections via services such as Twitter, there have also been recent examples of more concrete links between black activists and allies overseas. One particularly fruitful field of collaboration appears to be the emerging connection between Black Lives Matter activists and Palestinians resisting Israeli occupation.[52] In addition to organizing around the issue of political prisoners, Alex Lubin's study of black and Palestinian activism suggests that hip-hop and poetry are two contemporary examples of "[t]ranslational politics . . . [that] identify shared conditions produced by globalization and incarceration while also paying homage to previous generations' political imaginaries." Lubin optimistically concludes that "while globalization and neoliberalism have restricted the horizons of social movements in the public sphere, they have been unable to do so in the realm of cultural politics, where new geographies of liberation are being imagined."[53]

For all their promise, these new forms of transnational activism face many of the same challenges that the Panthers encountered as well as new problems of their own. A major factor in the ability of the BPP to continue propagating its messages despite severe government repression was the party's decision to maintain full control over the production, printing, and distribution of their own newspaper rather than relying on venues more susceptible to corporate or government control. The online activism associated with #BlackLivesMatter, however, is largely conducted through services such as Twitter, Tumblr, and Instagram that are controlled by large for-profit corporations. Even if these companies choose not to censor the content that they host, governments around the world have found ways of effectively controlling access to Internet services that they deem to be subversive.[54] Beyond censorship, corporations like Twitter have proven adept at finding ways to turn struggles that challenge the status quo into safe and profitable business opportunities. In June 2016, billionaire Twitter cofounder and CEO Jack Dorsey sat down for a discussion with Black Lives Matter activist Deray McKesson at the tech industry Code Conference.[55] Dorsey, who presided over a company where only 3 percent of the workforce was black or Latino and who had recently hired a white man as head of "diversity," marked the occasion by wearing a Twitter-branded "Stay Woke" T-shirt that appropriated a phrase associated with Black Lives Matter in service of raising his company's brand awareness. McKesson, meanwhile, has built a cozy online relationship with brands such as McDonald's, Apple, and Spotify that has drawn criticism from some within the movement.[56] For all of its struggles, late-period capitalism excels, if nothing else, at appropriating and commodifying dissenting cultural forms within the confines of the existing system. While corporate platforms like Twitter can perhaps be situationally employed to revolutionary ends, any movement that seeks changes on par with those pursued by the Panthers must have a plan for addressing the underlying material structures of political and economic power that organize life both online and in the streets of places such as Oakland and Ferguson.

Even in a best-case scenario, in which activists overcome technical hurdles, government repression, corporate co-optation, and the barriers of language and culture to form bonds across borders, the case of the BPP illustrates the limits of transnational organizing in the face of the power wielded by the U.S. government and its allies. While the Panthers' embrace of figures such as Kim Il-sung and Mao Zedong might seem naïve or ill-advised in retrospect, these alliances reflected the reality that those seeking revolutionary change needed more than goodwill and donations from foreign admirers if they wished to survive, much less topple, the U.S. government. For all the complications that they brought, connections to powerful and sympathetic revolutionary states were crucial to envisioning the possibility of a successful revolution in the United States. As historians Joshua Bloom and Waldo E. Martin observed, "Today, with few potential allies for a revolutionary black organization, the state could easily repress any Panther-like organization, no matter how disciplined and organized."[57] Any group seeking a revolutionary decolonization of American society would need to engage in a long-term project of organizing across borders in the hopes that such alliances might one day bring to power governments in other nations that could provide the kind of support sought by the BPP during its heyday.

The Black Panther Party in the late 1960s and early 1970s attempted nothing less than a revolution founded on the notion that the lives of people of color in the United States and around the world should not only matter but also be liberated from centuries of institutionalized white supremacy and state violence in all its forms. This was a monumentally ambitious task even in an age in which such a revolution seemed far more possible than it does today. Perhaps such change can take place without the kind of radical decolonization envisioned by the Panthers, though evidence thus far casts doubt on that proposition. The BPP failed in its central goal, but the history of the party and its members continues to hold valuable lessons for scholars and activists seeking to understand and change the conditions that prompted Huey Newton and Bobby Seale to action in the streets of Oakland in October 1966. While this story provides no easy or comforting answers, it nevertheless remains relevant for those committed to change that goes beyond the liberal reforms of the civil rights movement or a contemporary multiculturalism that often serves the interests of the status quo. Before his death in prison in April 2000, former BPP and BLA member Albert "Nuh" Washington reflected on the legacy of the party and its meaning for contemporary activists. "We've tried and in the trying, some died," he declared. "Others went on with their lives for good or bad, and some of us are still imprisoned. Is this then our legacy—failure? If so, then history and future generations will condemn us—not for failing, but for not trying again."[58]

Notes

Introduction

1. "What We Want Now! What We Believe," *Black Panther*, July 3, 1967.

2. Richard A. Couto, *Ain't Gonna Let Nobody Turn Me Round: The Pursuit of Racial Justice in the Rural South* (Philadelphia, 1992), 102–5.

3. For more on the other groups that took up the Panther name (particularly in San Francisco and New York), see Muhammad Ahmad, *We Will Return in the Whirlwind: Black Radical Organizations, 1960–1975* (Chicago, 2007), 167–74.

4. Joshua Bloom and Waldo E. Martin, Jr., *Black against Empire: The History and Politics of the Black Panther Party* (Berkeley, CA, 2013), 2. For purposes of clarity, I will use "Black Panther Party" and "BPP" for the entirety of this book.

5. Huey P. Newton, "To the Courageous Revolutionaries of the National Liberation Front and Provisional Revolutionary Government of South Vietnam We Send Greetings," *Black Panther*, January 9, 1971.

6. On the BPP's influence on other groups outside the United States see Nico Slate, ed., *Black Power beyond Borders: The Global Dimensions of the Black Power Movement* (New York, 2012).

7. United Press International, "Black Panther Party Greatest Threat to U.S. Security," *Deseret News*, July 16, 1969. For more on the somewhat curious circumstances surrounding Hoover's remarks, see Bloom and Martin, *Black against Empire*, 444n45.

8. United States Senate, Select Committee to Study Governmental Operations with Respect to Intelligence Activities, *Supplementary Detailed Staff Reports of Intelligence Activities and the Rights of Americans*, book 3 (Washington, DC, 1976), 188. On the CIA, MH/CHAOS, and

the BPP, see Frank J. Rafalko, *MH/CHAOS: The CIA's Campaign against the Radical New Left and the Black Panthers* (Annapolis, MD: Naval Institute Press, 2011).

9. House of Representatives, Committee on Internal Security, *Gun-Barrel Politics: The Black Panther Party, 1966–1971* (Washington, DC, 1971), 135.

10. "Memorandum of Conversation, Beijing, October 24, 1971, 9:23–11:20 p.m.," in *Foreign Relations of the United States, 1969–1976*, volume E-13, *Documents on China, 1969–1972*, http://2001-2009.state.gov/r/pa/ho/frus/nixon/e13/72503.htm. On State Department pressure on Algeria, see "Memorandum of Conversation," July 31, 1972, *Foreign Relations of the United States, 1969–1976 Volume E-5, Part 2, Documents on North Africa, 1969–1972*, Document 33, http://history.state.gov/historicaldocuments/frus1969-76ve05p2/ch2.

11. The literature on the party is too vast to cite here in its entirety. Though not without its flaws, the best single-volume history of the party is Bloom and Martin's *Black against Empire*. For a somewhat dated but still useful historiography, see David J. Garrow, "Picking Up the Books: The New Historiography of the Black Panther Party," *Reviews in American History* 35 (2007): 650–70.

12. Fred Hampton, "You Can Murder a Liberator, but You Can't Murder Liberation," in Philip S. Foner, ed., *The Black Panthers Speak* (New York, 1970), 139.

13. On Black internationalism, see Nikhil Pal Singh, *Black Is a Country: Race and the Unfinished Struggle for Democracy* (Cambridge, MA, 2005); Cheryl Higashida, *Black Internationalist Feminism: Women Writers on the Left, 1945–1995* (Urbana, IL, 2011); Roderick D. Bush, *The End of World White Supremacy: Black Internationalism and the Problem of the Color Line* (Philadelphia, 2009); Dayo F. Gore, *Radicalism at the Crossroads: African American Women Activists in the Cold War* (New York, 2011); Cynthia B. Young, *Soul Power: Culture, Radicalism, and the Making of U.S. Third World Left* (Durham, NC, 2006); Nico Slate, *Colored Cosmopolitanism: The Shared Struggle for Freedom in the United States and India* (Cambridge, MA, 2012); Robeson Taj Frazier, *The East Is Black: Cold War China in the Black Radical Imagination* (Durham, NC, 2015); Sohail Daulatzai, *Black Star, Crescent Moon: The Muslim International and Black Freedom beyond America* (Minneapolis, 2012). Key works examining the intersection of race and U.S. foreign relations include Penny M. Von Eschen, *Race against Empire: Black Americans and Anticolonialism* (Ithaca, 1997); Gerald Horne, *Black and Red: W.E.B. Du Bois and the Afro-American Response to the Cold War, 1944–1963* (Albany, NY, 1986); Gerald Horne, *Communist Front? The Civil Rights Congress, 1945–1956* (Madison, NJ, 1986); Brenda Gayle Plummer, *Rising Wind: Black Americans and U.S. Foreign Affairs, 1935–1960* (Chapel Hill, NC, 1996); Carol Anderson, *Eyes Off the Prize: The United Nations and the African American Struggle for Human Rights, 1944–1945* (Cambridge, UK, 2003); Thomas Borstelmann, *The Cold War and the Color Line: American Race Relations in the Global Arena* (Cambridge, MA, 2001); James H. Meriwether, *Proudly We Can Be Africans: Black Americans and Africa, 1935–1961* (Chapel Hill, NC, 2002); Mary L. Dudziak, *Cold War Civil Rights: Race and the Image of American Democracy* (Princeton, NJ, 2002); Brenda Gayle Plummer, *In Search of Power: African Americans in the Era of Decolonization, 1956–1974* (New York, 2013).

14. Singh, *Black Is a Country*, 53.

15. Huey P. Newton, "Functional Definition of Politics," *Black Panther*, May 15, 1967.

16. Ahmad Muhammad [Maxwell Stanford], "Message to African Heads of State from RAM—Revolution Action Movement—Black Liberation Front of the U.S.A.," n.d. [ca. spring 1965], in *The Black Power Movement, Part 3: Papers* of the Revolutionary Action Movement, LexisNexis database.

17. The concept of a U.S. Third World Left is deftly explored in Cynthia B. Young, *Soul Power: Culture, Radicalism, and the Making of U.S. Third World Left* (Durham, NC, 2006).

18. Eldridge Cleaver, "Pronunciamento," *Black Panther*, December 21, 1968.

19. Lee Lockwood, *Conversations with Eldridge Cleaver: Algiers* (New York, 1970), 54.

20. The best account of the delegation's journey is Judy Tzu-Chun Wu, *Radicals on the Road: Internationalism, Orientalism, and Feminism During the Vietnam Era* (Ithaca, NY, 2013), 107–92.

21. For a more recent analysis that shares a number of similarities with Newton's inter-communalism, see Michael Hardt and Antonio Negri, *Empire* (Cambridge, MA, 2000).

22. Untitled manuscript, Algiers [n.d., ca. 1972], Eldridge Cleaver Papers, Bancroft Library, University of California, Berkeley (hereafter Cleaver Papers), carton 2, folder 36.

23. Renato Rosaldo, "Imperialist Nostalgia," *Representations* 26 (Spring 1989): 107–22.

24. Eldridge Cleaver, "Solidarity of the Peoples until Victory or Death!," *Black Panther*, October 25, 1969; Cleaver, "Pronunciamento."

25. Mumia Abu-Jamal, *We Want Freedom: A Life in the Black Panther Party* (Cambridge, MA, 2004), 243.

26. Charlotte O'Neal, interview by Sean L. Malloy, September 23, 2014.

27. Elaine Brown, *A Taste of Power: A Black Woman's Story* (New York, 1992), 357.

28. Kathleen Neal Cleaver, "Women, Power, and Revolution," in *Liberation, Imagination and the Black Panther Party,* ed. Kathleen Cleaver and George Katsiaficas (New York, 2001), 126.

29. See, for example, Higashida, *Black Internationalist Feminism*.

30. Donald Cox, "The Man Question," *Voice of the Lumpen* 2, no. 3 (April 1972), 7; Denise Oliver, "To Our Brothers in Jail from the Sisters," *Voice of the Lumpen* 2, no. 3 (April 1972), 8–9.

31. "Separate Minority Views," *Gun-Barrel Politics*, 142; Tom Wolfe, "Radical Chic: That Party at Lenny's," *New York*, June 8, 1970, 26–56.

32. Randall L. Kennedy, "Protesting Too Much: The Trouble with Black Power Revisionism," *Boston Review*, March 23, 2015, http://bostonreview.net/books-ideas/randall-kennedy-protesting-too-much-black-power-revisionism.

33. Nico Slate, introduction to *Black Power beyond Borders*, 5; Young, *Soul Power*, 252.

34. Office of Policy Planning and Research, United States Department of Labor, *The Negro Family: The Case for National Action* (Washington, D.C., 1965), 5. For a nuanced discussion of the Moynihan report and its legacy, see Ta-Nehisi Coates, "The Black Family in the Age of Mass Incarceration," *Atlantic*, October 2015, http://www.theatlantic.com/magazine/archive/2015/10/the-black-family-in-the-age-of-mass-incarceration/403246.

35. David Hilliard, "Pig—An International Language," *Black Panther*, December 27, 1969.

36. Abu-Jamal, *We Want Freedom*, 233.

37. Nuh Washington, *All Power to the People* (Montreal, 2002), 41.

Chapter 1. "Every Brother on a Rooftop Can Quote Fanon"

1. Robert F. Williams, "Speech Delivered at the International Conference for Solidarity with the Peoples of Vietnam against U.S. Imperialist Aggression for the Defense of Peace," *Crusader* 6, no. 3 (March 1965), 2.

2. Ibid.

3. For an overview of the long history of black internationalism, see Singh, *Black Is a Country*; Roderick D. Bush, *The End of World White Supremacy: Black Internationalism and the Problem of the Color Line* (Philadelphia, PA, 2009).

4. W.E.B. Du Bois, *The Souls of Black Folk* (New York, 1961), 23.

5. James H. Meriwether, *Proudly We Can Be Africans: Black Americans and Africa, 1935–1961* (Chapel Hill, NC, 2002), 12–23; Penny M. Von Eschen, *Race against Empire: Black Americans and*

Anticolonialism (Ithaca, NY, 1997), 9–10; Paul Gilroy, *The Black Atlantic: Modernity and Double Consciousness* (Cambridge, MA, 1993), 24–25.

6. Vijay Prashad, *The Darker Nations: A People's History of the Third World* (New York, 2007), 6–7.

7. English-language histories of the conference include Christopher J. Lee, ed., *Making a World after Empire: The Bandung Movement and Its Political Afterlives* (Athens, OH, 2010); Jamie Mackie, *Bandung 1955: Non-Alignment and Afro-Asian Solidarity* (Singapore, 2005); See Seng Tan and Amitav Acharya, eds., *Bandung Revisited: The Legacy of the 1955 Asian-African Conference for International Order* (Singapore, 2008); Derek McDougall and Antonia Finnane, eds., *Bandung 1955: Little Histories* (Victoria, Australia, 2010). Also see "The Fate of Nationalisms in the Age of Bandung," Antoinette Burton, Augusto Espiritu, and Fanon Che Wilkins, eds., *Radical History Review* 95 (Spring 2006): 145–210.

8. "Speech by President Sukarno of Indonesia at the Opening of the Conference," in *Asia-Africa Speaks from Bandung* (Jakarta: National Committee for the Commemoration of the Thirtieth Anniversary of the Asian-African Conference, 1985), 8.

9. Cary Fraser, "An American Dilemma: Race and Realpolitik in the American Response to the Bandung Conference, 1955," in *Window on Freedom: Race, Civil Rights, and Foreign Affairs, 1945–1988*, ed. Brenda Gayle Plummer (Chapel Hill, NC, 2003), 131.

10. "Declaration of the Promotion of World Peace and Co-Operation," in *Asia-African Speaks from Bandung*, 148.

11. Jeffrey James Byrne, *Mecca of Revolution: Algeria, Decolonization and the Third World Order* (New York, 2016), 64.

12. John Grassi, ed., *Venceremos!: The Speeches and Writings of Che Guevara* (New York, 1968), 423. On the logic of Cuban support for external revolutions as part of its national security policy, Carlos Moore, *Castro, the Blacks, and Africa* (Los Angeles, 1988), 180; Jorge I. Domínguez, *To Make a World Safe for Revolution: Cuba's Foreign Policy* (Cambridge, MA, 1989), 116; Odd Arne Westad, *The Global Cold War* (Cambridge, UK, 2007), 175–79; Piero Gleijeses, *Conflicting Missions: Havana, Washington, and Africa, 1959–1976*, 21. On Guevara's theory of guerrilla warfare, see Che Guevara, *Guerrilla Warfare* (New York, 1969).

13. Domínguez, *To Make a World Safe for Revolution*, 130; Gleijeses, *Conflicting Missions*, 7, 32–36. On Algerian support for other insurgencies, see Matthew Connelly, *A Diplomatic Revolution: Algeria's Fight for Independence* (New York, 2002), 280; Chamberlin, *The Global Offensive: The United States, The Palestine Liberation Organization, and the Making of the Post–Cold War Order* (New York, 2012), 52–53; Westad, *The Global Cold War*, 106.

14. Moore, *Castro, the Blacks, and Africa*, 3, 15; Gleijeses, *Conflicting Missions*, 377; John A. Gronbeck-Tedesco, "The Left in Transition: The Cuban Revolution in US Third World Politics," *Journal of Latin American Studies* 40 (2008): 659, 665, 668; Young, *Soul Power*, 2006), 23; Henley Adams, "Race and the Cuban Revolution: The Impact of Cuba's Intervention in Angola," in *Race, Ethnicity, and the Cold War*, ed. Philip E. Muehlenbeck (Nashville, TN, 2012), 205–8.

15. Moore, *Castro, the Blacks, and Africa*, 62, 120; Gronbeck-Tedesco, "The Left in Transition," 662. For a broader discussion of the relationship between the Cuban revolution and African Americans, see Ruth Reitan, *The Rise and Decline of an Alliance: Cuba and African American Leaders in the 1960s* (East Lansing, MI, 1999); Young, *Soul Power*, 18–53; Brenda Gayle Plummer, "Castro in Harlem: A Cold War Watershed," in *Window on Freedom*, 133–56.

16. Frantz Fanon, *Wretched of the Earth* (New York, 2004), 5.

17. James H. Meriwether, *Proudly We Can Be Africans: Black Americans and Africa, 1935–1961* (Chapel Hill, NC, 2002), 125, 142–49.

18. Fanon, *Wretched of the Earth*, 81–82; Aristide Zolberg and Vera Zolberg, "The Americanization of Frantz Fanon," *Public Interest* 9 (Fall 1967): 50; Eldridge Cleaver, "Psychology: The Black Bible," in *Eldridge Cleaver: Post-Prison Writings and Speeches* (New York, 1969), 18.

19. Guevara, *Guerrilla Warfare*, 122.

20. Westad, *The Global Cold War*, 158–62; Max Elbaum, *Revolution in the Air: Sixties Radicals Turn to Lenin, Mao and Che* (New York, 2002), 45–53; Chen Jian, "China and the Bandung Conference: Changing Perceptions and Representations," in *Bandung Revisited: The Legacy of the 1955 Asian-African Conference for International Order*, ed. See Seng Tan and Amitav Acharya (Singapore, 2008), 140–41.

21. Laura Pulido, *Black, Brown, Yellow, and Left: Radical Activism in Los Angeles* (Berkeley, CA, 2006), 95, 135; Robin D.G. Kelley and Betsy Esch, "Black Like Mao: Red China and Black Revolution," *Souls* 1, no. 4 (Fall 1999): 9, 39.

22. Mao Zedong, "Statement Supporting the Afro-Americans in Their Just Struggle against Racial Discrimination by U.S. Imperialism," in *Afro-Asia: Revolutionary Political and Cultural Connections between African Americans and Asian Americans*, ed. Fred Ho and Bill V. Mullen (Durham, NC, 2008), 93.

23. Melani McAlister, "One Black Allah: The Middle East in the Cultural Politics of African American Liberation," *American Quarterly* 51 no. 3 (September 1999), 633.

24. Westad, *The Global Cold War*, 101, 107–8; Vijay Prashad, *The Darker Nations: A People's History of the Third World* (New York, 2007), 136–40; Borstelmann, *The Cold War and the Color Line*, 128–32.

25. "Riot in Gallery Halts U.N. Debate," *New York Times*, February 16, 1961; Cheryl Higashida, *Black Internationalist Feminism: Women Writers on the Left, 1945–1995* (Urbana, IL, 2011), 54; Peniel E. Joseph, *Waiting 'Til the Midnight Hour: A Narrative History of Black Power in America* (New York, 2006), 39–42; Brenda Gayle Plummer, *Rising Wind: Black Americans and U.S. Foreign Affairs, 1935–1960* (Chapel Hill, NC, 1996), 302–4; Singh, *Black Is a Country*, 186–87.

26. Plummer, *Rising Wind*, 303; "Riot in Gallery Halts U.N. Debate," *New York Times*, February 16, 1961.

27. "U.N. Takes Steps to Prevent Riots," *New York Times*, February 17, 1961; Higashida, *Black Internationalist Feminism*, 54.

28. Peniel E. Joseph, "Dashikis and Democracy: Black Studies, Student Activism, and the Black Power Movement," *Journal of African American History* 88, no. 2 (Spring 2003): 186; Young, *Soul Power*, 50.

29. Young, *Soul Power*, 50.

30. Lien-Hang Nguyen, "Revolutionary Circuits: Towards Internationalizing America in the World," *Diplomatic History* 39, no. 3 (2015): 420.

31. I.F. Stone, introduction to *Guerrilla Warfare*, by Che Guevara, xii. Also see George Katsiaficas, *The Imagination of the New Left: A Global Analysis of 1968* (Boston, 1987), 34.

32. As early as July 1964, a month before the Gulf of Tonkin incident and ensuing U.S. escalation, RAM congratulated the NLF "for their inspiring victories against U.S. imperialism in South Vietnam" and linked the two struggles to a "world revolution of oppressed peoples rising up against their former slavemasters." "Greetings to Our Militant Vietnamese Brothers, July 4, 1964," *Black America*, Fall 1964, 21.

33. David Kimche, *The Afro-Asian Movement: Ideology and Foreign Policy in the Third World* (Jerusalem, 1973), 211.

34. Subcommittee to Investigate the Administration of the Internal Security Act and Other Internal Security Laws, *The Tricontinental Conference of African, Asia, and Latin American Peoples* (Washington, DC, 1966), 79.

35. Ibid., 99, 131; "Declaration on the Rights of Afro Americans in the U.S.A., First Conference of Solidarity of the African, Asian and Latin American Peoples held in Havana, Cuba, Jan. 3 to 12, 1966," *Soulbook* 2, no. 2 (Summer 1966): 20.

36. George Breitman, ed., *Malcolm X Speaks: Selected Speeches and Statements* (New York, 1965), 52, 66, 69.

37. Ibid., 35.

38. Ibid., 73, 76–77.

39. Breitman, ed., *Malcolm X Speaks*, 75; Plummer, *In Search of Power*, 6; Mary L. Dudziak, *Cold War Civil Rights: Race and the Image of American Democracy* (Princeton, NJ, 200), 22; Manning Marable, *Malcolm X: A Life of Reinvention* (New York, 2011), 374.

40. Dayo Gore, "From Communist Politics to Black Power: The Visionary Politics and Transnational Solidarities of Victoria 'Vicki' Ama Garvin," in *Want to Start a Revolution? Radical Women in the Black Freedom Struggle*, ed. Dayo Gore, Jeanne Theoharis, and Kozomi Woodard (New York, 2009), 84. Also see Kevin Gaines, *African Americans in Ghana: Black Expatriates and the Civil Rights Era* (Chapel Hill, NC, 2008).

41. James Forman, *The Making of Black Revolutionaries* (Seattle, WA, 1997), 407–11; Clayborne Carson, *In Struggle: SNCC and the Black Awakening of the 1960s* (Cambridge, MA, 1981), 134–35.

42. Timothy B. Tyson, *Radio Free Dixie: Robert F. Williams and the Roots of Black Power* (Chapel Hill, NC, 1999), 223–31. For firsthand accounts of the Williams-led tour in July 1961, see Robert F. William, *Negroes with Guns* (New York, 1962), 69–72; LeRoi Jones, "Cuba Libre," *Home: Social Essays* (New York, 1966), 11–62; Harold Cruse, *The Crisis of the Negro Intellectual: A Historical Analysis of the Failure of Black Leadership* (New York, 1967), 356–58.

43. Tyson, *Radio Free Dixie*, 287–90.

44. Plummer, *Rising Wind*, 320; Mary Dudziak, "Birmingham, Addis Ababa, and the Image of America: International Influence on U.S. Civil Rights Politics in the Kennedy Administration," in Plummer, *Window on Freedom*, 190–91.

45. Gronbeck-Tedesco, "The Left in Transition," 672.

46. Tyson, *Radio Free Dixie*, 292–94; Domínguez, *To Make a World Safe for Revolution*, 77; Westad, *The Global Cold War*, 214; Reitan, *The Rise and Decline of an Alliance*, 5, 40–41, 80–81, 123.

47. "Speech by U.S. Negro Leader Robert Williams," *Peking Review*, no. 33 (August 12, 1966): 26.

48. Tyson, *Radio Free Dixie*, 300.

49. Breitman, ed., *Malcolm X Speaks*, 170.

50. Ibid., 38.

51. On the OAAU's aims at the time of its founding, see Malcolm X, *By Any Means Necessary* (New York, 1970), 57–96.

52. "The Robert F. Williams Case," *Crisis*, June/July 1959, 328; Williams, *Negroes with Guns*, 76.

53. Huey P. Newton and J. Herman Blake, *Revolutionary Suicide* (New York, 2009), 117; Julian Mayfield, "Challenge to Negro Leadership: The Case of Robert F. Williams," *Commentary*, April 1961, 299–301.

54. Robert F. Williams, "USA: The Potential of a Minority Revolution," *Crusader* 5, no. 4 (May/June 1964), 6; Williams, "Speech Delivered at the International Conference for Solidarity with the People of Vietnam," 2.

55. Cruse, *The Crisis of the Negro Intellectual*, 354.

56. Baraka quoted in Gronbeck-Tedesco, "The Left in Transition," 651.

57. McAlister, "One Black Allah," 650.

58. Jones, *Home*, 151; LeRoi Jones, "Black Art," in *Black Fire: An Anthology of Afro-American Writing*, ed. LeRoi Jones and Larry Neal (New York, 1968), 302.

59. Ibid., 85.

60. Ibid., 244, 248.

61. Ibid., 199, 153.

62. Ibid., 250.

63. Jones, *Home*, 201, 246.

64. Fanon, *The Wretched of the Earth*, 173.

65. Harold Cruse, *Rebellion or Revolution* (New York, 1968), 76.

66. Ibid.

67. Ibid., 95.

68. Martin R. Delany, *The Condition, Elevation, Emigration and Destiny of the Colored People of the United States* (Baltimore, MD, 1993), 12.

69. Earl Ofari Hutchinson, *Blacks and Reds: Race and Class in Conflict, 1919–1990* (Lansing, MI, 1995), 249. "Black Belt" thesis: "The 1929 Comintern Resolution on the Negro Question in the United States," From Marx to Mao, http://www.marx2mao.com/Other/CR75.html#s1, first published in *Daily Worker*, February 12, 1929.

70. Cruse, *Rebellion or Revolution*, 75.

71. Ibid., 13.

72. Ibid., 113; Cruse, *The Crisis of the Negro Intellectual*, 354.

73. Cruse, *Rebellion or Revolution*, 20; Young, *Soul Power*, 38.

74. Kelley and Esch, "Black Like Mao," 14; Amiri Baraka, *The Autobiography of LeRoi Jones/Amiri Baraka* (New York, 1984), 197.

75. Kelley and Esch, "Black Like Mao,"15; Muhammad Ahmad, *We Will Return in the Whirlwind: Black Radical Organizations, 1960–1975* (Chicago, IL, 2007), 111–14.

76. "The 12 Point Program of RAM (Revolutionary Action Movement) 1964," in *The Black Power Movement: Part 3: Papers of the Revolutionary Action Movement*, LexisNexis (hereafter RAM papers), Muhammad Ahmad (Max Stanford)—Writings, 1964. On the influence on Cruse and his essay on the development of RAM, see "Autobiography—Maxwell Stanford," RAM papers, Muhammad Ahmad Bio Materials (1).

77. "A New Philosophy for a New Age," *Black America*, Summer/Fall 1965, 10; Rolland Snellings, "Re-Africanization: Prelude to Freedom," *Black America*, November/December 1963, 17).

78. Charles Simmons, "To All the Freedom Loving People of the World," *Soulbook* 1, no. 2 (Spring 1965), 118.

79. "The World Black Revolution," [December 1966], RAM papers, Revolutionary Action Movement—External Documents (1).

80. Max Stanford, "Towards Revolutionary Action Movement Manifesto," *Correspondence*, March 1964, 3.

81. Donald Freeman, "The Politics of Black Liberation," *Black America*, November/December 1963, 18.

82. El Mahdi, "Dialectical Destiny of Afro-America," *Black America*, Summer/Fall 1965, 16.

83. Max Stanford, "We Can Win!," [circa June/July 1964], RAM Papers, Muhammad Ahmad (Max Stanford)—Writings, 1964.

84. "A New Philosophy for a New Age," 20. Emphasis in original.

85. Ibid.; "The Relationship of Revolutionary Afro-American Movement to the Bandung Revolution," *Black America*, Summer/Fall 1965, 11.

86. Kelley and Esch, "Black Like Mao," 20.

87. "We Can Win!," *Revolutionary Nationalist*, [circa 1965], 15, RAM papers, "Revolutionary Action Movement—External Documents (1). On the logic of interwar Anglo-American bombing strategy, see Sean L. Malloy, "Liberal Democracy and the Lure of Bombing in the Interwar United States," in *Making the American Century: Essays on the Political Culture of the Twentieth Century America*, ed. Bruce J. Schulman (New York, 2014), 109–23.

88. Ibid., 15.

89. Cruse, *The Crisis of the Negro Intellectual*, 397.

90. Ahmad, *We Will Return in the Whirlwind*, 113, 160.

91. Kenn M. Freeman, "The Colonized of North America: A Review-Essay of Fanon's *Studies in a Dying Colonialism*," *Soulbook* 1, no. 4 (Winter 1965/66): 307–8.

92. Freeman, "The Politics of Black Liberation," 18.

93. Maxwell Stanford, "Revolutionary Action Movement: A Case Study of an Urban Revolutionary Movement in Western Capitalist Society," master's thesis, Atlanta University, 1982, 82.

94. Robin D.G. Kelley, "Stormy Weather: Reconstructing Black (Inter) Nationalism in the Cold War Era," in *Is It Nation Time? Contemporary Essays on Black Power and Black Nationalism*, ed. Eddie S. Glaude (Chicago, IL, 2002), 87; Kelley and Esch, "Black Like Mao," 14–15.

Chapter 2. "Army 45 Will Stop All Jive"

1. Kenny Freeman quoted in Bobby Seale, *A Lonely Rage: The Autobiography of Bobby Seale* (New York, 1978), 126. Based on FBI surveillance reports, it seems likely that this rally was held on October 24, 1962, and also involved the Oakland chapter of the Young Socialist Alliance (YSA). San Francisco Field Office, 100-43450, "Young Socialist Alliance," December 13, 1961, Richard Aoki FBI files. On the evolution of PL (which eventually because the Progressive Labor Party), see Max Elbaum, *Revolution in the Air* (New York, 2002), 63–65; "The History of the Progressive Labor Party: Part One," *Progressive Labor* 10, no. 1 (August/September 1975): 55–70.

2. Newton and Blake, *Revolutionary Suicide*, 109–10; Bobby Seale, *Seize the Time: The Story of the Black Panther Party and Huey P. Newton* (New York, 1970), 13–14; Gene Marine, *The Black Panthers* (New York, 1969), 16–17.

3. Paul Alkebulan, *Survival pending Revolution: The History of the Black Panther Party* (Tuscaloosa, AL, 2007), 49.

4. Robert O. Self, *American Babylon: Race and the Struggle for Postwar Oakland* (Princeton, NJ, 2003), 6, 46, 50, 52.

5. David Hilliard and Lewis Cole, *This Side of Glory: The Autobiography of David Hilliard and the Story of the Black Panther Party* (Boston, 1993), 68.

6. James Edward Smethurst, *The Black Arts Movement: Literary Nationalism in the 1960s and 1970s* (Chapel Hill, NC, 2005), 251–52; Self, *American Babylon*, 78.

7. On the Bay Area's connections to the Cold War, see Rebecca S. Lowen, *Creating the Cold War University: The Transformation of Stanford* (Berkeley, CA, 1997); Stuart W. Leslie, *The Cold War and American Science: The Military-Industrial-Academic Complex at MIT and Stanford* (New York, 1994); Gary Brechin, *Imperial San Francisco: Urban Power, Earthly Ruin* (Berkeley, CA, 2006), 280–330; Self, *American Babylon*; Donna Jean Murch, *Living for the City: Migration, Education, and the Rise of the Black Panther Party in Oakland, California* (Chapel Hill, NC, 2010), 41–70.

8. For a good account of the HUAC demonstration in San Francisco, see Seth Rosenfeld, *Subversives: The FBI's War on Student Radicals and Reagan's Rise to Power* (New York, 2012), 77–87.

9. Ibid., 306.

10. Murch, *Living for the City*, 71, 81; Chris Rhomberg, *No There: Race, Class, and Political Community in Oakland* (Berkeley, CA, 2004), 82.

11. Self, *American Babylon*, 222; Smethurst, *The Black Arts Movement*, 260–62; Murch, *Living for the City*, 72–95.

12. Jason M. Ferreira, "'With the Soul of a Human Rainbow': Los Siete, Black Panthers, and Third Worldism in San Francisco," in *Ten Years that Shook the City: San Francisco, 1968–1978*, ed. Chris Carlsson (San Francisco, CA, 2011), 40, 43–44.

13. Murch, *Living for the City*, 80.

14. Bloom and Martin, *Black against Empire*, 39–43; Smethurst, *The Black Arts Movement*, 257–58; Murch, *Living for the City*, 76–77, 80, 82.

15. Baraka, *The Autobiography of LeRoi Jones/Amiri Baraka*, 248–56; Komozi Woodard, *A Nation within a Nation: Amiri Baraka (LeRoi Jones) & Black Power Politics* (Chapel Hill, NC, 1999), 70; Smethurst, *The Black Arts Movement*, 170.

16. Newton and Blake, *Revolutionary Suicide*, 68, 70.

17. Martha Biondi, *The Black Revolution on Campus* (Berkeley, CA, 2012), 41.

18. Murch, *Living for the City*, 97–103, 111.

19. Ibid., 106–7, 111.

20. Newton and Blake, *Revolutionary Suicide*, 77.

21. Murch, *Living for the City*, 8.

22. Seale, *Seize the Time*, 11–12; Seale, *A Lonely Rage*, 129–30.

23. Seale, *A Lonely Rage*, 130; Peniel E. Joseph, "Dashikis and Democracy: Black Studies, Student Activism, and the Black Power Movement," *Journal of African American History* 88, no. 2 (Spring 2003): 189; Kelley and Esch, "Black Like Mao," 16; *Living for the City*, 109; Smethurst, *The Black Arts Movement*, 262.

24. Newton and Black, *Revolutionary Suicide*, 110.

25. Editorial, *Soulbook* 1, no. 1 (Winter 1964): 3.

26. Bobb Hamilton, "That's Watts Happenin'!" *Soulbook* 1, no. 3 (Fall 1965): 151. On the development of *Soulbook* as well as a competing local journal, *Black Dialogue*, see Smethurst, *The Black Arts Movement*, 263.

27. Kenn M. Freeman, "The Real Reasons Tanganyika and Zanzibar United and Became Tanzania," *Soulbook* 1, no. 1 (Winter 1964): 37–45; Freeman, "Did the United Nations Benefit Congo?," *Soulbook* 1, no. 2 (Spring 1965): 87–104.

28. Cheikh-Anta Diop, "Africa, China and the U.S.," *Soulbook* 1, no. 3 (Fall 1965): 154–63; Alfredo Peña, "The Puerto Rican Revolution/La Revolución Puertorricqueña," *Soulbook* 1, no. 3 (Fall 1965): 208–19; Frantz Fanon, "Psychology and Négritude," *Soulbook* 1, no. 4 (Winter 1965–66), 246–53.

29. Kenn M. Freeman, "The Man from F.L.N.: Brother Frantz Fanon," *Soulbook* 1, no. 3 (Fall 1965): 171, 175.

30. Self, *American Babylon*, 170; Murch, *Living for the City*, 122.

31. Newton and Blake, *Revolutionary Suicide*, 75.

32. Seale, *Seize the Time*, xii.

33. Newton and Blake, *Revolutionary Suicide*, 19–20, 46–47, 76, 80–81, 95–96.

34. Ibid., 61, 71, 78–79, 103–4.

35. Ibid., 63, 70, 72.

36. Seale, *A Lonely Rage*, 145. On the origins and development of the SSAC, see Murch, *Living for the City*, 112; Bloom and Martin, *Black against Empire*, 31; Self, *American Babylon*, 224; Seale, *Seize the Time*, 26–27; Newton and Blake, *Revolutionary Suicide*, 72, 112.

37. Seale, *A Lonely Rage*, 146–51; Seale, *Seize the Time*, 27–29; Ronald Stone, "Uncle Sammy Call Me Full of Lucifer," *Soulbook* 1, no. 2 (Spring 1965): 129–30.

38. Newton and Blake, *Revolutionary Suicide*, 112–13; Seale, *Seize the Time*, 30–31, 34; Seale, *A Lonely Rage*, 15; Ahmad, *We Will Return in the Whirlwind*, 174.

39. Seale, *Seize the Time*, 24.

40. In addition to Newton and Seale's organization in Oakland, figures affiliated with RAM helped to found Black Panther organizations in New York and San Francisco while another independent Panther group sprang up in Los Angeles. Ahmad, *We Will Return in the Whirlwind*, 167–70; Donna Murch, "When the Panther Travels: Race and the Southern Diaspora in the History of the BPP, 1964–1972," in Slate, *Black Power beyond Borders*, 61–65.

41. Jeffrey O. G. Ogbar, *Black Power: Radical Politics and African American Identity* (Baltimore, MD, 2004), 85; Judson L. Jeffries, *Huey P. Newton: The Radical Theorist* (Jackson, MS, 2002), 11. The BPP program also bore some similarities to the earlier ten-point program enunciated by Robert F. Williams in North Carolina and the twelve-point program of the Revolutionary Action Movement (RAM). Williams, *Negroes with Guns*, 75–76; Kelley and Esch, "Black Like Mao," 18.

42. Breitman, ed., *Malcolm X Speaks*, 38.

43. "What We Want Now! What We Believe," *Black Panther*, July 3, 1967. The ten-point program was altered between March and September 1968 to include Cleaver's idea of a United Nations plebiscite for black America as part of point ten. The fact that the *Black Panther* subsequently (and incorrectly) published this modified version as the "October 1966 Black Panther Party Platform and Program" has been the cause of some confusion among historians.

44. "What We Want Now! What We Believe," 3.

45. Erik H. Erikson and Huey P. Newton, *In Search of Common Ground: Conversations with Erik H. Erikson and Huey P. Newton* (New York, 1973), 28. For examples of scholars who have accepted this argument, see Jeffries, *Huey P. Newton*, 62; Besenia Rodriguez, "'Long Live Third World Unity! Long Live International': Huey P. Newton's Revolutionary Intercommunalism," in *Transnational Blackness: Navigating the Global Color Line*, ed. Manning Marable and Vanessa Agard-Jones (New York, 2008), 152; Anne-Marie Angelo, "The Black Panthers in London, 1967–1972," *Radical History Review*, no. 103 (Winter 2009): 20.

46. Huey P. Newton, "Functional Definition of Politics," *Black Panther*, May 15, 1967.

47. Huey P. Newton, "Statement by Minister of Defense to the Black World," *Black Panther*, May 15, 1967.

48. Ahmad, *We Will Return in the Whirlwind*, 130–33.

49. Newton and Blake, *Revolutionary Suicide*, 116.

50. Seale, *Seize the Time*, 30.

51. Newton and Blake, *Revolutionary Suicide*, 63.

52. Huey P. Newton, "Guns Baby Guns," *Black Panther*, July 3, 1967.

53. Newton and Blake, *Revolutionary Suicide*, 117–18. For a good discussion of the influences on the BPP's decision to "pick up the gun," see Brigitte Baldwin, "In the Shadow of the Gun: The Black Panther Party, the Ninth Amendment, and Discourses of Self-Defense," in *In Search of the Black Panther Party: New Perspectives on a Revolutionary Movement*, ed. Jama Lazerow and Yohuru Williams (Durham, NC, 2006), 67–96.

54. Aristide Zolberg and Vera Zolberg, "The Americanization of Frantz Fanon," *Public Interest* 9 (Fall 1967): 61.

55. Huey P. Newton, "The Correct Handling of a Revolution," *Black Panther*, July 20, 1967; Newton, "In Defense of Self Defense," *Black Panther*, June 20, 1967; Newton and Blake, *Revolutionary Suicide*, 116–17.

56. Newton and Blake, *Revolutionary Suicide*, 113.

57. Seale, *Seize the Time*, 72. On Aoki, see Diane C. Fujino, *Samurai among Panthers: Richard Aoki on Race, Resistance, and a Paradoxical Life* (Minneapolis, MN, 2012). On allegations that Aoki was operating as an FBI informant at the time he helped arm the Panthers, see Rosenfeld, *Subversives*, 419–24.

58. Seale, *Seize the Time*, 82–83.

59. Newton and Blake, *Revolutionary Suicide*, 129.

60. For the RAM critique and Newton's response, see Newton, "The Correct Handling of a Revolution."

61. Ibid.

62. Self, *American Babylon*, 77–78; Bloom and Martin, *Black against Empire*, 38–39. Murch, "When the Panther Travels," 70. Similar efforts to patrol the police were also taking place in other cities with large African American populations at this time. See, for example, "Negroes Will Police in Detroit," *Chicago Tribune*, October 29, 1966.

63. Marine, *The Black Panthers*, 45.

64. Huey P. Newton, *Huey Talks to the Movement about the Black Panther Party, Cultural Nationalism, SNCC Liberals and White Revolutionaries* (Boston, 1968), 12.

65. Eldridge Cleaver, "Police Slaughter Black People," *Black Panther*, July 20, 1967.

66. Newton and Blake, *Revolutionary Suicide*, 146.

67. Eldridge Cleaver, "Independence for North Richmond Area," *Black Panther*, June 20, 1967.

68. "Black Activists in America," *Black Panther*, May 15, 1967. Also see Earl Anthony, "Core City Politics," *Black Panther*, June 20, 1967.

69. Cleaver, "Independence for North Richmond Area."

70. Newton, "Functional Definition of Politics."

71. Newton, "In Defense of Self Defense."

72. Seale, *Seize the Time*, 99–106.

73. Cruse, *The Crisis of the Negro Intellectual*, 354.

74. Bloom and Martin, *Black against Empire*, 57–59.

75. Newton, "Statement by Minister of Defense to the Black World."

76. Jerry Rankin, "Heavily Armed Negro Group Walks into Assembly Chamber," *Los Angeles Times*, May 3, 1967; Seale, *Seize the Time*, 155.

77. "Armed Negros Protest Gun Bill," *New York Times*, May 3, 1967.

78. "Only in America," *Washington Post*, May 6, 1967.

79. Newton and Blake, *Revolutionary Suicide*, 158.

80. Kathleen Cleaver, "A Picture Is Worth a Thousand Words," in *Black Panther: The Revolutionary Art of Emory Douglas*, ed. Sam Durant (New York, 2014), 52.

81. Hilliard and Cole, *This Side of Glory*, 3.

Chapter 3. "We're Relating Right Now to the Third World"

1. Eldridge Cleaver, "Pronunciamento," *Black Panther*, December 21, 1968.

2. "Interview with Masai," *Black Panther*, May 31, 1969.

3. Robeson Taj Frazier, *The East Is Black: Cold War China in the Black Radical Imagination* (Durham, NC, 2015), 12.

4. Eldridge Cleaver, *Soul on Ice* (New York, 1968), 4.

5. Ibid., 14.

6. Eldridge Cleaver, "Bunchy," Eldridge Cleaver Papers, Bancroft Library, University of California, Berkeley (hereafter Cleaver Papers), carton 2, folder 52.

7. Eldridge Cleaver, *Soul on Fire* (Waco, TX, 1978), 74; Cleaver, *Soul on Ice*, 57; Cleaver to *Rolling Stone*, May 27, 1976, Dr. Huey P. Newton Foundation Papers, Stanford University Special Collection, Stanford, California (hereafter Newton Papers), series 2, box 41, folder 10.

8. Cleaver referenced his communications with Donald Warden in Cleaver to Minister Bernard X, Muhammad's Mosque No. 26, San Francisco, August 18, 1964, Cleaver papers, box 3, carton 18. Also see his notes on a "Demonstration by members of A.A.A. at Oakland's McClymonds High School, Tuesday September 10, 1963," Cleaver papers, carton 1, folder 5.

9. Cleaver, *Soul on Fire*, 75.

10. Cleaver, *Soul on Ice*, 55–57; Cleaver, "Bunchy."

11. For Cleaver's prison reading lists, see Cleaver Papers, carton 1, folders 2, 5.

12. Cleaver, undated, handwritten notes [circa 1965], Cleaver Papers, carton 1, folder 1. Also see Cleaver to Beverly Axelrod, September 10, 1965 (box 2, folder 2); Cleaver to Axelrod, January 4, 1966 (box 2, folder 4); Cleaver to David Welsh, August 7, 1966 (box 3, folder 20).

13. Cleaver to Welsh, August 7, 1966.

14. Cleaver, for example, described homosexuality as "a sickness, just as are baby-rape or wanting to become head of General Motors." Cleaver, *Soul on Ice*, 110. His attitude toward women is summarized in a poem from his papers: "When a bitch learns / To stick her clitoris / Inside the head of my penis / Inside her vagina / She can fuck me all she wants / Till then, I'm fucking her." Cleaver Papers, "Undated Fragments," carton 2, folder 45.

15. Cleaver, *Soul on Ice*, 49. On Williams, see Tyson, *Radio Free Dixie*.

16. Cleaver, *Soul on Ice*, 130.

17. Ibid., 68.

18. Ibid., 123.

19. Ibid., 69, 81.

20. Ibid., 202, 204.

21. Ibid., 197.

22. On the history of *Ramparts*, see Peter Richardson, *A Bomb in Every Issue: How the Short, Unruly Life of 'Ramparts' Magazine Changed America* (New York, 2009).

23. Cleaver, *Eldridge Cleaver: Post-Prison Writings and Speeches*, 25; Cleaver, *Soul on Ice*, 19.

24. Elton C. Fax, *Black Artists of the New Generation* (New York, 1977), 256–70.

25. St. Claire Bourne, "An Artist for the People: An Interview with Emory Douglas," in Durant, ed., *Black Panther*, 202.

26. Amiri Baraka, "Emory Douglas: A 'Good Brother,' A 'Bad' Artist," in Durant, ed., *Black Panther*, 171, 177.

27. Marvin X, *Somethin' Proper: The Life and Times of a North American African Poet* (Castro Valley, CA, 1998), 121–25.

28. Cleaver, *Eldridge Cleaver: Post-Prison Writings and Speeches*, 36; Fax, *Black Artists of the New Generation*, 273–74.

29. Many of the BPP's varied ways of communicating its anticolonial vernacular, including the song quoted above, are on display in the short Newsreel Collective film *Off the Pig (Black Panther)*, DVD (1968, Oakland, CA:, 2006).

30. Cleaver, *Eldridge Cleaver: Post-Prison Writings and Speeches*, 129–30.

31. Alkebulan, *Survival pending Revolution*, 49; David Hilliard, preface in *The Black Panther Intercommunal News Service, 1967–1980* (New York, 2007), viii.

32. Cleaver, *Eldridge Cleaver: Post-Prison Writings and Speeches*, 20; "Speeding up Time," *Black Panther*, March 16, 1968.

33. Elaine Brown, "The Significance of the Black Panther Party," in Hilliard, ed., *The Black Panther Intercommunal News Service*, ix.

34. David Hilliard, "Pig—An International Language," *Black Panther*, December 27, 1969.

35. Seale, *Seize the Time*, 408.

36. Ibid., 409.

37. Masai Hewitt, "Seize the Time—Submit or Fight," *Black Panther*, December 13, 1969.

38. Aaron Dixon, *My People Are Rising: Memoirs of a Black Panther Party Captain* (Chicago, 2012), 94.

39. Amiri Baraka, "Black People!," in *The LeRoi Jones/Amiri Baraka Reader* (New York, 1991), 224.

40. Subcommittee to Investigate the Administration of the Internal Security Act and Other Internal Laws of the Committee of the Judiciary, United States Senate, *Testimony of Karl Dietrich Wolff* (Washington DC, 1969), 8. Also see Elijah Wald, *The Dozens: A History of Rap's Mama* (New York, 2012); Marcus Rediker, *Between the Devil and the Deep Blue Sea: Merchant Seamen, Pirates, and the Anglo-American Maritime World, 1700–1750* (New York, 1987), 167.

41. Benedict Anderson, *Imagined Communities* (London, 1991), 133.

42. Hewitt, "Seize the Time—Submit or Fight."

43. Steven Salaita, *Uncivil Rights: Palestine and the Limits of Academic Freedom* (Chicago, 2015), 42.

44. Cleaver, "Pronunciamento," 12–13.

45. Fanon, *The Wretched of the Earth*, 6. On the notion of black people in the United States as anticitizens, see David Roediger, *The Wages of Whiteness: Race and the Making of the American Working Class* (New York, 1991), 57.

46. Cleaver, *Eldridge Cleaver: Post-Prison Writings and Speeches*, 38, 133.

47. Seale, *Seize the Time*, 404.

48. Emory Douglas, "Support Your Local Police," *Black Panther*, May 15, 1967; Fax, *Black Artists of the New Generation*, 276.

49. Baraka, "Emory Douglas," 181.

50. Cleaver, *Eldridge Cleaver: Post-Prison Writings and Speeches*, 129–30.

51. Homi K. Bhabha, "Unsatisfied: Notes on Vernacular Cosmopolitanism," in *Postcolonial Discourses: An Anthology*, ed. Gregory Castle (Oxford, UK, 2001), 43.

52. Assata Shakur, *Assata: An Autobiography* (Chicago, 1987), 203.

53. Emory Douglas, "It's All the Same," *Black Panther*, March 16, 1968.

54. Emory Douglas, "We Are Advocates of the Abolition of War," *Black Panther*, September 28, 1968.

55. Colette Gaiter, "What Revolution Looks Like: The Work of Black Panther Artist Emory Douglas," in Durant, ed., *Black Panther*, 98, 101.

56. Baraka, "Emory Douglas," 180, 181.

57. Emory Douglas, "On Landscape Art," *Black Panther*, March 16, 1968.

58. Cleaver, "Information," *Black Panther*, October 26, 1968.

59. "The World of Black People," *Black Panther*, July 3, 1967.

60. Fanon, *The Wretched of the Earth*, 4–5.

61. "Armed Black Brothers in Richmond Community," *Black Panther*, April 25, 1967.

62. Huey P. Newton, "Functional Definition of Politics," *Black Panther*, May 15, 1967.

63. Rory Hithe, "Arm Yourself or Harm Yourself," *Black Panther*, August 30, 1969.

64. Young, *Soul Power*, 6.

65. See, for example, her illustrations in *Black Panther*, May 4, 1968 (p. 25), May 18, 1968 (p. 23), September 7, 1968 (p. 4), October 24, 1968 (p. 7), November 16, 1968 (p. 17, 18).

66. Examples of these types of illustrations can be found in Durant, ed., *Black Panther*, 80, 97, 102–3, 122, 144–59.

67. Mumia Abu-Jamal quoted in ibid., 4.

68. Cleaver, *Eldridge Cleaver: Post-Prison Writings and Speeches*, 66, 156.

69. George Murray, "For a Revolutionary Culture," *Black Panther*, September 7, 1968; Fred Hampton, "All Power to the People," *Black Panther*, July 19, 1969.

70. John Huggins, "Open Letter to L.A. Pig Chief," *Black Panther*, November 16, 1968; "Wanted Dead for Murder," *Black Panther*, November 2, 1968; David Hilliard, "If You Want Peace You Gotta Fight for It," *Black Panther*, November 22, 1969.

71. Matilaba (Joan Tarika Lewis), "Am I Doing It Right Mama?," *Black Panther*, December 7, 1968, Emory Douglas, "A Black Revolutionary Christmas," *Black Panther*, December 7, 1968.

72. Matilaba (Joan Tarika Lewis), "No More Riots," *Black Panther*, May 4, 1968.

73. Emory Douglas, "Revolutionary Art/Black Liberation," *Black Panther*, May 18, 1968.

74. Matilaba (Joan Tarika Lewis), "Before We Talk Reconstruction, Let's Accomplish the Ruins," *Black Panther*, December 21, 1968; Fanon, *Wretched of the Earth*, 1.

75. *Black Panther*, June 20, 1967.

76. "Chairman Bobby Speaks at May Day Rally to Free Huey," *Black Panther*, May 11, 1969.

77. George Murray, "Minister of Education," *Black Panther*, May 18, 1968. See also, for example, Brother Dynamite, "Police Use Gestapo Tactics," *Black Panther*, November 2, 1968; Fred Beaumont, "The Necessity of Unification," *Black Panther*, November 2, 1968.

78. Emory Douglas, "Get Out of the Ghetto, Get Out of Africa, Get Out of Asia, Get Out of Latin America," *Black Panther*, October 19, 1968.

79. Cleaver, *Eldridge Cleaver: Post-Prison Writings and Speeches*, 58.

80. Ibid., 67.

81. Young, *Soul Power*, 3, 13.

82. Eldridge Cleaver, "Information," *Black Panther*, September 28, 1968; Huey Newton, "Functional Definition of Politics," *Black Panther*, May 15, 1967; "An Exclusive Interview with Minister of Defense Huey P. Newton," *Black Panther*, March 16, 1968.

83. "What We Want Now! What We Believe," *Black Panther*, July 3, 1967, 3. On left-wing criticism of the BPP, see "A Statement by the Black Liberation Commission of the PLP: The Black Panther Party," *Progressive Labor* 6, no. 6 (February 1969): 32; Bob Avakian, *Summing up the Black Panther Party* (Cleveland, OH, 1979).

84. On tensions with white radicals, see Newton and Blake, *Revolutionary Suicide*, 143–44; Hilliard and Cole, *This Side of Glory*, 147. By September 1968 the *Black Panther* was forced to print an injunction to its readers to "stop vamping on the hippies" ("Warning to So-Called Paper Panthers," *Black Panther*, September 14, 1968). Also see Joel Wilson, "Invisible Cages: Racialized Politics and the Alliance between the Panthers and the Peace and Freedom Party," in Lazerow and Williams, ed., *In Search of the Black Panther Party*, 191–222; David Barber, "Leading the Vanguard: White New Leftists School the Panthers on the Black Revolution," in Lazerow and Williams, ed., *In Search of the Black Panther Party*, 223–51.

85. On polyculturalism, see Vijay Prashad, *Everybody Was Kung Fu Fighting: Afro-Asians and the Myth of Cultural Purity* (Boston, 2001).

86. See Jeffrey O. G. Ogbar, "Brown Power to Brown People: Radical Ethnic Nationalism, the Black Panthers, and Latino Radicalism," 1967–1973," in Lazerow and Williams, ed., *In Search of the Black Panther Party*, 252–88; Daryl J. Maeda, "Black Panthers, Red Guards, and Chinamen: Constructing Asian American Identity through Performing Blackness, 1969–1972," *American Quarterly* 57, no. 4 (December 2005), 1079–1103; Pulido, *Black, Brown, Yellow, and Left*.

87. Ferreira, "With the Soul of a Human Rainbow," in Carlsson, *Ten Years that Shook the City*, 36–37.

88. Seale, *Seize the Time*, 404, 411; "An Exclusive Interview with Minister of Defense Huey P. Newton."

89. Huey P. Newton, "In Defense of Self Defense," *Black Panther*, June 20, 1967. For similar sentiments, see Earl Anthony, "The Significance of the Black Liberation Struggle in Newark," *Black Panther*, July 20, 1967.

90. On tensions between the BPP and US, see Scott Brown, *Fighting for US: Maulana Karenga, the US Organization, and Black Cultural Nationalism* (New York, 2003), 107–30.

91. Anne McClintock, *Imperial Leather: Race, Gender and Sexuality in the Colonial Contest* (New York, 1995), 366–67.

92. Frazier, *The East Is Black*, 12.

93. Eldridge Cleaver, "Beauty Contests and the Third World," *Black Panther*, November 23, 1967.

94. Cleaver, *Eldridge Cleaver: Post-Prison Writings and Speeches*, 143. Also see Cleaver's attack on James Baldwin in *Soul on Ice*, 97–111.

95. Erika Doss, "'Revolutionary Art Is a Tool for Liberation': Emory Douglas and Protest Aesthetics at the *Black Panther*," in Cleaver and Katsiaficas, eds., *Liberation, Imagination and the Black Panther Party*, 178.

Chapter 4. "I Prefer Panthers to Pigs"

1. Hilliard and Cole, *This Side of Glory*, 3; Kathleen Cleaver, "A Picture Is Worth a Thousand Words," in Durant, ed., *Black Panther*, 52

2. Wilbert J. Weiskirch, "Black Panther Party for Self Defense," November 16, 1967, SF 100-58841, Richard Aoki FBI files.

3. Newton and Blake, *Revolutionary Suicide*, 181–82.

4. David Hilliard with Keith and Kent Zimmerman, *Huey: Spirit of the Panther* (New York, 2008), 2–4; Hilliard and Cole, *This Side of Glory*, 130.

5. For accounts of the incident, see Newton and Blake, *Revolutionary Suicide*, 184–87; Hilliard and Cole, *This Side of Glory*, 130–31; Hilliard, *Huey*, 2–5. For substantial coverage of the ensuing court case, see Lise Pearlman, *The Sky's the Limit: People v. Newton, the Real Trial of the 20th Century?* (Berkeley, CA, 2012).

6. The exact number of BPP local chapters is hard to pin down exactly. I have used the number provided by Bloom and Martin, *Black against Empire*, 2.

7. On the diverse local histories of Panther chapters outside Oakland, see James T. Campbell, "The Panthers and Local History," in Lazerow and Williams, ed., *In Search of the Black Panther Party*, 97–103; Judson L. Jeffries, ed., *On the Ground: The Black Panther Party in Communities across America* (Jackson, MS, 2010). The party's sometimes contentious relations with white radicals are covered in Joel Wilson, "Invisible Cages: Racialized Politics and the Alliance between the Panthers and the Peace and Freedom Party," in Lazerow and Williams, ed., *In Search of the Black Panther Party*, 191–222; David Barber, "Leading the Vanguard: White New Leftists School the Panthers on the Black Revolution," in Lazerow and Williams, ed., *In Search of the Black Panther Party*, 223–51.

8. On the BPP and its relations with the U.S. Third World Left, see Daryl J. Maeda, "Black Panthers, Red Guards, and Chinamen: Constructing Asian American Identity through Performing Blackness, 1969–1972," *American Quarterly* 57, no. 4 (December 2005): 1079–1103; Ferreira, "With the Soul of a Human Rainbow," 30–47; Ogbar, "Brown Power to Brown People," 252–88; Pulido, *Black, Brown, Yellow, and Left*; Bloom and Martin, *Black against Empire*, 269–87.

9. "Panthers on the Move Internationally: Free Huey at the UN," *Black Panther*, September 14, 1968. The BPP's UN demonstration was covered by photographer Howard L. Bingham. See Howard L. Bingham, *Howard L. Bingham's Black Panthers 1968* (Los Angeles, CA, 2009), 185–89.

10. On the rocky early history of black activism at the UN, Carol Anderson, *Eyes off the Prize: The United Nations and the African American Struggle for Human Rights, 1944–1955* (Cambridge, UK, 2003).

11. "Member States of the United Nations," UN News Center, http://www.un.org/en/members.

12. Breitman, ed., *Malcolm X Speaks*, 35.

13. "Remember the Worlds of Brother Malcolm," *Black Panther*, May 18, 1968.

14. Cleaver, *Eldridge Cleaver*, 67.

15. Eldridge Cleaver, "Political Struggle in America, 1968," *Black Panther*, March 16, 1968.

16. Huey P. Newton, "Communique No. 1," *Black Panther*, September 28, 1968. By September 1968 the UN plebiscite had been incorporated into point ten of the BPP program. See the somewhat misleadingly titled "October 1966 Black Panther Party Platform and Program," *Black Panther*, September 14, 1968; Seale, *Seize the Time*, 63.

17. The BPP first "drafted" Carmichael in June 1967, but he and Foreman received more prominent roles in the party in early 1968 as part of the "Free Huey" campaign. "Carmichael Drafted by Executive Mandate No. 2," *Black Panther*, July 3, 1967; Eldridge Cleaver, "Black Paper," *Black Panther*, May 4, 1968; Peniel E. Joseph, *Stokely: A Life* (New York, 2014), 231; Yohuru R. Williams, "American Exported Black Nationalism: The Student Nonviolent Coordinating Committee, the Black Panther Party, and the Worldwide Freedom Struggle, 1967–1972," *Negro History Bulletin* 60, no. 3 (July–September 1997): 13.

18. Clayborne Carson, *In Struggle: SNCC and the Black Awakening of the 1960s* (Cambridge, MA, 1981), 283–85; Joseph, *Stokely*, 237; James Foreman, *The Making of Black Revolutionaries* (Seattle, WA, 1985), 525–26; Seale, *Seize the Time*, 217–16.

19. Stokely Carmichael, with Ekwueme Michael Thelwell, *Ready for Revolution: The Life and Struggle of Stokely Carmichael (Kwame Ture)* (New York, 2003), 663; Joseph, *Stokely*, 240–41.

20. There are conflicting accounts of the Panther-Foreman meeting, and Foreman himself later denied that he had been threatened with a gun. There is no doubt, however, that the meeting ended badly and proved the final straw in the increasingly tenuous BPP-SNCC alliance. Foreman, *The Making of Black Revolutionaries*, 522–23, 535–38; Earl Anthony, *Spitting in the Wind: The True Story behind the Violent Legacy of the Black Panther Party* (Malibu, CA, 1990), 49; Dixon, *My People Are Rising*, 119–20; William Lee Brent, *Long Time Gone: A Black Panther's True-Life Story of His Hijacking and Twenty-Five Years in Cuba* (San Jose, CA, 2000), 108–12.

21. Dixon, *My People Are Rising*, 116–20.

22. Though it apparently never amounted to much in the way of formal collaboration, the BPP did attempt to coordinate with Mexican students in 1968–69. For examples, see "International Communique No. 1, October 3, 1968: To the Revolutionary Students and Freedom Fighters of Mexico," *Black Panther*, October 12, 1968; Bobby Seale, "Solidarity with Mexican Students," *Black Panther*, July 26, 1969; Eldridge Cleaver, *Soul on Fire*, 102; Central Intelligence Agency, "Situation Information Report," November 15, 1968, document provided under the Freedom of Information Act and in possession of author.

23. On the global development of New Left in this period, see George Katsiaficas, *The Imagination of the New Left: A Global Analysis of 1968* (Boston, 1987); Jeremi Suri, *Power and Protest: Global Revolution and the Rise of Détente* (Cambridge, MA, 2003).

24. Thomas R.H. Haven, *Fire across the Sea: The Vietnam War and Japan, 1965–1975* (Princeton, NJ, 1987), 54–67; Simon Andrew Avenell, *Making Japanese Citizens: Civil Society and the Mythology of the Shimen in Postwar Japan* (Berkeley, CA, 2010), 106–47; Claudia Derichs, "Japan: '1968'—History of a Decade," *Bulletin of the German Historical Society*, supplement 6 (2009), 90–91.

25. Yuichiro Onoshi, "The Presence of (Black) Liberation in Okinawan Freedom: Transnational Moments, 1968–1972," in *Extending the Diaspora: New Histories of Black People*, ed. Dawne Y. Curry et al. (Urbana, IL, 2009), 195.

26. Haven, *Fire across the Sea*, 119–20.

27. Avenell, *Making Japanese Citizens*, 110, 128–32.

28. "Kathleen to Japan," *Black Panther*, September 7, 1968; Earl Anthony, *Picking up the Gun: A Report on the Black Panthers* (New York, 1970), 140–41; Anthony, *Spitting in the Wind*, 51–55. "Statement—The Sanya Liberation Committee," *Black Panther*, November 15, 1969.

29. Anthony, *Picking up the Gun*, 151.

30. Haven, *Fire across the Sea*, 225; Avenell, *Making Japanese Citizens*, 129.

31. Anthony, *Picking up the Gun*, 149.

32. Big Man [Elbert Howard], "Press Release: Tokyo Japan," *Black Panther*, October 4, 1969.

33. Anthony, *Spitting in the Wind*, 60–61.

34. Ibid., 56.

35. "War Foes Close 3-Day Conference in Montreal," *Los Angeles Times*, December 2, 1968; "North Vietnamese Assail U.S. at Rally in Montreal," *New York Times*, November 30, 1968; Bryan Palmer, *Canada's 1960s: The Ironies of Identity in a Rebellious Era* (Toronto: University of Toronto Press, 2008), 351; Bloom and Martin, *Black against Empire*, 309.

36. Bobby Seale, "Complete Text of Bobby Seale's Address," *Black Panther*, December 21, 1968.

37. Bloom and Martin, *Black against Empire*, 310.

38. Raymond Lewis, "Montreal: Bobby Seale—Panthers Take Control," *Black Panther*, December 21, 1968.

39. "Antiwar Parley Repairs a Split," *New York Times*, December 1, 1968; Paul Lyons, *The People of This Generation: The Rise and Fall of the New Left in Philadelphia* (Philadelphia, 2003), 152.

40. Thomas Elman Jorgensen, *Transformation and Crises: The Left and the Nation in Denmark and Sweden, 1956–1980* (New York, 2008), 45, 55–56, 87.

41. Joseph, *Stokely*, 225; Jorgensen, *Transformation and Crises*, 98–99.

42. Robyn Spencer, "Merely One Link in the Worldwide Revolution: Internationalism, State Repression, and the Black Panther Party," in *From Toussaint to Tupac: The Black International since the Age of Revolution*, ed. Michael O. West, William G. Martin, Fanon Che Wilkins (Chapel Hill, NC, 2009), 220; Kathleen Cleaver, "Back to Africa: The Evolution of the International Section of the Black Panther Party (1969–1972)," in *The Black Panther Party Reconsidered*, ed. Charles E. Jones (Baltimore, MD: Black Classic Press, 1998), 228.

43. "Interview with Masai," *Black Panther*, May 31, 1969; Bobby Seale, "Chairman Bobby Seale and 'Masai' Hewitt Tour Scandinavian Countries," *Black Panther*, March 31, 1969; "Interview with Scandinavian Rep. of Black Panther Party: Connie Matthews," *Black Panther*, October 18, 1969.

44. Seale, "Chairman Bobby Seale and 'Masai' Hewitt Tour Scandinavian Countries."

45. Ibid. See also Bobby Seale, "Bobby Speaks to Scandinavia," *Black Panther*, October 25, 1969.

46. On Matthews's continuing work with the BPP in Scandinavia, see Connie Matthews, "Open Letter to the Danish Foreign Ministry," *Black Panther*, May 11, 1969; Connie Matthews, "Scandinavian Solidarity with the BPP," *Black Panther*, September 13, 1969.

47. Bloom and Martin, *Black against Empire*, 313.

48. Maria Höhn and Martin Klimke, *A Breath of Freedom: The Civil Rights Struggle, African American GIs, and Germany* (New York, 2010), 111.

49. Ibid., 113.

50. Ibid., 107–9; 112–13.

51. Christian Semler, "Statement: German SDS," *Black Panther*, November 15, 1969.

52. Höhn and Klimke, *A Breath of Freedom,* 116–17.

53. Ibid., 63–88, 143–70; Plummer, "Brown Babies: Race, Gender, and Policy after World War II," in Plummer, ed., *Window on Freedom,* 67–92.

54. Höhn and Klimke, *A Breath of Freedom, 111–12.*

55. Subcommittee to Investigate the Administration of the Internal Security Act and Other Internal Laws of the Committee of the Judiciary, *Testimony of Karl Dietrich Wolff,* 16.

56. "West German S.D.S. Supports Black Panthers and Black Liberation Movement," *Black Panther,* March 9, 1969.

57. Karl Dietrich Wolff, "Black Panther Party Solidarity Committee," *Black Panther,* December 13, 1969; Höhn and Klimke, *A Breath of Freedom,* 114–15, 119; Martin Klimke, *The Other Alliance: Student Protest in West Germany and the United States in the Global Sixties* (Princeton, NJ, 2010), 118–21.

58. On the British BPP, see Anne-Marie Angelo, "The Black Panthers in London, 1967–1972," *Radical History Review,* no. 103 (Winter 2009): 17–35.

59. Jean Genet, "The Black Panthers Are Preparing the Revolution with Precipitous Care: The Revolution Will Come; Time Is at Their Service," *Black Panther,* June 27, 1970. For more on Genet and the BPP, see Robert Sandarg, "Jean Genet and the Black Panther Party," *Journal of Black Studies* 16, no. 2 (March 1986): 269–82.

60. Höhn and Klimke, *A Breath of Freedom,* 148. Also see Klimke, *The Other Alliance,* 139–41.

61. Höhn and Klimke, *A Breath of Freedom,* 115. On the broad appeal of the BPP's particular invocation of American popular culture, see Jane Rhodes, *Framing the Black Panthers: The Spectacular Rise of a Black Power Icon* (New York, 2007).

62. On the persistence of nationalism within the context of revolution in the twentieth century, see Anderson, *Imagined Communities,* 2.

63. According to Eldridge Cleaver, "Stokely had told me flatly that the white Cubans were racists and that if I was thinking about going to Cuba I had better think again." Cleaver, "Slow Boat to Cuba" (unpublished manuscript), 15, Cleaver Papers, carton 2, folder 31. For Williams's critique of the Castro regime's attitude toward race, see "Speech by U.S. Negro Leader Robert Williams," *Peking Review,* no. 33 (August 12, 1966), 26.

64. Cleaver, "Slow Boat to Cuba," 17–18.

65. John A. Gronbeck-Tedesco, "The Left in Transition: The Cuban Revolution in US Third World Politics," *Journal of Latin American Studies* 40 (2008): 659–60.

66. Cleaver, "Slow Boat to Cuba," 29–30.

67. Landon Williams, "Panthers in Mexico, *Black Panther,* October 5, 1968.

68. "George Murray Press Conference" (reprinted from Granma News), *Black Panther,* October 12, 1968.

69. Juana Carrasco, "Huey P. Newton: Black Revolutionary Politics," (reprinted from Gramma News), *Black Panther,* October 12, 1968.

70. "Cubans Support Movement," *Black Panther,* October 19, 1968; "African, Asian and Latin-American Solidarity Group Appeals to OSPAAAL on Black American Revolution," *Black Panther,* September 7, 1968.

71. Colette Gaiter, "What Revolution Looks Like," 98, 101.

Chapter 5. "Juche, Baby, All the Way"

1. "Political Education, 21 March 1971, Eldridge Cleaver Discusses History of Black Panther Party," Cleaver Papers, carton 5, folder 12; "Transcript of Tape Recorder Notes, 28 March [1971]," Cleaver papers, carton 5, folder 12; Cleaver, "Uptight in Babylon," Cleaver Papers, carton 1, folder 56.

2. Eldridge Cleaver, "Slow Boat to Cuba," n.d. [circa 1969–1970], Cleaver Papers, carton 2, folder 31.

3. Hilliard and Cole, *This Side of Glory*, 177.

4. Photo caption, *Black Panther*, June 20, 1967, p. 4.

5. David Hilliard, "If You Want Peace You Gotta Fight for It," *Black Panther*, November 22, 1969.

6. Cleaver, *Soul on Ice*, 130.

7. Dixon, *My People Are Rising*, 126; Hilliard and Cole, *This Side of Glory*, 178.

8. Eldridge Cleaver, "Dig on This," *Black Panther*, November 23, 1967; "Beautiful News from Hunters Point," *Black Panther*, November 23, 1967; Emory Douglas, "Revolutionary Art/Black Liberation," *Black Panther*, May 18, 1968.

9. Cleaver, "Uptight in Babylon."

10. "Political Education, 21 March 1971"; Cleaver, "Uptight in Babylon"; Hilliard and Cole, *This Side of Glory*, 176, 183–84. Also see Eldridge Cleaver, "Letter to the Lumpen," *Voice of the Lumpen* 1, no. 9 (December 1971), 4.

11. Cleaver, *Eldridge Cleaver*, 9; Seale, *Seize the Time*, 223–25.

12. Huey P. Newton, "Police Run Amuck: Executive Mandate No. 3," *Black Panther*, March 16, 1968.

13. Hilliard, *Huey*, 128; Cleaver, *Eldridge Cleaver*, 9–11, 84.

14. Cleaver, *Eldridge Cleaver*, 74–75.

15. Ibid., 78.

16. Ibid., 71.

17. Hilliard, *Huey*, 129.

18. "Political Education, 21 March 1971"; Hilliard and Cole, *This Side of Glory*, 183; Hilliard, *Huey*, 131–32.

19. "Transcript of Tape Recorder Notes, 28 March."

20. Cleaver, *Eldridge Cleaver*, 86; Hilliard and Cole, *This Side of Glory*, 187; Hilliard, *Huey*, 134.

21. Cleaver, *Eldridge Cleaver*, 89–93.

22. Robert Scheer, introduction to Cleaver, *Eldridge Cleaver*, xxi.

23. Eldridge Cleaver, "Pronunciamento," *Black Panther*, December 21, 1968; Cleaver, *Eldridge Cleaver*, 117, 165.

24. Eldridge Cleaver to Bobby Seale, July 14, 1982 [unsent], Cleaver Papers, carton 3, folder 11; Cleaver, "Slow Boat to Cuba"; Eldridge Cleaver, *Soul on Fire*, 137.

25. Kathleen Cleaver, ed., *Target Zero: Eldridge Cleaver, a Life in Writing* (New York, 2006), 195.

26. Information on the Scheer-Cuba connection comes from Kathleen Cleaver, interview by Sean L. Malloy, March 13, 2014.

27. "Eldridge Cleaver Interview," November 9, 1977, Fresno to Waco Texas [telephone], Cleaver Papers, carton 9, folder 37; Cleaver, *Soul on Fire*, 107.

28. Cleaver, ed., *Target Zero*, 242, 245.

29. Chen Jian, *Mao's China & the Cold War* (Chapel Hill, NC, 2001), 78–84; Westad, *The Global Cold War*, 158–62; Max Elbaum, *Revolution in the Air: Sixties Radicals Turn to Lenin, Mao and Che* (New York, 2002), 45–53; Reitan, *The Rise and Decline of an Alliance*, 124.

30. Reitan, *The Rise and Decline of an Alliance*; Reitan, "Cuba, the Black Panther Party, and the U.S. Black Movement in the 1960s," in Cleaver and Katsiaficas, eds., *Liberation, Imagination and the Black Panther Party*, 164–74.

31. Williams quoted in Frazier, *The East Is Black*, 141.

32. Domínguez, *To Make a World Safe for Revolution*, 69.

33. Cleaver to Axelrod, January 4, 1966, Cleaver Papers, carton 2, folder 4.

34. Reitan, "Cuba, the Black Panther Party, and the U.S. Black Movement in the 1960s," 164–74; Reitan, *Rise and Decline of an Alliance*, 25–28. Carlos Moore offers a somewhat different take on internal Cuban politics in this period, but he agrees with Reitan that by 1968 Cuba had become highly dependent on the Soviet Union and increasingly conservative in its approach to supporting foreign revolutionary movements. Carlos Moore, *Castro, the Blacks, and Africa* (Los Angeles, 1988), 271.

35. Cleaver, "Slow Boat to Cuba;" Reitan, *Rise and Decline of an Alliance*, 65.

36. Kathleen Cleaver interview.

37. Mark Q. Sawyer, *Racial Politics in Post-Revolutionary Cuba* (New York, 2006), xvi–xviii; Alejandro de la Fuente, *A Nation for All: Race, Inequality, and Politics in Twentieth-Century Cuba* (Chapel Hill, NC, 2001), 99–171.

38. Esteban Morales Domínguez, *Race in Cuba: Essays on the Revolution and Racial Inequality* (New York, 2013), 61; Sawyer, *Racial Politics in Post-Revolutionary Cuba*, 53–57; Fuente, *A Nation for All*, 260–79.

39. Frazier, *The East Is Black*, 141–42.

40. Sawyer, *Racial Politics in Post-Revolutionary Cuba*, 30, 55

41. Ibid., 7; Fuente, *A Nation for All*, 279–84.

42. Frazier, *The East Is Black*, 143.

43. Fuente, *A Nation for All*, 279; Morales Domínguez, *Race in Cuba*, 21–22, 138–39; Sawyer, *Racial Politics in Post-Revolutionary Cuba*, 59–60.

44. Moore, *Castro, the Blacks, and Africa*, 259; Sawyer, 66–67.

45. "Cubans Support Movement," *Black Panther*, October 19, 1968.

46. Sawyer, *Racial Politics in Post-Revolutionary Cuba*, 50; Fuente, *A Nation for All*, 296–302.

47. Cleaver, "Slow Boat to Cuba"; Cleaver, *Target Zero*, 242–43.

48. Jennifer Van Vleck, *Empire of the Air: Aviation and American Ascendency* (Cambridge, MA, 2013), 275. The "skyjacking epidemic" of the late 1960s and early 1970s remains an understudied topic within the academic literature (outside of some dubious psychological and sociological studies of the hijackers published in the 1970s). One recent exception is Teishan A. Latner, "Take Me to Havana! Airline Hijacking, U.S.-Cuba Relations, and Political Protect in Late Sixties' America," *Diplomatic History* 39, no. 1 (January 2015), 16–44. Also see Chamberlin, *The Global Offensive*, for the non-Cuban context of this phenomenon.

49. Latner, "Take Me to Havana!," 17, 27, 30.

50. Fenton Wheeler, "Black Panthers Called Disenchanted with Cuba," *Washington Post*, June 26, 1969; "'Black Panther' in Cuba Is Called an FBI Agent by Party Chief," *Washington Post*, June 28, 1969.

51. Lockwood, *Conversations with Eldridge Cleaver: Algiers*, 21; Cleaver, ed., *Target Zero*, 244–47; Cleaver, "Back to Africa," in Jones, ed., *The Black Panther Party Reconsidered*, 221–22; Ahmad Maceo Eldridge Cleaver, *Soul on Islam* (Astoria, NY, 2006), 12.

52. Cleaver, *Soul on Fire*, 143; Cleaver, ed., *Target Zero*, 248; Sawyer, *Racial Politics in Post-Revolutionary Cuba* 94; Latner, "Take Me to Havana!," 32.

53. Kathleen Rout, *Eldridge Cleaver* (Boston, 1991), 107, 108–11. Kathleen Cleaver offered an alternative explanation for how the AP reporter found Cleaver, theorizing that the meeting was covertly set up by the Cuban government so that they claim that the exiled Panther had violated the agreement not to publicize his presence, thus giving the Cubans an excuse to eject him from the country. Kathleen Cleaver interview.

54. Eldridge Cleaver, "A Note to My Friends," *Ramparts*, September 1969, 29.

55. Cleaver, ed., *Target Zero*, 251; Cleaver, "Back to Africa," 226.

56. John P. Entelis, *Algeria: The Revolution Institutionalized* (Boulder, CO, 1986), 189; Matthew Connelly, *A Diplomatic Revolution: Algeria's Fight for Independence and the Origins of the Post–Cold*

War Era (New York, 2002), 280; Jeffrey James Byrne, *Mecca of Revolution: Algeria, Decolonization and the Third World Order* (New York, 2016).

57. Cleaver, "Back to Africa," 218; Domínguez, *To Make a World Safe for Revolution*, 181; Piero Gleijeses, *Conflict Missions: Havana, Washington, and Africa, 1959–1976* (Chapel Hill, NC, 2002), 134.

58. Samir Meghelli, "From Harlem to Algiers: Transnational Solidarities between the African American Freedom Movement and Algeria, 1962–1978," in *Black Routes to Islam* (New York, 2009), ed. Manning Marable and Hishaam D. Aidi, 113–14; Gleijeses, *Conflict Missions*, 134; Entelis, *Algeria*, 115–17.

59. Cleaver, "Back to Africa," 227.

60. Ibid., 119, 211–12; Rout, *Eldridge Cleaver*, 112–13.

61. Eric Pace, "Cleaver Assails Apollo Program," *New York Times*, July 21, 1969. For further BPP critique of the moon mission, see W.H. Sherman, "Astro Pigs on the Moon," *Black Panther*, July 26, 1969; Deputy Minister of Information, Des Moines Black Panther Party, "The Moon Belongs to the People," *Black Panther*, August 9, 1969.

62. Meghelli, "From Harlem to Algiers," 108; Cleaver, "Back to Africa," 213.

63. Eric Pace, "Cleaver Is Cheered in Algiers as He Denounces Israel as American Puppet," *New York Times*, July 23, 1969.

64. Cleaver, "Back to Africa," 213.

65. Del Hood, "Black Panther Candidate: Here's How He Stands," *Daily Californian* (El Cajon), July 30, 1968; Cleaver to Paul Jacobs, August 13, 1966, Cleaver Papers, box 3, folder 20.

66. Alex Lubin, *Geographies of Liberation: The Making of an Afro-Arab Political Imaginary* (Chapel Hill, NC, 2014), 26.

67. Ibid., 116–19; Clayborne Carson, *In Struggle: SNCC and the Black Awakening of the 1960s* (Cambridge, MA, 1981), 267–69.

68. "Eldridge Cleaver Interview," November 9, 1977, Cleaver Papers, carton 9, folder 37; Paul Thomas Chamberlin, *The Global Offensive: The United States, The Palestine Liberation Organization, and the Making of the Post-Cold War Order* (New York, 2012), 52–53.

69. Chamberlin, *The Global Offensive*, 62, 111, 130.

70. Cleaver, "Statement in Support of Palestinians," September 18, 1970, Cleaver Papers, carton 5, folder 9. See also "Al Fatah Speaks" and "Al Fatah Freedom Fighters," *Black Panther*, August 9, 1969; "Fifth Anniversary of Fat'h," *Black Panther*, February 7, 1970.

71. Donald Cox, "Statement of Black Panther Party to Palestinian Student Conference," Kuwait, February 13–17, 1971, Donald L. Cox FBI file, 1334053-0 Section 3.

72. "Black Panther Discussion with African and Haitian Liberation Fighters," *Black Panther*, August 23, 1969; *Eldridge Cleaver, Black Panther*, directed by William Klein (1970; Arte Éditions, 2010).

73. Eldridge Cleaver, "Somewhere in the Third World," *Black Panther*, July 12, 1969.

74. *Eldridge Cleaver, Black Panther*.

75. "Black Panther Discussion with African and Haitian Liberation Fighters."

76. Lockwood, *Conversations with Eldridge Cleaver: Algeria*, 95, 118.

77. Nathan Hare, "Algiers, 1969: A Report on the Pan-African Cultural Festival," *Black Scholar*, November 1969, 2–10. For a defense of the cultural approach to revolution, see Sékou Touré, "A Dialectical Approach to Culture," *Black Scholar*, November 1969, 11–26.

78. Eldridge Cleaver, "Open Letter to Stokely Carmichael," *Black Panther*, August 16, 1969; Joseph, *Stokely*, 280–81; Eric Pace, "Carmichael Tells of Meeting Cleaver in Algiers," *New York Times*, July 25, 1969.

79. "Black Panther Discussion with African and Haitian Liberation Fighters." Also see Cleaver's comments on "negritude and cultural nationalism [as] stumbling blocks to the people's

liberation struggles rather than assistances" in "Eldridge Cleaver Discusses Revolution: An Interview from Exile," *Black Panther*, October 11, 1969.

80. "Black Panther Discussion with African and Haitian Liberation Fighters."

81. On the shift toward "survival programs" and "survival pending revolution," see Bloom and Martin, *Black against Empire*, 179–98.

82. Sanche de Gramont, "Our Other Man in Algeria," *New York Times Magazine*, November 1, 1970, 113.

83. *Eldridge Cleaver, Black Panther*; Eldridge Cleaver, "On Meeting the Needs of the People," *Ramparts*, September 1969, 34. On his private reservations about survival programs, see "Slow Boat to Cuba," 24.

84. "Transcript of Tape Recorder Notes, 28 March."

85. Cleaver, "Back to Africa," 221–22; Byron Booth, "Beyond the Demarcation Line," *Black Panther*, October 25, 1969, 16–17.

86. Cleaver, "A Note to My Friends," 30.

87. Joseph, *Stokely*, 277.

88. Frazier, *The East Is Black*; Kelley and Esch, "Black Like Mao," 6–41; Wu, *Radicals on the Road*; Fred Ho and Bill V. Mullen, eds., *Afro-Asia: Revolutionary and Cultural Connections between Asian Americans and African Americans* (Durham, NC, 2008).

89. Wu, *Radicals on the Road*, 7.

90. Eldridge Cleaver, "Neither the People Inside Nor Outside the U.S.A. Will Tolerate Bobby Seale Being Condemned to Death," *Black Panther*, December 14, 1970.

91. Kathleen Cleaver interview.

92. Cleaver, "Back to Africa," 221.

93. Charles K. Armstrong, *Tyranny of the Weak: North Korea and the World, 1950–1992* (Ithaca, NY, 2013), 116, 139.

94. Ibid., 106, 144–45; Benjamin R. Young, "Juche in the United States: The Black Panther Party's Relations with North Korea, 1969–1971," *Asia Pacific Journal* 13, no. 2 (March 30, 2015), http://apjjf.org/2015/13/12/Benjamin-Young/4303.html.

95. Cleaver, "Back to Africa," 221.

96. Eldridge Cleaver, notebook (white cover), "International Conference of Journalists of the Whole World in the Fight against U.S. Imperialist Aggression," September 1969, Cleaver Papers, carton 4, folder 6.

97. Eldridge Cleaver, notebook (blue cover), Cleaver Papers, carton 5, folder 8.

98. Booth, "Beyond the Demarcation Line," 16.

99. Ibid.; Eldridge Cleaver, "We Have Found It Here in Korea," *Black Panther*, November 1, 1969.

100. "Report of Eldridge Cleaver," n.d., Eldridge Cleaver FBI File #100-HQ-447251, Section 17. This report, along with one by Byron Booth, was apparently seized from the Los Angeles office of the BPP during a police raid on December 8, 1969. While I have generally avoided citing FBI documents on the Panthers due to the well-known disinformation campaign waged by the bureau against the Panthers as part of COINTELPRO, the contents of these reports match closely both the private and public accounts of Cleaver and Booth, and I therefore take them to be genuine.

101. Cleaver, notebook (blue cover). For Cleaver's detailed strategy for guerrilla warfare, see the section on "Armed Struggled in Babylon" in "Eldridge Cleaver's Notes on Korea, 28 October, 1969," Wilson Center Digital Archive, http://digitalarchive.wilsoncenter.org/document/114563.

102. "Report of Eldridge Cleaver."

103. "Kim Il Sung on the Question of Firmly Establishing 'Juche' and Thoroughly Implementing the Mass Line," *Black Panther*, January 17, 1970.

104. "John McGrath Interviews Eldridge Cleaver," *Black Panther*, April 11, 1970.

105. "Report of [Byron Booth]," Eldridge Cleaver FBI File #100-HQ-447251, Section 17.

106. Eldridge Cleaver, "Witch Hour in Babylon" (fragments), n.d., Cleaver Papers, carton 4, folder 11.

107. "Manifesto from the Land of Fire and Blood: Introduction by Minister of Information Black Panther Party Eldridge Cleaver," *Black Panther*, March 15, 1970, special supplement; "Eldridge Cleaver, "Solidarity of the Peoples until Victory or Death!" *Black Panther*, October 25, 1969; "Peoples Republic of Korea," *Black Panther*, October 4, 1969; "Kim Il Sung on the Question of Firmly Establishing 'Juche' and Thoroughly Implement[ing] the Mass Line," *Black Panther*, January 17, 197; Judi Douglas, "Black People Must Incorporate the Idea of 'Juche,'" *Black Panther*, January 24, 1970; "Juche," *Black Panther*, January 31, 1970; "Birthday Greetings to Kim Il Sung," *Black Panther*, April 18, 1970; Kim Il Sung, "On Further Consolidating and Developing the Socialist System in the People's Republic of Korea," *Black Panther*, December 6, 1970.

108. "Telegram from Comrade Kim Il Sung," *Black Panther*, January 24, 1970; Young, "Juche in the United States."

109. Cleaver, "Back to Africa," 226.

110. *Eldridge Cleaver, Black Panther.*

111. Cleaver, "Back to Africa," 221, 222–23; Rout, *Eldridge Cleaver*, 112–13; Cleaver notebook (white cover).

112. Westad, *The Global Cold War*, 96–97, 190.

113. Lien-Hang T. Nguyen, *Hanoi's War: An International History of the War for Peace in Vietnam* (Chapel Hill, NC, 2012), 130, 148, 154, 158, 187–88.

114. Cleaver, *Soul on Fire*, 144; Cleaver, ed., *Target Zero*, 253.

115. Cleaver, "Back to Africa," 232.

116. Cleaver, *Soul on Fire*, 149–50; Cleaver, "Back to Africa," 230.

117. "Panther Political Prisoners for U.S. Prisoners of War," *Black Panther*, November 22, 1969.

118. Cleaver, *Soul on Fire*, 144; Cleaver, ed., *Target Zero*, 253, 256; Cleaver, "Back to Africa," 223–24, 232; Hilliard and Cole, *This Side of Glory*, 247.

119. On tensions with US and its feud with the BPP, see Scot Brown, *Fighting for US: Maulana Karenga, the US Organization, and Black Cultural Nationalism* (New York, 2003).

120. "Eldridge Cleaver's Notes on Korea, 28 October, 1969."

121. Eldridge Cleaver, *On the Ideology of the Black Panther Party* (San Francisco, CA, 1970), 1, 2.

122. David Hilliard, "What You Are Speaks So Loud I Hardly Hear Anything You Say," *Black Panther*, November 8, 1969.

Chapter 6. "Gangster Cigarettes" and "Revolutionary Intercommunalism"

1. Dave Monsees and Pat O'Brien, "Huey P. Newton's Release from Prison," KPIX News, San Francisco, CA, August 5, 1970, San Francisco Bay Area Television Archive, https://diva.sfsu.edu/collections/sfbatv/bundles/208428.

2. Cleaver, "Back to Africa," in Jones, ed., *The Black Panther Party Reconsidered*, 235.

3. On the groups outside the United States inspired by the BPP, see Michael L. Clemons and Charles E. Jones, "Global Solidarity: The Black Panther Party in the International Arena," in

Cleaver and Katsiaficas, eds., *Liberation, Imagination and the Black Panther Party*, 23–26; Slate, ed., *Black Power beyond Borders*.

4. Erik H. Erikson and Huey P. Newton, *In Search of Common Ground: Conversations with Erik H. Erikson and Huey P. Newton* (New York, 1973), 31–32, 34–35.

5. See, for example, the accounts of the Kissinger-Rogers rivalry with respect to policy in Vietnam and the Middle East in Chamberlin, *The Global Offensive*, 85–86; Nguyen, *Hanoi's War*, 133–34, 136, 145–46.

6. The delegation included Cleaver and Elaine Brown (representing the BPP), Robert Scheer and Jan Austen (*Ramparts*), Pat Sumi (Movement for a Democratic Military), Alex Hing (Red Guards), Andy Truskier (Peace and Freedom Party), Ann Froines (women's liberation movement and New Haven Defense Committee for the BPP), Randy Rappaport and Janet Kranzberg (New York Newsreel), and Regina Blumenfeld (women's liberation movement). "U.S. People's Anti-Imperialist Delegation," Cleaver Papers, carton 4, folder 6. The best account of the delegation's travels is Wu, *Radicals on the Road*, 107–92.

7. Cleaver, ed., *Target Zero*, 228.

8. Nikhil Pal Singh, "The Black Panthers and the 'Undeveloped Country' of the Left," in Jones, ed., *The Black Panther Party Reconsidered*, 83.

9. "Message from Anti-Imperialist Delegation of American People while Still Enroute to D.P.R.K.," *Black Panther*, August 8, 1970.

10. In addition to extensive coverage in *Black Panther* during August–October 1970, see "Cleaver and Black Panther Group Attend Hanoi Observance," *New York Times*, August 19, 1970; "Cleaver's Arrival in Hanoi Reported," *Sarasota Herald-Tribune*, August 16, 1970; "Cleaver Denounces Agnew's Asian Tour," *New York Times*, August 25, 1970; "Cleaver Pledges Fight against U.S. 'Fascism,'" [Baltimore] *Sun*, August 13, 1970; Jack Anderson, "Justice Department Uses Kid Gloves," *Fresno Bee*, October 15, 1970; Victor Riesel, "Black Panthers Are International," *Rome* [Georgia] *News-Tribune*, September 18, 1970; "Cleaver Meets with Hanoi's Premier," *Chicago Tribune*, September 5, 1970; "Black Panthers Open Office in Algiers," *New York Times*, September 14, 1970. The CIA monitored Cleaver's broadcast from North Vietnam, and a transcript was included in a series of documents obtained by the author via the Freedom of Information Act (FOIA). On U.S. government interest in the delegation, see Rafalko, *MH/CHAOS*, 116–19.

11. "An Interview with Elaine Brown, Deputy Minister of Information Black Panther Party," *Black Panther*, October 3, 1970, special supplement; Cleaver, "Back to Africa," 234.

12. "Statement to Anti-Imperialist Delegation Delivered July 15, 1970 by Comrade Krang Ryang Unk," *Black Panther*, October 10, 1970.

13. "Anti-Imperialist Delegation of American People Here," *Black Panther*, August 8, 1970; Cleaver, *Soul on Fire*, 148; Anti-Imperialist Delegation of American People Here; Wu, *Radicals on the Road*, 144.

14. "Statement by Eldridge Cleaver to GI's in South Viet Nam," *Black Panther*, September 26, 1970.

15. Wu, *Radicals on the Road*, 146. On war weariness and morale in the North Vietnam, see Nguyen, *Hanoi's War*, 154, 157.

16. Elaine Brown, "Anti-Imperialist Delegation—1970," Huey P. Newton Foundation Records, Stanford University Manuscripts Division, Stanford University, Stanford, California (hereafter Newton Papers), series 2, box 4, folder 17.

17. Wu, *Radicals on the Road*, 166–69, 174.

18. Cleaver, *Eldridge Cleaver: Post-Prison Writings and Speeches*, 143.

19. Wu, *Radicals on the Road*, 108.

20. Lien-Hang Nguyen, "Revolutionary Circuits: Towards Internationalzing America in the World," *Diplomatic History* 39, no. 3 (2015): 414; "Meeting with members of the central committee of the Vietnamese Women's Union, 8/22/70," Cleaver Papers, carton 5, folder 1; Wu, *Radicals on the Road*, 139.

21. "Elaine Brown and Andrew Truskier, Members of the U.S. People's Anti-Imperialist Delegation Speak before a War Crimes Tribunal at the University of California," *Black Panther*, December 14, 1970.

22. Wu, *Radicals on the Road*, 4.

23. "An Interview with Elaine Brown."

24. Wu, *Radicals on the Road*, 136–62.

25. Sanche de Gramont, "Our Other Man in Algeria," *New York Times Magazine*, November 1, 1970, 228; Cleaver, "Back to Africa," 230; "An Interview with Elaine Brown."

26. Cleaver, "Back to Africa," 235, 250; Cleaver, ed., *Target Zero*, 220.

27. Cleaver, "Back to Africa," 231.

28. Cleaver, *Soul on Fire*, 150–53; "Second Meeting with C. Salah, Wednesday am 16 August 1972," Cleaver Papers, carton 5, folder 40; Eldridge Cleaver to Cetewayo Tabor, September 24, 1972, Cleaver Papers, carton 5, folder 40; Charlotte O'Neal, interview with Sean L. Malloy, September 23, 2014.

29. Cleaver, *Soul on Fire*, 150.

30. "Eldridge Cleaver—Transcript of Tape Recorder Notes, 26 March [1971]," Cleaver Papers, carton 5, folder 19.

31. David Rosenzweig, "Ex-Panther Says He Saw Cleaver Kill a Man," *Los Angeles Times*, February 24, 2001; Elaine Brown, "Free Kathleen Cleaver," *Black Panther*, March 6, 1971; Rafalko, *MH/CHAOS*, 115–16; "Black Panther Party Factionalism," March 5, 1971, Eldridge Cleaver FBI File #100-HQ-447251, Section 20.

32. Kathleen Cleaver, "Reply to Article 'Free Kathleen,'" *Right On! Black Community News Service*, April 3, 1971; Kathleen Cleaver to Eldridge Cleaver, "Re: Letter from T.B.," August 23, 1969, Cleaver Papers, carton 5, folder 27.

33. Timothy Leary, *Flashbacks: An Autobiography* (New York, 1983), 301–10.

34. "Transcript of Telephone Conversation, Eldridge Cleaver with Radio KFRC, San Francisco, 2 February 1971," Cleaver Papers, carton 5, folder 22; "Interview between Curtice Taylor and Eldridge Cleaver," n.d. [circa 1974], Cleaver Papers, carton 5, folder 23; Leary, *Flashbacks*, 301–6; Robert Greenfield, *Timothy Leary: A Biography* (Orlando, FL, 2006), 395–98, 401–21.

35. Huey P. Newton, "To the Courageous Revolutionaries of the National Liberation Front and Provisional Revolutionary Government of South Vietnam We Send Greetings," *Black Panther*, January 9, 1971; Newton and Blake, *Revolutionary Suicide*, 314.

36. Huey Newton, "Repression Breeds Resistance," *Black Panther*, January 26, 1971.

37. George Jackson, *Soledad Brother: The Prison Letters of George Jackson* (New York, 1970), 167.

38. Bloom and Martin, *Black against Empire*, 364–65, 374–75.

39. Hilliard and Cole, *This Side of Glory*, 224.

40. On the NCCF, see Bloom and Martin, *Black against Empire*, 301–2; Alkebulan, *Survival pending Revolution*, 47–48.

41. "Situation Information Report," September 10, 1970," CIA files acquired under the Freedom of Information Act (FOIA) and in possession of the author.

42. "Huey P. Newton's Address at Boston College, November 18, 1970," *Black Panther*, January 23, 1971, special supplement. The first apparent public mention of intercommunalism came at the Revolutionary People's Convention in Philadelphia on September 4–5, 1970,

during which he called for "proportional representation in an inter-communalist framework." Huey P. Newton, "Towards a New Constitution," *Black Panther*, November 28, 1970.

43. Erikson and Newton, *In Search of Common Ground*, 30.

44. "Huey P. Newton's Address at Boston College."

45. Erikson and Newton, *In Search of Common Ground*, 30.

46. "Huey P. Newton's Address at Boston College."

47. Erikson and Newton, *In Search of Common Ground*, 31–32.

48. Ibid., 31.

49. Ibid., 31–32.

50. Ibid., 140.

51. Ibid., 35.

52. "Statement by Huey P. Newton, Minister of Defense of the Black Panther Party, Supreme Servant of the People at the Chicago, Illinois Coliseum, February 21, 1971," *Black Panther*, April 10, 1971.

53. Huey P. Newton, "On the Defection of Eldridge Cleaver from the Black Panther Party and the Defection of the Black Panther Party from the Black Community," *Black Panther*, April 17, 1971, special supplement.

54. See, for example, Kelley and Esch, "Black Like Mao," 26; Jeffries, *Huey P. Newton*, 78; Lubin, *Geographies of Liberation*, 111–41.

55. "Huey P. Newton's Address at Boston College."

56. On the evolution of the party's "survival programs," see Bloom and Martin, *Black against Empire*, 179–98.

57. "Statement by Huey P. Newton . . . at the Chicago, Illinois Coliseum."

58. "Huey P. Newton's Address at Boston College."

59. Shakur, *Assata*, 226.

60. David Hilliard recalled, "Huey's great in small sessions, enthusiastic, intense, funny. But before large groups he freezes; his voice gets high—the soprano that used to be a cause of fights back in school—and his style stiffens; he sounds academic, goes on incessantly, and becomes increasingly abstract, spinning out one dialectical contradiction after another. Hilliard and Cole, *This Side of Glory*, 302.

61. Shakur, *Assata*, 226.

62. Abu-Jamal, *We Want Freedom*, 74.

63. Erikson and Newton, *In Search of Common Ground*, 38.

64. Hilliard and Cole, *This Side of Glory*, 319; Robyn Spencer, "Merely One Link in the Worldwide Revolution: Internationalism, State Repression, and the Black Panther Party," in West, Martin, and Wilkins, eds., *From Toussaint to Tupac*, 224; Pulido, *Black, Brown, Yellow, and Left*, 152; Alkebulan, *Survival pending Revolution*, 23.

65. "A Letter from Huey to the Revolutionary Brothers and Sisters about the Women's Liberation and Gay Liberation Movements," *Black Panther*, August 21, 1970.

66. "Transcript of Tape Recorder Notes, 28 March," Cleaver Papers, carton 5, folder 19.

67. Eldridge Cleaver, "Neither the People Inside Nor Outside the U.S.A. Will Tolerate Bobby Seale Being Condemned to Death," *Black Panther*, December 14, 1970.

68. Kathleen Cleaver interview.

69. United States Senate, Select Committee to Study Governmental Operations with Respect to Intelligence Activities, *Supplementary Detailed Staff Reports*, book 3, 201; Rafalko, *MH/CHAOS*, 101–23; Ward Churchill and Jim Vander Wall, *The COINTELPRO Papers: Documents from the FBI's Secret Wars against Dissent in the United States* (Cambridge, MA, 2002), 150–59. A selection of declassified COINTELPRO documents detailing the FBI's efforts to exploit the tensions between Newton and Cleaver can be found in the Cleaver Papers, carton 24, folder 1.

70. "SAC, San Francisco (157–601) to Director, FBI, 2/25/71," Cleaver Papers, carton 24, folder 1.

71. Charlotte O'Neal interview; *Supplementary Detailed Staff*, book 3, 206.

72. Eldridge Cleaver to Huey P. Newton, December 20, 1970, Newton Papers, series 2, box 11, folder 10.

73. Bloom and Martin, *Black against Empire*, 342–46.

74. Gaidi Faraj, "Unearthing the Underground: A Study of Radical Activism in the Black Panther Party and the Black Liberation Army," PhD thesis, University of California, Berkeley, 2007, 144–45; "Free Geronimo—The Urban Guerrilla: Part I," *Right On! Black Community News Service*, April 3, 1971.

75. Bloom and Martin, *Black against Empire*, 356–62; "An Open Letter to the People from 'Bobby Hutton,'" *Right On! Black Community News Service*, April 3, 1971.

76. Eldridge Cleaver, "On the Weathermen," Cleaver Papers, carton 5, folder 10. On the Weather Underground's connection to Cleaver, see also Bernadine Dorn et al. to Eldridge Cleaver et al., December 6, 1970, Cleaver Papers, carton 5, folder 48.

77. Donald B. Thackrey, "Panther Leader[s] 'Disagree' on TV," *Afro-American*, March 6, 1971.

78. Newton, "On the Defection of Eldridge Cleaver."

79. A transcript of the Cleaver-Newton telephone conversation, which was recorded in Algiers, was reprinted in "On the Contradictions within the Black Panther Party," *Right On! Black Community News*, April 3, 1971. Also see Hilliard, *Huey*, 151.

80. These letters were enclosed in Elaine Brown to Martin Kenner, Committee to Defend the Panthers, March 20, 1971, Newton Papers, series 2, box 11, folder 10.

81. Washington, *All Power to the People*, 39.

82. "On the Assassination of Deputy Field Marshall Robert Webb," *Right On! Black Community News Service*, April 2, 1971; Huey P. Newton, "Eulogy for Samuel Napier," *Black Panther*, May 1, 1971; Bloom and Martin, *Black against Empire*, 362–64.

83. Washington, *All Power to the People*, 40.

84. Flores Alexander Forbes, *Will You Die with Me? My Life in the Black Panther Party* (New York: Washington Square Press, 2006), 56.

85. Mumia Abu-Jamal, *Live from Death Row* (New York, 1995), 153.

86. Bloom and Martin, *Black against Empire*, 373.

87. Abu-Jamal, *We Want Freedom*, 233–36.

88. "On the Contradictions within the Black Panther Party," 9.

Chapter 7. "Cosmopolitan Guerrillas"

1. *Right On! Black Community News*, April 3, 1971.

2. "Eldridge Cleaver—Transcript of Tape Recorder Notes, 26 March [1971]," Cleaver Papers, carton 5, folder 19.

3. Elaine Brown to Martin Kenner, Committee to Defend the Panthers, March 20, 1971, Newton Papers, series 2, box 11, folder 10; "Intercommunal Section Defects," *Black Panther*, March 20, 1971.

4. Cleaver, "Back to Africa," in Jones, ed., *The Black Panther Party Reconsidered*, 239.

5. "Eldridge Cleaver—Transcript of Tape Recorder Notes, 26 March [1971]."

6. Untitled manuscripts, Algiers, n.d. [circa 1972], Cleaver Papers, carton 2, folder 36.

7. "Freeman Forum—Transcript of [Eldridge Cleaver] Interview," n.d. [circa 1981], Cleaver Papers, carton 13, folder 70.

8. "Interview between [Curtice] Taylor and [Eldridge] Cleaver," n.d. [circa 1974], Cleaver Papers, carton 5, folder 23.

9. Suri, *Power and Protest*.

10. "Memorandum of Conversation, Beijing, October 24, 1971, 9:23–11:20 p.m.," *Foreign Relations of the United States, 1969–1976*, volume E-13, Documents on China, 1969–1972, document 52, U.S. Department of State, Office of the Historian, http://history.state.gov/historicaldocuments/frus1969-76ve13/d52.

11. "Eldridge Cleaver Interview, November 9, 1977, Fresno to Waco Texas," Cleaver Papers, carton 9, folder 37.

12. Eldridge Cleaver, "Greetings to the Black GI's," *Voice of the Lumpen* 1, no. 7 (1971): 20.

13. Eldridge Cleaver, "Towards a People's Army," *Babylon*, n.d. [circa 1971], 17, Cleaver Papers, oversize box 2.

14. Charles K. Armstrong, *Tyranny of the Weak: North Korea and the World, 1950–1992* (Ithaca, NY, 2013), 158, 168–69, 175.

15. Cleaver, "Back to Africa," in Jones, ed., *The Black Panther Party Reconsidered*, 244.

16. Nguyen, *Hanoi's War*, 261, 300–301.

17. "Freeman Forum—Transcript of [Eldridge Cleaver] Interview."

18. Cleaver, "Back to Africa," in Jones, ed., *The Black Panther Party Reconsidered*, 240–42.

19. Eldridge Cleaver, "On the Private Abuse of Public Power," Cleaver Papers, carton 2, folder 19.

20. Ernest Ndalla, "Message to Afro-Americans," *Message to the Afro-American People from the Peoples' Republic of Congo* (May 1971), 6, Cleaver Papers, carton 2, folder 5. On the filmmaking process, see "Participations diverses de Chris Marker à des films d'autres réalisateurs," Chris Marker, http://chrismarker.ch/participation/index.html#bv000125.

21. Cleaver, "On the Private Abuse of Public Power."

22. Eldridge Cleaver, "After Brother Malcolm," *Message to the Afro-American People from the Peoples' Republic of Congo*, 9–10, Cleaver Papers, carton 2, folder 5.

23. Eldridge Cleaver, "Afro-America and the Congo," *Message to the Afro-American People from the Peoples' Republic of Congo*, 20, Cleaver Papers, carton 2, folder 5.

24. Cleaver, "Back to Africa," in Jones, ed., *The Black Panther Party Reconsidered*, 242.

25. Huey P. Newton to Marien N'Gouabi, President of the People's Republic of Congo-Brazzaville, November 15, 1971, Newton Papers, series 2, box 7, folder 3.

26. Eldridge Cleaver, "Hidden Cancer," Cleaver Papers, carton 5, folder 17.

27. "What Is the Revolutionary Peoples Communications Network," September 13, 1971, Cleaver Papers, carton 5, folder 51.

28. "Kathleen Cleaver press conference, October 21, 1971," Eldridge Cleaver FBI File #100-HQ-447251, Section 22.

29. Contributor information comes from *Babylon*, n.d, Cleaver Papers, oversize box 2.

30. "Who the 'Voice of the Lumpen' Are," *Voice of the Lumpen* 1, no. 2 (1971): 6; Martin Klimke, *The Other Alliance*, 124

31. Höhn and Klimke, *A Breath of Freedom*, 148–49; Maria Höhn, "The Black Panther Solidarity Committee and the *Voice of the Lumpen*," *German Studies Review* 31, no. 1 (February 2008: 138.

32. Höhn, "The Black Panther Solidarity Committee and the *Voice of the Lumpen*," 133, 137–38.

33. Cleaver, "Greetings to the Black GIs," 19; "On the Prison Rebellions in Babylon," *Information Bulletin* [Revolutionary People's Communications Network] 1, no. 1.

34. Höhn and Klimke, *A Breath of Freedom*, 152.

35. Klimke, *The Other Alliance*, 126.

36. "Black GI Released from West German Prison to International Section Black Panther Party Algiers," *Voice of the Lumpen* 1, no. 8 (October 1971): 12. Jackson was convicted and sentenced to six years in prison. Klimke, *The Other Alliance*, 123.

37. Cleaver, "Back to Africa," in Jones, ed., *The Black Panther Party Reconsidered*, 243.

38. "The Kidnapping of Kathleen Cleaver," *Voice of the Lumpen* 1, no. 1 (1971): 2; Klimke, *The Other Alliance*, 124.

39. Kathleen Cleaver, "Daily Report, 12 March 1971," Cleaver Papers, carton 5, folder 46; Charlotte O'Neal interview.

40. "Participations diverses de Chris Marker à des films d'autres réalisateurs."

41. Donald Cox, "The Split in the Party, in Cleaver and Katsiaficas, eds., *Liberation, Imagination and the Black Panther Party*, 119.

42. *Babylon*, n.d., Cleaver Papers, oversize box 2.

43. Eldridge Cleaver, "On the Contradictions between the Outlaws and the Inlaws, between the Oldlaws and the Newlaws," Cleaver Papers, carton 4, folder 10.

44. Eldridge Cleaver, "Towards a People's Army."

45. "What Is the Revolutionary Peoples Communications Network."

46. André Moncourt and J. Smith, eds., *The Red Army Faction: A Documentary History*, vol. 1, *Projectiles for the People* (Oakland, CA, 2009), 44.

47. Ibid., 48; Jeremy Varon, *Bringing the War Home: The Weather Underground, the Red Army Faction, and Revolutionary Violence in the Sixties and Seventies* (Berkeley, CA, 2004), 20, 41–42, 63–66.

48. Stefan Aust with Anthea Bell, trans., *Baader-Meinhof: The Inside Story of the RAF* (New York, 2008), 66–75.

49. Ibid., 82.

50. Klimke, *The Other Alliance*, 132; Varon, *Bringing the War Home*, 209–11.

51. Kathleen Cleaver interview; Klimke, *The Other Alliance*, 127.

52. Moncourt and Smith, *Projectiles for the People*, 81.

53. Höhn and Klimke, *A Breath of Freedom*, 118.

54. Moncourt and Smith, *Projectiles for the People*, 82; Varon, *Bringing the War Home*, 206.

55. Moncourt and Smith, *Projectiles for the People*, 105; Klimke, *The Other Alliance*, 124

56. Klimke, *The Other Alliance*, 127.

57. Moncourt and Smith, *Projectiles for the People*, 105.

58. Varon, *Bringing the War Home*, 254–89.

59. Chamberlin, *The Global Offensive*, 149–50.

60. On Black September's "external operations," see ibid., 161–67, 185–93; John K. Cooley, *Green March, Black September: The Story of the Palestinian Arabs* (London, 1973).

61. Moncourt and Smith, *Projectiles for the People*, 205–36.

62. Chamberlin, *The Global Offensive*, 3.

63. Cleaver, "Statement in Support of Palestinians," September 18, 1970, carton 5, folder 9.

64. Cleaver, untitled manuscripts, Algiers, n.d. [circa 1970–71], Cleaver Papers, carton 2, folder 26.

65. Ibid.

66. Chamberlin, *The Global Offensive*, 172, 176, 192.

67. Cruse, *The Crisis of the Negro Intellectual*, 397.

68. Cleaver, "Towards a People's Army," 17.

69. Kelley and Esch, "Black Like Mao," 20.

70. Cleaver, "Towards a People's Army," 17. Emphasis in original.

71. Cleaver, "Back to Africa," in Jones, ed., *The Black Panther Party Reconsidered*, 243.

72. Ibid., 245; Brenden I. Koerner, *The Skies Belong to Us: Love and Terror in the Golden Age of Hijacking* (New York, 2013), 164–68.

73. "National Intelligence Estimate 62–71, July 31, 1971," in *Foreign Relations of the United States, 1969–1976*, volume E-5, part 2, *Documents on North Africa, 1969–1972*, document 27, U.S. Department of State, Office of the Historian, http://history.state.gov/historicaldocuments/frus1969-76ve05p2/d27; Samir Meghelli, "From Harlem to Algiers: Transnational Solidarities between the African American Freedom Movement and Algeria, 1962–1978, in *Black Routes to Islam* (New York, 2009), ed. Manning Marable and Hishaam D. Aidi, 114.

74. Koerner, *The Skies Belong to Us*, 174–76, 180–83.

75. Kathleen Cleaver, "Back to Africa," in Jones, ed., *The Black Panther Party Reconsidered*, 228; Kathleen Cleaver, "El Bair, 12:30 PM Dec 22 1971," Cleaver Papers, carton 5, folder 46.

76. Leary, *Flashbacks*, 303.

77. Cleaver, "Back to Africa," in Jones, ed., *The Black Panther Party Reconsidered*, 246.

78. Ibid.

79. Ibid., 247–48; Koerner, *The Skies Belong to Us*, 194.

80. Cleaver, *Soul on Fire*, 150.

81. "Memorandum of Conversation, July 31, 1972," in *Foreign Relations of the United States, 1969–1976*, volume E-5, Part 2, *Documents on North Africa, 1969–1972*, document 33, http://history.state.gov/historicaldocuments/frus1969-76ve05p2/d33.

82. Cleaver, "Back to Africa," in Jones, ed., *The Black Panther Party Reconsidered*, 246.

83. Ibid., 247.

84. Ibid., 249; Kathleen Cleaver interview; Charlotte O'Neal interview.

85. "Second Meeting with C. [*sic*] Salah, Wednesday am 16 August 1972," Cleaver Papers, carton 5, folder 40.

86. "Telegram 188030 from the Department of State to the Mission to the United Nations and the Interests Section in Algeria, October 14, 1972, "1933Z, in *Foreign Relations of the United States, 1969–1976*, volume E-5, Part 2, *Documents on North Africa, 1969–1972*, document 34, http://history.state.gov/historicaldocuments/frus1969-76ve05p2/d34.

87. "Situation Information Report," September 5, 1972," CIA files obtained by the author through FOIA.

88. Cleaver, "Back to Africa," in Jones, ed., *The Black Panther Party Reconsidered*, 250; James C. McKinley, Jr., "A Black Panther's Mellow Exile: Farming in Africa," *New York Times*, November 23, 1997; Gaidi Faraj, "Unearthing the Underground," 215–20.

89. Charlotte O'Neal interview; Cleaver, ed., *Target Zero*, 258–59; Larry Mack and Sekou Odinga to the Black Panther Party Coordinating Committee, September 18, 1972, Cleaver Papers, carton 5, folder 40.

90. Martin Luther King, Jr., "Beyond Vietnam: Address Delivered to the Clergy and Laymen Concerned about Vietnam at Riverside Church, April 4, 1967," in *A Call to Conscience: The Landmark Speeches of Dr. Martin Luther King, Jr.*, Martin Luther King, Jr. Research and Education Institute, Stanford University, http://kingencyclopedia.stanford.edu/kingweb/publications/speeches/Beyond_Vietnam.pdf.

91. "Transcript of Tape Recorder Notes, 28 March [1971]," Cleaver Papers, carton 5, folder 12.

92. Cleaver, "Towards a People's Army."

93. Charlotte O'Neal interview.

94. "Eldridge Cleaver—Transcript of Tape Recorder Notes, 26 March [1971]."

95. On Denise Oliver, see Johanna Fernández, "Denise Oliver and the Young Lords Party: Stretching the Political Boundaries of Struggle," in Gore, Theoharis, and Woodard, eds., *Want to*

Start a Revolution?, 271–93. On Connie Matthews, see Robyn Spencer, "Merely One Link in the Worldwide Revolution: Internationalism, State Repression, and the Black Panther Party," in West, Martin, and Wilkins, *From Toussaint to Tupac: The Black International since the Age of Revolution*, 220. For internal critiques of gender politics within the movement from the RPCN, see Donald Cox, "The Man Question," *Voice of the Lumpen* 2, no. 3 (April 1972): 7; Denise Oliver, "To Our Brothers in Jail from the Sisters," *Voice of the Lumpen* 2, no. 3 (April 1972): 8–9.

96. Kathleen Cleaver, "El Bair, 12:30 PM Dec 22 1971." Charlotte O'Neal offered a differing viewpoint, declaring, "I never had a problem with Eldridge. Some people might have, but I never did. He was a good brother. Very respectful." Charlotte O'Neal interview.

Chapter 8. The Panthers in Winter, 1971–1981

1. Central Intelligence Agency, "Situation Information Report," September 5, 1972, document provided under the Freedom of Information Act (FOIA) and in possession of the author.

2. Aaron Dixon, *My People Are Rising*, 257; Forbes, *Will You Die with Me?*, 6.

3. Newton and Blake, *Revolutionary Suicide*, 349, 352; Spencer, "Merely One Link in the Worldwide Revolution," in West, Martin, and Wilkins, eds., *From Toussaint to Tupac*, 227.

4. "Huey P. Newton, Servant of the People, Returns from the People's Republic of China," *Black Panther*, October 16, 1971.

5. Brown, *A Taste of Power*, 313.

6. Forbes, *Will You Die with Me?*, 6, 65.

7. Robert Seier, "Has China Betrayed the 'Revolution'?," *Black Panther*, April 15, 1972.

8. Bloom and Martin, *Black against Empire*, 381.

9. Forbes, *Will You Die with Me?*, 66.

10. Elaine Brown, "We Can Win on April 15!," *Black Panther*, February 15, 1975.

11. Self, *American Babylon*, 154–55.

12. "'We're Talking about Winning in Oakland': Sister Elaine Brown Speaks at Grove Street College," *Black Panther*, November 9, 1972; "Oakland: An All-American Example," Newton Papers, series 1, box 50.

13. Dixon, *My People Are Rising*, 269.

14. Huey P. Newton, "On the Defection of Eldridge Cleaver from the Black Panther Party and the Defection of the Black Panther Party from the Black Community," *Black Panther*, April 17, 1971, special supplement.

15. Brown, *A Taste of Power*, 313.

16. "We're Talking about Winning in Oakland."

17. Revised on March 29, 1972, the new program appeared in the pages of the *Black Panther* for the first time in the June 3, 1972, edition.

18. Forbes, *Will You Die with Me?*, 6.

19. "Make Your Vote Count on April 17: Elect Two Democrats," Newton Papers, series 2, box 45, folder 19.

20. "The Seale-Brown 14-Point Program to Rebuild Oakland," *Black Panther*, May 12, 1973.

21. "A Multi Ethnic International Trade and Cultural Center," *Black Panther*, April 7, 1973.

22. Bloom and Martin, *Black against Empire*, 381.

23. On Chavez's endorsement, see the press release in Newton Papers, series 2, box 45, folder 19.

24. Brown, *A Taste of Power*, 361–62, 401–16; Dixon, *My People Are Rising,* 252, 268; Hugh Pearson, *Shadow of the Panther: Huey Newton and the Price of Black Power in America* (New York, 1995), 274–75.

25. Huey P. Newton to Congressmen Robert N.C. Nix, April 17, 1972, Newton Papers, series 2, box 1, folder 2. Also see Charles B. Rangel to Newton, May 5, 1972, and John Conyers Jr. to Newton, May 1, 1972, both in Newton Papers, series 2, box 1, folder 2.

26. Forbes, *Will You Die With Me?*, 56, 69.

27. On the Oakland Community School, see Ericka Huggins and Angela D. LeBlanc-Ernest, "Revolutionary Women, Revolutionary Education: The Black Panther Party's Oakland Community School," in Gore, Theoharis, and Woodard, eds., *Want to Start a Revolution?*, 161–84.

28. "Statement by Huey P. Newton, Minister of Defense Black Panther Party, Servant of the People, to the Black Odyssey Festival," *Black Panther*, May 29, 1971.

29. Dixon, *My People Are Rising*, 250.

30. Brown, *A Taste of Power*, 3, 368–71.

31. Huggins and LeBlanc-Ernest, "Revolutionary Women, Revolutionary Education," 179.

32. "Why Gay People Should Vote for Bobby Seale and Elaine Brown," Newton Papers, series 2, box 45, folder 19. Also see Alkebulan, *Survival pending Revolution*, xv.

33. For a good selection of Douglas's 1970s artwork on behalf of the party, see Durant, ed., *Black Panther*, 144–59.

34. Bloom and Martin, *Black against Empire*, 386.

35. Self, *American Babylon*, 326.

36. "Introduction by Huey P. Newton, Servant of the People, Black Panther Party," *Black Panther*, April 29, 1972.

37. "Progressive Americans, Led by Panthers, Return from China," *Black Panther*, April 22, 1972, special supplement.

38. Lubin, *Geographies of Liberation*, 112; Frazier, *The East Is Black*, 44.

39. See, for example, the series of letters enclosed along with Elaine Brown to Martin Kenner, Committee to Defend the Panthers, March 20, 1971, Newton Papers, series 2, box 11, folder 10.

40. For an overview of the way in which the internationalism of the BPP influenced other groups, see Slate, ed., *Black Power beyond Borders*; Lubin, *Geographies of Liberation*, 130–41.

41. On the evolution of African Liberation Day and the global anti-apartheid struggle, see Brenda Plummer, *In Search of Power: African Americans in the Era of Decolonization, 1956–1974* (New York, 2013), 277–78; Borstelmann, *The Cold War and the Color Line*, 248–64; Donald R. Culverson, "From Cold War to Global Interdependence: The Political Economy of African American Antiapartheid Activism, 1969–1988," in Plummer, ed., *Window on Freedom*, 221–38.

42. "African Solidarity Conference Ignores Day to Day Issues," *Black Panther*, October 13, 1973.

43. "Interparty Memorandum #32," April 26, 1973, Newton Papers, series 2, box 4, folder 10.

44. Brown, *A Taste of Power*, 335; JoNina Albron to Huey P. Newton, November 11, 1978, "Re: OCLC Reception for Namibian Liberation Leader," Newton Papers, series 2, box 4, folder 11.

45. Bloom and Martin, *Black against Empire*, 374–76.

46. Romaine Fitzgerald, "Prospects for Intercommunal Warfare," *Black Panther*, May 8, 1971.

47. "The Spook Who Sat by the Door: Suicidal!," *Black Panther*, November 3, 1973.

48. "Statement by Huey P. Newton, Minister of Defense Black Panther Party, Servant of the People, to the Black Odyssey Festival," 12.

49. Forbes, *Will You Die With Me?*, 2, 76, 94, 125; Dixon, *My People Are Rising*, 250, 257–59.

50. Forbes, *Will You Die With Me?*, 6.

51. Hilliard, *Huey: Spirit of the Panther*, 200–201.

52. Forbes, *Will You Die With Me?*, 94, 109.

53. Bloom and Martin, *Black against Empire*, 382.

54. Central Intelligence Agency, "Situation Information Report," September 5, 1972.

55. Hilliard and Cole, *The Side of Glory*, 339.

56. Forbes, *Will You Die With Me?*, 93; Dixon, *My People Are Rising*, 244.

57. Dixon, *My People Are Rising*, 259.

58. Ibid., 284–85.

59. Faraj, "Unearthing the Underground." Also see Akinyele Omowale Umoja, "Repression Breeds Resistance: The Black Liberation Army and the Radical Legacy of the Black Panther Party," in Cleaver and Katsiaficas, eds., *Liberation, Imagination and the Black Panther Party*, 3–19; Russell Shoats, "Black Fighting Formations: Their Strengths, Weaknesses and Potentialities," in Cleaver and Katsiaficas, ed., *Liberation, Imagination and the Black Panther Party*, 128–40.

60. Bryan Burrough, *Days of Rage: America's Radical Underground, the FBI, and the Forgotten Age of Revolutionary Violence* (New York, 2015); John Castellucci, *The Big Dance: The Untold Story of Kathy Boudin and the Terrorist Family that Committed the Brink's Robbery Murders* (New York, 1986).

61. "Rules of the Black Panther Party," *Black Panther*, September 28, 1968.

62. Washington, *All Power to the People*, 36.

63. Jalil Muntaqim, *On the Black Liberation Army* (Montreal, 2002), 4.

64. "Bunchy," Cleaver Papers, carton 2, folder 52; Bloom and Martin, *Black against Empire*, 144.

65. Faraj, "Unearthing the Underground," 122–24, 143; Jack Olson, *Last Man Standing: The Tragedy and Triumph of Geronimo Pratt* (New York: Doubleday, 2000), 38.

66. Olson, *Last Man Standing*, 30–33, 37–39.

67. Ibid., 42, 53; "The Black Panthers: An Interview with Geronimo ji Jaga Pratt, 1992," in Joy James, ed., *The New Abolitionists: (Neo) Slave Narratives and Contemporary Prison Writings* (Albany, NY, 2005), 238.

68. Olson, *Last Man Standing*, 61–62.

69. Ibid., 69; Faraj, "Unearthing the Underground," 145–47; Abu-Jamal, *We Want Freedom*, 214. See also the account by Jalil Muntaqim, who dates the creation of a dispersed military wing of the BPP to late 1968 and early 1969. Muntaqim, *On the Black Liberation Army*, 3.

70. "The Black Panthers: An Interview with Geronimo ji Jaga Pratt, 1992," 241.

71. Abu-Jamal, *We Want Freedom*, 214.

72. Ibid., 199.

73. Huey P. Newton, "Pigs Run Amuck: Executive Mandate No. 3," *Black Panther*, March 16, 1968.

74. Shakur, *Assata*, 227.

75. Quoted in Umoja, "Repression Breeds Resistance," 10.

76. Washington, *All Power to the People*, 39.

77. Quoted in Burroughs, *Days of Rage*, 195.

78. Safiya Bukhari, *The War Before: The True Life Story of Becoming a Black Panther, Keeping the Faith in Prison and Fighting for Those Left Behind* (New York, 2010), 92.

79. Quoted in Burroughs, *Days of Rage*, 195.

80. Ibid.

81. *Kuwasi Balagoon: A Soldier's Story: Writings by a New Afrikan Anarchist* (Montreal, 2003), 69.

82. Ibid., 60, 69.

83. Dhoruba bin Wahad, "COINTELPRO and the Destruction of Black Leaders and Organization," in Joy James, ed., *Imprisoned Intellectuals: America's Political Prisoners Write on Life, Liberation, and Rebellion* (Lanham, MD), 100.

84. Black Liberation Army Coordinating Committee, *Message to the Black Movement* (Black Liberation Army, 1975), ii.

85. Quoted in Burroughs, *Days of Rage*, 176.

86. Huey P. Newton, "Functional Definition of Politics," *Black Panther*, May 15, 1967.

87. Muntaqim, *On the Black Liberation Army*, 11.

88. Washington, *All Power to the People*, 40.

89. Donald Cox, "Criticism of Your Communique of December 20, 1971," Donald L. Cox FBI file, 1334053-0 Section 4.

90. Quoted in Burroughs, *Days of Rage*, 538.

91. "'Madmen' Ambush, Kill Policemen in N.Y. Violence," *Tuscaloosa News*, May 22, 1971.

92. Muntaqim, *On the Black Liberation Army*, 12.

93. Ibid., 14. Writings by former BLA members on the issue of prison reform/abolition can be found in James, ed., *Imprisoned Intellectuals* and *The New Abolitionists*. Also see Dhoruba bin Wahad, Mumia Abu-Jamal, and Assata Shakur, *Still Black, Still Strong: Survivors of the U.S. War Against Black Revolutionaries* (South Pasadena, CA), 1993; Abu-Jamal, *Live from Death Row*.

94. Mutulu Shakur et al., "Biography of Mutulu Shakur," in James, ed., *Imprisoned Intellectuals*, 187.

95. There is little or no scholarly writing on this second incarnation of the BLA and its white allies. For journalistic accounts, see Castellucci, *The Big Dance*; Burroughs, *Days of Rage*.

96. Abu-Jamal, *Live from Death Row*, 147.

97. "Interview between [Curtice] Taylor and [Eldridge] Cleaver," n.d. [circa 1974], Cleaver Papers, carton 5, folder 23.

98. "The Golden Shower: The Testimony of Eldridge Cleaver," Valley Christian Center, Dublin, California, January 23, 1977, Cleaver Papers, carton 2, folder 84. For more on his unique pants (including sketches and photos), see Cleaver Papers, carton 13, folders 54, 56. The most complete account of Cleaver's winding and often bizarre post-Algerian journey is Rout, *Eldridge Cleaver*, 171–280.

99. "Interview with Eldridge Cleaver (1981)," in Anthony, *Spitting in the Wind*, 179.

100. "Impact 77," *Crusader*, June 1, 1977; "Eldridge Cleaver Joins Leary for Immortality Benefit," Cleaver Papers, carton 9, folder 6; The Anarchist Party of Canada (Groucho Marxist), press release, April 1977, carton 14, folder 32; Mike Campi (employment rep., Apple Computer), to Cleaver, February 2, 1981, Cleaver Papers, carton 13, folder 61.

101. Cleaver, ed., *Target Zero*, 289–92, 297–300.

102. Dixon, *My People Are Rising*, 292.

103. Jasmine Guy, *Afeni Shakur: Evolution of a Revolutionary* (New York, 2004), 66.

Epilogue

1. U.S. Department of Justice, Civil Rights Division, *Department of Justice Report Regarding the Criminal Investigation into the Shooting Death of Michael Brown by Ferguson, Missouri Police Officer Darren Wilson* (Washington, D.C., 2015), 5–7.

2. State of Missouri v. Darren Wilson, Grand Jury vol. 5 (St. Louis, 2014), 225, 228. Emphasis added.

3. U.S. Department of Justice, Civil Rights Division, *Department of Justice Report Regarding the Criminal Investigation into the Shooting Death of Michael Brown*, 5.

4. Aura Bagado, "Police Officer Calls Ferguson Protestors 'Animals,'" *Colorlines*, August 11, 2014, http://www.colorlines.com/.

5. Philip Carter, "Ferguson's Cops Are Armed Liked I Was in Iraq," *Daily Beast*, August 8, 2014, http://www.thedailybeast.com. Also see Thomas Gibbons-Neff, "Military Veterans See Deeply Flawed Police Response in Ferguson," *Washington Post*, August 14, 2014; Nick Wing, "Actual Military Veterans Say Cops in Ferguson Are Excessively Armed, Untrained Wannabes," *Huffington Post*, August 14, 2014, http://www.huffingtonpost.com/.

6. Taylor Wofford, "How America's Police Became an Army: The 1033 Program," *Newsweek*, August 13, 2014, http://www.newsweek.com/; Defense Logistics Agency, "1033 Program Overview," PowerPoint presentation, http://dispositionservices.dla.mil/leso/Documents/1033%20Program.pptx; Arezou Rezvani, Jessica Purovac, David Eads, and Tyler Fisher, "MRAPs and Bayonets: What We Know About the Pentagon's 1033 Program," National Public Radio, September 2, 2014, http://www.npr.org/.

7. Alicia Garza, "A Herstory of the #BlackLivesMatter Movement," *Feminist Wire*, October 7, 2014, http://www.thefeministwire.com/; Julia Craven, "Black Lives Matter Co-Founder Reflects on the Origins of the Movement," *Huffington Post*, September 30, 2015, http://www.huffingtonpost.com/; Jamilah King, "#blacklivesmatter: How Three Friends Turned a Spontaneous Facebook Post into a Global Phenomenon," *California Sunday Magazine*, March 2015, https://stories.californiasunday.com/.

8. Jon Swaine, Oliver Laughland, and Jamiles Lartey, "Black Americans Killed by Police as Likely to Be Unarmed as White People," *Guardian*, June 1, 2015.

9. Fredrick C. Harris, "The Next Civil Rights Movement?," *Dissent*, Summer 2015, 34.

10. New Black Panther Party, "Aims and Objectives," http://www.newblackpanther.com/. There is little scholarly writing on the NBPP. The best overview is D.J. Mulloy, "New Panthers, Old Panthers, and the Politics of Black Nationalism in the United States," *Patterns of Prejudice* 44, no. 3 (2010): 217–38. On the Huey P. Newton Gun Club, see Aaron Lake Smith, "The Revolutionary Gun Clubs Patrolling the Black Neighborhoods of Dallas," *Vice*, January 5, 2015, http://www.vice.com/.

11. Elbert "Big Man" Howard, "Concerning Reactionaries and Thugs," *San Francisco Bay View National Black Newspaper*, August 23, 2015, http://sfbayview.com/; Mulloy, "New Panthers, Old Panthers," 230–35; Southern Poverty Law Center, "New Black Panther Party," https://www.splcenter.org/.

12. Angela Y. Davis, *Freedom Is a Constant Struggle: Ferguson, Palestine, and the Foundations of a Movement* (Chicago: Haymarket Books, 2016), 2.

13. Young, *Soul Power*, 14. For similar critiques, see Alkebulan, *Survival pending Revolution*, 73; Frazier, *The East Is Black*, 10.

14. Keeanga-Yamahtta Taylor, *From #BlackLivesMatter to Black Liberation* (Chicago, IL, 2016), 196.

15. Cruse, *Rebellion or Revolution*, 76.

16. Michelle Alexander, *The New Jim Crow: Mass Incarceration in the Age of Colorblindness* (New York, 2012).

17. Richard Rothstein, *The Making of Ferguson: Public Policies at the Roots of Its Troubles* (Washington, DC, 2014), 2; "Ferguson (city), Missouri," United States Census QuickFacts, http://quickfacts.census.gov/qfd/states/29/2923986.html; Elizabeth Kneebone, "Ferguson, Mo. Emblematic of Growing Suburban Poverty, *The Avenue* (Brookings Institution), http://www.brookings.edu/blogs/the-avenue/posts/2014/08/15-ferguson-suburban-poverty.

18. Rothstein, *The Making of Ferguson*, 1.

19. Ibid., 2, 4, 28; Self, *American Babylon*; Thomas Sugrue, *The Origins of the Urban Crisis* (Princeton, NJ, 1996); Douglas S. Massey and Nancy Denton, *American Apartheid: Segregation and the Making of the Underclass* (Cambridge, MA, 1993).

20. Singh, *Black Is a Country*, 7.

21. Alexander, *The New Jim Crow*.

22. Rothstein, *The Making of Ferguson*, 22.

23. Self, *American Babylon*, 330.

24. U.S. Department of Justice, Civil Rights Division, *Department of Justice Report Regarding the Criminal Investigation into the Shooting Death of Michael Brown*, 2.

25. "An Exclusive Interview with Minister of Defense, Huey P. Newton," *Black Panther*, March 16, 1968.

26. U.S. Department of Justice, Civil Rights Division, *Department of Justice Report Regarding the Criminal Investigation into the Shooting Death of Michael Brown*, 2.

27. Ta-Nehisi Coates, "The Paranoid Style of American Policing," *Atlantic*, December 30, 2015, http://www.theatlantic.com/.

28. Fanon, *The Wretched of the Earth*, 3–4.

29. Jay Caspian King, "The Witnesses," *New York Times Magazine*, May 10, 2015, 37.

30. "Bree Newsome: As SC Lawmakers Debate Removing Confederate Flag, Meet the Activist Who Took It Down," Democracy Now!, July 6, 2015, http://www.democracynow.org/.

31. Ibid.

32. Sanjay Sharma, "Black Twitter? Racial Hashtags, Networks and Contagion," *New Formations* 78 (2013): 51. Also see Makeba Lavan, "The Negro Tweets His Presence: 'Black Twitter' as Social and Political Watchdog," *Modern Language Studies* 45, no. 1 (2015): 56–65.

33. King, "The Witnesses," 36.

34. Charlotte Alfred, "Protestors Say Ferguson Feels like Gaza, Palestinians Tweet Back Advice," *Huffington Post*, August 14, 2014, http://www.huffingtonpost.com/.

35. "FBI Deputy Director Speaks ahead of Brelo Verdict," WKCY News, May 14, 2015, http://www.wkyc.com/. For documents outlining government efforts to keep track of #BlackLivesMatter, see George Joseph, "Exclusive: Feds Regularly Monitored Black Lives Matter since Ferguson," *Intercept*, July 24, 2015, https://theintercept.com/.

36. Harris, "The New Civil Rights Movement?," 36–37.

37. Davis, *Freedom Is a Constant Struggle*, 86.

38. For a discussion of gender in the #BlackLivesMatter movement and #SayHerName, see Marcia Chatelain and Kaavya Aoka, "Women and Black Lives Matter: An Interview with Marcia Chatelain," *Dissent*, Summer 2015, 54–61; African American Policy Forum, *Say Her Name: Resisting Police Brutality against Black Women* (New York, 2015); African American Policy Forum, "*#SayHerName: Resisting Police Brutality against Black Women: A Social Media Guide* (n.d.); Taylor, *From #BlackLivesMatter to Black Liberation*, 165.

39. Tim Constantine, "Black Lives Matter Is a Terrorist Group," *Washington Times*, September 2, 2015, http://www.washingtontimes.com/; Katherine Krueger, "Frequent Fox News Guest: 'Black Lives Matter Will Join Forces with ISIS,'" Talking Points Memo, October 28, 2015, http://talkingpointsmemo.com/.

40. King, "The Witnesses," 52

41. Forbes, *With You Die with Me?*, 56.

42. Christopher B. Strain, *Pure Fire: Self-Defense as Activism in the Civil Rights Era* (Athens, GA, 2005), 166.

43. Eldridge Cleaver, "Towards a People's Army," Cleaver Papers, oversize box 2.

44. Shakur, *Assata*, 139.

45. Taylor, *From #BlackLivesMatter to Black Liberation*, 103.

46. Fanon, *The Wretched of the Earth*, 1.

47. Roqayah Chamseddine, "Understanding the US' Violent Response to Indignation over Ferguson," *Al-Akhbar English*, November 27, 2014, http://english.al-akhbar.com/node/22664.

48. Breitman, ed., *Malcolm X Speaks*, 129.

49. Harris, "The New Civil Rights Movement?," 39–40; Taylor, *From #BlackLivesMatter to Black Liberation*, 180.

50. Jordan T. Camp and Christina Heatherton, "We Charge Genocide: An Interview with Breanna Champion, Page May, and Asha Rosa Ransby-Sporn," in Camp and Heatherton, *Policing the Planet: Why the Policing Crisis Led to Black Lives Matter* (New York, 2016), 261.

51. Christina Heatherton, "#BlackLivesMatter and Global Visions of Abolition: An Interview with Patrisse Cullors," in Camp and Heatherton, *Policing the Planet*, 38–39.

52. Davis, *Freedom Is a Constant Struggle*, 139–40; Heatherton, "#BlackLivesMatter and Global Visions of Abolition: An Interview with Patrisse Cullors," 39; Dani McClain, "Why Black Lives Matter Activists Are Showing Up for a Palestinian Woman Threatened with Deportation," *Nation*, October 26, 2015, http://www.thenation.com/. Also see "Black on Palestine," http://blackonpalestine.tumblr.com/; "Black Solidarity with Palestine," http://www.blackforpalestine.com/.

53. Lubin, *Geographies of Liberation*, 162, 171.

54. On government filtering and denial of access to the Internet, see the various reports produced by the OpenNet Initiative, https://opennet.net/. Also see Moisés Naím and Philip Bennett, "The Anti-Information Age: How Governments Are Reinventing Censorship in the 21st Century," *Atlantic*, February 16, 2015, http://www.theatlantic.com/.

55. "Twitter and Black Lives Matter—Jack Dorsey and Deray McKesson—Code Conference 2016," YouTube, https://youtu.be/NqW45PsjXcE.

56. Mark S. Luckie, "Twitter Still Has a Major Problem with Employee Diversity," *Verge*, December 30, 2015, http://www.theverge.com/; "Is Deray a Corporate Shill?," DeployBurners, https://storify.com/DeployBurners/is-deray-a-corporate-shill.

57. Bloom and Martin, *Black against Empire*, 398.

58. Washington, *All Power to the People*, 41.

Index

Page numbers in *italic* refer to illustrations.

Abu-Jamal, Mumia, 13, 17, 93, 180, 185, 193, 238
African American exceptionalism, 44, 103, 104, 128, 148
African American GIs. *See* black GIs
African American separatism. *See* black separatism
African Liberation Day (ALD), 224
African National Congress (ANC), 22, 143, 150, 234
Afro-American Association (AAA), 46–52 passim, 56, 57, 74
Afro-Asian Conference, Bandung, 1955. *See* Bandung Conference, 1955
Ahmad, Muhammad, 39, 40, 44, 52, 53, 103
airline hijackers and hijacking, 141–42, 150, 171, 200–207 passim
Algeria, 11, 22, 42, 142–72 passim, 195; Afro American Information Center, 145, 150; Burrell, 195; Cleavers, 2, 10, 11, 131, 142–53 passim, 161–63 passim, 181–88 passim, 193, 201–10 passim, 232–33; Cox, 146, 170, 196, 232, 236; FLN, 22, 23, 33, 146; Malcolm X on, 29; natural gas, 143,

144, 203–7 passim; RAF in, 198; revolution, 23, 24, 25, 31, 34, 63, 144; secret police, 170, 171; skyjacking destination, 150, 198, 203–5; South Vietnamese relations, 143, 157–58; Timothy Leary in, 171; U.S. relations, 2, 143–44, 170, 203–4, 205, 207. *See also* international section of BPP; Pan-African Cultural Festival, Algiers, 1969
Allen, Ernest Mkalimoto, 52, 53, 56
Al-Mansour, Khalid, 49–50, 52, 56, 74
American exceptionalism, 12, 16, 239. *See also* African American exceptionalism
Anderson, Benedict, 83, 97
Angelou, Maya, 26, 30
Angola, 82, 121, 146, 173, 191, 223
Anthony, Earl, 107, 116–17
"anticolonial vernacular," 70–106 passim, 112, 131, 132, 148, 178; RAF use, 198–99
Anti-Imperialist Delegation. *See* U.S. People's Anti-Imperialist Delegation
antiwar movement. *See* Vietnam War: antiwar movement
Aoki, Richard, 61, 62
Apollo 11, 144

Arafat, Yasser, 2, 145, 146, 199
armed patrols (police monitoring), 6, 63–71
    passim, 75, 93–96 passim, 132, 178, 216;
    Gene Marine on, 64; Mulford Act effect
    on, 80, 84, 130, 132
armed self-defense, 5, 33, 50, 60–63, 92, 95,
    132; Douglas depiction, 93, *94*
armed struggle, 132, 133; backpedaling from,
    216; Cleaver views, 146, 149, 166, 183,
    202; Newton on, 173; Odinga on, 236;
    Palestinian, 199–200; Panther 21 on, 232;
    RAM vision, 43; Robert Williams views,
    34. *See also* guerrilla warfare
arms. *See* weapons
arrests, 57, 195, 250; Bree Newsome, 248;
    Cleaver, 181; Newton, 7, 9, 57, 101,
    108, 133; Pratt, 183, 230, 231; RAF, 199;
    Ramstein 2, 194; Sacramento
    protesters, 68, 69; Seale, 57, 134.
    See also house arrest
Asian-African Conference, Bandung, 1955.
    See Bandung Conference, 1955
Asian Americans, 102, 109, 122, 163
"Asian strategy" of BPP, 10, 131, 151–60
    passim, 165–73 passim, 208, 253
assassination, 200; attempt on witness, 227;
    attempts on Castro, 138; CIA plan (Lu-
    mumba), 25–26, Malcolm X, 74, 80; MLK,
    9, 130, 134–35; police, 12, 213, 233, 235
Axelrod, Beverly, 74–75, 78, 79, 139

Baader, Andreas, 198
Baader-Meinhof Gang. *See* Red Army
    Faction (RAF)
Babylon, 188, 193, 195, 196, 202
"Babylon" (label), 84, 87
Balagoon, Kuwasi, 233–34, 237
Bandung Conference, 1955, 5, 20–23 passim,
    27, 38
bank robbery, 198, 213, 237
Baraka, Amiri, 19, 35–37, 52, 54, 65; Black
    Political Convention, 221; Cuba visit, 30;
    on Douglas illustrations, 85, 89; RAM, 39;
    San Francisco, 35, 50, 78, 79; United Nations
    protest, 26; "up against the wall," 83
"Base of Operations" strategy, 212–24 passim
Beatles, 77
Beheiren, 115–17
Belgium, 25–26
Ben Bella, Ahmed, 22, 75, 143
Berkeley, 79, 134. *See also* University of
    California Berkeley (UCB)
Bhabha, Homi K., 85, 87
Bin Wahad, Dhoruba, 170, 232, 234, 243
Biondi, Martha, 51
Black America, 45

Black Arts Movement, 36, 39, 45, 50, 54,
    83; Black House and, 78; inspiration for
    Douglas, 79
Black Communications Project, 79
black GIs, 124, 126, 166, 182, 194–95, 198,
    230
Black House, 78, 79, 108
Black Liberation Army (BLA), 11–12, 186,
    197, 200, 209, 212–13, 228–39 passim, 250;
    Assata Shakur, 14, 228, 231, 232, 237, 248
Black Lives Matter, 242–55 passim
Black Panther, 7, 71–72, *71*, 81–84 passim,
    104–7 passim, 236, 251, 255; accessibility,
    178; Asian propaganda, 154–55, 158, 162,
    166, 173–74, 182; cafeteria-style inter-
    nationalism, 162; celebration of violence,
    92–97 passim, 149; circulation, 82; Dellums
    column, 219; inaugural issue, 81; interna-
    tional reach, 119; last issue, 238; Lumumba,
    25; mass audience, 54, 82, 96; Newton col-
    umns, 62; North Korea coverage, 154–55;
    post Cleaver-Newton split, 184, 187–88,
    220–26 passim; Third World solidarity, 103
Black Panther Solidarity Committee, Frank-
    furt, 124–25
Black Political Convention, Gary, Indiana,
    1972. *See* National Black Political
    Convention, Gary, Indiana, 1972
Black Power movement, 19–23 passim,
    27–35 passim, 45, 50–59 passim; black GIs,
    124; Cruse criticism, 38; Cuban
    relations, 138; Eldridge Cleaver views, 77,
    100; foreign relations, 109–10, 115, 120,
    123, 124; Merritt College, 56, 79;
    RAM role, 39; SFSU, 108; UCB, 50.
    See also Black House
black press, 82. *See also Black Panther*
black separatism, 34, 38, 59, 111, 112, 234,
    243. *See also* Garvey, Marcus; Nation of
    Islam (NOI)
black soldiers. *See* black GIs
Black September, 11, 186, 188, 199–202
    passim, 208
Black Student Union (BSU), San Francisco
    State University. *See* San Francisco State
    University (SFSU): Black Student Union
    (BSU)
black studies, 50, 51, 56–57, 147
"Blacktags" (social media), 249
Blake, J. Herman, 50
Bloom, Joshua, 221, 256
Boggs, James and Grace Lee, 40, 65
bombing and bombings, 43–44, 201, 202; by
    BLA, 213, 235–36; Black September, 200;
    Weather Underground, 183, 232; West
    Germany, 198

Booth, Byron, 150, 153–54, 155
Boumédiène, Houari, 143, 157, 170, 203–6 passim
Bousselham, Abdel Kader, 205–6
Bouteflika, Abdelaziz, 207
breakfast program. *See* free breakfast program
British Black Panthers, 125
Brown, Elaine, 11, 14, 149, 166–69 passim, 179, 181, 185, 220; "Base of Operations" strategy, 212–21 passim; *Black Panther*, 82, 220; on China, 168, 213, 216; China visit, 213; denunciation of NBPP, 243; departure from BPP, 228; leadership, 220, 226, 227; on Oakland, 215
Brown, George, 207
Brown, Jerry, 219
Brown, Michael, 241–42, 252, 254
Brown Berets, 102, 109
Buddha Samurai, 212, 226
Bukhari, Safiya, 232–33
Burrell, William, 194–95
Byrne, Jeffrey James, 21

California legislation. *See* Mulford Act
California State Capitol protest.
    See Sacramento protest, May 1967
Canada, 118, 131, 137, 162, 239
Carmichael, Stokely, 19, 113, 120–21, 149–51 passim, 158, 192; African Liberation Day, 224; BPP split, 147; criticism of BPP, 72; Cuba, 127, 141, 274n63; Dialectics of Liberation Conference, 123; Japanese relations, 115; Lowndes County, Alabama, 1; UCB, 50
Carter, Alprentice "Bunchy," 229–30
Castro, Fidel, 22, 32, 62, 184; Chinese relations, 139; Eldridge Cleaver and, 75, 137; U.S. visit, 23; view of black Cubans, 140
Central Intelligence Agency. *See* CIA
Chamberlin, Paul Thomas, 200
chants, 26, 81, 83, 118, 136, 145
Chavez, Cesar, 218
Chicago, 95, 102, 155, 172. *See also* Illinois/ Chicago BPP
Chicanos, 102, 109, 122
China, 20, 24–25, 214, 253; as Asian vanguard, 121; BPP visits, 163, 185, 213, 222, 223; Cuban relations, 139, 141; Cultural Revolution, 155, 168; Elaine Brown on, 168, 213, 216; embassy in Algeria, 169; Nixon/U.S. relations, 11, 177, 188–90, 196, 213; North Korean relations, 152; Malcolm X view, 29; People's Delegation, 10, 163, 167; PLO relations, 145–46; RAM and, 42;

Robert Williams in, 32; Soviet relations, 24, 42, 138, 153, 154, 155; Tricontinental Conference, 28; United Nations, 213
Christianity, 219, 238–39
CIA, 92, 211–12; Algiers operations, 189, 207; Congo operations, 25; domestic intelligence, 174, 227; MH/CHAOS program, 182; view of Boumédiène, 143
Civil Rights Act of 1964, 18
Civil Rights Congress, 48, 63, 111, 254
civil rights movement, 5, 28, 29, 33–38 passim, 47–55 passim, 83, 246, 247, 256; Cruse criticism, 38; Hithe view, 92; Japanese relations, 115; RAM view, 59
Cleaver, Eldridge, 91, 93, 99–100, 107, 199–213 passim, 250; abuse of women, 74, 75, 166–67, 171, 210, 287n96; African Liberation Day, 224; Algeria, 2, 10, 11, 131, 142–53 passim, 161–63 passim, 181–88 passim, 193, 201–10 passim, 232–33; birth and early years, 73–74; April 6, 1968, shootings, 9, 130–31, 135–36, 147, 148, 216; Asian strategy, 10, 131, 151, 158–60 passim, 165, 169, 172, 253; Asian tour, 1970, 10, 156, 157, 161–68 passim, 210; BLA and, 186, 197, 232; "black colony," 99–100, 245; Black September and, 11, 186, 188, 199–202 passim, 208; Bunchy Carter relations, 229; commitment to revolution, 196–97; Congo, 191; Cuba, 9–10, 127–28, 131, 137–43 passim, 274n63; declaration of war, 134–35; Douglas relations, 79–80; "embryonic sovereignty," 112; France, 11, 208; "Gangster Cigarettes," 163; on guns, 75, 95, 146–47, 149, 209, 251; homophobia, 106, 181, 268n14; influence on RAF, 199; on internal colonialism, 82; Japan invitation, 116, 117; joining of BPP, 71, 73; last years, 238–39; on moon walk, 144; murder plots and rumors, 166, 171; on Newton, 80, 159; Newton split, 10–11, 14, 181–87, 211–12, 214, 232; Newton split run-up, 172–81; "North American Liberation Front," 10, 179; on North Richmond, 66; North Vietnam, *164*; parole, 74, 78–80 passim, 108–9, 116, 131, 132, 136; Peace and Freedom Party, 101; "pig" (word), 85; profanity, 70, 83, 84; public speaking, 106, 179, 249; rapes, 74, 75; relations with Kathleen, 166–67, 171, 210; sexism, 106; sexual attitudes, 106, 167, 210, 268n14; SFSU, 50; *Soul on Ice*, 75, 77, 101, 133; ten-point program critique, 159; Third World relations, 7, 70; twenty-first-century analog, 249; United Nations visit, 110–14 passim; views of Black Power

Cleaver, Eldridge (*continued*)
movement, 77, 100; views of violence,
75–76, 132
Cleaver, Kathleen, 10, 14, 69, 104; Algeria, 11,
131, 143, 144, 150, 161, 181–86 passim,
204–6 passim; BPP Central Committee,
220; Congo conference, 191; on Cuba,
139; on FBI provocation, 182; France, 11,
208, 238; in iconography, 73; on international section of BPP, 161, 181; Japan
invitation, 116, 117; on "life of the marooned," 204; New York, 195; relations
with Eldridge, 166–67, 171, 210; RPCN,
188, 192–93, 196, 202–3; on skyjackers,
205; travel restrictions, 195; West Germany
visits, 124, 194
Cleveland, 39, 45, 242, 250
Coates, Ta-Nehisi, 247
cocaine, 216, 238
COINTELPRO, 2, 13, 113, 183, 214, 235,
249; international section and, 209; Pratt
murder and, 230
Cold War, 34, 48–50 passim, 111, 127, 162,
168, 177, 253; Asia, 151, 188, 190, 213;
Black Power movement, 39; Cuba, 138;
Eldridge Cleaver, 74, 159–60, 173, 174,
179, 190, 193
Comfort, Mark, 50, 65
Communist International, 37, 41
Communist Party USA (CPUSA), 24, 31, 32,
37, 40, 47, 72, 101; Audley Moore, 113;
PL and, 46
Community Action Patrol (CAP). *See* Los
Angeles: Community Action Patrol (CAP)
community service programs. *See* survival
programs
Congo, 25–26, 49, 53, 111, 188, 190–91, 196
Congressional Black Caucus, 219
Conyers, John, 219
Council on African Affairs (CAA), 19, 34, 41
Cox, Donald, 146, 170, 196, 232, 236
crime. *See* "hustling" (petty crime); organized
crime; murder; theft
Crusader, 18, 30, 34
Cruse, Harold, 5, 19, 37–41 passim, 52–59
passim, 175, 244; Cuba visit, 30, 37, 70;
cultural revolution call, 39, 77–78; on
slavery, 245; view of bombing as tactic, 43,
202; view of guns, 34, 67
Cuba, 22, 109, 114, 126–29, 253; Algerian
relations, 22, 143; art, 79, 89; Assata Shakur,
228, 237; Bay of Pigs, 27, 141; Carmichael, 127, 141; Chinese relations, 139,
141; Cullors, 252; Eldridge Cleaver, 9–10,
128, 137–44 passim; as Latin American
vanguard, 121; missile crisis, 46; Newton,

64, 129, 185, 223; Progressive Labor (PL),
49, 52; RAM, 42, 44; revolution, 22–34
passim, 64, 129, 137, 142; Robert Williams,
18, 30–32, 34, 127; Second Declaration of
Havana, 141; Soviet relations, 32, 138–40
passim; Tricontinental Conference, 27–28,
42, 50, 127, 139; United Nations, 111;
white supremacy, 140, 274n63. *See also* Fair
Play for Cuba Committee
Cullors, Patrisse, 252, 254
Cyril, Janet, 193

Davis, Angela, 142, 197, 203, 244, 250
Deacons for Defense and Justice, 61, 132
Delany, Martin R., 19, 37
Dellums, Ron, 219
Democratic Party, 217–19 passim, 238
Democratic Republic of North Korea
(DPRK). *See* North Korea
Democratic Republic of Vietnam (DRV).
See North Vietnam
demonstrations. *See* protests
Denmark, 119–20
Detroit, 39, 45, 193, 204–5, 230
Dixon, Aaron, 83, 132, 215–16, 219,
227–28, 239
Dominican Republic: U.S. intervention,
27, 111
Dorsey, Jack, 255
Doss, Erika, 106
Douglas, Emory, 7, 71–72, 79–81 passim, 88–93
passim, 101, 106–9 passim, 178, 223;
Algiers, 145; armed struggle iconography, 93, *94*; Baraka on, 85, 89; birth and
early years, 78–79; China visit, 222; on
"deadly pictures of the enemy," 96–97;
demilitarization of images, 220; depiction
of women, *94, 105*; joining of BPP, 73;
pig iconography, *86–88*, 88, 92–93, *96*, 98;
in police raid, 133–34; posters, *8*, 129; on
shootings of police, 133; twenty-first-century
analog, 249; United Nations visit, 110
Dowell, Denzil, 65, 81, 92
DPRK. *See* North Korea
draft, military. *See* military draft
drugs, 170, 171, 216, 226; Newton, 11, 228,
238. *See also* marijuana
Du Bois, David Graham, 222
Du Bois, Shirley Graham, 5, 14, 30, 222
Du Bois, W.E.B., 19, 20, 21, 34, 41, 77,
169, 222
Dutschke, Rudi, 123

Economic Policy Institute, 245–46
Egypt, 25, 26
electoral politics, 212–21 passim, 250, 252

Elzie, Johnnetta, 251
Empire (Hardt and Negri), 178
England: Dialectics of Liberation Conference, 1967, 123
Everett, Ronald. *See* Karenga, Maulana
exceptionalism, American. *See* American exceptionalism

Fair Play for Cuba Committee, 30, 50
Fanon, Frantz, 23–24, 32, 33, 59–61 passim, 73, 132, 216; as Baraka inspiration, 36; Cleaver reading, 75, 131; on colonial world, 247; on decolonization, 84, 252; Elaine Klein relations, 144; "Fanonismo," 54; McClintock on, 104; Murray invocation of, 97; *Soulbook*, 53; view of lumpenproletariat, 23–24, 60; view of passivity of colonized, 23, 93; on violence, 23, 91; *Wretched of the Earth*, 23–24, 51, 61, 63, 252
Faraj, Gaidi, 228, 229
Fatah, 2, 143, 145, 150, 199–200, 201
FBI, 2, 10, 44, 182–85 passim, 189, 211, 236, 249–50; informants, 107, 116, 117; Robert Williams indictment, 30. *See also* COINTELPRO
Featherstone, Ralph, 115
Federal Republic of Germany, 122–25, 162, 193–94. *See also* Red Army Faction (RAF)
feminism, 180–81, 250
Ferguson, Missouri, 241–51 passim
Ferreira, Jason M., 50
film and video, 195–96, 225, 242
firearms. *See* guns
Fitzgerald, Romaine, 225
FLN. *See* Front de Libération Nationale (FLN) (Algeria)
Forbes, Flores Alexander, 213–19 passim, 227
Ford, Joudon, 128
Foreman, James, 30, 113
France, 196, 208, 238. *See also* Algerian revolution
Fraser, Cary, 21
Frazier, Roberson Taj, 73, 104, 151
free breakfast program, 148, 149, 166, 212
Freeman, Donald, 39, 41, 44, 103
Freeman, Kenn M. *See* Lumumba, Mamadou (Kenn Freeman)
Frey, John, 108, 133
Front de Libération Nationale (FLN) (Algeria), 22, 23, 33, 146
Frye, Paulette, 193

gangs, 55, 74, 229
Garvey, Marcus, 19, 36, 38, 49
Garvin, Vicki, 5, 14, 19, 30, 34, 169

Gary, Indiana: Black Political Convention, 1972. *See* National Black Political Convention, Gary, Indiana, 1972
gay bashing. *See* homophobia
gay liberation and gay rights, 180–81, 220
gender, 13, 73, 75, 104, 180–81, 149, 220, 250. *See also* patriarchy
Genet, Jean, 125–26
German SDS. *See* Sozialistischer Deutscher Studentenbund (SDS)
Germany, West. *See* Federal Republic of Germany
Ghana, 30, 50, 75, 112, 192, 224
The Godfather (Puzo), 227
Gronbeck-Tedesco, John, 31
guerrilla warfare, 178, 186, 231; Cleaver plans and views, 137–41 passim, 148, 150, 154, 179–84 passim, 197–202 passim, 251; in Cuban and Algerian revolutions, 22; *foco* theory, 22; Forbes view, 219; party purges and, 182; RAM, 43–44; rejection of, 176, 212, 219, 225; urban, 199, 209; urged by Robert Williams, 34
Guerrilla Warfare (Guevara), 7, 24
Guevara, Ernesto "Che," 22, 24, 32, 33, 59, 60, 138; absence from Cuba, 139; Eldridge Cleaver reading, 75; *Guerrilla Warfare*, 7, 24; Newton on, 61; on solidarity, 85
Guinea, 112, 120, 128, 147
guns, 60–71 passim, 93, 102, 130, 132, 226, 227; in Algeria, 170; Elaine Brown on, 216; Eldridge Cleaver on, 75, 95, 146–47, 149, 209, 251; Eldridge's in Cuba, 142; Hewitt on, 148; iconography, *94*, 95, *96*, 97, 98; Murray on, 128; Newton on, 60, 61, 173, 177, 184; North Korea, 154; police, 242; Pratt, 230; public carrying of, 6, 57, 61–65 passim, 68–69, 80; Robert Williams, 33, 61; Second Amendment, 61, 62. *See also* Mulford Act (California)

Hampton, Fred, 3, 95
Hansberry, Lorraine, 5, 14, 19
Hardt, Michael, *Empire*, 178
Hare, Nathan, 147
Harris, Elihu, 49
Harris, Fredrick C., 242–43, 250
Hayden, Tom, 124
Haywood, Harry, 40, 54
Heanes, Herbert, 108
Hemispheric Conference to End the War in Vietnam, Montreal, 1968, 117–19
Hewitt, Raymond "Masai," 72, 83, 84, 120, 121; Algiers, 145; China visit, 222; on guns, 148

hijackers, airline. *See* airline hijackers
Hilliard, David, 48, 102, 107, 173; on
    adventurism, 131; Algiers, 145, 149; on
    armed struggle debate, 133; on BPP
    organized crime, 226; Cleaver-Newton
    split run-up, 172, 180, 184; Cuba trip
    attempt, 128; departure from BPP, 228;
    Eldridge Cleaver criticism/call for murder
    of, 166; fund-raising ideas, 108; on *God-
    father*, 227; house arrest of Anthony, 117;
    on language "born out of oppression," 83;
    Marxism-Leninism, 159; Montreal confer-
    ence, 118; Newton shooting and, 108; on
    Newton's public speaking, 282n60; op-
    position to Cleaver's police ambush plans,
    135, 149; Scandinavian tour, 120; "we will
    kill," 95
Hilliard, June, 166
Hinckle, Warren, 78
Hithe, Rory, 92
Ho Chi Minh, 72, 77, 101, 156, 173
Höhn, Maria, 126, 198
Holder, Willie Roger, 203, 204, 207
homophobia, 84, 106, 180, 181, 268n14
Hoover, J. Edgar, 2
house arrest, 117, 171, 206–7
House Committee on Un-American
    Activities Committee (HUAC), 49
Howard, Elbert "Big Man," 117, 124, 243
Howell, Donna, 14, 219
Huggins, Ericka, 14, 149, 181, 212, 219, 220
Huggins, John, 95
Hussein, King of Jordan, 200–201
"hustling" (petty crime), 108, 170, 205, 238.
    See also prostitution
Hutton, Bobby, 81, 130, 136

Illinois/Chicago BPP, 3, 95
imagined communities, 84, 97, 99
imperialism: Newton on, 174–75
imprisonment. *See* prison and jail time
India, 20, 162, 223
Indonesia, 20, 21, 152. *See also* Bandung
    Conference, 1955
"intercommunalism" (Newton), 11, 161,
    162, 174–81 passim, 188, 193, 201, 223;
    first public mention, 281–82n42
International Conference of Journalists,
    Pyongyang, 1969, 153, 154
international section of BPP, 122–23, 131,
    161, 163, 169–71 passim, 178, 208; expul-
    sion by Newton, 184; "Intercommunal
    Section," 181; Leary on, 204; legacy,
    207–10; post Cleaver-Newton split, 186,
    186, 192
internecine violence, 184–85, 225–28 passim

intersectionality, 14, 40
Iraq War, 242, 243
Irish, 37, 222, 233–34
Israel, 143, 145, 200, 222, 223, 249

Jackson, Edward Lawrence, 194
Jackson, George, 173, 224–25
Jackson, Jonathan, 173, 285n36
jail and prison time. *See* prison and jail time
Japan, 114–18 passim, 162, 190, 253
Ji-Jaga, Geronimo. *See* Pratt, Geronimo
Johnson, Lyndon B., 27, 88, 89, *90*, 246
Johnson, Raymond, 142
Jordan, 2, 198, 200
Jørgensen, Thomas Elman, 120
Juche, 154–55, 158, 172
Judaism, 145
Justice Department. *See* U.S. Department
    of Justice (DOJ)

Kang Ryang-uk, 165
Kansas City, 13, 170, 185, 207
Karenga, Maulana, 49, 72, 104, 158
Kelley, Joan, 14, 220
Kelley, Robin, 39, 42, 45, 151
Kennedy, Randall L., 15
Kennedy, Robert F., 89, *90*
Kenya, 23, 30, 50, 62, 82
Kerkow, Catherine Marie, 203, 204
Kimche, David, 27–28
Kim Il-sung, 4, 152–59 passim, 178, 184,
    208, 223, 256; Newton view, 208;
    Nixon-Mao meeting and, 190;
    uncle, 165–66
King, Jay Caspian, 249
King, Martin Luther, Jr., 209, 248;
    assassination, 9, 130, 134–35
King Hussein. *See* Hussein, King of Jordan
Kissinger, Henry, 2, 16, 188–91 passim
Klein, Elaine, 144, 152, 156, 162, 195, 210
Klimke, Martin, 123, 126, 198
Korea. *See* North Korea; South Korea
Ku Klux Klan, 18, 30
Kuwait, 2, 146

Lamp Post (Oakland nightclub), 227
land ("land question"), 99–100, 111–12, 114
Lara, Luis, 129
Leary, Timothy, 2, 171, 204, 239
Lewis, John, 30, 77
Lewis, Raymond, 119
Lewis, Tarika, 7, 71–72, 81, 88, 93–97
    passim, 104, 249
Lin, J. Frank, 193
"Little Red Book." *See* *Quotations from
    Chairman Mao Tse-Tung*

Los Angeles: BLA, 232; BPP chapter, 95, 109, 133, 163, 182–83, 184, 229–30; Brown Berets, 102; Community Action Patrol (CAP), 63. *See also* Watts uprising, 1965
Lowndes County Freedom Organization, 1, 58
Lubin, Alex, 145, 254–55
lumpenproletariat, 23–24, 60, 83, 101, 159. See also *Voice of the Lumpen*
Lumumba, Mamadou (Kenn Freeman), 52, 53, 54
Lumumba, Patrice, 25–26, 27, 50, 59, 111

Mack, Larry, 170
Mailer, Norman: *The White Negro*, 77
Malcolm X, 28–41 passim, 47, 52, 59, 60, 65, 73; assassination, 74, 80; birthday demonstration, 57; Cuba, 129; echoed by ten-point program, 58; influence on Eldridge Cleaver, 74, 75, 78; influence on New York BPP, 231; on international power, 253; UCB visit, 49, 50; views of Third World solidarity, 103, 192; views of United Nations, 111
Mansour, Khalid al-. *See* Al-Mansour, Khalid
Maoism, 24–25, 42, 46, 53, 59, 155
Mao Zedong, 25, 59–63 passim, 73, 97, 159, 213, 214, 256; Cleaver reading, 75; Newton and Seale reading, 51, 131; Newton on, 60, 61; Nixon relations, 189; *Quotations from Chairman Mao Tse-Tung*, 7, 51, 62, 66–67, 97; quoted in Douglas illustration, 88, *89*
Marighella, Carlos, 186, 231
marijuana, 74, 108, 163
Marker, Chris, 196
Marshall, Wanda, 39
Martin, Trayvon, 242, 254
Martin, Waldo, 221, 256
Marvin X, 36, 78, 79
Marx, Karl, 56, 101, 133, 176
Marxism, 23, 38, 59, 72, 100–101; Carmichael, 113, 121; Congo, 191–92; Cuba, 140; Eldridge Cleaver, 79, 131, 159; Merritt College, 51; Newton, 177–78; North Korea, 153, 158. *See also* Maoism
mass media, 15, 68, 69, 237; West Germany, 198. See also *New York Times*
Matthews, Connie, 120, 122, 124, 125, 162, 166, 210, 223
May, Page, 254
Mayfield, Julian, 33
McAlister, Melanie, 35
McClintock, Anne, 104
McKesson, Deray, 255
McNamara, Robert S., 16, 89, *90*

media. *See* black press; film and video; mass media; *Radio Free Dixie*; underground and alternative press
Meinhof, Ulrike, 198
Merritt College (Oakland City College), 46, 49, 51, 52, 55–57, 75, 108, 136; Newton on, 61. *See also* Soul Students Advisory Council (SSAC)
Mexico, 114, 128. *See also* Olympic Games: Mexico City, 1968
military bases, U.S. *See* U.S. military bases
military draft, 57, 58, 118
military service of BPP members, 52, 182, 230
misogyny, 14, 106, 167, 226. *See also* rape
Montreal antiwar conference. *See* Hemispheric Conference to End the War in Vietnam, Montreal, 1968
moon walk, 1969. *See* Apollo 11
Moore, Audley, 40, 113–14
Moore, Isaac, 52
Moore, Richard. *See* Bin Wahad, Dhoruba
"motherfucker" (word), 83, 84, 85
Muhammad, Elijah, 28, 74
Muhammad Speaks, 54, 82
Mulford Act (California), 7, 68, 69, 71, 80–81, 93, 130, 132
Munich Olympics. *See* Olympic Games: Munich, 1972
Muntaqim, Jalil, 229, 235, 237
Murch, Donna, 51, 52
murder, 184; Newton charges, 108, 130, 227, 238; plots and rumors, 166, 171, 227. *See also* assassination
Murray, George, 50, 54, 95, 97, 99, 128–29
Muslims, 231. *See also* Nation of Islam

Nasser, Gamal Abdel, 25, 26
National Association for the Advancement of Colored People (NAACP), 18, 33, 34, 46, 50, 52, 111, 168
National Black Political Convention, Gary, Indiana, 1972, 221–22
National Committees to Combat Fascism, 174
National Liberation Front (NLF). *See* South Vietnam: National Liberation Front (NLF)
Nation of Islam (NOI), 28, 32–41 passim, 49–58 passim, 65, 231, 243; Bunchy Carter in, 229; Eldridge Cleaver in, 74–75; Farrakhan, 239; NBPP compared, 243
natural gas, 143, 144, 203–7 passim
Ndalla, Claude-Ernest, 191
Neal, Larry, 36, 54
Negri, Antonio, *Empire*, 178
Neil, Earl A., 134
New Black Panther Party, 243
New Haven BPP, 92

New Left, 27, 78, 79, 108, 115–25 passim;
Europe, 119–23 passim, 197. *See also* Students for a Democratic Society (SDS)
Newsome, Bree, 248
Newton, Huey P., 46–49 passim, 80, 131,
149, 208; arrests, 9, 101, 108, 130; "Base of
Operations" strategy, 212, 219, 250; birth
and early years, 55; bodyguards, 226; BPP
founding, 1, 2, 47, 56–61
passim, 73; China, 213, 223; Cuba, 64, 129,
223; drug addiction/abuse, 11, 228, 238;
Eldridge Cleaver on, 80, 159; Eldridge
planned police ambush and, 135; Eldridge
split, 10–11, 14, 181–87, 211–12, 214,
232; Eldridge split run-up, 172–81 passim;
"Free Huey," 101, 109, 111, 114, 128–29,
131; guns and, 60–64 passim, 80; on guns,
60, 61, 173, 177, 184; Kissinger reference
to, 2, 189; Merritt College, 51, 55–58
passim; murder charges, 108, 130, 227, 238;
murder of, 238; North Vietnam, 158, 161;
on occupation by police, 92; "only [blacks]
can free the world," 103, 118; order to
Eldridge to flee U.S., 136; organized crime,
226–27; parole/probation, 56, 107–8; "pig"
(word) and, 84–85; portrait with M1, 97;
prison release, 161, 172–73, 231; public
speaking, 174–75, 179–80, 282n60; purges,
182–83, 231, 232; response to Mulford
Act, 68; Robert Williams influence on, 33;
Seale on, 55; shootings of Oct. 28, 1967,
108, 133; on symbolic violence, 102; Timothy Leary and, 171; trial, 9, 109, 119, 130;
Vietnam War, 2, 118, 161, 173, 225, 234;
view of guerrilla warfare and spontaneous
violence, 93, 135; view of police, 92, 247;
view of profanity, 83, 104; view of United
Nations, 112. *See also* "intercommunalism"
(Newton)
New York City, 45; attacks on police, 197,
233, 234; *Babylon* correspondent, 193;
BPP chapter, 12, 109, 110, 128, 133, 170,
183, 184, 231–33 passim;
killings by police, 242; RAM, 39;
Young Lords, 102
New York Times, 26, 119, 234
New Zealand, 223
Ngouabi, Marien, 191, 192
Nguyen, Lien-Hang, 27, 157, 167
Nix, N.C., 219
Nixon, Richard, 88, 235; Chinese relations,
2, 177, 188
Nkrumah, Kwame, 30, 50, 75, 77, 112,
128, 192
NLF. *See* South Vietnam: National Liberation
Front (NLF)

Non-Aligned Movement (NAM), 42
North Carolina, 18, 30, 132
North Korea, 4, 128, 151–59 passim, 190,
253; Elaine Brown on, 168; embassy in
Algeria, 169, 170; People's Delegation, 10,
163–67 passim
North Oakland, 46, 51, 58. *See also* Merritt
College
North Richmond, California, 65–66
North Vietnam, 151, 158, 166, 190; embassy
in Algeria, 170; at Montreal antiwar conference, 117, 118; Newton relations, 158,
161; People's Delegation, 10, 163–67
passim, *164*; Robert Williams in, 18–19
nuclear weapons, 16, 25, 91, 123

Oakland, 46–49 passim, 81, 92, 185, 238,
239; "Base of Operations" strategy, 212–24
passim, 250; *Black Panther*, 82; BPP office,
107; Elaine Brown on, 215; electoral poli-
tics, 212–21 passim, 250; Matthews, 122;
mayors and mayoral elections, 49, 216, 218,
219; organized crime, 226–27; port, 215–16.
See also North Oakland; West Oakland
Oakland City College. *See* Merritt College
Oakland Community Learning Center
(OCLC), 220
Oakland Community School, 219, 220
Oakland Police Department (OPD), 63, 252;
April 6, 1868 shootings, 130–31, 133,
135–36
Oda, Makoto, 115, 116
Odinga, Sekou, 170, 205, 207, 236
oil industry: Algeria, 144, 203
Oliver, Denise, 14, 186, 191, 193, 196, 210, 223
Olympic Games: Mexico City, 1968, 91;
Munich, 1972, 200, 201
O'Neal, Charlotte, 13, 170, 207, 210, 287n96
O'Neal, Pete, 170, 207
Onishi, Yuichiro, 115
Organización de Solidaridad con los Pueb-
los de Asia, África, y América Latina
(OSPAAAL), 8, 89, 127, 128–29, 165
Organization of African Unity (OAU),
29–30, 41, 42
Organization of Afro-American Unity
(OAAU), 33, 78
organized crime, 226–27, 228, 238

Palestine and Palestinians, 11, 143, 145–46,
173, 222, 249, 254. *See also* Black
September; Fatah; Palestine Liberation
Organization (PLO)
Palestine Liberation Organization (PLO), 2,
22, 181–82, 198, 201; BLA compared, 233;
Chinese relations, 145–46

Pan-African Cultural Festival, Algiers, 1969, 144–56 passim
pan-Africanism, 20, 21, 79, 113, 121, 147, 158; New York, 231
Pan Africanist Congress of Azania, 224
panther icon, 1, 58, 198
Panther 21, 183, 232
party split, 10–11, 14, 181–87, 211–12, 214, 232; run-up, 172–81
passports and visas. *See* visas and passports
patriarchy, 13, 14, 44, 104, 106, 167, 210, 244; acknowledgment and rejection of, 180, 220, 226, 227; in BPP iconography, 73; of Eldridge Cleaver, 75, 167, 210
"patrolling the pigs." *See* armed patrols
Peace and Freedom Party, 101, 109, 113, 116, 163
People's Anti-Imperialist Delegation. *See* U.S. People's Anti-Imperialist Delegation
People's Republic of the Congo. *See* Congo
Pham Van Dong, 166, 184
Philadelphia, 39, 174, 185, 193
"pig" (word), 84, 85, 88, 198–99
pigs, iconography of, 78, 85, *86–88*, 92–93, *96, 98*
police, 133; Algeria, 170, 171, 205, 206–7; assassination of, 12, 213, 233, 235; Berkeley, 134; Fanon view, 91; Los Angeles, 182–83, 230; Mexico, 128; militarization, 242, 247; NCCF and, 174; Newton view, 92, 247; New York City, 183, 197, 233; "pigs" and pig iconography, 85, *88*, 93; San Francisco, 80, 133–34; West Oakland, 63, 118, 135. *See also* armed patrols (police monitoring); Oakland Police Department; police brutality; shootings by police; shootings of police
police brutality, 67, 72, 84, 92, 149, 156, 174, 209; Berkeley, 57; highlighted by Malcolm X, 29; not covered in *Soulbook*, 54; Oakland, 55, 63, 67, 85, 92; self-defense against, 95
popular culture, American, 77, 126
posters, 88, 97, 127, 132, 194; by Douglas, *8*, 88, 89, 129, 145
Prashad, Vijay, 101
Pratt, Geronimo, 182–83, 226, 230–31, 232
PRG. *See* South Vietnam: Provisional Revolutionary Government (PRG)
prison and jail time, 237; Davis, 203; Douglas, 78; Eldridge Cleaver, 74–78 passim, 136, 139, 238; escape attempts and escapes, 224–25, 198, 237; George Jackson, 173, 224–25; Newton, 56, 128, 133–36 passim, 158, 161, 172, 230; Seale, 69, 108, 158, 172
prisoners of war (POWs), 158, 165

profanity, 57, 70, 83–85, 104
Progressive Labor Movement (PL), 46, 48, 51, 52, 56, 72, 101
property, 128. *See also* sabotage, property destruction, etc.
prostitution, 226–27
protests, 67; anti-draft, 118; antiwar, 49, 67, 198; Ferguson, Missouri, 242; Merritt College, 46; Richmond, California, 65; Sacramento, 59, 68–69, 80–81, 130; SSAC, 57; United Nations, 26, 110–11; West Germany, 124, 198; West Oakland, 67
Puerto Rican nationalists, 53, 102. *See also* Young Lords
purges, 182–83, 231, 232
"pussy power" (Eldridge Cleaver), 106, 167, 210
Puzo, Mario: *The Godfather*, 227

Quotations from Chairman Mao Tse-Tung, 7, 51, 62, 66–67, 97

Radio Free Dixie, 18, 30
Ramparts, 64, 78, 80, 101, 137, 163, 166
Ramstein 2, 194–95
Rangel, Charles B., 219
ransoms, 203–6
rape, 74, 75
Reading, John, 218
Reagan, Ronald, 13, 68, 69, 83, 84, 88, 136; presidential election and presidency, 238, 239, 246–47
Red Army Faction (RAF), 188, 197–201 passim, 209
Red Guards, 102, 109, 163
Republic of New Afrika, 185, 234
Revolutionary Action Movement (RAM), 5, 19, 27, 34, 39–45, 56–67 passim, 82, 244; African American exceptionalism, 103, 148; Audley Moore mentorship, 113–14; influence on BPP, 47, 56; Oakland chapter, 52–53, 59; SSAC relations, 57
"revolutionary nationalism," 5–6, 12, 47, 52–56 passim, 64–66 passim, 108, 116, 148, 243, 252–53; anticolonial vernacular and, 72; BLA, 233, 235, 237; Black House and, 79; Cruse, 5, 37–40 passim, 56; pan-Africanism clash with, 113, 147; RAM, 5, 40, 45, 56, 64–65; shift from, 221
Revolutionary People's Communications Network (RPCN), 11, 14, 188, 193–97, 202–3, 239; *Information Bulletin*, 194; legacy, 207–10
Revolutionary People's Constitutional Convention, 174
Richmond, California, 65

Right On!, 188, 191, 195
robbery, 55, 198, 213, 229, 235, 237
Roediger, David, 84
Rogers, William P., 163, 207
romanticization, 9, 12, 106, 125–27 passim,
　137, 189; of Asia and Asians, 168;
　of violence, 44, 209
Rosaldo, Renato, 12
Rusk, Dean, 89, *90*

sabotage, property destruction, etc., 43–44,
　200, 201, 229, 235–36
Sacramento protest, May 1967, 59, 68–69,
　80–81, 130
Salah, Si, 207
Salaita, Steven, 84
Sanchez, Sonia, 36, 50, 54, 78
San Francisco: *Babylon* correspondent, 193;
　Baraka in, 79; BLA, 232; Chicanos, 102;
　HUAC hearings, 49; mayors, 88; police, 80,
　133–34; Red Guards, 102. *See also* Black
　House
San Francisco City College, 79
San Francisco Mime Troupe, 136
San Francisco State University (SFSU), 35, 109;
　Black Student Union (BSU), 50, 79, 108
San Quentin State Prison (California), 74–75,
　173, 224–25
Scandinavia, 119–22, 162, 223
Scheer, Robert, 78, 137, 163
Scott, Jessica, 195
SDS. *See* Students for a Democratic Society
　(SDS)
SDS (Germany). *See* Sozialistischer Deutscher
　Studentenbund (SDS)
Seale, Bobby, 46–62 passim, 73, 149; arrests,
　57, 134; "Base of Operations" strategy,
　212–13, 216, 217; birth and early years,
　52; Black Political Convention, 221; BPP
　founding, 1, 47, 56–61 passim; denuncia-
　tion of NBPP, 243; departure from BPP,
　228; disavowal of skyjacker, 142; Dixon
　on, 132; on Fanon, 60; Malcolm X assas-
　sination anniversary event, 80; mayoral
　campaign, 216–21 passim; Merritt College,
　51; military service, 52; Montreal confer-
　ence, 118–19; on "motherfucker" (word),
　83; on Newton, 55; North Vietnam, 158;
　on "pig" (word), 84–85; prison, 69, 108,
　158, 172; public speaking, 97, 118–19,
　179; Sacramento demonstration, 1967, 68;
　Scandinavian tour, 120, 121, 125; *Soulbook*,
　53; SSAC, 57; on symbolic violence, 102;
　United Nations visit, 110, 113
Seattle BPP, 83, 109, 132, 133, 215

Seidler, William and Miriam, 196
Self, Robert O., 215, 221, 246, 247
self-defense, armed. *See* armed self-defense
Semler, Christian, 123
separatism, black. *See* black separatism
sex (gender). *See* gender
sexual attitudes of Eldridge Cleaver. *See*
　Cleaver, Eldridge: sexual attitudes
sexual violence. *See* rape
Shabazz, Betty, 80, 221
Shakur, Afeni, 240
Shakur, Assata, 14, 87–88, 179, 231, 232, 240,
　252; Cuba, 228, 237; legacy, 248; on New-
　ton speeches, 180; prison break, 237
Sharma, Sanjay, 249
shootings by police, 213, 242; Denzil Dowell,
　65, 81, 92; Michael Brown, 241–42, 252
shootings of police, 108, 133, 198, 201, 233;
　Newton, T.K. *See also* assassination: of police
Sibeko, David, 224
Los Siete de la Raza, 102, 109
Sihanouk, Norodom, 166, 184
Singh, Nikhil Pal, 5, 164, 246
skin color, 140, 147–48
skyjackers. *See* airline hijackers
Slausons (L.A. gang), 229
slavery, 37, 245
Smethurst, James, 48
Smith, Clinton, 150, 171
SNCC. *See* Student Nonviolent
　Coordinating Committee (SNCC)
Socialist Student League of Germany.
　See Sozialistischer Deutscher
　Studentenbund (SDS)
Socialist Workers Party, 48
social media, 242, 249, 254, 255
soldiers, black. *See* black GIs
Soledad State Prison (California), 74, 229
Soulbook, 53–59 passim, 67
Soul on Ice (Cleaver), 75, 77, 101, 133
Soul Students Advisory Council (SSAC),
　56–61 passim, 75
South Africa, 34, 222, 224. *See also* African
　National Congress
South Carolina, 124, 242, 248
South Korea, 152, 155, 190
South Vietnam: Algerian relations, 143,
　157–58; National Liberation Front (NLF), 2,
　22, 61, 63, 132, 156–59 passim, 173; Provi-
　sional Revolutionary Government (PRG),
　151, 156–58 passim, 169, 173, 190, 196
Soviet Union, 24–25, 31, 120; Chinese
　relations, 24, 42, 138, 153, 154, 155;
　Congolese relations, 25; Cuban
　relations, 32, 138–40 passim; North

Korean relations, 152; People's Delegation, 163; Seale on, 121; *Soulbook* view of, 53; Tricontinental Conference, 28; U.S. détente, 7, 177

Sozialistischer Deutscher Studentenbund (SDS), 122–24, 194, 197

The Spook Who Sat by the Door, 225

Stanford, Max. *See* Ahmad, Muhammad

Stanford University, 48

State Department. *See* U.S. Department of State

Stevens, William, 191

Stone, I. F., 27

Stone, Ronald, 57

Strain, Christopher B., 251

Student Nonviolent Coordinating Committee (SNCC), 1, 45; African tour, 30; BPP split, 113; Germany, 123; Japan, 115; Scandinavia, 120; split with BPP, 113; Vietnam War opposition, 27, 115, 123, 156

Students for a Democratic Society (SDS), 39, 50, 117, 123, 235

Suez crisis, 1956, 25

Sukarno, 21

surveillance, 107, 211, 250

survival programs, 162, 172, 177, 216, 219, 220, 251; Eldridge Cleaver criticism of, 166. *See also* free breakfast program

Sweden, 119–20, 223

symbolic violence, 91–99 passim, 132

Tabor, Connie. *See* Matthews, Connie

Tabor, Michael Cetewayo, 122, 170, 191, 207

Tanzania, 110, 111, 114, 207

Taylor, Keeanga-Yamahtta, 244–45, 252

ten-point program (BPP), 1, 13, 58, 217, 244, 252; modification, 112, 158–59

Texas, 203, 230

theft, 56, 74, 170, 241. *See also* robbery

"Third World" (term), 20

Touré, Askia M., 36, 50, 78

Touré, Sékou, 128

treaty organizations, 92

trials: BLA, 237; Davis, 203; Eldridge Cleaver, 136, 238; Newton, 7, 9, 108–10 passim, 119, 120, 130, 161; Panther 21, 183; Ramstein 2, 194–95

Tricontinental Conference of Asian, Africa and Latin American Peoples, 1966, 27–28, 42, 53, 139

Ture, Kwame. *See* Carmichael, Stokely

twelve-point program (RAM), 40

Twist (dance), 77

Twitter, 242, 249, 254, 255

Tyson, Timothy B., 32

UCLA, 230

underground and alternative press, 188, 191–96 passim, 202; West Germany, 198. See also *Black Panther*; *Ramparts*

uniform of the BPP, 6, 66, 81, 106, 226

United Nations, 9, 21, 109–14 passim, 254; in *Black Panther*, 222; China, 213, 216; Civil Right Congress petition, 48; Congo, 25; Cuba, 23; Malcolm X views, 29; protests, 26–27, 111; UNESCO, 120

Universal Negro Improvement Association (UNIA), 19, 49, 65

University of California, Berkeley (UCB), 48–49, 50, 51, 66–67, 109

"The Urban Guerrilla Concept" (RAF), 199

U.S. Congress. *See* Congressional Black Caucus; U.S. House of Representatives; U.S. Senate

U.S. Constitution, 34, 59; Second Amendment, 61, 62

U.S. Department of Justice (DOJ), 241, 247

U.S. Department of State, 2, 163, 205; Rusk, 89, *90*

U.S. House of Representatives, 219. *See also* House Committee on Un-American Activities Committee (HUAC)

U.S. interventionism, 25, 111, 253–54

U.S. military bases, 124, 194, 209, 253–54

US Organization, 49, 72, 104, 158, 230

U.S. People's Anti-Imperialist Delegation, 10, 156, 157, 161–71 passim; roster, 280n6

U.S. Senate: subcommittee on Internal Security Act, 124

USSR. *See* Soviet Union

vanguardism, 63, 67, 118–25 passim, 164, 176, 221, 224; Cruse views, 5, 38; Odinga on, 236; RAM views, 5, 41, 44, 54, 118

video. *See* film and video

Viet Cong. *See* South Vietnam: National Liberation Front (NLF)

Vietnam, North. *See* North Vietnam

Vietnam, South. *See* South Vietnam

Vietnam Day Committee, 49

Vietnam War, 13, 16, 19, 27, 49, 76, 157, 252; antiwar movement, 57, 58, 101, 115–19 passim, 125, 156, 165, 190, 198; Baraka and, 36; fragging (urged by Eldridge Cleaver), 166; German views, 123–26 passim, 198; Japanese views, 116; Newton offer of Panther soldiers, 161, 173, 225; Port of Oakland and, 215; Pratt in, 230; SSAC and, 57; as unifying force, 224; West Germany, 194–95; winding down, 190

Vietnam Workers Party (VWP), 157
violence, internecine. *See* internecine violence
violence, symbolic. *See* symbolic violence
visas and passports, 116, 127, 169, 170, 193, 195
Voice of the Lumpen, 188, 191, 194, 195

Warden, Donald. *See* Al-Mansour, Khalid
Washington, Albert "Nuh," 17, 184–85, 229,
     232, 256
Washington Post, 69
Watts, Daniel, 24, 26
Watts uprising, 1965, 19, 28, 44, 63, 75, 82;
     OSPAAAL celebration, *8*, 128, 165
weapons: public display of, 93; Second
     Amendment, 61, 62; Third World, 10, 206.
     See also armed patrols; armed self-defense;
     armed struggle; guns
Weather Underground, 171, 183, 200, 201,
     209, 231–32
We Charge Genocide, 248, 254
Weems, Donald. *See* Balagoon, Kuwasi
West Germany. *See* Federal Republic of
     Germany
West Oakland, 55, 67, 93, 216; BPP origins,
     2, 4, 16; DeFremery Park, 49, 81; NOI, 49;
     police, 63, 118, 135
white allies, 108, 116, 117, 224; Bay Area,
     109; BLA and, 237; Carmichael
     criticism, 72; Cleaver, 76–77, 79, 101, 108;
     Seale view, 122. *See also*
     New Left; Weather Underground
The White Negro (Mailer), 77
white supremacy, 76, 116, 209, 245; capitalism
     and, 100, 101; Cuba, 140

Williams, Landon R., 128
Williams, Robert F., 18–19, 28–39 passim, 52,
     60–61, 66, 67, 73, 109–10; China, 25, 32,
     139; Cuba, 18, 30–37 passim, 52, 127, 139,
     140–41; Eldridge Cleaver building upon,
     76; "ninety-day war," 42–43, 202, 209, 235;
     North Vietnam, 18–19; UCB, 50
Wilson, Lionel, 219
Windom, Alice, 30
Wolfe, Tom, 15
Wolff, Karl Dietrich, 83, 124, 125, 193–94
women, Eldridge Cleaver abuse of. *See*
     Cleaver, Eldridge: abuse of women
women, iconography of, 73, *94, 105*
women and men. *See* gender
women's liberation. *See* feminism
The Wretched of the Earth (Fanon), 23–24, 51,
     61, 63, 252
Wu, Judy, 151, 166, 167, 168, 169
Wu Hsueh-chien, 28

X, Malcolm. *See* Malcolm X
X, Marvin. *See* Marvin X

Yates, Ashley, 248
Yazid, Mohammed, 157–58
Yoshiyuki, Tsurumi, 115, 116
Young, Cynthia, 27, 92, 100, 244
Young Lords, 102, 109, 191
Young Socialist Alliance, 48

Zhou Enlai, 2, 189, 213
Zionism, 145
Zolberg, Aristide and Vera, 61

peer toward regime — the activity
when they gave up arms

COLD WAR — moment of opp for
Black Panthers 229

243 was BPP's intervention really
key to its growth?

What doom them
— end of CW — lost of state allies
— state repression
— own weakness   neolib?

Failure + need to explain failure
+ speak to the present seem to
hold this study back. So
much to learn from the
ideas + efforts to form transnat'l
a with

p200 – Cleaver + state us anti-colonial
violence
Black Sept: guerilla movement –
inspired by Palestinian movement

TECHNOLOGY
plane hijackings
206
Detente – makes drugs harder f/
Cleaver in Algeria
p 208-9 relative power of stateless grp
(TERRORISTS)

p209 – Case for revolutionary
251 violence??
How to deal w/ subjects like
this?
218-9 – from guns to running for office
– return to '66 roots
221 – They abandoned critique of
liberalism + hope for fundamental Δ
by running for office
also p. 222 (Judging)

1970 - relationformations @ state level
+ w. informal transmill orgs
cafeteria style internationalism

162 -163 How style / method of politic
was changing (US. earlier in
senate)

167 - limit to the transmittlin
- comm state always involved

168 - sacrifice of autonomy for state
level support

175 - intercommunin - Nauton
- US expid so pervasive
- don't matter of you're a
nation state

179 practicalists question - is that
really the wrad return?
Nauton expelled from int'l sectn
- clever toutmes

(p 209) Loot for floor lattn

what does trans do here >
Put in rela to Goebels >
as geopol environ Δs - new formation
of black radical politics - melding
of nationalism w. Third Wld - deasled
politics

- problem of ideas → action >
- vs. PA (Hall) - cosmopolitans + their
                                    limits
- how to Be cosmo + popuhcol p 58-59
p 63-4- How he shows link b/w BPP +
     3rd wld politics
How serious was their interest in 3rd wld
     pol + the influence of it on them?

77-78 role of <u>culture</u>
     vs. anti - cap.
     vs guns

Keeps saying that how this would lead
to new is unclear but isn't dev
of these pol + wld view a revolution
          ANTI colonial venurelan

CPSIA information can be obtained
at www.ICGtesting.com
Printed in the USA
LVOW12s0137080417
530105LV00001B/12/P

9 781501 713422